# KIDDING A Santa Fe

## A YOUNG PERSON'S GUIDE TO THE CITY

SUSAN YORK

ILLUSTRATED BY SALLY BLAKEMORE

**John Muir Publications**
Santa Fe, New Mexico

***This book is lovingly dedicated to:*** *Maggie Rose and Ryan*
***With boundless apprecia-tion to:*** *Chris Worth*
***Deep thanks to:***
*Valerie Brooker*
*Kathy Costa*
*Melanie Demmer*
*Ellyn Feldman*
*Ms. Gomez and her 5th grade class, Salazar Elementary School*
*Dee Gregory*
*Kathy Haaland*
*Erica and Eliza Kretzmann*
*Jess Lacey*
*Jennifer Lewis*
*Joey & Matthew Lewis*
*Avra Leodas*
*Melina Leodas-Whelan*
*Sarah Lovett*
*Anne McCormick*
*Gordon McDonough*
*Ricardo Padilla, Hyde State Park*
*Cecilia Portal*
*Orlando Romero*
*Allen Schwartz*
*John Sherman*
*Dr. David Snow*
*Craig Stamm*
*Karen Tasaka*
*Peggy van Hulsteyn*
*Jeffrey Worth*
*Bette Yozell and her Middle School art classes, Santa Fe Preparatory School*

John Muir Publications, P.O. Box 613, Santa Fe, NM 87504


Printed in the United States of America
First edition. First printing

Library of Congress Cataloging-in-Publication Data

York, Susan.
Kidding around Santa Fe : a young person's guide to the city / Susan York ; illustrated by Sally Blakemore. — 1st ed.
p. cm.
Summary: Offers cultural and historical information about Santa Fe and describes a variety of sites of interest to young people.
ISBN 0-945465-99-8
1. Santa Fe (N.M.)—Description—Guide-books—Juvenile literature. 2. Children—Travel—New Mexico—Santa Fe—Juvenile literature. [1. Santa Fe (N.M.)—Description—Guides.] I. Blakemore, Sally, ill. II. Title.
F804.S23Y67 1991
917.89'560453—dc20 91-6651
CIP
AC

Designer: Joanna Hill
Typeface: Trump Medieval
Typesetter: Copygraphics, Inc., Santa Fe, New Mexico
Printer: Guynes Printing Company of New Mexico

Distributed to the book trade by
W. W. Norton & Company, Inc.
New York, New York

# Contents

# 1. Bienvenidos / Welcome

*If you want to see one of the biggest adobe buildings in the world, go to* ***Cristo Rey Church****. The 180,000 bricks were made the traditional way, from the earth the church stands on.*

*Bienvenidos a Santa Fe.* Welcome to Santa Fe. "The City of Faith" was first founded by the Spanish on a place of ancient Indian settlements. It was established on its current site in 1609, eleven years before the Pilgrims landed at Plymouth Rock! More than four hundred years before that, Indians had created a home here.

Santa Fe is a multicultural community, and while you're here, you'll hear many languages and sample new kinds of food. Even the buildings are different from those in most American cities since many of them are built with brown adobe and look handmade.

You might think you're in a foreign country. You're not alone. Sometimes, mail doesn't get to New Mexico because people still think it's part of Old Mexico. People from other places often ask, "Where are the bullfights?" Rodeos *are* held here, but not bullfights. Even though parts of Santa Fe may make you feel like you're in Spain or south of the border, the city has been a part of the United States since 1846.

The wide open spaces go on for miles, so try to spot a mesa, which means table in Spanish (and plateau in geology). If you're driving from Albuquerque and reach La Bajada, remember that

early settlers used to stop at the bottom of this hill, spending the night before the hard climb into Santa Fe. The highway department blasted the top of it away many years ago, so it's not as steep as it was then. Stop at the rest area on your way into town and you'll see a dramatic view at the top of the hill. If you travel into Santa Fe at night, look into the sky. Because there are no large cities nearby, the night sky is as black as ink. In the winter, look for the Big Dipper. In the summer, look for Draco the Dragon.

***Adobe Brick Recipe***

*Mix wet Santa Fe earth with a little straw. Squish the mud into a wooden frame. Push it out of the frame and let it dry. After 4 days, stand it on one side, then the other so it will stay flat. Build with it after it has dried for 6 weeks in the sun.*

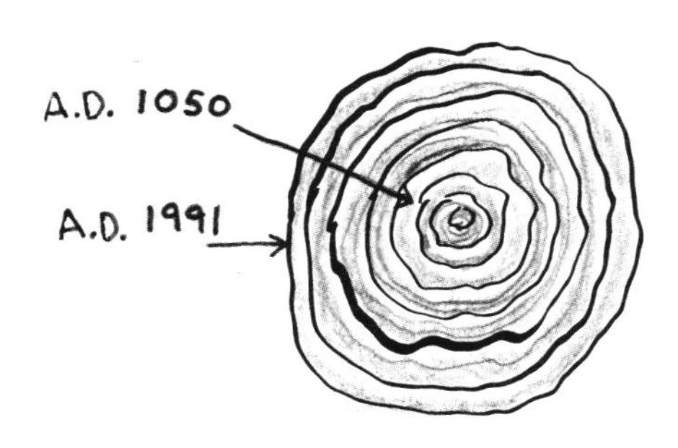


***Arroyo Negro**, the site of an ancient Indian pueblo, was located at what is now West Alameda Street. Anthropologists counted tree rings found at the site and concluded it was started between A.D. 1050 and 1150.*

Because Santa Fe is distinctly Spanish, you'll hear that language often during your visit. If you speak Spanish or have studied it in school, this is the place to practice. Keep your eyes peeled for street names like Paseo de Peralta, Don Diego, and Coronado, which represent the city's rich Spanish and Mexican heritage. Listen for the lilting sound of Tewa, the language of several Indian pueblos, or Keresan, which is spoken by the people of Santo Domingo, Cochiti, and San Felipe pueblos.

The city has seen lots of change during its long history, having been governed by Spaniards, Indians, Mexicans, Americans, and even Confederate soldiers. At different times, the leaders of these groups ruled from the Palace of the Governors, which stands on the north side of the plaza (pronounced plah-za) in the center of the city.

Put on your walking shoes, because that's the easiest way to see this old city with your family. Go inside the old buildings and listen to the quietness that comes from three-foot-thick adobe walls. Wander up Canyon Road and see the artists painting on the street or in their studios. Watch the dances at the Indian pueblos and be a part of hundreds of years of history and tradition. Take hikes through high canyons or feel the wind rush against you as you bicycle down country lanes. All of this can be a part of your visit to Santa Fe, so get ready, get set, go!

# 2. Yesterday

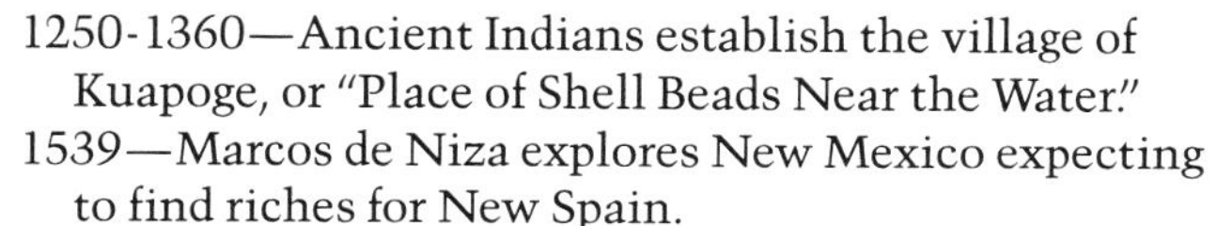

1250-1360—Ancient Indians establish the village of Kuapoge, or "Place of Shell Beads Near the Water."

1539—Marcos de Niza explores New Mexico expecting to find riches for New Spain.

1540—Wearing gilded armor, Francisco Vasquez de Coronado, leads an expedition into New Mexico. The Spaniards are disappointed to find mud huts instead of gold.

1598—A group of colonists led by Don Juan de Oñate ride their horses from Mexico through the desert of the Southwest. They establish the first Spanish settlement in the Santa Fe area (near San Juan Pueblo).

1609—Governor Pedro de Peralta moves the Spanish colony to Santa Fe, officially named La Villa Real. The Spaniards impose their culture and religion, which causes resentment among Native Americans.

1645—Nearly forty Indians refuse to give up their ancient religion and are beaten and hanged by the Spaniards. Historians think this contributed to the Pueblo Revolt.

1680—The Pueblo Revolt is led by San Juan Pueblo Indian leader, Popé. The Indians cut off the water supply to the Spanish settlers and force them to retreat to El Paso.

1680-1693—Native Americans occupy Santa Fe and destroy or damage churches in the same way that their own religious symbols had been destroyed by the Spanish. They build two kivas in the plaza area.

1692—Don Diego de Vargas rides up the Rio Grande with his army, in what is known as the First Entrada

(entry). He meets with Indian leaders and concludes that Spanish settlers can now safely return to Santa Fe.

1693—An expedition of families, soldiers, and priests arrives in Santa Fe during a cold December. Led by de Vargas, they are disappointed to find that the Indians haven't left Santa Fe and end up camping on a hill above the town. De Vargas and his army attack Santa Fe in a violent battle and take it back for Spain.

1712—Old friends and soldiers of de Vargas meet in a leaky room and write a proclamation announcing an annual fiesta (party) in his honor. The first Fiesta de Santa Fe is celebrated; it has taken place nearly every year since.

1821—Mexico becomes independent from Spain; New Mexico is now a part of Mexico. The Santa Fe Trail opens; foreign explorers and traders are now welcomed to Santa Fe.

1837—Mexican Governor Albino Perez imposes laws that oppress Hispanic and Indian New Mexicans. During the Rebellion of 1837, these New Mexicans rebel and kill the governor.

1846—New Mexico becomes a territory of the United States.

1847—Governor Bent is killed in Taos by a coalition of Hispanics and Indians who resist American rule.

1862—Confederate soldiers ride into Santa Fe, taking over the Palace of the Governors for a few weeks before their defeat at the Battle of Glorieta.

1879—The Santa Fe Railroad enters New Mexico.

1912—New Mexico becomes a state, an event that is celebrated by a week-long fiesta.

1920—*Los Cinco Pintores* (The Five Painters), join the already thriving art colony in Santa Fe and gain prominence.

1926—Artist Will Shuster creates the first Zozobra, a ghostlike figure that symbolizes gloom and is burned in a big fire during Fiesta.

1957—A Historical Zoning Ordinance is enacted which keeps most buildings in the historical area three stories or less, flat roofed and brown.

1960-1990—Santa Fe's art community continues to grow. At last count, there were over 200 galleries in the city.

# 3. The End of the Trail

Begin at the **plaza**, even though it was the end of the trail for early travelers and merchants who arrived in town on the Santa Fe Trail. The plaza is the geographic and social center of Santa Fe. So many teenagers (older and younger people, too) like to cruise the plaza that cars aren't allowed in the area during the summer. You'll see skateboarders, roller-skaters, and an assortment of people sitting on the white iron benches. If you're lucky, you might even see an international kazoo contest. During the summer, a bandstand is erected and a lot of different musicians and dancers perform in free concerts.

*Lowriders often cruise the plaza. If you're lucky, you'll see their cars, which ride inches from the ground and without warning hop up and down on hydraulic jacks. The cars are often painted with murals and covered with 100 layers of clear lacquer. If you look inside, you might see crushed velvet upholstery and a 6-inch circle of chain that is the steering wheel. There's even a lowrider car in the Smithsonian Institution!*

Although the plaza is now square, it was originally a rectangle that reached east to the Saint Francis Cathedral. Copied after the Spanish *plaza mayor* (great public square), it was created for military and religious ceremonies that needed lots of room for horses.

You'll see many Native Americans sitting under the portal of the **Palace of the Governors** selling their crafts. They sit in front of blankets covered with carefully made silver and turquoise bracelets, earrings and necklaces, pottery, and sometimes Indian bread. Buying crafts directly from the artists is fun because you can tell them how much you like their work.

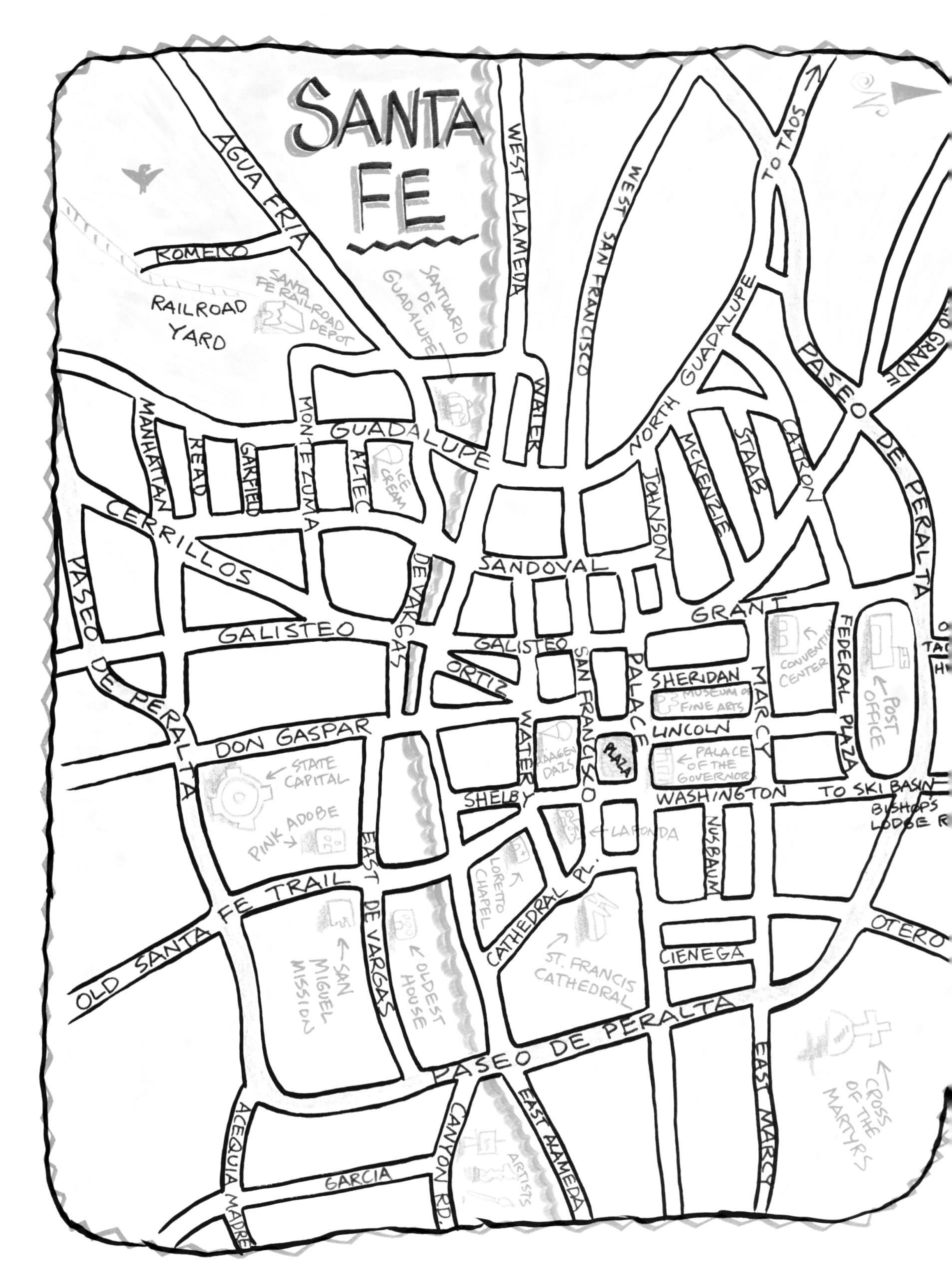

SANTA FE
AGUA FRIA
ROMERO
RAILROAD YARD
SANTA FE RAILROAD DEPOT
SANTUARIO DE GUADALUPE
WEST ALAMEDA
WEST SAN FRANCISCO
TO TAOS
NORTH GUADALUPE
PASEO DE PERALTA
MANHATTAN
READ
GARFIELD
MONTEZUMA
GUADALUPE
AZTEC
ICE CREAM
WATER
JOHNSON
MCKENZIE
STAAB
CATRON
CERRILLOS
DE VARGAS
SANDOVAL
GRANT
PASEO DE PERALTA
GALISTEO
GALISTEO
ORTIZ
SAN FRANCISCO
PALACE
SHERIDAN
MUSEUM OF FINE ARTS
MARCY
CONVENTION CENTER
FEDERAL PLAZA
POST OFFICE
LINCOLN
DON GASPAR
WATER
HAAGEN DAZS
PLAZA
PALACE OF THE GOVERNOR
STATE CAPITAL
PINK ADOBE
SHELBY
WASHINGTON
TO SKI BASIN
LA FONDA
NUSBAUM
LORETTO CHAPEL
CATHEDRAL PL.
EAST DE VARGAS
OLD SANTA FE TRAIL
SAN MIGUEL MISSION
OLDEST HOUSE
ST. FRANCIS CATHEDRAL
CIENEGA
OTERO
PASEO DE PERALTA
EAST MARCY
CROSS OF THE MARTYRS
ACEQUIA MADRE
GARCIA
CANYON RD.
ARTISTS
EAST ALAMEDA

If you like history, you'll enjoy the Palace of the Governors, which is the oldest public building in the United States (in constant use). Roaming through the rooms, which have thick adobe walls, you can imagine the people who sat in the wooden chairs in the Mexican Governor's Office or waited in 1893 in the Reception Room of Governor Prince. There are muskets, a *carreta* (wooden cart), and even a carved black wooden hearse.

Outside in the courtyard you'll see a covered wagon and an old chuckwagon used by ranchers to cook and serve meals in the old west. In the

***Biscochitos-"Official New Mexican Cookie"***

*Mix 1 cup of lard, ¾ cup sugar, and 2 teaspoons anise seeds (as in licorice). Beat in 1 egg. Add 3 cups of flour, 1½ teaspoons baking powder, and ½ teaspoon salt. Roll out ¼" to ½" thick and cut in circles or funny shapes. Dip in cinnamon sugar (¼ cup sugar, 1 teaspoon cinnamon) and bake for 10 minutes at 350°.*

**Palace Print Shop**, you can watch while books are printed on an old-fashioned letterpress and then handbound. Before you leave, check out the gift shop and its Navajo beaded turtle pins, silver bracelets, and tiny pots from Jemez Pueblo.

Did you see the big Spitz clock that stands on the northwest side of the plaza? It's actually the third one to be placed there. In 1881, the first one stood in front of the Spitz Jewelry Store, and years later, the second one was knocked down by Santa Fe's first motorized truck.

The clock stands in front of the **Museum of Fine Arts**, a building inspired by the church at Acoma Pueblo. Originally, money for the building was raised from donations by the townspeople. Because of this, the museum at that time let any artist hang his or her work on its walls. But in recent years, Hispanic, Indian, and women artists have complained that the museum doesn't exhibit their work enough. Decide if you agree or disagree with them, as you look through the rooms of the galleries. Kids rave about the art

*One of the most exciting moments of Fiesta is the burning of* ***Zozobra****. The 44-foot-tall monster burns up in a flurry of fire, groans, and fireworks. Dressed in a long white robe and glowing eyes the size of pizza pans, Zozobra is called Old Man Gloom because he symbolizes fear and uncertainty. Santa Fe burns its worries and woes when it sets the monster on fire.*

classes the museum sometimes offers. They will show you how to make collages, paint murals, and sculpt.

During many mornings in the summer, you can sit in on free rehearsals of the **Santa Fe Chamber Music Festival** in the adjoining Saint Francis Auditorium. The Festival also offers free youth concerts in various locations. You can listen to a concert and talk to your favorite musicians after you hear them play.

Parades and pageants march through the streets of the plaza in all seasons. **Fiesta** has taken place nearly every year since 1712 and marks the time in 1692 when Don Diego de Vargas took Santa Fe back from the Native Americans. This moment is reenacted in early September, and de Vargas and his conquistadors (played by local residents) ride into the plaza in the full military dress of that time.

Join Santa Fe kids in the Fiesta's **Pet Parade**. Bring your favorite pet or dress as one. Kids have been known to bring their stuffed animals, as well as their live snakes and llamas. You might see kids dressed as prairie dogs, riding in a wagon surrounded by chicken wire.

During the spring, **All Species Day**, an environmental celebration, takes place on the plaza and at Fort Marcy. Join the parade by dressing up as a lizard or a bird and walk through the center of town. Look for kids and adults on stilts and in costume. See giant buffalo along with beautiful storks. Watch puppet shows that explain what we need to do to help our environment.

Wander down Palace Avenue and look in the big windows of different art galleries. You may see giant paintings, pottery that's as big as you, or a little girl you can hold hands with, even though she's made of bronze.

The **Saint Francis Cathedral** stands at the end of San Francisco Street east of the plaza. In 1869, Archbishop Lamy wanted it designed so that he could be reminded of his native country, France. If you think the church looks like it's missing its steeples, you're right. They never got around to building two towers that would have risen 160 feet. Archbishop Lamy is buried underneath a tall altar inside the church.

East of the cathedral is the **La Fonda Hotel** whose hallways are brightly painted with flowers. You can eat your lunch in a dramatic atrium in the hotel restaurant. The hotel was known as "The Inn at the End of the Trail" because it marked the end of the Santa Fe Trail, which began in Missouri and wound its way 750 miles through prairies and over mesas and mountains to its destination at the plaza.

Freight wagons, stagecoaches, and mail wagons traveled the Santa Fe Trail, leaving wheel marks that can still be seen today. Keep your eyes peeled for them when you go to the Folk Art Museum (chapter 4). The trail used to pass right over what is now its parking lot. There's still an unpaved portion to the west where you can see the long grassy ridges that the wheels left over a century ago. You have to be a real explorer to find these because they aren't marked and seem to disappear into the grass.

Near the La Fonda is **UNICEF-All the World's Children**, where you help children in need by buying cards, dolls, and crafts from all over the world. Walk toward the plaza from here, and you can look in the many shop windows or buy T-shirts. **Woolworth's** is a favorite place for kids who like to buy frito pies from the take-out window or get popcorn to feed to the pigeons on the plaza.

The most popular hang-out for Santa Fe teenagers is **Haagen-Dazs**. During the first day of Indian Market in August, 9,000 people walk through its doors, and the workers serve 5,000 scoops of ice cream!

Down Don Gaspar Avenue you'll find **Capt. Kid Toys**, where you might get to play with the owner or workers who are really grown-up kids. Next door is the **Mineral and Fossil Gallery of Santa Fe**. Here you might see a geode, which is just a plain-looking rock on the outside, but on the inside, it has a crystalline secret treasure.

Entering **Doodlet's** seems like walking into grandmother's attic. Bird cages hang from the ceilings, and unusual postcards are stacked next to lots of stuff that costs less than a dollar.

*Sopaipillas (sop-ah-pee-yaz) are like deep fried bread. Be sure to pour honey inside the tiny "pillow."*

Whether you're in the mood to put on your dress-up clothes or not, don't miss afternoon tea at the **Hotel Saint Francis**. Relax in the comfy wingback chairs and sample scones or finger sandwiches while drinking tea from china cups. If you're in Santa Fe at Christmas time, you can sit in front of the roaring fire while Santa Fe schoolchildren sing carols.

Do you need some peace and quiet? Try the **Santa Fe Public Library**. It used to be a fire station as well as a jail. Can you figure out where the fire truck used to park? Yikes! Were prisoners jailed on the spot where you're reading? Go to the Children's Room on the second floor and relax in big rocking chairs in front of a fireplace. The library also has story hour.

*Chile rellenos (chee-leh ray-eh-nos) are green chiles stuffed with cheese, fried in batter, and covered with chile sauce and cheese.*

Order anything from enchiladas to hamburgers to apricot pie at **Josie's Casa de Comida**. Josie's was voted as having the best desserts in town by the readers of the *Santa Fe Reporter*, a good free newspaper that tells you what's happening in Santa Fe. Buy the daily paper, the *New Mexican*, on Friday for a complete listing of the following week's events.

If you want to run around or have a picnic with your family, try the park next to the **Federal Courthouse**. Look for the tall stone column in front of the courthouse. It doesn't look a thing like **Kit Carson**, but it's a monument to him anyway. Go inside the courthouse and check out the historic murals. You'll see a painting of a wagon train coming to town on the Old Santa Fe Trail.

You might be wondering what that Pepto-Bismol pink building is north of the park. The **Scottish Rite Temple** was built at the turn of the century and modeled after a castle (the Alhambra) in Santa Fe, Spain. Touring its large auditorium is like a trip into fantasy land. Tiny stars sparkle in the ceiling, painted to look like the sky. The temple welcomes large and small groups for tours; you'll get the best tour if you come before lunch.

A short stroll from the Scottish Rite Temple on Paseo de Peralta, the **Cross of the Martyrs** is a historical walk that winds its way up a steep hill. Take the hundreds of steps and stop at markers that chart the history of Santa Fe from A.D. 500 to now. You'll learn how much the United States paid Mexico for New Mexico, Arizona, and California. Because the cross was built in their honor, you'll find out the names of the twenty-one Franciscan friars who died during the Pueblo Revolt. The view from the top is the best.

No one seems to know exactly when it was built (or if it really is the oldest), but for more than a hundred years, Santa Feans have called the house at 215 East de Vargas Street the **Oldest House**. By counting tree rings in the *vigas* (ceiling beams), it's estimated that the trees were cut

*In the dining room of the Scottish Rite Temple, look for the Tiffany lamps that were made by Louis Tiffany in 1911. Forty years later, the temple ordered two more from the Tiffany Studios, hoping they would match. But Mr. Tiffany died with the secret of how the bottom part of the lamp was made. Can you tell which are the new ones?*

La Conquistadora *(sometimes translated as The Conquerer), a 28-inch statue, was first brought to Santa Fe in 1625. During Fiesta, a replica of the statue is carried from the cathedral to the Cross of the Martyrs.*

*Look for old and new postcards at the **Marcy St. Card Shop**. Almost next door, the **Marcy St. Toy Shop** has an incredible assortment of stuffed animals.*

before 1767. The interior has a low ceiling and a dirt floor. The house now adjoins a curio shop, and you can walk through it on any day but Sunday.

When the **Loretto Chapel** was completed in 1878, there wasn't any way to get to the choir loft because there wasn't enough room for a regular staircase. When the nuns put out the word that they needed help, a mysterious carpenter appeared. He built a beautiful spiral stairway but left without being paid and before the nuns found out who he was. You won't find a nail or any outside support in this structure, and that's why many call it the miraculous stairway. Legend had it that St. Joseph, the carpenter saint, built the staircase, but historians think it was actually an Austrian man named Johann Hadwiger.

If you want to take an organized tour, several companies offer guided tours of the Santa Fe area. Lots of kids love to ride the yellow **Grayline Tours** bus around town. During the summer, Grayline uses open-air buses that are especially fun. Visit haunted buildings downtown at dusk with **Santa Fe Adventures for Children**. Or take a raft ride down the Rio Grande with them, stopping at Santa Clara Pueblo for lunch, or go to an artist's studio and work with clay for a morning. This company specializes in tours for kids—with or without adults. The desk in La Fonda Hotel has information on many tours, as does the Chamber of Commerce.

If you're in the mood for seeing the town on foot, Waite Thompson's **Santa Fe Walks** will give you a good introduction to the city. Discover Santa Fe by walking down major streets and little-known alleys with someone who can keep you from getting lost.

# 4. P-P-Pots, Papooses, & Puccini

*If you like dolls, trains,* retablos *(paintings of saints), circuses, masks, needlepoint, or weavings, you'll find them in the Museum of International Folk Art, which has the largest collection of folk art in the world! You may see demonstrations of a Hispanic tin worker making beautiful frames in the museum, a Native American forming pots, or a Nigerian drummer playing his talking drum.*

While you're in Santa Fe, you can visit lots of museums and see handmade crafts of New Mexico as well as from countries all over the world. There are special activities for kids at most of these places, especially at the Santa Fe Children's Museum. Explore the New Mexico State Capitol during the day, or stay up late and listen to famous opera singers at the Santa Fe Opera.

"The Art of the Craftsman Is a Bond Between the Peoples of the World" is written above the door of the **Museum of International Folk Art**, and that unity is especially evident in the many dolls that you can see all over the museum. Made in every country you can think of, the dolls have one thing in common: most of them were made for a child to carry around. But that's where the similarity ends, because they are made from wood, cloth, straw, clay, and even beads. Many of the faces show the Hispanic, Native American, Anglo-American, Asian, East Indian, or African-American origins of its maker.

Be sure to touch the adobe fireplace on the TV screen in the museum and learn all about adobes. You can register for workshops with folk artists who will teach you how to make everything

from toy coffins and skull masks for the Days of the Dead (November 1 & 2) to *papel picado*, cut paper banners. The store at the museum has lots of unusual things from all over the world for under five dollars.

Next door, the **Museum of Indian Arts and Culture** is filled with beautiful pottery, baskets, weavings, and jewelry made by Native Americans. These are the kind of arts and crafts that we usually only see in books, so wander through the museum and discover a pot made in A.D. 400 or just a few months ago. Sit down at a table in the Kid's Corner and put together puzzles in the shape of black pottery, draw on the chalkboard, or make a pot. Pearl Sunrise (a renowned weaver) is the curator of the Resource Center and will show you how to grind corn in a *metate* or weave on a traditional Navajo loom. In the Resource Center, you can also touch the weavings, card wool, and even play a drum. Zuni beaded dolls and many books on Indian legends as well as tiny Acoma pots are for sale in the gift shop.

Walk from the Museum of Indian Arts and Culture down a dirt road to the nearby **Wheelwright Museum**. Built in the eight-sided shape of a traditional Navajo hogan, the high ceiling is made of stacked logs. The first floor is filled with changing exhibits of everything from sandpaintings to sculpture made by American Indians. Sometimes there may even be potters or weavers demonstrating their work in the museum.

Downstairs, go backward in time at the Case Trading Post, which is a replica of a turn-of-the-century trading post. Concho belts (silver medallions strapped to a leather belt) hang from poles, and pottery fills another cabinet. You can buy tapes of Indian songs and stories or cloth Navajo dolls wearing velvet shirts and turquoise necklaces. There are even tiny papoose pins and painted wooden tomahawks for sale.

The museum sometimes offers classes for kids in such things as how to make a paintbrush from a yucca stalk. Before you leave, go outside and walk through the round doorway of a tipi; look at the sky through the hole in its cone-shaped roof. On summer evenings, you can sit in front of it and listen to Joe Hayes tell stories like "The Day It Snowed Tortillas."

*If you eat some chile that's too spicy, take a piece of tortilla or bread instead of water. It will cool your mouth down faster.*

The **Santa Fe Children's Museum**, located on Old Pecos Trail, is recommended as a must-see by kids of all ages. Outside you'll see fierce-looking animal sculptures and in warm weather, the museum turtle. Two big purple "sound dishes" stand forty feet away from each other near the museum's entrance. If you talk into the metal ring on one dish, your friend can hear you through the other one, which is nearly half a block away! Inside the two-story interior of the museum, you can pull huge bubbles over your head from the giant soap table. If you put on a rock-climbing helmet and rope, members of the **Santa Fe Mountain Center** will help you climb sixteen feet straight up on the specially designed ceramic climbing wall. The Climbing Wall isn't open all the time, so call first to make sure you can use it. You can also observe leaves, bugs, and bones through a microscope or run your hands across thousands of blunt nails in the Pin Screen for a creepy feeling.

*On Saturdays, at the Santa Fe Children's Museum, you can work with a Santa Fe artist and learn to paint, weave, make pottery masks, and more. Scientists also come to the Children's Museum and bring special snakes, birds, animals, and fossils. You might do floating water experiments with a physicist or learn about lizards from a herpetologist (a person who studies reptiles). On many Friday evenings, you'll find puppeteers, musicians, story tellers, and dancers performing for noisy audiences of kids and parents of all ages.*

*Did you see the glass dome, sixty feet above you, in the rotunda of the Capitol? Can you guess what's above it? If you guessed green plants, you're right. Flowers and plants for the grounds are grown in a greenhouse here. The grounds of the New Mexico State Capitol are very unusual because they are covered with native plants that form secret gardens where you can hide away or picnic.*

The museum is home to a variety of creatures, from giant hissing Madagascar cockroaches (don't let them out!) to corn snakes you can carry around your neck. Watch exotic fish in the aquarium and talk to a colorful parrot. Before you leave, look in the Museum Store, which has colorful T-shirts, a cyclone in a bottle, and lots of games for you to buy and take home.

The **State Capitol Building**, on Paseo de Peralta, is just a short drive from the Children's Museum. It's built in the round shape of the Zia Pueblo sun symbol whose four arms represent the four directions. Look for the red Zia sun symbol on the yellow New Mexico flag and see how the building's round shape mirrors the flag. You can tour the Capitol on your own or with a tour guide (no charge) whose desk is on the ground floor.

*Being short will help when it comes to looking at the state seal, which is inlaid in turquoise, brass, and marble in the floor of the State Capitol. Why does the eagle have a snake in its mouth? Aztec legend says that whenever you see an eagle with a snake in its mouth, that's where the gods want you to settle and where an empire will be founded. Did you find the Mexican eagle? That's on the state seal because New Mexico was once a part of Old Mexico.*

During the summer, the **Santa Fe Opera** saves final dress rehearsals for kids. In fact, an adult needs to bring four kids to get in! The opera house is an outdoor amphitheater, and while many seats have a roof, others do not. The performance doesn't begin until sunset, so be sure to bring a rain poncho and lots of warm sweaters because you'll probably be there until the cold midnight hour. There's nothing like the Santa Fe Opera when it comes to beautiful sets, awesome costumes, and out-of-this-world singing.

During dress rehearsal at the Santa Fe Opera,

the technical staff wears headphones and sits at a "tech table." They're telling backstage workers to change the lighting or asking a singer to move over a little. After a dress rehearsal, opera workers will sometimes completely repaint scenery or make a new costume.

Looking for a bargain? Then hit the **flea market** (north of town by the opera) held every weekend during the warm months, and bargain for everything from tennis shoes to old jewelry to a book you can't live without. You won't see many tourists here. But you'll see lots of different Santa Feans. Old and young, weird and not so weird.

# 5. Planes, Trains, & Posole

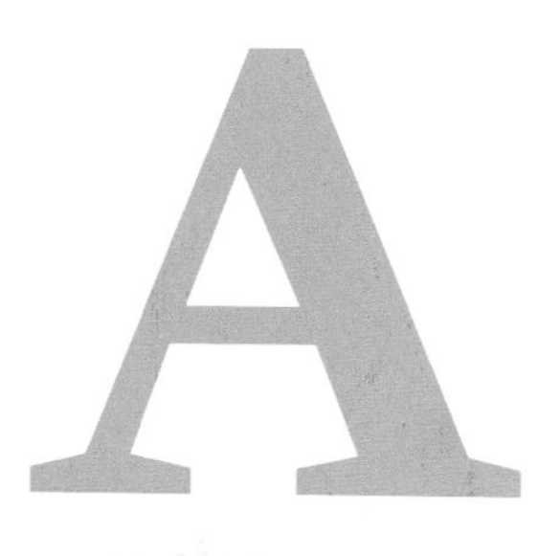

s you walk to **Guadalupe Street** from the plaza, you can't miss the **Santuario de Guadalupe**, which stands at the corner of Guadalupe and Agua Fria streets. Built in 1795, it is probably the oldest shrine to the Virgin of Guadalupe in the United States. The vigas, long logs that support the roof, were actually cut down twenty-three years before the United States became independent from Great Britain.

*During Christmastime, farolitos (paper bags that hold a lit candle imbedded in sand) line Canyon Road. These beautiful glowing lanterns light the way for the Christ child. Small bonfires called luminarias also burn along the streets on Christmas Eve.*

The Virgin of Guadalupe, the patron saint of Mexico, is said to have appeared before a poor farmer and given him a bouquet of fresh roses in the middle of winter. Although the Santuario is no longer used as a church, a painting of the Virgin hangs above where the altar once was. The **Santa Fe Desert Chorale** performs here in the summer.

As you walk up Guadalupe Street with your grown-up, you'll see antique shops, clothing stores, and restaurants. Look for the **Guadalupe Cafe**, which serves good New Mexican food, or the **Zia Diner**, where you can sit at an old-fashioned soda fountain. If you've ever taken a snapshot, be sure to look at the excellent photos in the **Scheinbaum and Russek Gallery of Photography**. Seeing these pictures might have you taking your next photo from down on the floor or in a crowd of strangers. Next door is **Horizons**, a store that has science kits, toys, and a good selection of books on the environment.

Take a detour down Montezuma Street and explore the **Sanbusco Market Center**. It used to be a run-down warehouse, but now it's fixed up and filled with a lot of different stores. There's a sidewalk café as well as a restaurant and clothing store. **Los Llanos Bookstore** has an excellent selection of books. At **Pookanoggin**, you can play with many of the toys before you buy them: fly a plane around the room or push a train on its tracks.

When you go back up Montezuma Street, you'll walk over the railroad tracks. You can look down into the railroad yard, which has occasional freight trains moving through it. You'll probably spot a railroad car or two on the tracks. In the yard is the old railroad station, which is now **Tomasita's Restaurant**, where you can find New Mexican food. A local newspaper poll said that the restaurant had the best chile rellenos and sopaipillas, and also the longest wait.

On the corner of Montezuma and Guadalupe streets is the **State Records Center and Archives Building**. Does that sound boring? Maybe it is on the inside, but on the outside, five Santa Fe artists have painted a huge mural that covers one wall of the building. Look closely and you'll see a medicine man, a corn goddess, and a railroad train practically chugging out of the wall.

Across the street is **Santa Fe Pottery**. Inside you can look at everything from handmade casseroles to hanging lamps to mugs. The person at the counter is probably one of the potters, and he or she might demonstrate "throwing" a pot.

*Every Tuesday and Saturday during the summer and early fall, you'll find the south parking lot of Sanbusco Center crowded with pickup trucks laden with fruits, vegetables, and baked goods. This* ***Farmer's Market*** *is an old-fashioned growers market where you'll meet the farmer who grew the watermelon, corn, honey, chile, or apples she or he is selling. You'll see flowers of all colors, braids of garlic, and lots of kids. The Farmer's Market is a chance for you to see a part of New Mexico that is usually found only by exploring narrow dirt roads.*

Wander down the side streets and you're sure to discover some surprises. You can walk back to the plaza through the **Santa Fe River Park**. You'll know you're there when you see the fountain made by Linda Wilde, a sculpture of two kids playing. On hot days, you may see real kids wading in the fountain. Keep going north on Guadalupe and you can sample awesome chocolate brownies at the **Chocolate Maven** or pizza at **El Primo**.

If you follow Guadalupe Street to the south, you'll end up on Cerrillos Road. Going southwest on Cerrillos, you'll see the fenced grounds of the New Mexico School for the Deaf and the Santa Fe Indian School. On the grounds of the Indian School is the **Museum of the Institute of American Indian Arts**, a two-year art college that has taught some of the most prominent Native American artists in the world. See the work of famous artists like Allan Houser and T. C. Cannon. (In 1992, look for the museum near the plaza at Cathedral Place and San Francisco Street.)

Are X Men, Spiderman, Batman, or Conan your favorite comic book heroes? Then head over to **Book Mountain** on Cerrillos Road where you'll find stacks of old and new ones as well as tons of used books. If you collect baseball cards, turn on St. Michael's Drive and go to **Santa Fe Trail Coin and Currency**. You'll often find the shop filled with kids buying and trading baseball, football, and hockey cards. For cheap and good fast food, go back to Cerrillos Road; order a soft shell taco or a Vitari fruit cone at **Baja Taco**.

Do you know what a Jackalope is? You can find postcards and a sculpture of the imaginary creature (half jackrabbit, half antelope) at **Jackalope Pottery**. Many kids recommend it as a place

Original mural design director, Zara Kriegstein; mural artists, Marian Berg, Olen Perkins, Felipe Cabeza de Vaca, and David Pratt

to lay in Mexican hammocks or look at birds in a huge cage that fills part of a room. There are hundreds of big and little things you can take home and an outdoor café that has reasonably priced lunches and homemade lemonade. You can get beaded belts that say "Santa Fe" on them or Christmas lights shaped like red chile peppers. Before you leave, check out the pottery yard's stacks and stacks of all sizes of pots.

The **Villa Linda Mall**, farther down Cerrillos, has an old-fashioned carousel to ride as well as a video arcade. Pretend you're a pilot in the airplane cockpit (at the arcade), pushing buttons and pulling switches, or play countless video games. There are also six movie theaters in case you're in the mood to sit in the dark.

*Watch for the huge mural showing some of New Mexico's history on the side of* ***Empire Builder's Supply*** *on Cerrillos Road. A giant eagle dancer rises in front of his pueblo while conquistadors look toward him. Scientists stand in front of bombs and a pueblo-style church sits serenely in the landscape.*

# 6. Burros, Birds, & Bugs

*The **Historic Santa Fe Foundation** recommends taking an architectural tour of Santa Fe. The **Fort Marcy Officer's Residence** (116 Lincoln Ave.) copied the Spanish pueblo style, while the **Randall Davey House** on upper Canyon Road was built in the territorial style. Look for these and other types of buildings as you walk up Canyon Road.*

If you like arts and crafts, then **Canyon Road** will be heaven. It begins with the little carved turquoise sign at the intersection with Paseo de Peralta which says, "Canyon Road," and continues with the many galleries and artist's studios that line the road.

Before the Spanish came to Santa Fe, Canyon Road was a trail the Indians used which followed the Santa Fe River over the Sangre de Cristos to the Pecos Pueblo. Ruins are all that remain of the pueblo, but Canyon Road became *el camino del cañon*. Until the middle of the 1950s, you would have seen burros loaded down with firewood making their way slowly down the road. They were led by woodcutters who were bringing firewood to keep Santa Fe residents warm.

The compound at **two twenty-five Canyon Road** is filled with many different art galleries. Exhibits change often, so whenever you go, a surprise is in store. You may see giant marble sculptures or paintings of New Mexico landscapes. Or you might be able to hold the tail of a ceramic cat that is also a teapot.

Look for the red brick **First Ward Schoolhouse** at 400 Canyon Road. If it's open to the public, wander through the rooms and imagine what it was like to be a student in 1906. Where did the

teacher stand? Where do you think the wood stoves stood which kept the kids warm? Did the children play in the yard? What did they learn in those rooms? Do you think they ever ditched school? Since the school closed in 1928, the building has been a gallery, a theater, and an apartment house.

Back on Canyon Road, you'll see lots of galleries filled with Indian rugs, baskets, handmade furniture, and pottery. There might even be a show of sculpture outside which looks like rockets and spaceships. Peek through high fences and spy into secret gardens.

When you see the white picket fence, you'll know you're close to **El Zaguán**, where Adolph and Josephine Bandelier lived a hundred years ago. Walk through the *zaguán*, which is a roofed area joining separate buildings. Bandelier National Monument (see chapter 9) is named after Adolph Bandelier, who was an ethnologist, a person who studies human cultures. Explore the formal Victorian garden that was probably planted by him originally. When gardeners replanted it, samples of the soil were actually examined under a microscope in order to see which pollen and seeds were growing in the garden a century ago.

*How are anthills like adobe houses? The* El Temporal Guide *of the Audubon Center says harvester ants work very hard and dig up big hills of dirt around their nest entrance. Like adobe houses, this "wall of dirt" helps protect the ants against hot and cold. Does the south side of the anthill seem to have a longer slope than the north? This helps collect more of the sun's heat in the wintertime.*

Take a walk on one of the diagonal brick walkways in the garden. Because the property is owned by the **Historic Santa Fe Foundation**, you can picnic on the grounds and smell the flowers. They publish an activities book on historical preservation especially for fourth graders. It tells how you can help save historical buildings.

The **Bookroom** (616 Canyon) has a shelf of books specializing in New Mexico folktales as well as tapes of southwestern stories. In the back, you can have a drink in the coffee bar, or take a muffin into the garden.

**The Stables-Working Artists Studios** (821 Canyon) is filled with artists doing everything from making pottery to painting on silk. These shops are small; usually the artist whose work is on sale is working right there. Talk to them, ask them questions. Is it fun to be an artist? Why does the glaze get shiny in the kiln?

The studio of **Frederico Vigil** (1107 Canyon) is filled with colorful paintings created by this prominent artist. Be sure to call first to make sure he's there. You never know what you may see in Frederico's studio because he may be painting or preparing a fresco. Look for his mural at the **Acequia Madre School**.

The **Randall Davey Audubon Center** on Upper Canyon Road offers lots of special activities for kids on its 135 acres. (Randall Davey was an artist and you can see the studio where he worked.) The Audubon Center offers natural history activities. Try their (costly) Summer Camp (week-long sessions, 9 a.m.-4 p.m.) and leave your parents to sightsee while you learn about animal habitats and go on expeditions. Among other things, you'll learn how to read and take bearings on a compass and how to follow a map. During (inexpensive) Saturday morning sessions, you might play the Recyling Game where you "become" aluminum and are made into a tin can. What happens to you after you're thrown away?

Go to the **Hands-on Interactive Center** and curl up in a cubbyhole with headphones while you listen to bird songs. Walk to the creek or up and down hills. Remember to stay on trails. No picnicking is allowed here. Get the **El Temporal Trail Guide** and take your family on your own self-guided walk. Before you go, check out the bookstore for a good selection of natural history books. On your way home, look for the big reservoir on the right. That's the water supply for all of Santa Fe.

*The best place to look for birds at the Audubon Center is in the orchard and gardens. More than 150 different types of birds have been spotted here, and if you're really lucky, you might see a bald eagle or a yellow warbler, which have only been seen a few times in the last five years.*

# 7. Kivas, Koshares, & Kachinas

Going to an Indian pueblo is sometimes like walking into another century. The Pueblo Indians' early relatives were the *Anasazi*, or "ancient ones." The languages you hear might sound the same to you if you don't know them, but the Pueblo Indians actually speak three different languages, Keresan, Kiowa-Tanoan, and Zuni. When you go to a pueblo where Kiowa-Tanoan is spoken, you'll even hear different dialects called Tewa, Tiwa, and Towa. Sound like too much? Most of the Native Americans you meet will also speak English, but it's fun to listen to the musical sound of their languages.

When you go to the dances, remember that they are sacred ceremonies that help the Indians give thanks for being part of the earth, sky, and water. They consider the earth to be their grandmother and the animals to be their brothers and sisters.

During the **Deer Dance**, you'll watch deer climb down a hill only to discover that they are really men transformed from deer! They wear antlers on their heads and walk on deerlike legs that they hold in their hands. The **Matachines Dance** is a mixture of Spanish and Indian cultures and often has a fiddler making music while

*You may see traditionally dressed people dancing on top of a kiva at* ***Nambe Pueblo****, which is twenty miles from Santa Fe. If you go to nearby* ***Nambe Falls****, think of the legend of the maiden who was loved by two men: a warrior and a hunter. The warrior was jealous and killed the hunter. When the maiden prayed for revenge, the earth swallowed both of them. The maiden's tears are said to have made the falls and pools.*

the dancers wear black fringe over their eyes and beaded costumes. In some pueblos, this dance is performed by Native Americans as well as Hispanics. Dances are not always performed on the same day every year, so call the pueblo for the exact date of the dance you want to attend.

When you visit a pueblo, remember that you're in a very special place and unless you happen to be a resident there, it has a different culture and tradition from yours. Here are some things you need to remember while you're visiting a pueblo.

- Be sure to go to the dances, but don't forget they are religious ceremonies. It's fine to dress casually, but don't wear clothes (such as shorts) that you wouldn't wear to church, synagogue, or school.
- The kiva is a sacred building, so don't walk in or on top of it.
- Dances may begin when the sun comes up or after the dancers have prayed in the kiva. Pretend you're in a place before clocks were invented, because the dances don't always begin according to the time on watches. Be patient, and remember that the ceremony will be worth waiting for.
- When the dances begin, keep a respectful distance, and try not to block anyone's view. Don't touch the dancers or imitate them. If you want to talk to a friend, talk quietly. Wait until the ceremony's over to run and jump.
- The residents of the pueblos are very generous people and usually cook for days before a feast day. There isn't enough food for them to serve all guests, so there are food booths where you can buy traditional Indian foods. If you go to these booths, be sure to buy the delicious Indian bread that is baked in hornos.

*The* koshare *are clowns who paint their bodies with gray paint and black stripes. They are important leaders in the pueblo and watch the dancers to make sure everyone is doing it right.*

*The Pilgrims landed at Plymouth Rock twenty-two years after* **San Juan Pueblo** *became the capital of New Mexico. In the main plaza, you'll see two rectangular kivas next to the Catholic church. You can go to the Feast Day on June 24 or see the Buffalo Dance the night before. While you're at San Juan, be sure to look at the beautiful carved red pottery or the stone carvings in the* ***O'ke Oweenge Arts and Crafts Cooperative****.*

*The Pueblo Indian dances are related to the four seasons. During spring, summer, and autumn dances, the people offer their thanks for the planting season and the harvest by dancing the Blue Corn Dance and the Harvest Dance. The Elk Dance and the Buffalo Dance are winter dances that celebrate animals.*

• If a pueblo resident invites you to eat in his house, it is impolite to refuse. Enjoy your meal and then go back outside because another guest is probably waiting for your seat. Of course, it is not OK to walk into someone's house uninvited.

• If you want to take pictures, sketch, or use a video camera, you need to ask permission. If it's OK, you'll be asked to pay a fee. Some pueblos don't want anyone to take pictures of their kiva or the surrounding area, so always ask permission before you click the shutter.

There are many pueblos in the Santa Fe area. Only a few are listed below; if you want to visit other Native American villages, contact the Eight Northern Pueblos Council or the individual pueblos.

**Cochiti Pueblo**

On your way to Cochiti Pueblo, look for giant water tanks painted like the famous Cochiti drums. The Keresan-speaking tribe has a long history of resisting Spanish rule. About thirty years before the Pueblo Revolt, the Spaniards uncovered a plot that the Cochiti, Jemez, and Apache had created to drive them away. When it was discovered, the Spanish governor had many of the Indian leaders hung and turned others into slaves. Historians believe this contributed to the Pueblo Revolt.

Visit the pueblo on July 14, and you can celebrate the Feast of San Buenaventura. An elaborate mass is held in the beautiful old Spanish-Indian church. This is followed by a long day of dancing and feasting. The pueblo is known for its wonderful ceramic storyteller dolls. These figures are usually seated women who have kids climbing up their arms, clinging to their shoulders, crying

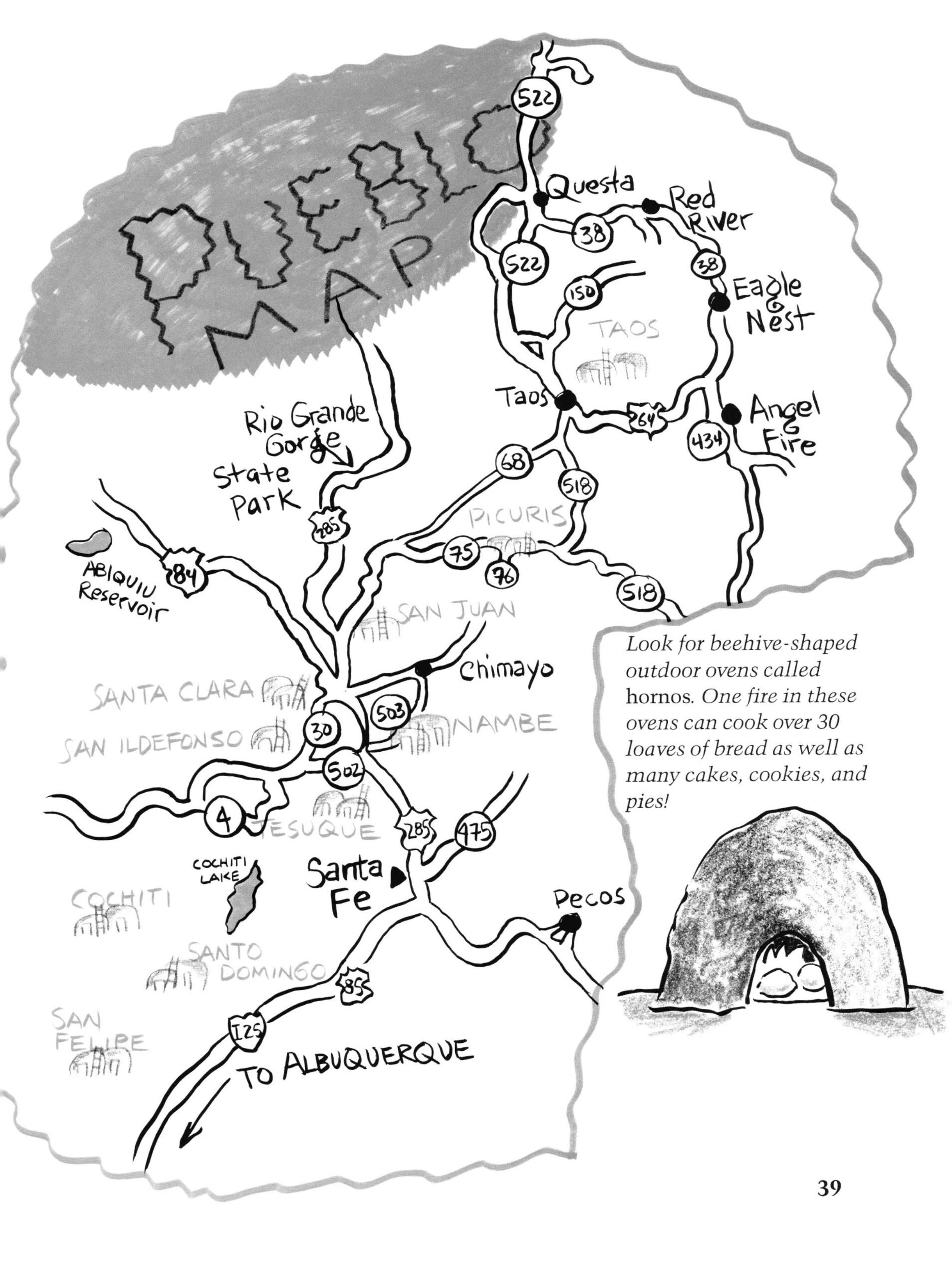


*Look for beehive-shaped outdoor ovens called* hornos. *One fire in these ovens can cook over 30 loaves of bread as well as many cakes, cookies, and pies!*

*You might especially wish you were a member of a pueblo on a Feast Day (which takes place on the same day every year), because it's usually a school holiday for the kids who live there. Long before the Spaniards came to New Mexico, the pueblo people celebrated their Feast Days, but it was the Spanish priests who named the Pueblo Feast Days for Catholic saints. The pueblos also have names for their Feast Days in the Tewa or Keresan languages.*

in their ears, and dangling from their legs! Would you like to be the storyteller?

**San Ildefonso Pueblo**

Located on a spectacular mesa twenty-four miles northwest of Santa Fe, San Ildefonso Pueblo is called *Po-woh-ge-oweenge* in Tewa, which means "Where the Water Cuts Through." (The nearby Rio Grande is the water that cuts through.) The pueblo is famous for its pottery, which becomes jet black in a special firing method that was rediscovered by Maria Poveka Martinez and her husband, Julian.

See the black or red pottery in the **San Ildefonso Pueblo Museum** or the **Popovi Da Studio of Indian Arts**. Can you find the *avanyu*, or water serpent, designs on the pots? January 23 is the Feast Day at this pueblo, and that's when you can watch the Comanche and Animal Dances. The people of San Ildefonso ask the spirits to bless their pueblo on this day. You can also fish on the **San Ildefonso Fishing Lake** or picnic nearby.

**Santa Clara Pueblo**

Indians were living in the Puye Cliff Dwellings 240 years before Christopher Columbus "discovered" America. Put your feet in the same holes these ancient people used to climb to their high caves. Climb ladders to the top level of the mesa. Stand in the great courtyard of Santa Clara Pueblo in August and watch the Puye ceremonial dances.

## Santo Domingo Pueblo

The Green Corn Dance on August 4 at Santo Domingo Pueblo honors St. Dominic and Iyatiko, the mother figure of the tribe who is often symbolized by corn. After the Pueblo Revolt, many Santo Domingo Indians fled to high mesas in the Jemez Mountains. This has helped them keep their strong traditions, which are especially evident on their Feast Day and on the many days during the year when the pueblo is closed while the tribe privately honors its sacred beliefs. The *cacique*, who is an honored elder, leads the ceremonies. All spring and summer he has fasted (on and off) and meditated to get ready for this day.

Santo Domingo kids suggest you look for two kivas in their pueblo, one of the squash people and the other of the turquoise people. During the dances, see the men from these groups who are painted orange or turquoise! Look for tiny round shell necklaces called *heishi*, which are a specialty of the pueblo jewelers.

## Tesuque Pueblo

You and your family could ride your bikes to the **Pueblo of Tesuque**, *Teh Tsu Geh* (grove of trees close together), because it's only nine miles north of Santa Fe. During Spanish rule, Tesuque was a revolutionary pueblo. Two of its leaders were runners who warned the other pueblo chiefs when the Pueblo Revolt would begin.

Their Feast Day is November 12 and begins with mass in the church, followed by dances on the plaza later in the day. Look for the beautiful vegetable gardens where the members of this Tewa-speaking pueblo are farming everything from blue corn to pumpkins.

***Pueblo Green Chile Stew***
*Fry 2 pounds of pork with 1 chopped onion, 2 diced squash, and 2 diced potatoes. Add 3 cups of water and cook covered for 1 hour. Add 1 cup of diced green chile, 1 can of tomatoes, and 1 can of corn. Cook for 30 minutes.*

*Kivas, ceremonial prayer chambers (kind of like churches), are usually round or rectangular and built partway into the ground. They are made out of adobe bricks and often have domed ceilings.*

**Taos Pueblo**

Going to Taos Pueblo is like walking into a history book. The ancient pueblo with its stacked, boxlike adobe buildings and blue-trimmed doors and windows seems to stand still in time. The residents of this old part of the pueblo still draw their water from the Rio Pueblo, choosing not to change the buildings by adding plumbing or electricity. On San Geronimo Feast Day, September 30, you can watch as boys your age climb to the top of a pole or run races.

You can see dancers and singers from all over the United States and Canada participate in the Annual Taos Pueblo Pow-Wow the second weekend in July. Taste warm bread baked in the horno or have some green chili stew at one of the stands in the Pueblo Plaza. Be sure to go to a shop and beat one of the handmade Taos Pueblo drums.

The **Taos Indian Horse Ranch Company** will take you on horseback rides off into the sunset, winter sleigh rides, or summer hay wagon cookouts. An Indian storyteller, along with traditional Native American dancers, may join your group.

# 8. Good Sports

The high mountains, roaring rivers, and open mesas that surround Santa Fe offer places for all kinds of sporting activities. You can climb up a cliff, saddle a horse, or hear the crack of your baseball bat hitting a hard line drive. In the winter, go downhill and cross-country skiing, or try snowshoeing, ice skating, or sliding down a hill in a big inner tube. In the warm months, go white-water rafting down the Rio Grande or windsurfing on Cochiti Lake. Tired of taking chances? Then go bowling or play a round of miniature golf. Santa Fe's parks have basketball and tennis courts, too.

**Winter Sports**

Snap your skis on at the **Santa Fe Ski Area**, and if you want a lesson, stop at Chipmunk Corner. Whether you're just learning or want someone to help you run on moguls or speed through gates, as long as you're over three and under thirteen, this is the place to get a lesson. Ski through cones or play games with your class, and then whiz down Alpine Bowl with your family.

Want to glide through the snow without waiting in line for the chair lift? Santa Fe has lots of cross-country ski trails nearby. (When you go,

*The ice at the Los Alamos Ice Skating Rink is created by ice skaters who spray the water on with hoses during the coldest part of the night and skate over the new ice until it's smooth. You'd like this job if 3:00 in the morning is your favorite time to get up and out.*

follow the safety rules in chapter 9.) The **Nordic Ski Trail** (14 miles from Santa Fe on State Road 475) was created just for cross-country skiers. The beginner's trail is good to learn on because it's fairly flat and even. You can test your skills on the advanced trail, which has a few steep spots. Both of these trails are short, so you may want to practice on them and then take nearby **Aspen Vista** for a longer trip.

**The Southwest Nordic Center** offers cross-country skiing lessons for kids during the winter. Doug MacLennan will teach you how to put your skis on, go down hills, and make turns. Intermediate and advanced lessons are also available. Ski rental is provided with the lesson. They're located in Taos, but they'll give you lessons in Santa Fe as well.

If you'd like to try your hand at figure eights, take your skis off, and head over to the **Los Alamos Ice Skating Rink**. It's an outdoor rink shaded by a mountain, so it stays cold throughout the winter. Rent single- and double-bladed skates, or bring your own. Whiz around the rink by yourself or take lessons, and learn how to figure skate or play hockey or broom ball (hockey with a broom). If you need a schedule, call the Los Alamos Department of Parks and Recreation.

Back in Santa Fe, **Hyde Park** also has a skating rink and a tubing area behind the Evergreen Lodge, but the skating pond isn't open regularly. Be sure to call first to make sure you can use the rink. Otherwise, blow up a big inner tube, or bring a sled, and glide down the bowl near the rink, or try the other tubing area above the ski area parking lot.

**Spring, Summer, and Fall Sports**

Whether you're hiking, picnicking, or watching the aspen trees turn golden, you can ride up 10,000 feet on the chair lift at the **Santa Fe Ski Area**. At the top of the mountain, you'll be treated to more dramatic views and you can also look through some telescope-like pipes that will point you all the way toward Sandia Peak in Albuquerque and other faraway spots. Bring a jacket; riding through high mountain areas can be cold, no matter what time of year it is.

After seeing all those mountains, you may want to try climbing up the side of a cliff. Don't try it until you've had lessons from professionals, like those who teach at the **Santa Fe Mountain Center**. You'll learn how to safely climb up and rappel down a cliff. They'll also show you how to use climbing equipment and teach you important safety lessons. This all-day outing is expensive, so you'll need to save your money for it.

*Have you ever wanted to get on a windsurfing board and sail across the water? **Santa Fe Windsurfing** says kids learn windsurfing quickly, partly because of their low body weight. If you weigh sixty pounds or more, they will teach you about safety, emergency stops, and steering in their two-hour ground school. The next day, they'll take you to Cochiti Lake where you can catch the wind in your sail all day long. This class is expensive (so save up your money) and qualifies you for national certification, which you need to rent sailboards.*

*If you're a "mountain kid"—that means an intermediate skier who rides the chair lift—then you can go to* ***Children's Adventureland*** *in the Santa Fe Ski Area. Explore snow caves, crawl through tunnels, or slide up and down on the Rio Grande Roller Bumps. You can hide in Totemoff's Tipi, and when you get cold, warm up by the big fireplace inside the cabin. After you get warm, speed down the roller coaster of Pecos Gulch. It's like a water slide made of snow.*

**New Wave Rafting Company** will pick you up near the plaza and take you white-water rafting on the Rio Grande. If you're over seven years old and can get your parents to sign a release form, New Wave will take you without your mom and dad! Kids get special treatment from the guides, who are licensed by the Bureau of Land Management. Float on 11- to 15-foot inflatable rafts. Help paddle the raft around rocks as you see the Rio Grande from a rare vantage point.

Now that you've sped down a river, how about a game of good old American baseball? If you're tired of being a tourist and want to meet some kids from Santa Fe, **Dynos-Baseball** welcomes boy and girl visitors six to thirteen years old (a little older or younger is okay, too). They play Tuesday and Thursday evenings for eight weeks during June, July, and August. On Tuesdays, parents are welcome as spectators, and on Thursdays, you can bring Mom and Dad to play with you. Be sure to call Vince Demmer at Dynos (471-0137) for time and location.

**Year-Round**
Another way to see the Santa Fe area from an unusual spot is to put your feet in the stirrups and go horseback riding. Chery Fenley of the **Medicine Horse Ranch** (south of Santa Fe) will teach you how to saddle and get to know your horse. The ranch has miniature paint ponies and other special horses just for kids. After you mount up, Fenley will teach you the ABC's of riding. If you've dreamed of riding through wide open spaces like in the cowboy movies, then **Camel Rock Ranch** (north of Santa Fe) is the place for you. When you see an outcropping of rocks shaped like a camel, you'll know you're near the ranch where you can ride through 7,000 acres of mesa land.

*The City of Santa Fe owns a large area north of town where cyclists like to ride. From the plaza, drive with your family north on St. Francis to Camino de las Crucitas west. Follow this road several miles until you see a park just before the city landfill on your left-hand side. Park here and take your bike back out onto Camino de las Crucitas turning left. When the road forks, take an immediate right. Now look for trails and explore. Every way is the right way, and it's easy to get lost and found here. Remember to ride toward the Sangres if you want to get home, and stay with your family at all times.*

*Be sure to wear your bicycle helmet and take a grown-up with you while you're riding. Most bicycle injuries can be prevented or reduced if the rider has a helmet on.*

If you need a break from the adults in your life, consider the **Children's Adventure Company**. You can make art, act in plays, go rock-climbing, kayak, and even experience wilderness survival with skilled leaders. You have to sign up for at least one week; summer hours are from 8:00 a.m. to 6:00 p.m. Monday through Friday.

Ready to whiz through town on your bike? With its narrow roads, busy streets, and lack of bike lanes, Santa Fe isn't the best town to bicyle in. But there are some good trails and roads that will take you to beautiful spots. If you want to rent a bike, go to **Downtown Bike Shop** (719 Paseo de Peralta) where you can rent a mountain bike by the hour, day, or week. A helmet is included in the rental cost.

If you plan to stay on roads (as opposed to mountain trails), there are several routes to choose from. Pick up a City of Santa Fe Bicycle Map at the city libraries, **rob and charlies**, or the Downtown Bike Shop. This map shows you which streets are the best for road riding and mountain biking, places where you need to be especially careful, and intersections to avoid. If you need more information about biking or want to ride with a group, call the **Sangre de Cristo Bicycle Club** (471-3394).

Road cyclists suggest taking Bishop's Lodge Road to Tesuque. This is a pretty ride to take with grown-ups in all four seasons. It has narrow shoulders, slow traffic, and lots of ups and downs. Stop along the way to enjoy the views, or wait until you're in Tesuque and choose from several spots to visit (see chapter 10).

# 9. Hiking

Do you want to get out of town? Or go to places only your feet can take you? Then put on your walking shoes, because in the Santa Fe area you can hike up to 13,000 feet or down to 6,000 feet! Four wilderness areas (Pecos, Bandelier, Dome, and San Pedro parks) are within a ninety-minute drive. The Santa Fe National Forest is only minutes away, and you'll find one and one-half million acres of land ready to be hiked.

Remember to follow safety rules. Never go alone. Be sure your family or an adult friend goes with you. Plan your route before you go, and tell someone where you are going and when you expect to return. People who've lived in New Mexico all of their lives get lost every year while hiking. The New Mexico Department of Game and Fish can recommend safe places to go during hunting season. Storms can come quickly, so be sure to stay off peaks during a lightning storm.

*Remember! Respect the animals' homes. Do not handle any animals in the wild.*

Even if you go in the summer, take extra wool clothes as well as a rain poncho, a small first aid kit, sunscreen, and a flashlight. When you go into the wilderness, take waterproof matches, a map, a compass, a pocketknife, a whistle to call attention to yourself if you get separated from your group, a candle, and extra water and food.

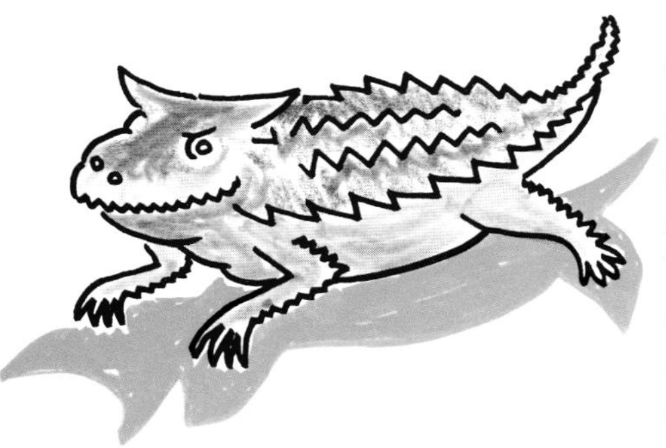

*Look closely at horned toads, which are actually lizards, and you can imagine that they roamed the Earth at the same time as the dinosaurs. Their rough, earth-colored skin camouflages them so well in New Mexico's landscape that they are usually hard to see. To find them, walk in a spiral away from anthills (where they're waiting for ants to eat). Keep your eyes peeled, because if the horned toad sees you, he will stay completely still, blending in with the landscape.*

If you've come to New Mexico from a low altitude, wait several days until you go into the mountains. Many people experience altitude sickness if they go too high too fast. If you, or anyone in your group, experiences diarrhea or vomiting or feels very ill, get down the mountain and to a hospital. Hypothermia or exposure is another problem. If someone in your group experiences shivering followed by difficulty in walking, get him warm right away.

It's unlikely you or anyone in your group will have anything but a good time on your travels. Following safety rules like these can prevent big problems. Got your hiking boots or your walking shoes laced up? Get ready. Get set. Go!

The **Sierra Club** welcomes everyone on their group hikes, which are rated strenuous, moderate, and easy. The club publishes their schedule in all the local newspapers and recommends that you try an easy hike to start. Go on a Saturday or Sunday hike or a weekend backpacking trip. During the winter, the hikes sometimes become cross-country ski tours. Anyone under sixteen needs to go with their parents. You don't have to join the Sierra Club to go, but all hikers share in paying for gas since they car pool to the trailhead.

Some of the Sierra Club hikes take place in **Hyde Park**, which is in the Sangre de Cristo

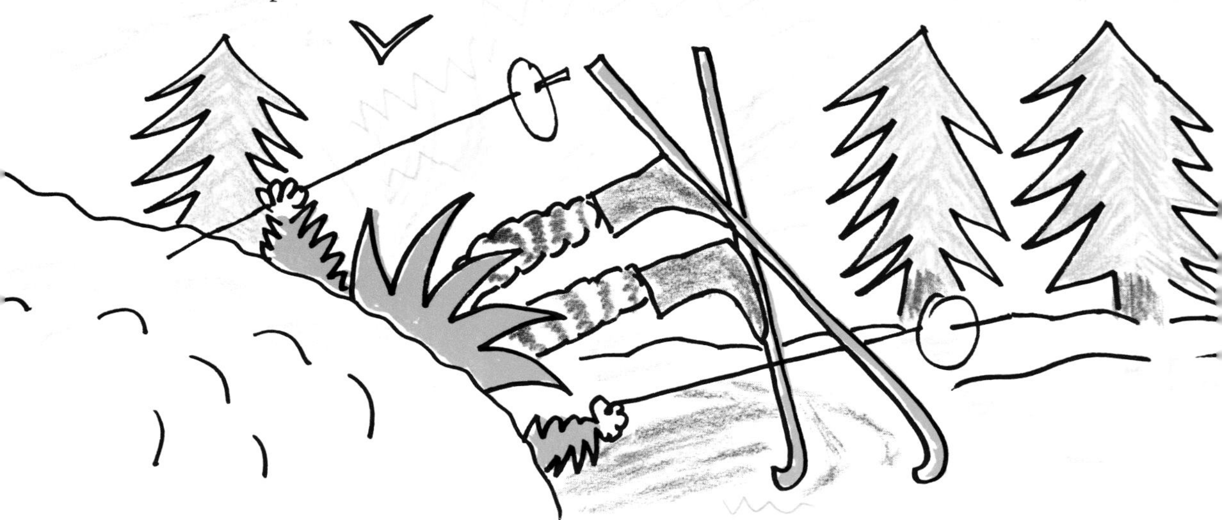

(Blood of Christ) mountains. Almost every trail in this area is good for hiking and picnicking, and the small fee you put into the payment box helps pay for park maintenance.

From the **Hyde Memorial State Park Headquarters** (Washington Avenue to Artist's Road, east for 7.2 miles), you can take the **Girl Scout Nature Trail**. This trail was created by the Girl Scouts about twenty years ago. The trees are tagged, so test yourself! All trees with needles are the same? Right? Wrong. Check out the signs. On the nature trail alone, find these different trees with needles: Douglas fir, white fir, limber pine, and ponderosa pine. Look for the Oregon grape, which is called a "living fossil" because its form is found in so many fossils.

If you want to hike in a warmer spot, try **Tentrocks** (40 miles south of Santa Fe off the Cochiti exit to State Road 16). It looks like a set from a movie about extraterrestrials. The tall round rock spires rise high into the sky. What once was a hundred-foot cliff of welded volcanic glass called tuff has been eroded by wind and rain into cones shaped like giant tents. Climb under massive boulders or through narrow canyons. Keep your eyes peeled for petroglyphs (ancient rock carvings) of handprints and serpents. Remember not to take any rocks from here.

*Whiptail lizards live in lower areas like Tentrocks. Look for their jerky walk and thin forked tongue. If you get too close, they'll do "push-ups" to scare you off.*

*Look for tarantulas. You may see these spiders migrating, especially in fall.*

*Don't look for beans in* "Rito de Frijoles" *even though it means "Little River of Beans" or "Bean Creek."*

**Bandelier National Monument**, an hour northwest of Santa Fe, is the site of an Indian settlement that thrived from A.D. 1100 to 1550. To this day, no one really knows why they left the site, though anthropologists (people who study native languages and cultures) think the dwellers of Bandelier had to leave for a variety of reasons including overpopulation and drought.

Bandelier is a great place to experience history while you hike or camp. The National Park Service manages Bandelier and offers a lot of activities for kids. In the **Ruins Ranger Program**, you can earn a special patch by doing a variety of activities, from identifying trees and plants to writing about what it might have been like to be an Indian living at Bandelier.

**Campfire talks** take place at night around the fire, and you might see a Park Ranger telling stories, showing slides, or talking about the plants and animals in Bandelier. **Kids Stuff** is a ranger-guided program that happens in the summer and includes lots of different activities from nature walks to making pottery. This program is for kids only, so you'll have to ask the adults who are with you to keep out of trouble while you participate. Call ahead to find out when this program takes place.

On the **Frijoles** (Beans) **Canyon** walk, you can actually climb up long ladders to caves where these ancient people lived. Feel the cool, protected air inside the caves which made them

comfortable homes during hot summers and cold winters. Walk in grooves in the volcanic rock which were worn there by the ancient dwellers. This trail is partly accessible by wheelchair. Self-guiding trail bookets in six languages, including braille, are available at the trailhead or in the Visitor's Center.

Pretend you're one of the residents as you climb ladders to the **Ceremonial Cave**, 150 feet above the canyon. Imagine what these people did in their caves. Did they chant and meditate? Did they cook their dinners? Did they tell stories to their children?

Like Bandelier, **Pecos National Historical Park** (25 miles southeast of Santa Fe, 8 miles west of Glorieta exit) is the site of what was a thriving Indian settlement. At one time, the pueblo housed from 1,500 to 2,000 people, but they were killed by diseases brought by the Europeans and a war with the Comanche Indians.

Walk along the **Pecos Ruins Trail**, which begins at the Visitor's Center. Go inside the kiva; push a button, and you'll be surrounded by Indian chants. Archaeologists continue to explore the site. They have discovered two large semi-underground houses that they think were used during the summers. These pit houses were probably built in the ninth century. That's twelve hundred years ago!

In the Visitor's Center, be sure to handle the pottery shards and tools on the "Please Touch" table. You'll love the diorama (miniature three-dimensional scene) of the pueblo when it was thriving. Look for the hunting party returning with their game and the people weaving, making pottery, or shucking corn. Does the church look different from what you imagined?

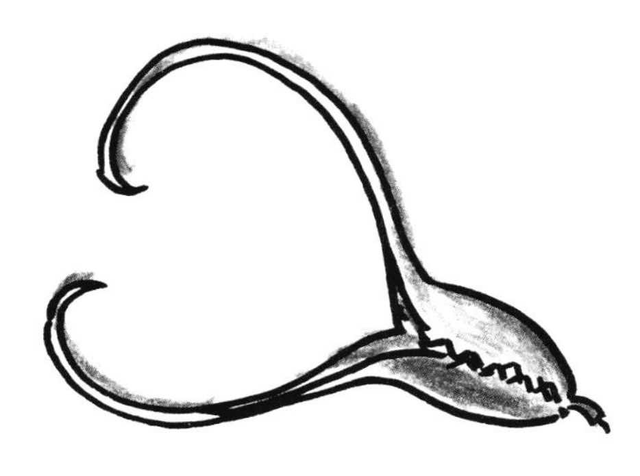

*Devil's claws grow near Tentrocks. Look for these creepy-looking curved seed pods that look like their name.*

*When Gaspar Castaño de Sosa visited the* ***Pecos Pueblo*** *in 1590, he said, "The houses are four and five stories. They go up little ladders that can be pulled up by hand through the hatchways. Every house has 3 or 4 apartments so that from top to bottom each house has 15 or 16 rooms. The rooms are. . . white-washed."*

*Don't stand under* Viscum album *unless you want to get kissed! Why? That's Latin for mistletoe, and it grows on ponderosa pine trees.*

# 10. Outer Limits

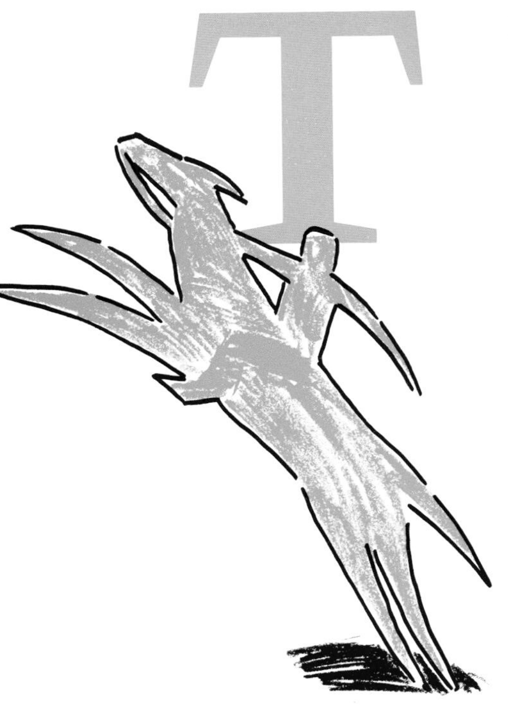

Find clay by looking for cracked earth that curls up a lot at the edges. Good places to spot it are where water runs down, washing the soil away.

There are several towns just a hop, skip, and jump from Santa Fe. Tesuque is a country village that's only five miles north of town. La Cienega is a community filled with farmers, craftspeople, and others who are lucky enough to have an enormous old ranch in their town. Madrid, a little farther away, looks like a town cut right out of an old cowboy movie, while Albuquerque, an hour away, is the largest city in New Mexico.

The grounds of **Shidoni Foundry and Galleries** in **Tesuque** are covered with sculptures of all kinds, many of which have been made right there in the foundry. Walk inside a house sculpture or touch one of the huge bronze figures. If you go on a Saturday afternoon, you can watch a sculpture being cast. On weekdays, tour the foundry during the workers' breaks from 10:30 to 10:45, 12:00 to 1:00, or 3:00 to 3:15. A paid tour includes a guide through all of the foundry and a detailed explanation of how a clay or wax sculpture is turned into bronze.

Before you leave Shidoni, be sure to stop next door at **Tesuque Glassworks**, where Charlie Miner makes beautiful handblown glass. Admire the shape of his delicate goblets, and visit his studio. You can watch Charlie and his friends

***Dixon Apple Farm** is located between Santa Fe and Albuquerque (south of La Cienega, off the Cochiti Lake exit). During the fall apple harvest, you can watch cider being made and learn how apples are picked on a big farm. Don't forget to save your tree climbing for somewhere else: the trees are the Dixons' livelihood and only apples and birds get to hang from them.*

*Get up close to giant snakes in the snake house of the **Rio Grande Zoo** in Albuquerque, or watch exotic birds in the aviary. Concerts take place on the grounds in the summer and you can bring a picnic while you listen to everything from folk to classical music.*

put long pipes into raging furnaces and roll molten glass into hot orange balls. If you stay long enough, you'll get to see them gently blow air into the ball and form one of the glasses you saw on the shelves inside the shop.

If you haven't eaten yet, try the **Tesuque Village Market**, which has a small restaurant. You can eat inside or take out deli food for a picnic. While you're here, visit nearby **Tesuque Pueblo** (chapter 8) or hike on trails that wind around the surrounding hills.

**La Cienega** is an old community that used to be a stopping point for travelers on their way to Santa Fe. Eleven miles south of the city, **El Rancho de las Golondrinas**, the Ranch of the Swallows, has been a working ranch since 1710. Originally purchased by a Spanish couple from the king of Spain, the ranch has spectacular views and is a must-see because it brings history to life in a whole different way.

If you go to the ranch on one of the festival days during the first weekend of June or October, you will get to see people dressed in old-fashioned clothes making rope, candles, and soap or baking bread in hornos. You might also see a blacksmith pounding metal, a weaver dying and spinning wool, or a wheelwright making wagon wheels. From April to August, you can walk through the rancho's old buildings and see the giant waterwheel that grinds grain. A one-room schoolhouse rests above the ranch. It's easy to imagine kids sitting at the desks with their small blackboards. When you see the large dunce cap shaped like an ice cream cone, you might be glad you didn't go to school there.

Coal mining began in **Madrid** (25 miles south

of Santa Fe) in the late 1800s, and the town grew to 3,000 residents. But hard times fell after World War II because the United States didn't use as much coal. Madrid became a ghost town and was put up for sale. In 1975, a land office was set up and the town was sold off piece by piece to all kinds of interesting people. Look for the wooden cabins where miners used to live. They were brought into town in sections on the train and have been turned into galleries, shops, and restaurants.

Go to the **Old West Museum** and inspect the equipment from the coal mine. You can even go inside a mine shaft and see a seam of coal. Look for the saws miners used to cut the coal out of the ground. Outside, go in the train, a 1906 Baldwin

*A.V. Kidder excavated part of Pecos Pueblo beginning in 1915. He dug carefully through the layers of trash near the pueblo and while noting changes in pottery through time, was able to figure out how the culture developed.*

*The* ***Sandia Mountains*** *rise 5,000 feet above the city of Albuquerque. Geologists think that millions of years ago, the Earth's crust shifted and the mountains were suddenly uplifted 20,000 feet. Albuquerque sits on 15,000 feet of these eroded rocks. You can get to Sandia Crest by car or on the Sandia Peak Tramway, a cable car that suspends you in midair as you glide up the mountain.*

*Q. Why is Albuquerque's nickname the "Duke City"?*
*A. The city was named for the Duke of Albuquerque, who lived in Mexico and was the 34th viceroy of New Spain.*

steam engine. Get in the cab and be the train engineer, sitting high above the tracks. If you're visiting in the summer, you might have a chance to walk in the **4th of July Children's Parade** and celebrate the holiday with other kids.

**Albuquerque**, the largest city in New Mexico, is an hour from Santa Fe and has lots of activities for kids. At the **New Mexico Museum of Natural History**, you can walk through a volcano. Smell it burn, and see streams of "lava" flow under your feet. Look for the life-size moving dinosaur. Don't be surprised when it roars! In the Naturalist Center, you can make bird prints in sand and inspect the giant ant farm or beehive.

If you like baseball, you'll love the **Albuquerque Dukes**, the Triple-A farm team for the Los Angeles Dodgers. The stadium is small, and you can get great seats for less than the cost of a movie ticket. Sit by the dugout and see your favorite player close up, or try to catch home runs out at the family area where you can sit on your car and watch the game.

**Los Alamos** is 45 minutes northwest of Santa Fe, and besides hiking, skiing, and ice skating, you can also go to the **Bradbury Science Museum** where there are lots of hands-on exhibits for you to explore. Line up a laser beam, talk to a computer, or pinch plasma in the museum. Before World War II, the only human life at Los Alamos was a boy's school. It was closed by the U.S. government because they wanted to use it to work on Project Y, the code name for the secret development of the atomic bomb. It's really scary to think about a nuclear bomb, but it's also important to never forget about it. When you enter Los Alamos, look for two guard towers that are left over from the time when guards let people in and out of town.

# 11. Adiós / Good-bye

As the high mountains and the low adobe buildings of Santa Fe fade into the distance, pack away your postcards but not your memories. Maybe you climbed a ladder to a kiva or put on a helmet and went straight up the wall at the Children's Museum. Perhaps you saw a sacred ceremony.

One of the greatest things about traveling is being exposed to cultures that are different from yours. That means you meet a whole world of people who have new ideas and ways of seeing the world. Whether your background is African, Anglo, Asian, Hispanic, Native American (or from somewhere else), chances are you met someone in Santa Fe completely unlike yourself.

When you find that your way of living is not the only one, you may appreciate something special about your own life. Or maybe you saw a kid doing something in Santa Fe that you want to try at home. Whether you respectfully watched a Native American dance or spoke Spanish with another child, these are memories of a place that is rich in culture. These differences, after all, are what makes the whole world such an interesting place!

# Year-Round Calendar

Dates are subject to change. Call the Santa Fe Convention and Visitor's Bureau at 984-6760 for specific dates and times.

**January**

Jan. 1: Various dances, Transfer of Canes (most pueblos)
Jan. 6: King's Day Celebration to honor new tribal officers (most pueblos)
Jan. 7: Dances at many pueblos
Jan. 22: Vespers at church, evening Buffalo and Animal Dances at the plaza (San Ildefonso)
Jan. 23: San Ildefonso Pueblo Feast Day, Comanche and Animal Dances (San Ildefonso)

**February**

Animal, Buffalo, and Deer Dances (most pueblos)

**March**

Dances at many pueblos

**April**

Spring skiing at the Santa Fe Ski Area until Easter

**May**

El Rancho de los Golondrinas Spring Festival
Santa Cruz Day, Corn Dance (Cochiti and Taos Pueblos)
Corn Dance (late May or early June at Tesuque Pueblo)
All Species Day

**June**

Vespers and Evening Dances, Buffalo Dances (San Juan Pueblo)
St. Anthony's Feast Day, Comanche Dance (Santa Clara, San Juan, San Ildefonso, Taos pueblos)
Corn Dance (Taos Pueblo)
Santa Fe Desert Chorale (through August) Santa Fe Opera (late June through August)

**July**

Spanish Market
Storytelling with Joe Hayes, early July through late August (Wheelwright Museum)
Jan. 14: San Buenaventura Feast Day, Corn Dance (Cochiti Pueblo)
High Country Arts & Crafts Festival (Picuris Pueblo)
Nambe Falls Celebration (Nambe Pueblo)
Rodeo de Santa Fe
Taos Pueblo Pow-Wow
The Chamber Music Festival (through August)
Eight Northern Pueblos Arts & Crafts Show, San Ildefonso Pueblo
Santiago's Day, various dances (San Ildefonso)

**August**

Aug. 4: Santo Domingo Feast Day, Green Corn Dance (Santo Domingo Feast Day)
Indian Market
Santa Fe Banjo and Fiddle Contest
Pueblo Plaza Fiesta (Picuris Pueblo)
Sunset Dance, San Lorenzo Feast Day-dances and pole climbing (Picuris Pueblo)
Aug. 12: Santa Clara Feast Day, various dances (Santa Clara Pueblo)
Corn Dances, late August or early September (San Ildefonso)

**September**

Fiesta de Santa Fe:
- Burning of Zozobra
- Pet Parade
- Hysterical Historical Parade
- Arts & Crafts Show

Feast of San Geronimo, pole climbing, early morning races (Taos Pueblo)

# Appendix

**October**

El Rancho de los Golondrinas Fall Festival

Oct. 4: St. Francis Feast Day (Nambe Pueblo)

International Hot Air Balloon Fiesta (Albuquerque)

**November**

Dixon New Mexico Artist Studio Tours

Nov. 12: San Diego Feast Day, Comanche and Animal Dances (Tesuque Pueblo)

Santa Fe Ski Area opens (Thanksgiving)

**December**

Dec. 12: Guadalupe Feast Day (Pojoaque Pueblo)

Christmas at the Palace of the Governors

Las Posadas, Palace of the Governors

Dec. 24: Sundown Torchlight Procession, Picuris, San Juan, Taos Pueblos

Dec. 24: Luminarias and Farolitas, Acequia Madre, Plaza

Dec. 25: Matachines or various dances, Santo Domingo, San Ildefonso, Santa Clara, Taos, and Tesuque Pueblos

Dec. 26: Turtle Dance, San Juan Pueblo

The area code for the telephone numbers listed below is 505, unless otherwise noted. Many places are closed on holidays. Call first to double check information.

**Bandelier National Monument**
National Park Service, Los Alamos 87544
672-3861, some areas are handicapped accessible

**Bradbury Science Museum**
Tues. through Fri. 9:00-5:00; Sat., Sun., Mon., 1:00-5:00
Handicapped accessible, no admission charge
667-4444

**Camel Rock Ranch**
Tesuque Pueblo
986-0408

**Capt. Kid Toys**
112 Don Gaspar Ave.
982-2212

**Children's Adventure Company**
828 Gonzales Rd.
984-8870

**Chocolate Maven**
222 N. Guadalupe St.
984-1980

**Cochiti Pueblo**
Pena Blanca, N.M. 87041
465-2255

**Cristo Rey Catholic Church**
1107 Cristo Rey St.
983-8528

**Dixon Apple Farm**
(I-25 S. to exit 264)
465-2976
Peña Blanca, N.M. 87041

**Doodlet's Shop**
120 Don Gaspar Ave.
983-3771

**Downtown Bike Shop**
107 E. Marcy St.
983-2255

**Dynos-Baseball**
Vince Demmer
Rt. 10, Box 881
Santa Fe, NM 87505
471-0137

**Eight Northern Pueblos Council**
(Nambe, Picuris, Pojoaque, San Juan, Santa Clara, San Ildefonso, Tesuque, and Taos Pueblos)
P.O. 969
San Juan Pueblo, NM 87566
852-4265

**II El Primo Pizza**
234 N. Guadalupe St.
988-2007

**Farmer's Market**
Sanbusco Market Center
Pam Roy
471-4711

**Grayline Tours of Santa Fe**
313 Guadalupe St.
983-9491

**The Guadalupe Cafe**
313 Guadalupe St.
982-9762

**Haagen-Dazs Ice Cream Shoppe**
56 E. San Francisco St.
988-3858

**Historic Santa Fe Foundation**
545 Canyon Road
983-2567

**Hotel St. Francis**
210 Don Gaspar Ave.
983-5700

**Hyde State Memorial Park**
P.O. 1147, 87504
983-7175

**Institute of American Indian Arts Museum**
1369 Cerrillos Rd.
988-6281
Handicapped accessible

**Jackalope Pottery**
2820 Cerrillos Rd.
471-8539

**Josie's Casa de Comida**
225 E. Marcy St.
983-5311

**La Fonda Hotel**
100 E. San Francisco St.
982-5511

**Loretto Chapel**
219 Old Santa Fe Trail
984-7971

**Los Alamos Ice Skating Rink**
Los Alamos Dept. of Parks & Recreation
662-8170; rink: 662-4500

**Los Llanos Bookstore**
500 Montezuma St.
982-9542

**Marcy St. Card Shop**
85 W. Marcy St.
982-5160

**Marcy St. Toy Shop**
99 W. Marcy St.
988-5292

**Medicine Horse Ranch**
Chery Fenley
Rt. 22, Box 33 CF
Santa Fe, NM 87505
983-5662

**Mineral and Fossil Gallery of Santa Fe**
118½ Don Gaspar Ave.
984-1862

**Museum of Fine Arts**
107 E. Palace Ave.
Santa Fe, 87501
505-827-4455
10:00-5:00 daily, handicapped accessible
Admission, children under 16 free
Discount for N.M. residents first Sunday of each month

**Museum of Indian Arts and Culture**
708 Camino Lejo
827-8941
10:00-5:00 daily
Admission, children under 16 free
Discount for N.M. residents first Sunday of each month
Handicapped accessible

**Museum of International Folk Art**
706 Camino Lejo
Ph. 505-827-8350
10:00-5:00, 7 days a week, except Mon. in January
Admission, children under 16 free, scholarships available for workshops
Handicapped accessible

**New Mexico Museum of Natural History**
1801 Mountain Rd. N.W., Albuquerque
841-8837
Handicapped accessible

**New Wave Rafting Company**
107 Washington Ave. (summer)
984-1444

**Old West Museum**
Madrid, N.M.
473-0743

**Palace of the Governors**
North Side of the Plaza
827-6474
10:00-5:00 daily, handicapped accessible
Admission, children under 16 free
Discount for N.M. residents, first Sunday of each month

**Pecos National Historical Park**
(26 mi. S.E. of Santa Fe on I-25)
P.O. Drawer 418
Pecos, NM 87552-0418

**Pookanoggin**
500 Montezuma St.
988-3228

**Rancho de las Golondrinas**
Spring Festival, first weekend of June; Fall Festival, first weekend of October
Old Cienega Village Museum
Rt. 14, Box 214, Santa Fe 87505
471-2261
Open April 1-October 31; April-May, by appointment; June-August, Wed. through Sunday 10:00-4:00

**Randall Davey Audubon Center**
Upper Canyon Road
983-4609

**Rio Grande Zoological Park**
903 10th S.W., Albuquerque, N.M.
843-7413
Handicapped accessible

**rob & charlies**
1632 St. Michael's Dr.
471-9119

**Sangre de Cristo Bicycle Club**
471-3394

**Santa Fe Adventures for Kids**
610 Caminito del Sol
983-0111

**Santa Fe Chamber Music Festival**
640 Paseo de Peralta
983-2075
Handicapped accessible

**Santa Fe Children's Museum**
1050 Old Pecos Trail
989-8359
Handicapped accessible
Thurs.-Sun. 10:00-5:00
Admission

**Santa Fe Desert Chorale**
219 Shelby St.
Box Office: 988-7505
Handicapped accessible

**Santa Fe Mountain Center**
Rt. 4, Box 34 C
Santa Fe, NM 87501
983-6158

**Santa Fe Opera**
(no. of Santa Fe on U.S. 84-285)
Box Office: 982-3855
Handicapped accessible

**Santa Fe Public Library**
145 Washington Ave.
984-6780
Handicapped accessible

**Santa Fe Reporter**
132 E. Marcy St.
988-5541

**Santa Fe Ski Area**
Located 16 miles N.E. of Santa Fe on Highway 475
982-4429
Lift open 10:00-3:00
Open during ski season & Thursdays through Sundays from July 4-Oct. 1

**Santa Fe Walks**
La Fonda Hotel Lobby
983-6565

**Santa Fe Windsurfing**
905 St. Francis Dr.
986-1611

**Santo Domingo Tribal Office**
Box 99
Santo Domingo Pueblo, NM 87052
465-2214

**Santuario de Guadalupe**
100 Guadalupe St.
505-988-2027

**Scheinbam & Russek Gallery of Photography**
328 Guadalupe St.
988-5116

**Scottish Rite Temple**
463 Paseo de Peralta
982-4414

**Shidoni Foundry & Galleries**
5 miles north of the Plaza
Tesuque, N.M.
988-8001

**Sierra Club Santa Fe**
440 Cerrillos Rd.
983-2703

**Southwest Nordic Center**
Doug MacLennan
P.O. Box 3212
Taos, NM 87571
758-4761

**St. Francis Cathedral**
131 Cathedral Pl.
982-5619
6:00-6:00 daily, side doors
Call the rectory for a tour guide

**State Capitol Building**
Paseo de Peralta & Old Santa Fe Trail
827-4011
Handicapped accessible

**Taos Indian Horse Ranch Company**
Cesario Stormstar Gomez
P.O. Box 3019
Taos, NM 87571
758-3212

**Ten Thousand Waves**
P.O. Box 6138
988-1047

**Tesuque Glassworks**
Tesuque, NM
988-2165

**The Wheelwright Museum**
704 Camino Lejo
982-4636
Mon.-Sat. 10:00-4:45; Sun. 1:00-4:45
Admission by donation
Handicapped accessible

**Tomasita's Restaurant**
500 S. Guadalupe St.
983-5721

**Woolworth's**
58 E. San Francisco St.
982-1062

**Zia Diner**
326 S. Guadalupe St.
988-7008

## Kidding Around with John Muir Publications

We are making the world more accessible for young travelers. In your hand you have one of several John Muir Publications guides written and designed especially for kids. We will be *Kidding Around* other cities also. Send us your thoughts, corrections, and suggestions. We also publish other books about travel and other subjects. Let us know if you would like one of our catalogs. All the titles below are 64 pages and $9.95, except for *Kidding Around the National Parks of the Southwest*, which is 108 pages and $12.95.

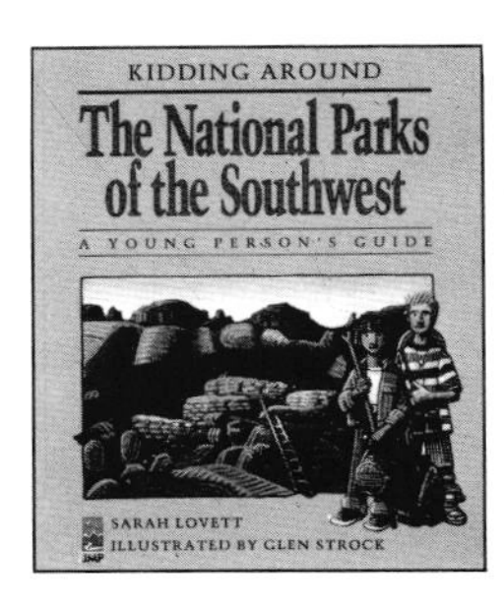

TITLES NOW AVAILABLE IN THE SERIES

**Kidding Around Atlanta**
**Kidding Around Boston**
**Kidding Around Chicago**
**Kidding Around the Hawaiian Islands**
**Kidding Around London**
**Kidding Around Los Angeles**
**Kidding Around the National Parks of the Southwest**
**Kidding Around New York City**
**Kidding Around Paris**
**Kidding Around Philadelphia**
**Kidding Around San Francisco**
**Kidding Around Santa Fe**
**Kidding Around Seattle**
**Kidding Around Washington, D.C.**

**Ordering Information**
Your books will be sent to you via UPS (for U.S. destinations). UPS will not deliver to a P.O. Box; please give us a street address. Include $2.75 for the first item ordered and $.50 for each additional item to cover shipping and handling costs. For airmail within the U.S., enclose $4.00. All foreign orders will be shipped surface rate; please enclose $3.00 for the first item and $1.00 for each additional item. Please inquire about foreign airmail rates.

**Method of Payment**
Your order may be paid by check, money order, or credit card. We cannot be responsible for cash sent through the mail. All payments must be made in U.S. dollars drawn on a U.S. bank. Canadian postal money orders in U.S. dollars are acceptable. For VISA, MasterCard, or American Express orders, include your card number, expiration date, and your signature, or call (800) 888-7504. Books ordered on American Express cards can be shipped only to the billing address of the cardholder. Sorry, no C.O.D.'s. Residents of sunny New Mexico, add 5.875% tax to the total.

Address all orders and inquiries to:
John Muir Publications
P.O. Box 613
Santa Fe, NM 87504
(505) 982-4078
(800) 888-7504

JMP
Enriching Independent Spirits

TRAVEL/CHILDREN

Santa Fe, famous for its painters and writers, is also a great place for kids. In *Kidding Around Santa Fe,* Susan York helps kids of all ages discover the best this area has to offer—Indian pueblos, museums, outdoors fun that includes white water rafting and fabulous hiking trails, New Mexican cooking, wagon wheel marks left by settlers westward bound on the Old Santa Fe Trail. Join us for a fun-filled, eye-opening Southwestern adventure.

*"A combination of practical information, vital statistics, and historical asides."*

—New York Times

*"This new series of guides for young travelers, ages eight and older, makes a perfect pre-trip gift. Combining history and geography with sights and sounds in a delightful and interesting format, they will make your kids preeminent members of your vacation planning committee."*

—Family Travel Times

*"For some fresh, offbeat ideas, we suggest the* Kidding Around *city guidebooks. Although the guides are intended for kids over eight, they also appeal to grown-ups . . . . Each listing is so well researched that you'll probably learn a thing or two yourself, even about your home city."*

—Condé Nast Traveler

*"Some travel guidebooks forget about the smallest members of the family—the kids. But with the* Kidding Around *series, the world is more accessible than ever before to young travelers."*

—Family Circle

ISBN 0-945465-99-8

**J... ...blications** Santa Fe, New Mexico

# Licences and Insolvency

A Practical Global Guide to the Effects of Insolvency on IP Licence Agreements

Consulting Editors **Marcel Willems, Matthias Nordmann** and **Ulrich Reber** on behalf of the International Bar Association

**Consulting editor**
Marcel Willems, Matthias Nordmann and Ulrich Reber on behalf of the International Bar Association

**Managing director**
Sian O'Neill

**Commissioning editor**
Katherine Cowdrey

**Editorial services director**
Carolyn Boyle

**Production manager**
Neal Honney

**Group publishing director**
Tony Harriss

***Licences and Insolvency: A Practical Global Guide to the Effects of Insolvency on IP Licence Agreements***
**is published by**
Globe Law and Business
Globe Business Publishing Ltd
New Hibernia House
Winchester Walk
London SE1 9AG
United Kingdom

Tel +44 20 7234 0606
Fax +44 20 7234 0808
Web www.globelawandbusiness.com

Printed and bound by CPI Group (UK) Ltd, Croydon, CR0 4YY

ISBN 9781909416253

# Table of contents

# Preface

**Marcel Willems**
Kennedy Van der Laan
**Matthias Nordmann**
**Ulrich Reber**
SKW Schwarz

The International Bar Association is called the global voice of the legal profession. It was at its annual conference in Boston that the idea to commission this publication on licence agreements in bankruptcies came up. It was felt that despite a growing harmonisation of intellectual property (IP) law throughout most parts of the world as a result of international treaties, insolvency law still seemed to be a domestic domain. In addition, an increasing number of cross-border licence transactions has created a need for answers on the destiny of licence agreements if one of the contracting parties becomes insolvent. The mere fact that a company faces liquidation in country A might unexpectedly have a serious impact on its contracting party that resides in country B. And an increasing amount of case law shows that a party may be disappointed in finding out that it is not always the law chosen by the parties in their licence agreement that determines who will continue to own the rights that are subject to that agreement.

What we discovered is that hardly anything had been written yet about the effects of insolvency on IP licences; hence the idea to try and fill the gap. This publication, while not attempting to be a scientific analysis of all of the problems and challenges associated with the IP licence/insolvency scenario, is intended to be a practical guide providing the reader with a summary of what a party may encounter if a licence agreement is affected by insolvency in a particular jurisdiction.

In preparing this guide, we identified a number of questions relating to those issues that may be at stake if an insolvency of a company occurs in a particular jurisdiction. Each contributor was nonetheless entirely free to modify the chapter concerned in a way that covered the topics most appropriately for the relevant jurisdiction. Even so, most country chapters conform to the standard organisational structure we set out at the start.

Each contribution first sets out the general principles of the insolvency law that it covers. The reader will notice that this has resulted in the use of varying terminology in the different jurisdictions – eg, an insolvency practitioner is sometimes called a trustee, sometimes an administrator, sometimes a liquidator, and so on. So be it; that happens when one tries not so much to compare various jurisdictions but to compile a guide consisting of descriptions of the legal systems of a great number of countries.

Beyond terminology, the reader will discover a wide range of systemic differences in the insolvency regime in each country presented in this publication. While some countries essentially have just one general insolvency proceeding, other countries have up to seven, and the line between involuntary formal proceedings and a voluntary shareholder-driven liquidation process is often not easy to discern. Then some jurisdictions have preliminary proceedings that can trigger legal effects on both the company and its creditors; in other countries this concept is unknown. Also, the role and powers of courts, authorities and insolvency practitioners vary greatly between the different jurisdictions. These variations clearly have a certain impact on how licence agreements are treated if they become part of the insolvency estate of one of the contracting parties.

The most striking difference lies between jurisdictions where there is little impact on an existing licence agreement – instead, rights and obligations continue as before with little room for intervention by an insolvency trustee – and other jurisdictions which provide far-reaching powers to the insolvency trustee or simply automatically result in an end to the enforceability of a licence agreement altogether, including a possible reversion of rights to the non-insolvent party. So while a growing harmonisation of IP laws over recent years has certainly helped bring together common concepts in this area, this publication is evidence that when a licence agreement is suddenly affected by the insolvency of one of its contracting parties, it may be the insolvency laws in the respective countries that suddenly govern the destiny of the IP rights.

Our hope is that all those who regularly have to deal with insolvencies and/or intellectual property in an international context will appreciate the choices we have made in the structure and selection of topics. We believe this book will be a guide for them. We also express our sincere gratitude to all those who have contributed to this publication. Without their time and effort, this guide would never have seen the light of day.

*Marcel Willems started his professional career in 1988. In 1992 he co-founded Kennedy Van der Laan, now one of the leading independent law firms in the Netherlands. Mr Willems has broad experience in insolvency, banking and finance, and dispute resolution – mostly in a cross-border setting. He publishes and lectures regularly. Mr Willems has been active in the Insolvency, Restructuring and Creditors' Rights Section of the International Bar Association for a number of years, and is currently senior vice-chair for conference quality.*

*Matthias Nordmann is focused on both strategic transactions and mergers and acquisitions as a Certified Expert for Corporate and Commercial Law. He is frequently being recommended or named as a leading lawyer by many prominent lawyer rankings for information technology and e-business law in Germany. Dr Nordmann is a member of the Executive Committee of the International Bar Association (IBA) and a past chair of the IBA's Intellectual Property and Entertainment Law Committee.*

*Ulrich Reber assists and represents domestic and foreign enterprises in the field of civil and commercial law, in particular in litigation and dispute resolution matters. A special focus is on cross-border lawsuits and representation in the competent courts. Clients from the publishing, music and games industries rely on Dr Reber's competence in the fields of media, entertainment and copyright law. He also assists clients in bankruptcy and restructuring matters.*

# Australia

**Christopher Brown**
Lonsdale Chambers
**Timothy Creek**
**Rodney De Boos**
Davies Collison Cave Law

---

## 1. Overview

### 1.1 Relevant legislation governing intellectual property and bankruptcy

There is no legislation specifically addressing the impact of insolvency on intellectual property or transactions involving intellectual property. The Bankruptcy Act 1966 (Cth) deals with the administration of bankruptcy of individuals, whereas the Corporations Act 2001 (Cth) deals with the insolvency of corporate entities registered under that act and which are therefore subject to the procedures provided for by that act. This chapter deals with the impact of the insolvency of a company on intellectual property rights and intellectual property transactions only, rather than the effect of the bankruptcy of an individual.

### 1.2 Types of insolvency procedures

There is a range of different types of insolvency procedure available where a company is insolvent. In broad terms, corporate insolvency can lead to receivership, voluntary administration or liquidation, each of which is described further below. Where a company is subject to one or more of these appointments, it is said to be under 'external administration'.

#### *(a) Receivership*

There are two forms of receivership: court-appointed receivers and privately appointed receivers. A court-appointed receiver is appointed by a court (typically the Federal Court of Australia, or the supreme court of a state or territory) that has the power to make such appointments in particular circumstances, such as an appointment over partnership assets in circumstances where there is a partnership dispute. Private receivership of a company registered under the Corporations Act 2001 occurs where a secured creditor holding a security interest over some or all of a company's assets appoints a person as a receiver, or as a receiver and manager, to collect and sell sufficient of the company's assets which are charged by the security in order to satisfy the debt owed to the secured creditor. A receiver will be called a 'receiver and manager' if the terms under which it is appointed also give the power to manage the affairs of the company.

Private receivership arises out of a private contractual arrangement (a security agreement) between the company and a secured creditor who has the right to appoint a receiver and manager in certain situations. A security agreement should comply with the requirements of Section 20 of the Personal Property Securities Act 2009 (Cth) – for example, where it contains a description of the particular collateral and has been signed or adopted by the grantor. Appointment under the security agreement usually occurs in the event of a default. One such event of default would normally be the insolvency of the company.

Once an appointment is made, the powers of the receiver and manager are governed by the security agreement and Part 5.2 of the Corporations Act 2001. For instance, the security document might give extensive powers to a receiver and manager in terms such as these:

> *... Such receiver and any receiver so appointed shall without any consent on the part of the Company have power to do anything in respect of the Assets in respect of which the security is held that the Company could do, including without limitation: take possession of, collect and get in the whole or any part of the Assets in respect of which the security is held, carry on or concur in carrying on the business of the Company and do all acts which the Company might do in the ordinary conduct of its business for the protection or improvement of the Assets in respect of which the security is held or for obtaining income or returns therefrom.*

A receiver has broad powers to do everything necessary or convenient for the attainment of the objective for which the receiver was appointed, subject to the provisions of the security document or court order under which the receiver was appointed. Thus a receiver can take the property which has been charged in a particular case, and sell it in order to satisfy a company's obligation to a secured creditor.

The terms of the security agreement under which a receiver is appointed will determine the powers of the directors of the company during the receivership. Where the charge is over all (or almost all) of the assets of the company, the receiver would effectively have control of the company; however, the directors would still have responsibilities and duties and may retain residual control. Once the receivership is completed and in the absence of the company going into liquidation, full control of the company is handed back to the directors.

When appointed, a receiver or a receiver and manager is deemed to be the agent of the company in respect of which the appointment is made. However, this agency will not arise if a liquidator is appointed first and will cease if a liquidator is appointed subsequently.

For the purposes of this chapter, we will assume that the receivership is a private appointment by a secured creditor over all of the assets as this is most common form of appointment.

### *(b) Voluntary administration*

Voluntary administration is a process usually initiated by the directors of a company; however, a liquidator or a secured creditor can also initiate the process. When entering into voluntary administration, an independent and qualified person is appointed to take control of the company with a view to investigating the company's affairs and making recommendations as to the future of the company. The objective of the provisions in the Corporations Act 2001 relating to voluntary administration is to provide a cooperative approach to satisfying the debts of a company or to restructure a company so as to make it a viable ongoing concern.

Once appointed, an administrator has a relatively short statutory time frame within which to hold an initial creditors' meeting (first meeting), investigate the affairs of the company, prepare a report for the creditors, make a recommendation to the creditors on the future of the company and hold a further meeting of creditors (second meeting) so that creditors can vote on the future of the company. The usual time frame for this process is 20 business days, although the period may be extended by an application to the court.

Once an administrator is appointed, no one else (including a director) can perform any function or power as an officer. However, a receiver or a receiver and manager appointed before the voluntary administration may still deal with the property that is the subject of the security arrangement under which the receiver or receiver and manager was appointed.

An administrator will typically present creditors with the following three options at the second meeting of creditors:

- to return the company to the directors and remove it from voluntary administration;
- to accept a deed of company arrangement, whereby the creditors' debts are extinguished in return for, usually, only part payment of their debt (eg, 10 cents in the dollar) and the company is allowed to trade on, subject to the terms of the deed; or
- to place the company into liquidation.

The most common outcomes of voluntary administration are entry into a deed of company arrangement or the liquidation of the company.

### *(c) Liquidation*

Liquidation is the process whereby a liquidator is appointed to take control of and wind up a company in an orderly and fair way for the benefit of creditors. There are two types of liquidation for insolvent companies. The first is a creditor's voluntary liquidation and the second is a court-initiated liquidation.

The most common form of liquidation is a creditor's voluntary liquidation, which can be brought about by:

- a vote of creditors following a voluntary administration; or
- a terminated deed of company arrangement; or
- the vote of more than three-quarters of the company's shareholders attending a properly convened meeting in person or by proxy.

The other way in which an insolvent company can be wound up is by order of a court. Such an order would usually be the result of an application to the court by a creditor for the winding-up of the company.

In most situations where liquidation is ordered by the court, the applicant to the court for such an order must be able to show that the company is insolvent or deemed to be insolvent. A court can also order liquidation of a company in other circumstances but these are not dealt with in this chapter because they do not usually concern insolvency.

Liquidators have broad powers under the Corporations Act 2001, and the appointment of a liquidator effectively removes all powers from the directors of the company. One task of the liquidator is to realise all of the assets of the company with a view to satisfying creditors to the greatest extent possible. A liquidator has an obligation to end trading by the company and wind up its affairs in a quick but commercially practical way. However, a liquidator may choose to continue trading the company for a period so as to allow for a sale of the business as a going concern.

### 1.3 Grounds of bankruptcy

A company is insolvent if it is unable to pay all of its debts as and when they become due and payable. A company is presumed to be insolvent if it fails to comply with a statutory demand by a creditor in respect of a debt owed by the company to that creditor.

Where a company is insolvent, it can be placed into liquidation by a resolution of creditors or by order of a court.

Section 461 of the Corporations Act 2001 also provides for a number of additional grounds on which a company can be wound up, which are not dealt with in this chapter.

### 1.4 Filing for bankruptcy

In the context of insolvency, the entry into each of the different external administrations is typically made as follows:

- The appointment of a receiver will be made by a secured creditor.
- The appointment of a voluntary administrator will be made by the directors of the insolvent company.
- An application for the appointment of a liquidator will be made to the court by a creditor.

The appointment of a receiver is usually a private appointment by a secured creditor under the terms of a charge over the assets of the company. A court can appoint a receiver in a variety of circumstances, but usually this would occur where the assets are at risk and there is a dispute over them.

Voluntary administration is usually initiated by the directors of a company in circumstances where the company is insolvent or at risk of becoming insolvent. Voluntary administration may also be initiated by a liquidator, usually in circumstances where a deed of arrangement is proposed. Voluntary administration may also be initiated by a secured creditor.

Applications for the appointment of liquidators and matters relating to the conduct of liquidators, receivers and administrators can be dealt with by the Federal Court of Australia or the supreme court of a state or territory.

The appointment of a liquidator can be made voluntarily by the company, on the application of creditors, by a court as relief for oppression (Section 233 of the Corporations Act 2001) or on other grounds specified in Section 461 of that act.

### 1.5 Administrators and other appointed persons

Persons appointed – whether as receivers, receivers and managers, administrators or liquidators – are invariably registered liquidators under the Corporations Act 2001.

Liquidators and administrators take control of the company and the directors' powers are suspended. Receivers also usually take control of the company, but their powers will depend on the document under which they were appointed (usually a charge) or the terms of the court order under which they were appointed.

## 2. Licence agreements in the phase between filing and declaration of bankruptcy

### 2.1 Effects on licence agreements in the licensor's bankruptcy

Before a receiver, a receiver and manager or a liquidator is appointed, a licensor under a licence agreement might, by the terms of that agreement, experience an event of default. Such events commonly found in licence agreements are:

- the filing of a creditors' petition with the court against the company (which may lead to liquidation);
- the filing of a winding-up application with the court (which may lead to the appointment of liquidator); and
- insolvency (ie, an inability to pay debts when due).

There is no statutory effect on the operations of a company until a formal appointment is made. If the event of default specified in the licence agreement occurs, the consequences provided for in the agreement would be available to the licensee. In general terms, there is no restriction on what events might be included as events of default in a licence agreement. However, if, for instance, under the terms of a licence an unsecured licensor was required to pay money to a licensee on an event of default occurring to the licensor – perhaps as liquidated damages to provide for the Licensee to access alternative technology – and that payment was made within six months of the appointment of a liquidator, that payment will be susceptible to recovery by the liquidator as a preference payment (to be repaid to the company in liquidation and equally distributed amongst all creditors, including the licensor).

### 2.2 Powers of administrators or receivers in the licensor's bankruptcy

An external administrator of any description may choose simply to allow the licensor company to breach a licence agreement (if the act of appointment did not already qualify as a breach), whereupon the licensee would merely become an unsecured creditor of the licensor company in the amount of any loss or damage arising from the breach.

A receiver, or a receiver and manager, of a company which has granted a licence under an intellectual property right has no right to disclaim or terminate the licence unless entitled to do so by the terms of that licence. However, a receiver or a receiver and manager may have power to dispose of the assets of the company under the terms of the document by which that person was appointed. In that event, the receiver or receiver and manager may have power to assign intellectual property rights licensed to a third party under a license agreement. The assignment of that right without recognition of the licence would likely place the company in breach of the licence unless assignment was permitted by the licence itself.

In the case of patents and trademarks, if the licensee had its interest as licensee recorded under the Patents Act 1990 (Cth) or the Trade Marks Act 1995 (Cth) respectively, the purchaser would acquire the intellectual property rights subject to the licence. This provision is, however, contingent on the assignee being a purchaser in good faith for value and not having notice of any fraud on the part of the assignor, which in this case would include the receiver and manager because they are deemed to be the agent of the company. There is no provision for the recordal of copyright licences in Australia and no statutory provision dealing with the recognition of the rights of licensees of copyright.

An administrator of a company which has granted a licence under an intellectual property right has no right to disclaim or terminate the licence unless entitled to do so by the terms of that licence. However, an administrator has rights to dispose of assets of the company, similar to that of a receiver (as discussed above).

A liquidator has certain rights to disclaim the property of a company, including contracts. However, the liquidator cannot disclaim a contract (except unprofitable contracts) without leave of the court. An unprofitable contract is in this context one which imposes continuing financial obligations on the company which are regarded as detrimental to creditors or which will delay the winding-up of the company's affairs because performance would take place over a substantial period of time or would involve unrecoverable expenditure (see Transmetro Corp Ltd v Real Investments Pty Ltd [2000] 2 Qd R 555).

### 2.3 Effects on licence agreements in the licensee's bankruptcy

The same basic position applies as for section 2.1 above when a licensee (rather than a licensor) faces bankruptcy. The terms of the licence agreement prevail and there is no statutory consequence for either party until an external administrator is appointed.

However, the provisions regarding preferential payments are more likely to be relevant to the insolvency of a licensee in so far as royalty payments are concerned. In liquidation and personal bankruptcy, one has to be wary of unfair preference payments which can be recovered by the liquidator/trustee (see Sections 588FE and FF of the Corporations Act and Section 122 of the Bankruptcy Act). Payments that are made by a company or individual to unsecured creditors in the six months before the liquidation/bankruptcy are voidable and repayable to the liquidator/trustee to effectively go back into the pool of assets of the company for distribution to all creditors. This would usually apply to payments received by a licensor from a licensee where the licensee is subsequently wound up or made bankrupt.

A licensor may have a defence if it had no reasonable grounds for suspecting that the licensee was insolvent at the time that the payment was received.

### 2.4 Powers of administrators, receivers or trustees in the licensee's bankruptcy

Prior to a formal appointment – whether by order of a court, resolution of creditors or shareholders, or appointment by a secured creditor – the relevant controller or liquidator has no power. However, following appointment, the relevant external administrator has the same powers as are described in section 2.2 above in relation to licensor bankruptcy.

### 2.5 Impact of registration

Licences can be recorded under the Patents Act 1990 (Cth) and the Trade Marks Act 1995 (Cth). Recordal is mandatory under the Patents Act but not under the Trade Marks Act. The main advantage of recordal is that it puts third parties on notice of licensees' interest. This has advantages for a licensee in that any dealing in the patent or trademark would be subject to that interest. If a particular item of intellectual property, such as a licence agreement, is not recorded under the Patents Act, the licensee's interest is not affected; rather, the Patents Act provides that any such particulars are not admissible in any proceeding as proof of title to the patent or an interest in it (unless a court directs otherwise).

Entities can register an interest in intellectual property where that interest is a security interest pursuant to the Personal Property Securities Act 2009. If an entity has a registered security interest over intellectual property and the intellectual property has been licensed, the licence will be considered proceeds under Section 31 of the foregoing act and therefore the security interest in the intellectual property will extend to the licence granted (Section 32 of the same act). In that event, the security holder will have a paramount interest over later-secured parties and all unsecured parties.

A security interest can be created over intellectual property licences concerning patents, registered trademarks, registered designs, plant breeders' rights, circuit layouts and copyright (Section 106 of Personal Property Securities Act). This is contrary to most other statutory licences (see Section 8(1)(k) of the same act).

## 3. Licence agreements in the phase after declaration of bankruptcy

### 3.1 Treatment of intellectual property rights

There is no distinction in insolvency between the various intellectual property rights. They are all treated as assets of the insolvent company.

As noted above, liquidators can disclaim assets, including intellectual property rights. However, as mentioned in section 2.2 above, licences (which are dealt with further below) are typically considered as contracts and therefore can only be disclaimed where the contract is unprofitable or with leave of the court. Intellectual property rights other than licences are likely to be readily able to be disclaimed by the liquidator, particularly in circumstances where the asset is unsaleable or not readily saleable, or where the costs and expenses of realising the intellectual property would exceed the proceeds of sale (Section 568(1) of the Corporations Act).

The effect of the liquidator disclaiming the asset is that it is no longer an asset of the company (the insolvent party). Usually, if the asset has any residual value, a disclaimer occurs because there are other interested parties, eg a secured creditor, whose interest will prevail over any interest of the company.

Furthermore, intellectual property licences may be subject to recordal if they relate to patents or trademarks or separate security interests (irrespective of the intellectual property right involved) registered under the Personal Property Securities Act. As noted above, these recordals or registrations will affect how licences can be dealt with.

### 3.2 Effects on licence agreements in the licensor's bankruptcy

It is common for licence agreements to provide that the appointment of an external administrator is an event of default enabling the licensee to terminate. Limited exceptions may apply to entities with a security interest (Sections 441A and 441B of the Corporations Act).

An administrator does not have the power to disclaim an intellectual property licence but can repudiate it. In such a case the licensee would merely have an unsecured claim against the company for damages.

#### (a) *Voluntary Administration*

Where an administrator is appointed, the main task of the administrator is to investigate the affairs, report to creditors and make a recommendation as to the future of the company. The administrator also has power to continue to trade and to sell assets of the company (subject to any security interest in the assets). If the administrator continues to trade, then the administrator may become liable for amounts payable under a licence agreement. Section 443B of the Corporations Act gives an administrator five business days within which to give an owner of intellectual property notice that the company does not propose to exercise rights in relation to any property subject to a licence agreement. Such a notice relieves the administrator from liability for amounts payable under the licence, but not the company. However, if the company exercises rights in relation to the particular intellectual property, the notice ceases to have effect.

The purpose of the provisions relating to voluntary administration is to allow the affairs of the company to be administered in a way that maximizes the chance of the business continuing in existence and/or maximizes the return to company creditors (see Section 435A of the Corporations Act). To achieve this objective, the Corporations Act applies strict controls on the powers of creditors during the period of administration, including:

- restrictions on secured parties and lessors executing rights over property (Section 440B);
- a stay of any court proceedings (Section 440D);
- the suspension of any enforcement process (Section 440F); and
- a moratorium on the enforcement of any guarantee provided by the directors or a spouse in relation to the company (section 440J).

#### (b) *Liquidation*

In the case of liquidation, the liquidator may have the power to disclaim the licence under Section 568 of the Corporations Act 2001. However, as already noted, a licence agreement is typically a contract and can only be disclaimed in circumstances where it is unprofitable or with leave of the court (Section 568(1A) of the act).

A contract is deemed unprofitable in this context if it imposes on the company continuing financial obligations which do not confer a reciprocal benefit on the company. This could occur where an upfront licence fee has been paid and the licence is still in effect with its attendant obligations. Furthermore, a contract may be deemed unprofitable where performance of the contract may delay the winding-up of the company and involves expenditure that may not be recoverable.

### *(c) Receivership*

A receiver has no power to disclaim contracts. However, if the company repudiates a licence agreement, the licensee's right to damages would merely be an unsecured debt of the company, which would rank behind the debts owing to secured creditors (including the secured creditor who has appointed the receiver).

### *(d) General consideration: proof of debt*

If a contractual dispute arises involving an insolvent party which becomes the subject of administration or liquidation, the other party to the licence agreement would effectively be restricted to submitting a proof of debt for any damages claim under the licence agreement if there was a breach. The solvent party would not be permitted to commence court action against the company (Section 440D of the Corporations Act in respect of administration, Section 500 of the act in respect of voluntary liquidation and Section 471B of the act in respect of a court-ordered winding-up) without leave of the court (or permission of the administrator in a case of administration, pursuant to Section 440D of the same act).

In any event, even where the solvent party successfully sues the insolvent company in liquidation, administration or receivership, the judgment debt would merely be an unsecured debt of the company and would not be afforded any priority over other unsecured creditors. Hence, the proof-of-debt process referred to above, which can include the liquidator/administrator determining a fair value of damages in relation to any non-liquidated damages claim, is likely to be a more efficient means of recovering at least some of the debt.

If a liquidator or administrator denies proof of debt, under Section 1321 of the Corporations Act the party lodging the proof has the right to apply to the court for review of the decision of the administrator or liquidator. This would occur in an Australian court regardless of the terms of the licence agreement involved.

## 3.3 Powers of an administrator, receiver or trustee in the licensor's bankruptcy

The powers of a liquidator or controller of a licensor are the same as those described in section 2.2 above.

If the liquidation/receivership/administration is not an event of default leading to termination under the terms of the licence, the liquidator/administrator/receiver can choose to continue to perform the licence agreement.

## 3.4 Powers and rights of creditors in a licensor's bankruptcy

The creditors of an insolvent licensor under a licence agreement have no direct rights in respect of the licence agreement. However, they may be able to influence the position taken by a liquidator or controller in respect of the licence. This would be particularly so in the case of voluntary administration, where the creditors meet to resolve whether they will enter into a deed of company arrangement and agree the terms of that arrangement.

An entity which has a licence agreement with a company in liquidation can apply to the court to discharge the contract or rescind the contract on terms that the court deems proper (Section 568(9) of the Corporations Act).

### 3.5 Effects on licence agreements in the licensee's bankruptcy

Typically, the appointment of a receiver to, or the voluntary administration or liquidation of, a licensee under an intellectual property licence is an event of default entitling the licensor to terminate the licence. In the absence of the right to terminate or, where there is such a right, actual termination, the potential effect on the licence of one of these events will vary depending upon the type of event.

As has been noted above, only a liquidator has the power to disclaim a contract and this power is regulated by the Corporations Act 2001. Although an administrator or receiver does not have the power to disclaim a contract, an administrator has the ability to avoid further liability for the company by giving notice to a licensor that the company will not continue to use the intellectual property in its business. Under Section 443B of the Corporations Act, this must be done within five days of appointment. Moreover, if an administrator or receiver repudiates a licence agreement, rightfully or wrongfully, the licensor may well be left as an unsecured creditor in the event of liquidation of the licensee.

Licensors should also be wary of payments being made under a licence agreement immediately before liquidation, as they might be treated as unfair preference payments that could be subject to recovery by a liquidator. The right to recover preference payments applies to payments that are made six months before entering into liquidation. Any such payments successfully recovered by a liquidator will go into the pool of assets which will ultimately be distributed for the benefit of all creditors.

### 3.6 Powers of an administrator, receiver or trustee in the licensee's bankruptcy

The powers of external administrators are the same as described in section 2.2 above.

### 3.7 Powers and rights of creditors in a licensee's bankruptcy

The position is as described in section 3.4 above.

### 3.8 Exclusive and non-exclusive licences

There is no distinction between exclusive and non-exclusive licences for insolvency purposes in Australia.

### 3.9 Perpetual and non-perpetual licences

There is no difference between perpetual and non-perpetual licences for insolvency purposes in Australia. A liquidator, administrator or receiver can repudiate a licence agreement and the licensor would merely become a creditor for any damages suffered as a result.

### 3.10 Effects on a sub-licence in a licensor's bankruptcy

The position of a sub-licence will depend upon the fate of the head licence. Thus, unless the eventuality is specifically covered in the sub-licence (such as by providing for automatic novation to the head licensor), the termination of a head licence would automatically terminate a sub-licence in most cases.

### 3.11 Effects on a sub-license in a licensee's bankruptcy

The position is the same as is described in section 3.10 immediately above.

### 3.12 Impact of registration

The position on registration is described in section 2.5 above.

As noted, entities can register an interest in intellectual property where that interest is a security interest pursuant to the Personal Property Securities Act. If an entity has a registered security interest over intellectual property and the intellectual property has been licensed, the licence will be considered proceeds (pursuant to Section 31 of that act) and therefore the security interest in the intellectual property will extend to the licence granted (pursuant to Section 32 of the act).

A licence is not in itself a security interest for the purposes of the Personal Property Securities Act (see Section 12(5) of that act). However, a security interest can be created over an intellectual property licence (Section 10 of the act) contrary to most statutory licences (Section 8(1)(k) of the act).

## 4. Contractual arrangements in deviation from the law

### 4.1 Exceptions

There are no exceptions for particular types of intellectual property licences in general terms in so far as insolvency is concerned. However, know-how licences and other 'licences' dealing with non-statutory rights will not be treated as intellectual property licences for the purposes of the Personal Property Securities Act.

### 4.2 Scope to alter statutory mechanisms

There is very little freedom in Australia for parties to agree to matters which alter the position under the relevant statutes in the context of insolvency. An external administrator has certain powers and is entitled to exercise those powers irrespective of what is contained in an intellectual property licence. This is particularly so given the power of a liquidator or court to set aside transactions which provide a creditor with an undue preference over other creditors of equal standing.

### 4.3 Termination rights and automatic reversions

The parties can provide that insolvency is a ground for termination of a licence agreement.

## 5. Cross-border aspects

### 5.1 Foreign law and foreign jurisdiction

A controller or liquidator is not bound by a choice-of-law clause in so far as it would affect the procedures, rights and obligations in insolvency. This is because Australian law applies to the administration of Australian companies.

However, in the event of receivership, the company in receivership would be bound by the same terms of the licence as it would before it entered into receivership.

The general considerations set out in section 3.2(d) above apply equally to cross-border transactions where the company that is the subject of receivership, administration or liquidation proceedings is an Australian company.

# Austria

**Axel Anderl**
**Felix Hörlsberger**
Dorda Brugger Jordis

---

## 1. Overview

### 1.1 Relevant legislation governing intellectual property and bankruptcy

Under Austrian law, the most relevant legislation governing intellectual property rights are the Copyright Act, the Trade Marks Act, the Patents Act, the Utility Patent Act and the Designs Act. The relevant legislation governing Austrian insolvency law is the Insolvency Act, which entered into force on July 1 2010.

With the exception of the Copyright Act, which stipulates only very selected and limited deviations from the general rules, Austrian intellectual property law does not provide for any special provisions for cases of insolvency. Thus, the general rules according to the Insolvency Act apply.

### 1.2 Types of insolvency procedure

Under Austrian law, there are two types of insolvency proceeding applicable to companies as debtors: reorganisation proceedings and bankruptcy proceedings (each described further below). Where the insolvent debtor is an individual, special provisions apply.

#### *(a) Reorganisation proceedings*

A debtor can apply for the opening of reorganisation proceedings if that debtor provides a reorganisation plan as part of the application. Such a plan needs to offer to the creditors at least a quota of 20%, payable within two years.

In the event that the debtor does not want to lose its power to dispose of its assets, the company needs to additionally apply for a grant of self-administration. In this case, a list of assets, a status report and a financial plan for the next 90 days need to be attached to the application for reorganisation proceedings. Furthermore, the debtor must offer a minimum quota of 30% (instead of 20%) payable within two years.

Reorganisation proceedings aim to reorganise the debtor's business, but they can be converted into bankruptcy proceedings if the reorganisation plan is either rejected by the creditors or cannot be fulfilled by the debtor.

#### *(b) Bankruptcy proceedings*

Bankruptcy proceedings lead to the complete sale of the debtor's assets and, subsequently, to the distribution of the proceeds to the creditors on a proportionate basis. The business may be continued only if continuation is not disadvantageous to the creditors.

At any time during the proceedings, the debtor can submit a (new) reorganisation plan – for example, if the debtor finds an investor which would allow for the debtor to service a quota of 20% or more within two years.

Bankruptcy proceedings will end either with a successful reorganisation (reorganisation plan approved by the creditors) or with the liquidation of the company. In a case of liquidation, the insolvency administrator distributes the proceeds to the creditors on a proportionate basis.

## 1.3 Grounds of bankruptcy

Under Austrian insolvency law, insolvency proceedings must be opened if the debtor is either insolvent (ie, unable to pay its due debts) or over-indebted and has no positive outlook to remain a going concern.

## 1.4 Filing for bankruptcy

Where a company is insolvent or over-indebted and with no positive outlook, the management is obliged to file for the opening of insolvency proceedings in a timely manner but at the latest after 60 days, calculated from the moment the preconditions for filing for insolvency are met. In addition, it is also possible for a company to file for the opening of restructuring proceedings where there is an imminent inability to pay debts when due.

Furthermore, any creditor of an insolvent company can initiate the opening of insolvency proceedings with the competent insolvency court. In this event, the creditor must substantiate that it has a claim (even if not due) against the debtor and that the debtor is either insolvent or over-indebted.

However, filing for bankruptcy does not automatically lead to the opening of insolvency proceedings: the competent court can refuse to open proceedings "if the available assets are not likely to be sufficient to cover the costs of the court proceedings". In this event, the debtor or the creditor who files for bankruptcy can make a deposit, which is determined by the court and which is likely to cover the anticipated costs.

In the event that the debtor's main interest is situated within the territory of Austria, the courts of Austria will have jurisdiction to open insolvency proceedings.

Under Section 63 of the Insolvency Act, the Austrian court of first instance in which district the insolvent or over-indebted debtor runs its business or has its habitual residence is competent to open insolvency proceedings. Austria also has jurisdiction if the debtor neither runs its business nor has its habitual residence within the territory, so long as it has a branch or property in Austria.

## 1.5 Administrators and other appointed persons

Austrian insolvency law distinguishes between two relevant phases:

- The phase between the party's material insolvency and the opening of insolvency proceedings by the court, once an application has been filed; and
- The phase after insolvency proceedings have been initiated by the insolvency court.

As the procedural provisions only apply once the court has opened insolvency proceedings, under Austrian law there are no preliminary insolvency proceedings starting with the filing for insolvency. In particular, there is no preliminary insolvency administrator or other person appointed upon filing for insolvency.

With the opening of insolvency proceedings by the competent court, the debtor loses its power to dispose of its assets. This power is instead conferred on an insolvency administrator, appointed by the insolvency court after insolvency proceedings have been initiated. Transactions concluded by the debtor after the opening of insolvency proceedings are void with respect to its creditors. Under certain circumstances the court may also appoint a creditors' committee, which exists to represent all creditors.

The insolvency administrator is obliged to assess the economic status of the debtor as a first step. In the event that the debtor is an entrepreneur, the administrator needs to assess whether the continuation of the business is disadvantageous to the creditors. If this is the case, the debtor is obliged to shut the business down prior to the first creditors' meeting, to sell all assets of the debtor and to distribute the proceeds to the creditors. After the first creditor's meeting, the insolvency court may shut down the business if the continuation inevitably leads to further disadvantage to the creditors.

The insolvency administrator is entitled to examine all claims that have been lodged by the creditors at the competent court during the lodging time given in the insolvency declaration. The administrator can either accept or contest a lodged claim. After the examination process, the administrator must list all lodged claims in a register of creditors.

Under Austrian insolvency law, the insolvency administrator is entitled to declare as null and void certain transactions undertaken by the debtor during specified periods of time prior to the opening of insolvency proceedings.

The relevant provisions in Section 27 and following of the Insolvency Act aim to prevent preferential treatment of individual creditors and to thus ensure equal satisfaction to all of them.

## 2. Licence agreements in the phase between filing and declaration of bankruptcy

### 2.1 Effects on licence agreements in the licensor's bankruptcy

As material insolvency itself does not have a direct legal effect on any contracts (including licence agreements), any licence agreements as well as the rights and obligations thereunder remain valid and effective despite insolvency.

However, practice shows that, between the point in time where the undertaking is materially insolvent (or even before that) and the opening of insolvency proceedings by the court, there is a substantial risk that:

- the insolvent party sets aside or dissipates assets, and hence causes disadvantages to its creditors;
- the insolvent party enters legal obligations which cause disadvantages to some of the creditors and thus breaches the principle of equal treatment; and

- a creditor tries to pressure the debtor to satisfy any claims or to grant securities, which may also lead to discrimination against other creditors.

These risks are particularly important in relation to intellectual property rights, as they concern no physical goods; thus no physical transfer is necessary. Further, the grant of a licence does not even require the registration in a register as such a registration is merely declarative. Thus, there is a serious risk that the value of an insolvent party's assets is substantially lowered by grants of a licence.

To safeguard the interests of not only licensors or licensees but also the insolvent party's creditors in general, Austria's insolvency law provides for the possibility of contesting and getting annulled legal acts that the insolvent party has concluded before insolvency proceedings were initiated and which are liable to cause disadvantage to creditors. This, of course, also relates to licence agreements. The various circumstances under which a debtor's acts may be contested are set out in Sections 27–31 of the Insolvency Act.

### 2.2 Powers of administrators, receivers or trustees in the licensor's bankruptcy

As described in the preceding paragraph, Sections 27–31 of Austria's Insolvency Act set forth various circumstances for a contestation/avoidance of agreements, which also apply to any licence agreements and the rights and obligations thereunder. Under Section 28 of the same act, the insolvency administrator may challenge such legal acts if they caused a disadvantage to creditors and the debtor's intention to cause disadvantage was known or ought to have been known to the counterparty. Where actual knowledge by the counterparty exists, this applies to legal acts in the 10 years prior to the opening of the insolvency proceedings (Section 28(1)); if there is no actual knowledge, the relevant period is the two years prior to the opening of the insolvency proceedings (Section 28(2)).

Further, legal acts are also challengeable if entered into or performed by the insolvent party without consideration (Section 29) in the two years before the opening of the insolvency proceedings. Such transactions may be challenged irrespective of whether the receiving party knew about the debtor's situation and the risk of causing disadvantage to creditors.

Therefore, any licence agreements concluded before the conditions for opening insolvency proceedings have been fulfilled by the debtor may be challenged on the basis of the foregoing provisions. In this case, the validity of the whole licence agreement may be contested, not just performance of the contract or the rights and obligations thereunder. As a result, any licence agreement or transfer of intellectual property rights is at risk of being invalidated by the insolvency administrator if entered into with an entity which is in financial trouble. This is to protect the creditors of the insolvent party and to warrant an equal treatment of all creditors concerned in the insolvency proceedings.

Austrian insolvency law also provides for the possibility of challenging legal acts entered into by which the insolvent party is giving one or more creditors preferential treatment after it is materially insolvent. This is of great practical significance and is based on the idea that creditors must be treated equally, not only after insolvency proceedings have been opened but also once the conditions for such insolvency proceedings are fulfilled. The grant of preferential treatment to one or more creditors is a rather common phenomenon in practice. As already indicated in section 2.1 above, this is particularly easy when licences for intellectual property rights are granted, as no physical transfer or entry in a register is necessary.

The satisfaction or collateralisation of a creditor or licensor may also be challengeable if it was done after the emergence of the material insolvency (ie, the inability to pay or over-indebtedness) on the day of filing for the opening of bankruptcy proceedings or in the 60 days prior to any of such events. Section 31 of the Insolvency Act also allows the challenging of legal acts because the other party had knowledge – or negligently did not know – of the insolvent party's inability to pay his due debts. Section 31 does not require any negligent or wilful conduct by the insolvent party; it is sufficient that the other party knew (or ought to have known) of the insolvent party's financial situation – particularly, that it fulfilled the requirements of material insolvency.

Under Section 31 the following two legal acts are challengeable:

- the satisfaction/performance or collateralisation of a creditor, whereby an exchange of performances in a concurrent manner (ie, licence agreements with regular payment of the licence fees) is again exempted (as in such a case the other party is not deemed to have become a creditor); and
- disadvantageous transactions or contracts concluded by the insolvent party with a third party. Under this alternative, congruent transactions are also challengeable. Both 'directly disadvantageous' transactions (whereby the disadvantage is already present at the time of entering into the contract) and 'indirectly disadvantageous' transactions or contracts (whereby the disadvantage emerges after the transaction/contract is entered into, but was objectively predictable) fall within the scope of this provision.

The rights to contest legal acts by the insolvent party that are mentioned in this section are exclusive rights of the insolvency administrator. Because licence agreements – or a transfer/assignment of intellectual property rights – may be contested and annulled if such agreements fall under any of the foregoing provisions, both the licensor and the licensee need to act with due care if they enter into any such agreements with parties that are – or that potentially may be – at risk of becoming insolvent.

### 2.3 Effects on licence agreements in the licensee's bankruptcy

As set out in section 2.1 above, whether the licensor or the licensee is a materially insolvent party has no direct effect on the validity of the licence agreement itself.

### 2.4 Powers of administrators, receivers or trustees in the licensee's bankruptcy

The powers of the insolvency administrator – the only relevant person under Austrian law in this respect – in a case of a licensee's insolvency are the same as those set out in section 2.2 above.

## 2.5 Impact of registration

The legal situation as set out under section 2.2 above remains unaffected regardless of whether the licence agreement is registered.

# 3. Licence agreements in the phase after declaration of bankruptcy

## 3.1 Treatment of intellectual property rights

Once insolvency proceedings have been initiated by the insolvency court's order, all intellectual property rights form part of the insolvency assets among all other assets of the insolvent debtor. The only exceptions are any author's moral rights, which will always remain with the author.

With the exception of the Copyright Act, which stipulates for copyright licences very selected and limited deviations from the general rules (see next paragraph), Austrian intellectual property law does not provide for any special provisions in a case of insolvency. Thus, the general rules according to the Insolvency Act will apply.

The Copyright Act provides for an exception of the usual rules of the Insolvency Act in its Section 32 for insolvency of a licensee only. This provision applies if the licence agreement cannot be qualified as a rental agreement and is thus qualified as an agreement unperformed by both parties (see section 3.3 below). In this case the Copyright Act stipulates that the application of the provisions for contracts unperformed by both parties is not precluded merely because the work to be reproduced has already been transferred. Thus, even if the work has been transferred, the agreement is still deemed to be unperformed.

Further, according to Section 32(2) of the Copyright Act the author of the work has a special right of withdrawal. If at the time of the initiation of insolvency proceedings the reproduction of the work has not yet been started by the licensee, then the author may withdraw from the contract. If the author does not declare whether he wants to withdraw from the contract, the insolvency administrator may ask the court to set a deadline after which withdrawal is not possible.

## 3.2 Effects on licence agreements in the licensor's bankruptcy

The two governing principles of Austrian insolvency law are the aim of satisfying creditor's claims and the aim of preserving the business entity by reorganising it. Therefore, in a case of insolvency, all contracts in general remain intact, valid and enforceable. This means that the mere initiation of insolvency proceedings by the court's order does not in itself have a direct effect on any licence agreement.

## 3.3 Powers of an administrator, receiver or trustee in the licensor's bankruptcy

While there is no direct effect on licence agreements once insolvency proceedings have been started by the court's order, Austrian law stipulates certain extraordinary rights of termination. The consequences therefrom depend on whether the licensor or the licensee becomes insolvent, how the contract may be qualified, and which of the parties is trying to terminate the contract.

The Insolvency Act provides special rights to the insolvency administrator to preserve the insolvent undertaking. Whether the insolvency administrator has an extraordinary right to terminate the contract if insolvency proceedings have been started by the licensor depends on the distinction made between rental agreements and agreements unperformed by both parties. Austrian law makes a distinction as to whether a licence may be classified as comparable with a rental agreement (Section 23 of the Insolvency Act) – and if it cannot be so classified, the fall-back provision for agreements unperformed by both parties (under Section 21) applies. While this is a distinction that may be a contentious matter and may also lack legal predictability and certainty, the consequences can be severe.

The prevailing view of this doctrine and in the courts in Austria is that licence agreements may be classified as rental agreements because of the similarity of such contracts. However, an individual assessment is necessary in each and every case to determine whether the licence agreement contains all the necessary elements of a rental agreement that allows an equal treatment in respect to the statutory provisions of the Insolvency Act. Such a classification is therefore necessary for each licence on its own, and it is not possible to generalise the assessment. However, as the provisions concerning rental agreements are *lex specialis* in relation to the provisions for agreements unperformed by both parties, the latter are only applicable if the former do not apply.

According to current thinking, a licence may be treated equally to a rental agreement if the licensee receives a right to use, the grant of rights is for consideration and there is an element of permanence to the agreement. It is, however, necessary to examine whether the contract in question is solely aimed at granting a right to use the intellectual property, or whether other elements are also concerned. For example, in the case of a licence agreement for a copyrighted movie the law distinguishes between a mere rental agreement and a contract under which the licensee is also obligated to exploit the work. If, therefore, the grant of rights is not the main focus of the contract, the provisions for agreements unperformed by both parties will apply in the case of insolvency of either party.

Further, as already stated above, it is crucial whether a continuing obligation is provided for under the contract. If the whole licence fee is paid upfront, the contract has a very strong tendency in the direction of a sales contract. In a case of mixed contracts, the economic emphasis of the contract will have a bearing on which provisions apply.

If the licence can indeed be classified as a rental agreement, Section 24 of the Insolvency Act applies. This means that, in the case of a licensor's insolvency, the insolvency administrator does not have an extraordinary right of termination. Therefore, both parties have to comply with any contractually stipulated rights to terminate, and each party may only terminate in accordance with such a licence agreement.

If the licence does not qualify as a rental agreement, Section 21 of the Insolvency Act will apply. This provision stipulates the consequences for bilateral contracts unperformed by the parties at the time insolvency proceedings have been opened. The legal effects also depend on whether only one of the parties has not yet fulfilled its obligations, or both. If the licensor has already fulfilled its obligations under the licence, the licensee still has to fulfil its own obligations, and will thus usually have to pay the relevant licence fees. If, on the other hand, the licensee has already fully paid its obligations, it may then only lodge an insolvency claim.

If both parties have not yet entirely fulfilled their obligations, the insolvency administrator is automatically granted an option to terminate the licence. He then has the power to terminate the contract with immediate effect, such that the contract becomes legally void and no further obligations under the contract arise. The licensee would, however, have a claim for damages which, as an insolvency claim, is unsecured. If it is advantageous to creditors to continue with the contract, the insolvency administrator may also perform the licensor's obligations and demand performance by the licensee. Moreover, if it is an even better option commercially, the insolvency administrator may sell the intellectual property rights.

### 3.4 Powers and rights of creditors in a licensor's bankruptcy

In a case of the licensor's bankruptcy, the licensee does not receive any extraordinary rights to terminate the licence agreement in order to safeguard the continuation of the insolvent party. As a general principle, any creditors – ie, licensees in this case – do not have any rights to influence the decisions of the insolvency administrator.

### 3.5 Effects on licence agreements in the licensee's bankruptcy

Similar to licensor insolvency, in a case of a licensee's insolvency all contracts and licence agreements remain intact, valid and enforceable. Therefore, the mere starting of insolvency proceedings by a court order does not in itself have a direct effect on the licence agreement. However, termination of a contract in line with contractual or statutory provisions is only possible if it does not jeopardise the continuation of the company that filed for insolvency. Otherwise, the licensor would be bound for six months and could, before that, only terminate for good cause. Impairment of the licensor's financial situation or its default in services is expressly excluded by the Insolvency Act from being a good cause. This is a mandatory provision, from which the parties may not deviate.

### 3.6 Powers of an administrator, receiver or trustee in the licensee's bankruptcy

In a licensee's insolvency, the consequences are slightly different and quite drastic. As already mentioned in section 3.4 above, the licence itself remains valid. However, if the licence qualifies as a rental agreement, Section 23 of the Insolvency Act applies, which stipulates that the insolvency administrator may, notwithstanding any claims for damages, terminate the agreement by observing the statutory termination period, or a shorter period if so contractually agreed. The statutory termination period for termination of licences is 24 hours, after which the insolvency administrator may declare the termination. Any claims for damages by the licensor must be filed with the competent insolvency court.

### 3.7 Powers and rights of creditors in a licensee's bankruptcy

In a licensee insolvency, the licensor may either terminate as contractually agreed or, otherwise, according to the statutory provision mentioned in section 3.6 above. This is subject to the limitation mentioned in section 3.5 above, namely that the continuation of the insolvent company must not be jeopardised.

As a general principle, any creditors – in this case, licensors – do not have any rights to influence the decisions of the insolvency administrator.

### 3.8 Exclusive and non-exclusive licences

Austrian Law does not draw a distinction between exclusive and non-exclusive licences in the event of bankruptcy.

### 3.9 Perpetual and non-perpetual licences

When the fee for a licence has to be paid upfront, meaning that during the lifespan of the licence no further payments to the licensor have to be made by the licensee, the qualification of the agreement pursuant to the Insolvency Act is affected. As already pointed out under section 3.1 above, the licence agreement will then most likely be considered as similar to a sales contract and, as a legal consequence, the Insolvency Act rules for contracts unperformed by the parties will apply. Otherwise, an assessment has to be made as to whether the provisions of the Insolvency Act for rental agreements will apply. For example, in a case of a licence agreement for a copyrighted movie under which the licensee has to pay the whole fee in advance and neither party has completely fulfilled its obligations (for instance, because the licensee is obligated to exploit the work), the provisions for agreements unperformed by both parties will apply.

If the agreement for a perpetual licence is unilaterally performed, the consequences depend on which party became insolvent. In the event that the licensor has become insolvent and the licence fee has already been paid, then the licensee may only lodge an insolvency claim. In a case of the licensee's insolvency where the licensee has already fully paid, the licensee may then further rely on the licence granted.

### 3.10 Effects on a sub-licence in a licensor's bankruptcy

Austrian law does not stipulate any special provisions concerning sub-licenses. Therefore the same rules as set out in sections 3.3 and 3.6 above will apply.

In general, termination of a licence agreement by the owner of the intellectual property rights as a result of the owner's insolvency will affect any sub-licensee. This is because in such a case the sub-licensee's contractual partner, ie the sub-licensor, will lose its own rights under the licence and is no longer entitled to forward its rights to third parties. However, subject to the provisions of the sub-licence, the sub-licensee may claim damages against the sub-licensor.

### 3.11 Effects on a sub-licence in a licensee's bankruptcy

As there are no special provisions concerning sub-licences in the Austrian legislation, in a case of a licensee's bankruptcy the general rules as described in sections 3.3 and 3.6 above apply without restriction.

### 3.12 Impact of registration

With one exception (see next paragraph), it does not make any difference during insolvency proceedings whether a licence or sub-licence is registered. License agreements for patents, utility patents, designs and trademarks can generally be registered in the respective Austrian registers, which are maintained by the Austrian Patents Office with its seat in Vienna. In contrast, owing to the lack of registers for these intellectual property rights, licences for copyrighted works or for know-how cannot be entered into a register under Austrian law.

There is one exception to the foregoing general position, in that whether a licence agreement that can qualify as a rental agreement is registered has an effect on its validity and the termination rights if the intellectual property right is transferred during insolvency proceedings. If the transferred licence is entered into the register, the licence will generally continue to be valid to its full extent. If, however, the transferee acquires an intellectual property right which is not registered, the prevailing view is that the new owner of such intellectual property rights may terminate any licence agreements that fall under the provisions of rental agreements by observing the statutory termination period of 24 hours. The licensee may then claim damages from his contractual partner and previous owner of the intellectual property rights, but no other party.

## 4. Contractual arrangements in deviation from the law

### 4.1 Exceptions, and scope to alter statutory mechanisms

The foregoing provisions apply to all licence agreements equally (with the exception of copyright licences as described in section 3.1). There are no licence agreements that are subject to a regime different from the regime applicable to regular licence agreements.

### 4.2 Termination rights and automatic reversions

As explained above, the provisions of the Insolvency Act are mandatory; thus, parties to an agreement cannot validly deviate from the rules that are laid down. Specifically, Section 25b(2) of the Insolvency Act states that contractual agreements between two parties, which entitle a party to terminate an agreement or which provide for the automatic termination of an agreement in a case of the opening of insolvency proceedings over the assets of a counterparty, are invalid.

The Austrian insolvency law aims to facilitate the continuation of an insolvent company and its restructuring. If the termination of a contract might harm the continuation of the company, a creditor may only terminate the contract after six months following the opening of insolvency proceedings for important reasons caused after the opening of insolvency proceedings. The Insolvency Act makes clear that the deterioration of the debtor's financial situation or the non-fulfilment of a claim that has become due prior to the opening of insolvency proceedings may never be considered as an important cause and therefore do not entitle a creditor to terminate the contract.

## 5. Cross-border aspects

### 5.1 Foreign law

Following the principles of international law, it is admissible under Austrian law to elect foreign material law to govern a licence agreement. However, the parties cannot validly agree on deviating procedural law in the case of a party's insolvency; moreover, the parties cannot agree on the applicability of a foreign law on insolvency proceedings initiated in Austria. Therefore, a stipulation of a right to terminate a licence agreement in the event of the licensor's or licensee's insolvency is unenforceable.

### 5.2 Foreign jurisdiction

Austrian courts have jurisdiction in insolvency proceedings if the insolvent debtor either runs its business or has its habitual residence in Austria; moreover, Austrian courts are competent in a case where the debtor has a branch or property in Austria. In these circumstances, agreements between parties on the exercise of a different jurisdiction with reference to the opening of insolvency proceedings are invalid. The competent insolvency court or the insolvency administrator would therefore not be bound by the election of a foreign jurisdiction with reference to insolvency proceedings in a licence agreement.

# Belgium

**Yves Lenders**
**Annick Mottet Haugaard**
Lydian

---

## 1. Overview

### 1.1 Relevant legislation governing intellectual property and insolvency

Belgium does not have specific legislation governing the effects of insolvency on intellectual property. These effects are governed by the general legislation applicable to insolvency and intellectual property, ie:

- The Law on Continuity of Companies of January 31 2009, published in the *Official State Gazette* of February 9 2009 and in effect as of April 1 2009;
- The Bankruptcy Law of August 8 1997, published in the *Official State Gazette* of October 28 1997 and in effect as of January 1 1998; and
- the Copyright and Neighbouring Rights Law of June 30 1994, which sets out provisions relating to insolvency but only applicable to specific cases (publishing contracts, and the insolvency of the producer of an audiovisual work) and not to licence agreements as such.

### 1.2 Types of insolvency procedure

Belgian law provides three main regulated procedures: pre-insolvency proceedings, insolvency proceedings and liquidation. Each is described further next.

#### *(a) Pre-Insolvency proceedings*

The Law on Continuity of Companies provides that any company can enter into an amicable out-of-court settlement with at least two of its creditors to redress its financial situation or to reorganise its undertaking. Such a voluntary agreement benefits from some legal limitations to contract with a pre-insolvent entity. These agreements will be protected against possible clawback actions under the Bankruptcy Law. Under that law, any transactions of valuable consideration where the third party was aware of the cessation of payments of the company, as well as payments in cash for undue debts (including waivers of payments or payment terms), can be declared unenforceable against the bankruptcy estate if they were performed by the debtor during the suspect period. These clawback actions are not possible against the aforementioned agreements.

#### *(b) Insolvency proceedings*

The Law on Continuity of Companies provides for different types of judicial reorganisation (or composition) of a company in financial difficulties:

- an amicable settlement with two or more creditors;
- a collective settlement with all creditors, resulting in the approval of a reorganisation plan; and
- the transfer of all or part of the activities of the distressed company to one or more third parties.

If a rehabilitation of the company is considered impossible, the bankruptcy procedure may take effect and the provisions of the Bankruptcy Law will apply.

### (c) *Liquidation*

Liquidation follows the dissolution of a company in order to divide or realise the assets of the company and distribute them among its creditors and, possibly, its shareholders. As a principle, so-called 'liquidation in deficit' is also accepted as an alternative to bankruptcy. A liquidation in deficit is a liquidation whereby the liabilities exceed the assets. The legal proceedings do not vary from an ordinary liquidation.

## 1.3 Grounds of insolvency

### (a) *Judicial reorganisation*

The court can grant a moratorium to any debtor that is 'in distress' – ie, one that has difficulties to meeting its financial obligations in the short term, irrespective of its cause. It is sufficient that the continuity of the company is endangered. The Law on Continuity of Companies provides that financial difficulties are assumed if the net asset value of the company has dropped below 50% of its share capital as a direct result of incurred losses. A company that is from a theoretical point of view bankrupt can also be the subject of a moratorium.

### (b) *Bankruptcy*

The court may declare a debtor bankrupt if the following conditions are met:

- The debtor is engaged in commercial activities;
- The debtor has suspended payments to its creditors; and
- The debtor is no longer creditworthy, so he will continue not to meet his obligations to creditors.

### (c) *Liquidation*

A general meeting of shareholders can decide, on a discretionary basis, to start a liquidation procedure. In exceptional circumstances, liquidation can be ordered by a court when the net assets of the company have decreased below a certain amount or when the company has failed to file its annual accounts for at least three consecutive years.

## 1.4 Filing for insolvency

### (a) *Judicial reorganisation*

The debtor (ie, the person who can legally represent the company) or its lawyer can file a request for judicial reorganisation before the Commercial Court of the jurisdiction of the debtor's registered offices.

### *(b)* *Bankruptcy*

The debtor itself must file for bankruptcy within one month of the suspension of payments – there are significant civil and criminal sanctions if the debtor fails to do this. The filing must be done before the Commercial Court of the jurisdiction of the registered offices of the debtor. In the case of a company, the filing must be done by the person who can legally represent the company, which would be a director or the board of directors. A special power of attorney can also be given.

Apart from the possibility of filing for bankruptcy, a company can also be summoned in bankruptcy by a creditor, the Public Prosecutor, a court-appointed administrator appointed as a provisional measure, or the trustee of the main bankruptcy in a case of an international bankruptcy.

Indeed, the Bankruptcy Law provides for the possibility for the President of the Commercial Court to appoint an administrator *ex officio* or upon unilateral request of an interested party as a provisional measure if there are strong indications that the conditions for bankruptcy are met and bankruptcy is not filed by the company itself. The authorities of this administrator will be defined in the President's decision and the designation remains valid only if the administrator files for bankruptcy within 15 days of his appointment.

### *(c)* *Liquidation*

The decision to dissolve and liquidate a company, when taken by the shareholders' meeting of the company, triggers the dissolution of the board of directors.

All interested parties or the Public Prosecutor can request the court to dissolve a company when it has failed to submit its annual accounts for three years in a row.

## 1.5 Administrators and other appointed persons

### *(a)* *Judicial reorganisation*

During the composition procedure, the directors and shareholders of the debtor stay in charge of the company. Upon filing of the request for judicial reorganisation, a judge is appointed by the Commercial Court to supervise the procedure.

There are certain exceptions to this general arrangement, as follows:

- The debtor may request the court to appoint a mediator to assist the company during its reorganisation process or, upon a creditor's request, a court-appointed judicial officer. Interested third parties (such as creditors) can request the court to appoint a judicial officer in the case of apparent serious shortcomings of the debtor or its representatives that may endanger the continuity of the company.
- If the debtor or, in exceptional circumstances, the Public Prosecutor, a creditor or an acquiring company chooses a composition by way of transfer of (part of) the undertaking, a judicial officer is appointed to represent the undertaking for this (part) transfer.

- In a number of circumstances, the court may appoint a judicial officer to the insolvency proceedings. The powers of a judicial officer are determined on a case-by-case basis.

*(b)* ***Bankruptcy***

Upon filing for bankruptcy, no specific person (such as a trustee, receiver or administrator) is appointed. Moreover, when a company files for bankruptcy, as the filing is not a confession, the court still has to examine whether the conditions for bankruptcy are met and it does not imperatively have to declare the company bankrupt.

Once the court has declared the bankruptcy of the debtor, the court appoints one or more trustees, which then take full control over the company with the aim of collecting outstanding debts, realising the assets of the bankrupt estate and distributing the proceeds to the creditors.

*(c)* ***Liquidation***

A liquidator is appointed by the shareholders' meeting when dissolving a company. The liquidator takes over the mandate of the directors with the aim of realising the assets and completing the subsequent liquidation. The liquidator might already be specified in the company's articles of association.

Appointment must be approved by a court, which is rarely refused. The ground for refusal is that that the liquidator is not deemed 'honourable' or 'sincere'.

Generally, a lawyer or accountant is appointed as liquidator. A director can also be appointed as liquidator, but this might result in a conflict of interest, as a liquidator is entitled to start liability actions against the director if there are grounds to do so.

The liquidation is followed up by the court and the final report must be approved by the court.

## 2. Licence agreements in the phase between filing and declaration of insolvency

### 2.1 Effects on licence agreements in case of the licensor's insolvency

*(a)* ***Judicial reorganisation***

As a principle, a composition aims to preserve the continuity of a company as a going concern. Hence, the initiation of a composition as a result of a licensor's insolvency cannot terminate any contracts.

However, penalty clauses such as default interest cannot be enforced during the suspension period. Moreover, clauses automatically ending the agreement if the debtor requests a composition have no effect.

The Law on Continuity of Companies further provides for a 'remedy period' – ie, a period of 15 days (taking effect as of notification of default) during which the debtor in composition may cure a contractual default that occurred prior to the composition. Consequently, the creditor cannot terminate the contract on the basis of such default if and when the debtor under composition fulfils its contractual obligations within the remedy period.

***(b) Bankruptcy***

In Belgian bankruptcy law, no specific rules apply for the phase between filing and declaration of bankruptcy. Moreover, as previously mentioned, the court will only declare a company bankrupt if the appropriate conditions are met (see section 1.3(b) above).

***(c) Liquidation***

In the case of liquidation of a company, the court or the shareholders immediately decide to dissolve the company, but the liquidation does not automatically end the ongoing agreements unless contractually agreed otherwise or the agreement is *intuitu personae* (ie, the identity of the other party constitutes an essential element upon the signing of the contract). Even so, as the company after the appropriate legal steps exists merely to complete liquidation, the liquidator will most likely terminate all agreements.

**2.2 Powers of administrators, receivers or trustees in the licensor's insolvency**

***(a) Judicial reorganisation***

As previously mentioned, a debtor usually remains in possession even during insolvency, apart from in the following three circumstances:

- A judicial officer has been appointed by a court, with the officer's powers determined on a case-by-case basis. The board retains full company powers, save for the judicial officer's tasks.
- Part or all of the undertaking is being transferred.
- The directors and shareholders have lost control over the company as a direct consequence of the composition by transfer of the company.

***(b) Bankruptcy***

The question of authoritative powers is not applicable in Belgian bankruptcy law as no specific person (such as a trustee, receiver or administrator) is appointed upon filing for bankruptcy.

The powers of an administrator appointed as a provisional measure (see section 1.4(b) above) should be clearly defined in the decision of the President of the Commercial Court appointing this administrator. At any given time, the President can modify these powers upon request of the administrator. The creditor seeking its appointment can ask for specific tasks to be granted to the administrator, but these should always be limited in scope in view of the performance of the main task of the administrator, namely verifying whether the bankruptcy conditions are met.

***(c) Liquidation***

This is a non-issue in case of liquidation of a company, as a court or the shareholders immediately decide to dissolve the company. No powers are therefore grantable between filing and declaration, unless necessary in view of the liquidation of the company.

## 2.3 Effects on licence agreements in case of the licensee's insolvency

### (a) *Judicial reorganisation*

The effects within a judicial reorganisation under a licensee's insolvency are the same as those described in section 2.1(a) above for a licensor's bankruptcy.

### (b) *Bankruptcy*

In Belgian bankruptcy law, no specific rules apply for the phase between filing and declaration of bankruptcy. Moreover, as previously mentioned, the court will only declare a company bankrupt if the conditions are met.

### (c) *Liquidation*

This is a non-issue in case of liquidation of a company as the court or the shareholders immediately decide to dissolve the company.

## 2.4 Powers of administrators, receivers or trustees in the licensee's insolvency

### (a) *Judicial reorganisation*

The effects are the same as in case of the licensee's bankruptcy.

### (b) *Bankruptcy*

This is a non issue in Belgian bankruptcy law as no specific person such as a trustee, receiver or administrator is appointed upon filing for bankruptcy.

The powers of the administrator appointed as a provisional measure are clearly defined in the President's decision appointing this administrator. At any given time, the President can modify these powers upon request of the administrator. The creditor seeking its appointment could ask for specific tasks to be granted to the administrator, but all limited in view of the performance of the main task of administrator (ie, verifying whether the bankruptcy conditions are met. The creditors do not have a say in this).

### (c) *Liquidation*

This is a non-issue in the case of liquidation of a company as the court or the shareholders immediately decide to dissolve the company and thus terminate all agreements.

## 2.5 Impact of registration

Registration is not relevant in this context because during the phase between filing and declaration of bankruptcy nothing will happen and the licence agreement will continue at least for the time being.

## 3. Licence agreements in the phase after declaration of insolvency

### 3.1 Treatment of intellectual property rights

Belgian law does not set forth specific provisions relating to intellectual property rights and licences when insolvency arises. There is therefore no difference between intellectual property rights during or outside insolvency. The only thing to note in a case of bankruptcy is that, for registered intellectual property rights (ie, trademarks, patents and designs), a licence has to be registered in the official register in order to be opposable by third parties.

### 3.2 Effects on licence agreements in case of the licensor's insolvency

#### (a) *Judicial reorganisation*

As a principle, a composition aims to preserve the continuity of a company as a going concern. Hence, the initiation of a composition does not terminate any contracts as such.

However, penalty clauses such as default interest cannot be enforced during the suspension period. Moreover, clauses automatically ending the agreement if the debtor requests for a composition and/or obtains such a composition, have no effect.

The Law on Continuity of Companies further provides for a 'remedy period' – ie, a period of 15 days (taking effect as of notification of default) during which the debtor in composition may cure a contractual default that occurred prior to the composition. Consequently, a creditor cannot terminate the contract on the basis of such default if and when the debtor under composition fulfils its contractual obligations within the remedy period.

There is an exception to the foregoing, in that a debtor has the right to no longer execute a contract during the composition, and may consequently deviate from the general rule of continuity of contracts, if the following two circumstances hold: the debtor notifies the creditor of its intention to no longer carry out its obligations under the contract; and such decision is necessary in order for the debtor to be able to implement a reorganisation plan or to transfer the company into other hands. If the debtor decides to terminate the agreement according to Article 35 of the Law on Continuity of Companies, the indemnity due to the licensee is not privileged.

#### (b) *Bankruptcy*

The basic assumption in Belgian insolvency law is the continuity of all ongoing agreements (ie, the contracts existing before the commencement of bankruptcy proceedings), so these agreements continue to exist notwithstanding the initiation of bankruptcy. It will be up to the appointed trustee to terminate the ongoing contract in accordance with the terms and conditions of such agreement.

If the trustee fails to take a decision whether it will terminate the agreement, the contracting party is allowed to force the trustee to take a position. The trustee must decide within 15 days of receiving this notice of default (although this period can by convention be prolonged). If the trustee fails to take a decision within the given term, the agreement is deemed to be terminated as of the expiration of the delay.

The trustee may even choose to continue the business of the debtor, and by consequence not to terminate the agreements, if the trustee receives authorisation of the court and the continuation of the company does not cause any prejudice to the creditors.

*Intuitu personae* contracts (ie, contracts whereby the identity of the other party constitutes an essential element upon the signing of the contract) are automatically terminated as of the bankruptcy judgment since the debtor is no longer in charge of the company. Parties can, however, agree on continuing such contracts. Sometimes, licence agreements can be *intuitu personae*.

Licence agreements will therefore not automatically end on declaration of a licensor's bankruptcy unless otherwise stipulated in the agreement.

#### (c) *Liquidation*

The liquidation procedure does not terminate existing contracts; the liquidator decides whether the contracts will be terminated. However, *intuitu personae* contracts can be terminated by the counterparty (and this could be stipulated in the agreement).

### 3.3 Powers of an administrator, receiver or trustee in the licensor's insolvency

#### (a) *Judicial reorganisation*

A debtor usually remains in possession, apart from in the following two situations:

- The debtor may request the court to appoint a mediator to assist the company during its reorganisation process or, upon a creditor's request, a court-appointed judicial officer. Interested third parties (such as creditors) can request the court to appoint a judicial officer in the case of apparent serious shortcomings of the debtor or its representatives that may endanger the continuity of the company.
- If the debtor or, in exceptional circumstances, the Public Prosecutor, a creditor or an acquiring company chooses a composition by way of transfer of the undertaking, a judicial officer is appointed to represent the undertaking in this (part) transfer.

#### (b) *Bankruptcy*

A trustee in bankruptcy has full authority to represent the bankrupt company. The trustee's powers are, for some decisions, subject to prior approval by the supervising judge. If the trustee wishes to terminate a licence agreement in the case of the licensor's bankruptcy, it must do so in accordance with the terms and conditions of that agreement. The trustee must thus respect the rights given to the licensee if the licence is opposable by third parties. The licence agreement will therefore not be terminated by the bankruptcy unless agreed as such in the licence agreement.

For termination of a software licence agreement which is really crucial for the licensee, the latter may propose to the trustee to buy the source code of such software in order to let the latter continue functioning. This does not constitute a statutory right of the licensee and the trustee is not obliged to sell the source code, but it could be considered an abuse of right if it is software that is tailor–made for the licensee.

#### *(c)* *Liquidation*

As of its appointment by the general shareholder meeting, the liquidator takes over the mandate of the directors with the aim of realising the assets and completing the liquidation.

### 3.4 Powers and rights of creditors in a licensor's insolvency

#### *(a)* *Judicial reorganisation*

A judicial reorganisation has no automatic impact on the performance of ongoing agreements. The licensor is expected to continue to perform its agreement.

If the licensor is in breach of contract, the licensee can perform all contractual remedies. However, if the breach of contract is from before the opening of insolvency proceedings, the licensee must issue a notice of default and, if the licensor does not remedy the breach within 15 days, the licensee can terminate the agreement.

The licensor is further entitled to suspend (and, according to legal scholars, terminate) the licence agreement if this action is required for ensuring the continuity of the licensor's business. The damages resulting from that suspension or termination will be a claim which falls in the moratorium.

#### *(b)* *Bankruptcy*

The bankruptcy trustee will decide, shortly after its appointment, whether to continue or end ongoing agreements. A contracting party can issue a notice of default to the trustee to take that decision. If the trustee fails to reply within 15 days, the agreement is considered terminated at the expense of the bankruptcy estate.

#### *(c)* *Liquidation*

No specific regulation applies, other than what is set out above in section 2.1(c).

### 3.5 Effects on licence agreements in case of the licensee's insolvency

#### *(a)* *Judicial reorganisation*

The effects on licence agreements when a licensee's insolvency arises and is subject to a judicial reorganisation are the same as apply for a licensor's reorganisation.

#### *(b)* *Bankruptcy*

As previously mentioned, the basic assumption in Belgian insolvency law is the continuity of agreements despite the insolvency. Licence agreements will therefore not end by operation of law in a case of a licensee's bankruptcy, except when the agreement is *intuitu personae.*

Indeed, a licence agreement is not as such an *intuitu personae* agreement for the licensee: this will have to be assessed on a case by case basis. For instance, a trademark owner will not grant a trademark licence to just anyone: he will first verify whether the potential licensee is able to offer the same level of quality, so that trademark licence agreement is considered to be an *intuitu personae* agreement. If the licence agreement does not allow the licensee to grant a sub-licence, it will in principle be also considered an *intuitu personae* agreement. However, a standard Microsoft software licence will not be considered as an *intuitu personae* agreement.

In order to avoid any discussion on the *intuitu personae* character (or otherwise) of the agreement, it is advisable to stipulate in the licence agreement that the agreement will end in the event of the licensee's bankruptcy.

***(c) Liquidation***

The liquidation procedure does not terminate the existing contracts; the liquidator decides whether or not the contracts will be terminated. However, *intuitu personae* contracts can be terminated by the counterparty. As already mentioned, a licence agreement can be *intuitu personae* (ie, it is concluded exclusively in consideration of the individual entity who signs the agreement for the licensee). This could be a cause of early termination stipulated in the licence agreement.

**3.6 Powers of an administrator, receiver or trustee in the licensee's insolvency**

***(a) Judicial reorganisation***

As mentioned above, the debtor usually remains in possession apart from in the following three circumstances:

- A mediator is appointed by the court to help the debtor in its reorganisation process. The power of such a mediator does not affect the powers of the debtor, unless otherwise specified in the appointment order at the request of the debtor.
- A judicial officer is appointed by the court. The powers of a court-appointed officer vary, depending on the basis of such appointment. The court has extensive discretionary powers to define the powers of the judicial officer, and thus the impact of the powers of the debtor.
- (Part of) the undertaking is being transferred. The judicial official will decide what will be sold to whom, following the court's approval. The debtor has only an advisory role in the process.

***(b) Bankruptcy***

A bankruptcy trustee does not have any specific powers in the event of a licensee's bankruptcy. As the licence agreement is not always terminated in such circumstances (because this depends on the provisions of the agreement), the trustee is in principle allowed to continue, terminate or transfer the licence. In order to avoid, however, the licence being transferred to an unwanted contracting party (eg, a competitor of the licensor), a clause of limitation of transfer or termination in the event of bankruptcy of the licensee could be inserted in the licence agreement.

***(c) Liquidation***

As of its appointment by the general shareholders meeting, the liquidator takes over the mandate of the directors with the aim of realising the assets and completing the liquidation. The liquidator can thus terminate the licence agreement.

## 3.7 Powers and rights of creditors in a licensee's insolvency

### *(a) Judicial reorganisation*

Judicial reorganisation has no automatic impact on the performance of ongoing agreements. The licensee is expected to continue to perform its agreement.

If the licensee is in breach of contract, the licensor/creditor can perform all contractual remedies. However, if the breach of contract is from before the opening of the insolvency proceedings, the licensor/creditor must issue a notice of default and, if the licensor does not remedy the breach within 15 days, the licensee can terminate the agreement.

The licensee is further entitled to suspend (and, according to legal scholars, terminate) the licence agreement if this action is required for ensuring the continuity of the licensee's business. The damages resulting from that suspension or termination will be a claim which falls in the moratorium.

### *(b) Bankruptcy*

When a licensee's bankruptcy arises, creditors have the same powers and rights as in the event of a licensor's bankruptcy (see section 3.4(b) above).

### *(c) Liquidation*

No specific regulation applies, other than what is set out above in section 2.1(c).

## 3.8 Exclusive and non-exclusive licences

There is as no difference in Belgian law between exclusive and non-exclusive licences.

In practice, though, it is clear that the termination of an exclusive licence has more impact than a non-exclusive licence, so a licensee is likely to do its best in order to retain continuation of the licence.

## 3.9 Perpetual and non-perpetual licences

There is as no difference in Belgian law between perpetual and non-perpetual licences. In practice, though, it is clear that when bankruptcy of the licensor arises, a licensee is likely to do its best in order to retain continuation of a perpetual licence.

## 3.10 Effects on a sub-licence in a licensor's insolvency

As previously mentioned, the basic assumption in Belgian insolvency law is the continuity of the agreements. Sub-licence agreements will therefore not end by operation of law in the event of a licensor's insolvency.

However, if the initial licence agreement stipulated that it would automatically come to an end in the case of the licensor's bankruptcy or liquidation, the sub-licence agreement must immediately also come an end. The sub-licensee is then entitled to claim damages, but such a claim is not privileged.

## 3.11 Effects on a sub-licence in a licensee's bankruptcy

As previously mentioned, the basic assumption in Belgian insolvency law is the continuity of the agreements. Sub-licence agreements will therefore not end by operation of law in the event of a licensee's insolvency.

However, if the initial licence agreement can be terminated because of the licensee's bankruptcy or liquidation, it is clear that any sub-licence will immediately come an end as well in such circumstances, because the licensee cannot transfer more rights than it has.

### 3.12 Impact of registration

As described in section 2.5 above, for registered intellectual property rights (trademarks, patents and designs), a (sub-)licence has to be registered in the official register in order to be opposable by third parties.

## 4. Contractual arrangements in deviation from the law

### 4.1 Exceptions

In relation to exceptional circumstances, Belgian legislation provides for a specific regime for publishing agreements.

According to Article 30 of the Copyright and Neighbouring Rights Law and Article 46 of the Bankruptcy Law, in the case of bankruptcy of a publisher any one of its authors may terminate the publishing agreement between them within 15 days, by registered letter with acknowledgment of receipt.

The author has a preferential right to buy all copies or reproductions that are protected by copyright. In the event of disagreement between the bankruptcy trustee and the author on the purchase price, the latter will be determined by the court at the request of either party and, if necessary, on the advice of one or more experts. Expert fees will be shared between the (bankrupt) publisher and the author. The author loses his preferential right of purchase if he does not inform the trustee that he wishes to exercise his right within 30 days of receipt of the offer. The offer and acceptance must be made by writ or by registered mail with acknowledgment of receipt. The author of the work may waive his right of preferential purchase, by writ or by registered mail addressed to the trustee.

Such arrangements apply also in a case of judicial reorganisation or liquidation, according to Article 30 of the Copyright and Neighbouring Rights Law.

### 4.2 Scope to alter statutory mechanisms

Since, under Belgian law, there is no statutory mechanism for altering agreements, parties are free to determine the rules applicable to their licence agreement provided that they respect the principle of equality among the creditors (see also section 4.3 below).

### 4.3 Termination rights and automatic reversions

Parties can provide that, in the event of the bankruptcy of one of the parties, their licence agreement is automatically terminated.

However, parties cannot provide that, in the case of bankruptcy of the licensor, the intellectual property rights covered by the licence agreement will automatically be transferred in ownership to the licensee, because this will be contrary to the principle of equality among the creditors. It is nonetheless permitted that the transfer can occur provided the licensee buys those intellectual property rights at the market price, so that there is in principle no disadvantage to the creditors.

## 5. Cross-border aspects

### 5.1 Foreign law

If a licence agreement is continued despite the licensor's or licensee's insolvency, the law applicable to the licence agreement remains the law chosen by the parties. However, if the trustee or debtor wishes to terminate the licence agreement, the rights of termination of the trustee or debtor and the consequences thereof will be determined by Belgian insolvency law. Indeed, Article 4.2(e) of EU Council Regulation 1346/2000 of May 29 2000 on insolvency proceedings explicitly stipulates that the law of the state of the opening of insolvency proceedings shall determine the effects of the insolvency proceedings on current contracts to which the debtor is party.

If the licensor or licensee is declared insolvent in Belgium, Belgian insolvency law will apply irrespective of the law chosen by the parties in the licence agreement.

### 5.2 Foreign jurisdiction

If a licence agreement is continued despite the licensor's or licensee's insolvency, the appointed trustee remains bound by the election of any foreign jurisdiction over the licence agreement, because the continuity of agreements is the predominant rule in Belgian insolvency law.

However, if litigation between the parties concerns a contesting by the trustee of a creditor's claim filed in the insolvency, the case will be heard by the Belgian Commercial Court that opened the insolvency proceedings.

# Canada

**Craig J Hill**
Borden Ladner Gervais LLP

## 1. Overview

### 1.1 Relevant legislation governing intellectual property and bankruptcy/insolvency

There are three principal federal statutes in Canada governing intellectual property in the context of bankruptcy or insolvency: the Bankruptcy and Insolvency Act,[1] the Companies' Creditors Arrangement Act[2] and the Winding-up and Restructuring Act.[3] The Winding-up and Restructuring Act is rarely utilised as it applies to winding up federally regulated entities such as banks, trust companies and insurance companies.

### 1.2 Types of insolvency procedure

There are three principal types of insolvency proceedings in Canada:

- debtor-initiated restructuring proceedings under the Companies' Creditors Arrangement Act or under the proposal proceedings set out in Part III of the Bankruptcy and Insolvency Act;
- liquidating bankruptcies under the Bankruptcy and Insolvency Act; and
- creditor-initiated receivership proceedings under the Bankruptcy and Insolvency Act.

Restructurings or proposal proceedings are initiated for insolvent persons, generally defined as a debtor that is unable to meet its obligations as they become due, has ceased paying its current obligations in the ordinary course of business or where the liquidation value of its property is not sufficient to enable payment of all of its obligations.

### 1.3 Grounds of bankruptcy/insolvency proceedings

In order to be eligible to commence proposal proceedings under the Bankruptcy and Insolvency Act, a debtor company must be able to show that:

- it is not bankrupt (ie, a bankruptcy order has not been made against it);
- it resides, carries on business or has property in Canada;
- its liabilities to creditors provable as claims under the Bankruptcy and Insolvency Act amount to no less than $1,000; and
- it is insolvent.[4]

1 Revised Statutes of Canada (RSC) 1985, c B-3, as amended.
2 RSC 1985, c C-36, as amended.
3 RSC 1985, c W-11, as amended.
4 Bankruptcy and Insolvency Act, Sections 2, 50 and 50.4.

Only an insolvent person may make an assignment to commence a voluntary liquidating bankruptcy.[5] The criteria for being an insolvent person are the same criteria as are applied when determining whether a debtor company is eligible to commence a Bankruptcy and Insolvency Act proposal proceeding.[6]

In order to be eligible to file for Companies' Creditors Arrangement Act protection, a debtor company or a group of affiliated debtor companies must show that:

- they are insolvent;
- they are incorporated under the laws of Canada or have assets or do business in Canada; and
- they have claims against them which exceed C$5 million in the aggregate.[7]

If the debtor companies can meet the applicable criteria, they may apply to the court for what has come to be known as an 'initial order'.

## 1.4 Filing for bankruptcy

Any creditor owed at least C$1,000 may apply for a bankruptcy order against a debtor under the Bankruptcy and Insolvency Act. Any person may apply to the court for an initial order to be made against a debtor under the Companies' Creditors Arrangement Act. Only a secured creditor may apply to the court for the appointment of a receiver or a 'receiver and manager' under Section 243 of the Bankruptcy and Insolvency Act.

Under both the Companies' Creditors Arrangement Act and the Bankruptcy and Insolvency Act, jurisdiction for insolvency proceedings is conferred on the superior courts in the relevant provinces and territories.

## 1.5 Administrators and other appointed persons

A licensed trustee in bankruptcy is appointed under both proposal proceedings and bankruptcy proceedings under the Bankruptcy and Insolvency Act. A monitor must be appointed by the court in an initial order made under the Companies' Creditors Arrangement Act; the monitor must be a licensed trustee in bankruptcy. Any receiver appointed by the court pursuant to the Bankruptcy and Insolvency Act must be a licensed trustee in bankruptcy.

The primary function of a trustee in bankruptcy is to liquidate the assets of the bankrupt debtor and distribute the proceeds in accordance with the statutory scheme of distribution set out in the Bankruptcy and Insolvency Act. A court-appointed receiver carries out a similar task in terms of the liquidation of assets, but typically distributes the proceeds to secured creditors of the debtor.

The primary functions of a monitor in Companies' Creditors Arrangement Act proceedings or a trustee under proposal proceedings are to assist the debtor in possession with its restructuring, whether that is taking the form of a balance sheet

---

5 Bankruptcy and Insolvency Act, Section 49(1).
6 Bankruptcy and Insolvency Act, Sections 2, 50 and 50.4.
7 Companies' Creditors Arrangement Act, Sections 2–3.

restructuring through a plan of compromise, or through an arrangement (or proposal) to compromise the claims of creditors, or through a liquidation of the assets by the debtor accompanied by oversight by the monitor/trustee.

Receivers, trustees and monitors are all considered to be officers of the court, have fiduciary duties to all creditors and are considered by the court to be its 'eyes and ears' in the insolvency process. Receivers/trustees/monitors report to the court on the status of the proceedings and with respect to material matters as the process develops. It is possible to have overlapping appointments – for example, it is common to have a receiver appointed to liquidate the assets but convert the receivership to a bankruptcy at the stage where distribution occurs so as to benefit from the statutory scheme of distribution in the Bankruptcy and Insolvency Act.

## 2. Licence agreements in the phase between filing and declaration of bankruptcy

With respect to debtor-initiated restructuring proceedings under the Companies' Creditors Arrangement Act, the proposal proceedings set out in Part III of the Bankruptcy and Insolvency Act, voluntary liquidating bankruptcies under the Bankruptcy and Insolvency Act, and creditor-initiated receivership proceedings under the Bankruptcy and Insolvency Act, there is no interim phase in the proceedings: the insolvency proceedings commence upon the filing or the order being made by the Court. Since the insolvency representative is appointed at the commencement of the proceeding, there is no point in time where an insolvency proceeding has been commenced but an insolvency representative has not been appointed.

The only insolvency proceeding that presents the prospect of a procedural gap between the filing and the bankruptcy order occurs when a creditor issues an application for a bankruptcy order and the debtor does not immediately consent to the bankruptcy order. In that case, a delay of 10 days can occur before a bankruptcy order is made. However, the trustee in bankruptcy named in the bankruptcy application does not have authority to exercise statutory powers in the interim.

## 3. Licence agreements in the phase after declaration of bankruptcy

### 3.1 Treatment of intellectual property rights

There is no distinction made with respect to different intellectual property rights in terms of how they are treated in the event of a bankruptcy or insolvency proceeding. 'Intellectual property' is not defined in any of the insolvency statutes, which has resulted in similar principles being applied to all forms of intellectual property.

### 3.2 Effects on licence agreements in the licensor's bankruptcy

The restructuring parts of the Bankruptcy and Insolvency Act and the Companies' Creditors Arrangement Act permit debtor licensors to terminate or disclaim contracts, including licence agreements. If a debtor has the approval of the relevant trustee/monitor, notice of the termination of the agreement can be given by the debtor to the licensee. The licensee then has 15 days to seek an order of the court to prohibit the termination. In the event that the debtor does not have the approval of the trustee/monitor, it must obtain an order from the court approving the termination. The court considers, among other things, whether the disclaimer would facilitate the restructuring efforts of the debtor and whether the disclaimer would cause significant financial hardship to the contract counterparty.

Each of the Bankruptcy and Insolvency Act (as relevant to restructuring) and the Companies' Creditors Arrangement Act also contains statutory protections for the licensee's right to continue to utilise the licensed intellectual property for the length of the agreement, notwithstanding the disclaimer. Any disclaimer does not affect the right to use the intellectual property, as long as the debtor continues to perform its obligations under the contract in relation to the use of the intellectual property.

The liquidation provisions of the Bankruptcy and Insolvency Act and the case law relating to the common-law powers of trustees in bankruptcy and receivers confirms their power to disclaim contracts, including licence agreements. However the statutory protection for the licensee to continue to utilise the licensed intellectual property is not extended to liquidating bankruptcies and receiverships.

The commencement of restructuring proceedings under the Bankruptcy and Insolvency Act by a licensor automatically creates a statutory stay of proceedings that prohibits the termination of all contracts with the debtor, including licence agreements. The standard form of initial order under the Companies' Creditors Arrangement Act and standard form of receivership order under the Bankruptcy and Insolvency Act also contain terms that prohibit the termination of contracts with an insolvent debtor. There is no similar statutory prohibition on termination of contracts in the event of a bankruptcy. The trustee in bankruptcy is given a brief period of time to determine whether it wants to adopt the contract, failing which the contract counterparty is entitled to treat the contract as breached and terminate it.

### 3.3 Powers of an administrator, receiver or trustee in the licensor's bankruptcy

As noted in section 3.2 above, trustees in bankruptcy and receivers have been held to possess the common-law power to disclaim contracts, including licence agreements. More importantly, there is Canadian precedent for the power of trustees in bankruptcy and receivers to transfer the debtor licensor's rights under a licence agreement to a third-party purchaser, free and clear of the rights of the licensee.

### 3.4 Powers and rights of creditors in a licensor's bankruptcy

All of the rights and powers to terminate or continue licence agreements in a licensor's bankruptcy belong to the trustee or receiver, or can be exercised by the restructuring debtor with the input of the monitor or trustee. The creditors do not have any independent rights with respect to dealing with licence agreements.

### 3.5 Effects on licence agreements in the licensee's bankruptcy

The restructuring parts of the Bankruptcy and Insolvency Act and the Companies' Creditors Arrangement Act permit debtor licensees to terminate or disclaim contracts, including licence agreements. If the debtor has the approval of the trustee/monitor, notice of the termination of the agreement can be given by the debtor to the licensor.

The licensor then has 15 days to seek an order of the court to prohibit the termination. In the event that the debtor does not have the approval of the trustee/monitor, it must obtain an order from the court approving the termination.

The commencement of restructuring proceedings under the Bankruptcy and Insolvency Act by a licensee automatically creates a statutory stay of proceedings that prohibits the termination of all contracts with the debtor, including licence agreements. The standard form of initial order under the Companies' Creditors Arrangement Act and standard form of receivership order under the Bankruptcy and Insolvency Act also contain terms that prohibit the termination of contracts with an insolvent debtor.

### 3.6 Powers of an administrator, receiver or trustee in the licensee's bankruptcy

As noted in section 3.2 above, trustees in bankruptcy and receivers have been held to possess the common-law power to disclaim contracts, including licence agreements. There is Canadian precedent for the power of trustees in bankruptcy and receivers to transfer the debtor's rights under a licence agreement to a third-party purchaser, free and clear of the rights of the counterparty to the licence agreement. For example, a transfer of a debtor licensor's rights to a purchaser has been effective to terminate the pre-existing rights of a licensee under the contract. Similar authority would extend the principle to the prospect that a transfer of a debtor licensee's rights to a purchaser can be performed in spite of any objection by the licensor.

### 3.7 Powers and rights of creditors in a licensee's bankruptcy

All of the rights and powers to terminate or continue licence agreements in a licensee's bankruptcy belong to the trustee or receiver, or can be exercised by the restructuring debtor with the input of the monitor or trustee. The creditors do not have any independent rights with respect to dealing with licence agreements.

### 3.8 Exclusive and non-exclusive licences

There is no distinction between exclusive and non-exclusive licences in a bankruptcy or insolvency proceeding in Canada.

### 3.9 Perpetual and non-perpetual licences

There is no distinction in Canada in the treatment of the rights and obligations of the debtor under perpetual and non-perpetual licences in the event of a bankruptcy.

However, the fact that the licence fee has been paid upfront may have an impact on the court's consideration of whether to approve a termination, by the debtor licensor, of a perpetual licence.

### 3.10 Effects on a sub-licence in a licensor's bankruptcy

There are no specific provisions in the Bankruptcy and Insolvency Act or the Companies' Creditors Arrangement Act relating to sub-licences. As a result, the comments set out above with respect to the stay of proceedings, termination of agreements and transfer of agreements would also be applicable with respect to a sub-licence.

### 3.11 Effects on a sub-licence in a licensee's bankruptcy

See the comments in section 3.10 above.

### 3.12 Impact of registration

The registration (or not) of a licence does not affect the treatment of the licence agreement in an insolvency proceeding.

## 4. Contractual arrangements in deviation from the law

### 4.1 Exceptions

As noted in section 3.1 above, there is no distinction made with respect to different intellectual property rights in terms of how they are treated in the event of a bankruptcy or insolvency proceeding. The term 'intellectual property' is not defined in any of the insolvency statutes, which has resulted in similar principles being applied to all forms of intellectual property.

### 4.2 Scope to alter statutory mechanisms

Any contractual provision triggered by an event of insolvency or bankruptcy that has the effect of depriving creditors of value that would otherwise be available is void as being against public policy. The court's general approach to insolvency legislation is to provide a liberal interpretation to its provisions. As a result, any provision of an agreement that could be interpreted as negatively affecting the value of the debtor's estate is at significant risk of being unenforceable.

### 4.3 Termination rights and automatic reversions

See the comments in section 4.2 above.

## 5. Cross-border aspects

### 5.1 Foreign law

The superior courts of Canada have an extensive record of deferring to the choice-of-law provisions in contracts and attempting to resolve through the application of foreign law any disputes that are to be determined, so long as the foreign law can be proved in the domestic insolvency proceeding. However, there is an exception in that the Canadian superior court may refuse to implement any foreign law that would be contrary to public policy in Canada.

### 5.2 Foreign jurisdiction

The court has interpreted the legislative policy of the Bankruptcy and Insolvency Act and the Companies' Creditors Arrangement Act as being in favour of 'single control' – namely one court controlling the assets, property, claims and litigation of an insolvent estate. In the event that the Canadian court had proper jurisdiction with respect to the debtor, the trustee/monitor would not be bound by the election of foreign jurisdiction in the licence agreement.

# China

**Brian Sullivan**
**Yin Zhengyou**
W&H Law Firm

---

## 1. Overview of Bankruptcy Law in China

### 1.1 Relevant legislation governing intellectual property and bankruptcy

The passing of the Enterprise Bankruptcy Law by the People's Republic of China (PRC) in 2006 brought the biggest change to the bankruptcy code in China since the 1986 law, which only pertained to state-owned enterprises (SOEs). With the current law, all legal person enterprises (both state-owned and private) are able to participate in bankruptcy proceedings that offer liquidation, reorganisation and reconciliation (compromise). For financial institutions, there are some special requirements to initiate insolvency proceedings, along with approval from relevant government agencies. For listed companies, there are some additional arrangements for initiating reorganisation proceedings, including approval from the China Securities Regulatory Commission.

The Enterprise Bankruptcy Law does not provide specific articles for intellectual property (IP). PRC legislation governing IP comes from numerous laws, none of which include any provisions for bankruptcy, as follows:

- the Patent Law;
- the Trademark Law;
- the Copyright Law;
- the Law Against Unfair Competition;
- the Regulations for Computer Software Protection;
- the Regulations for the Protection of Layout Design of Integrated Circuits;
- the Copyright Collective Management Regulations;
- the Regulations for the Administration of Audio-Visual Products;
- the Regulations for the Protection of New Varieties of Plants;
- the Regulations for the Customs Protection of IP rights; and
- the Regulations for the Administration of Special Signs.

#### *(a) Judicial Interpretations*

Starting in 2011, the Supreme People's Court (SPC) began a series of so-called 'judicial interpretations' in order to clear up disputes affecting the Enterprise Bankruptcy Law. Entitled "Provisions of the Supreme People's Court on Certain Issues Relating to the Application of the Enterprise Bankruptcy Law of the PRC", the first judicial interpretation established judicial guidelines on provisions for the acceptance of bankruptcy cases. The main issue that was to be dealt with involved the challenge of having local courts delaying – or even ignoring – bankruptcy petitions. Focusing on eligibility and application in the Enterprise Bankruptcy Law, as a result of the judicial interpretation it was possible to apply to an immediately higher court in the event of the lower court declining a case or not providing a response to the application in an appropriate time period. The purpose was to address concerns over a sharp drop in the number of accepted bankruptcy cases after implementation of the Enterprise Bankruptcy Law.

The Supreme People's Court plans to publish several interpretations during a multi-year timetable, and in 2013 the court released its second interpretation – Provisions of the Supreme People's Court on Certain Issues Relating to the Application of the "Enterprise Bankruptcy Law of the People's Republic of China" (II). In this interpretation of the Enterprise Bankruptcy Law, the court clarified provisions relating to debtors' property, including "revocation of rights, recall rights, set-off rights, discontinuance of preservation measures, and suspension of enforcement procedures against the debtor's property, along with derivative trials related to the debtor".[1] The court also aims to avoid actions that may reduce the value of the debtor's property, including limiting the actions of creditors from the date the debtor's application is accepted by the People's Court for bankruptcy protection. Furthermore, in order to encourage greater efficiency in bankruptcy proceedings, any lawsuits brought during such insolvency proceedings shall be heard by the same court that originally accepted the case.

Another judicial interpretation regarding further development of the bankruptcy administrator system is on the way and, among other things, will focus on introducing the right for applicants to recommend eligible attorneys/accountants to work as temporary bankruptcy administrators. This third interpretation is currently in the approval process and will be issued before the end of 2014.

### 1.2 Types of insolvency procedure

The Enterprise Bankruptcy Law contains 12 chapters with 136 articles. The provisions applicable for each procedure in the event of bankruptcy or impending bankruptcy are set out in:

- Chapter 8: Reorganisation;
- Chapter 9: Reconciliation (Compromise); and
- Chapter 10: Bankruptcy Liquidation.

Improvements were made in creating a strong reorganisation regime that allows for a debtor or creditor to petition the court to initiate proceedings. Additionally, Chapter 8 provides the opportunity for debtors or shareholders of the debtor which hold 10% or more of the registered capital of the debtor to petition the court to convert a liquidation proceeding into reorganisation. This is done after the acceptance of the bankruptcy case by the courts, but before the declaration of bankruptcy. In some situations, the debtor is then able to maintain control of its assets and business with the approval of the People's Court.

---

1 CCH China, "Supreme Court Issues Judicial Interpretation of Enterprise Bankruptcy Law", *Shanghai Business Review*, November 4 2013.

Chapter 9's 'compromise' is the reconciliation tool used to negotiate the debts of the debtor. The Enterprise Bankruptcy Law, as the name suggests, only pertains to enterprises and at present China does not have a personal or individual bankruptcy law. Although personal bankruptcy has been considered in the past and officials have stressed the need for such a law, there have not been any serious steps taken so far to enact such a law.

### 1.3 Grounds of bankruptcy

The Enterprise Bankruptcy Law establishes the grounds of bankruptcy for a debtor, with further articles provided under the first judicial interpretation.

Article 2 of the Enterprise Bankruptcy Law outlines eligibility for bankruptcy: where an "enterprise legal person cannot pay off [its] debts due and [its] assets are not enough for paying off all the debts, or [it] apparently lacks the ability to pay off [its] debts, the debts shall be liquidated according to the provisions of this Law".

In 2011 the first judicial interpretation further clarifies the conditions for bankruptcy: a debtor is deemed unable to repay its due debts, as set out in Article1of the interpretation, where its assets are insufficient to pay off all its liabilities or where the debtor apparently lacks capacity for repayment.

There are no specific conditions for bankruptcy with regard to the amount of assets or claims.

### 1.4 Filing for bankruptcy

The Enterprise Bankruptcy Law allows for both a debtor and its creditors to petition the court for bankruptcy. Absent from the bankruptcy law is a specific requirement for those that are required to file for bankruptcy, which includes shareholders and directors of the debtor. Although the duties of a director do not include pre-insolvent trading or a need to file for bankruptcy, directors found to be "hindering" the bankruptcy proceedings such that serious damages result will be investigated for criminal liability.

In relation to the proper authority for receiving petitions of bankruptcy, Article 3 of the Enterprise Bankruptcy Law states: "A bankruptcy case shall be under the jurisdiction of the People's Court at the place where the debtor is domiciled." In most cases, the place where the debtor is registered should be regarded as the place of the domicile. In certain cases, if the principal place of business can be determined explicitly and is different from the place of registration, the principal place of business will be presumed to be the place of the domicile.

#### *(a) Dedicated bankruptcy divisions*

China currently does not have a specialised or dedicated bankruptcy court in place to hear cases. As a new independent court is not permitted under current Chinese law, one solution is to establish a dedicated division within the Intermediate People's Court or some important county level court. The Supreme People's Court has promulgated "Guidance on Providing Judicial Guarantees for Corporate Mergers and Acquisitions", dated June 3 2014, to promote the establishment of dedicated bankruptcy divisions within local people's courts.

## 1.5 Administrators and other appointed persons

The Enterprise Bankruptcy Law introduced the Bankruptcy Administrator System, through which, on the date the bankruptcy case is accepted, the People's Court designates a bankruptcy administrator to oversee the case. As there are some disadvantages to this process of selection by the People's Court, a new judicial interpretation has been drafted to encourage a more market-oriented approach by including the applicant's recommendation. The third judicial interpretation of the Enterprise Bankruptcy Law may well be promulgated before the end of 2014 and will most likely allow for an applicant (creditor or debtor) to recommend a qualified law or accounting firm to work as a temporary bankruptcy administrator. When the People's Court makes the decision to accept a bankruptcy petition, at the same time it usually makes a decision to designate a firm as the (temporary) bankruptcy administrator for the case.

The People's Court will examine whether there are any specific situations under which a recommended firm is not qualified to be designated as the temporary administrator. If there are no issues, then the People's Court will directly appoint the temporary bankruptcy administrator until the first creditors' meeting. In the first creditors' meeting, if there is no resolution to change the temporary bankruptcy administrator, then the temporary administrator will become the designated bankruptcy administrator for the case.

With an administrator appointed by the courts (also through random selection from an approved list), it is now possible to oversee the day-to-day affairs of a debtor. Chapter 3 of the Enterprise Bankruptcy Law outlines the duties and responsibilities of the bankruptcy administrator, where the court-appointed administrator will take over the operations and assets of the debtor during bankruptcy proceedings. Furthermore, the bankruptcy administrator will oversee the operations of the debtor unless approved otherwise by the People's Court in giving the debtor further control over its assets and business under the supervision of the administrator.

Prior to a declaration of bankruptcy, the administrator will present its report to the People's Court. The court will then evaluate the case to make sure that the debtor not only meets the grounds for bankruptcy (Article 2 of the Enterprise Bankruptcy Law), but also to determine whether it is feasible for the debtor to go through reorganisation or reconciliation. Upon this application for bankruptcy, the People's Court will make a decision on whether to declare the debtor bankrupt.

## 2. Licence agreements in the phase between filing and declaration of bankruptcy

Bankruptcy in China involves a three-step procedure: first, a filing for bankruptcy, then the acceptance of the bankruptcy petition, and finally the declaration of bankruptcy. Unlike many jurisdictions where automatic stay or other actions are taken upon the filing for bankruptcy, in China these actions are only taken upon acceptance of the bankruptcy petition by the People's Court. As a result, prior to the acceptance of the bankruptcy case, licence agreements under both the licensor and licensee will not be affected. This changes once the petition has been accepted and a bankruptcy administrator has been appointed.

For reorganisation and reconciliation proceedings, there is no declaration of bankruptcy unless the reorganisation or reconciliation fails.

### 2.1 Effects on licence agreements in the licensor's bankruptcy

A licence agreement will still be valid after the acceptance of the licensor's bankruptcy case. However, the agreement will not be enforceable unless it complies with the utmost interests of the creditors (determined by the bankruptcy administrator). The licensor also has the power to terminate the licence agreement, which is generally done by the administrator.

In the event that the licensor wishes to continue to perform the licence agreement, then the licensee may ask the licensor or the bankruptcy administrator to provide sufficient securities or guarantees for the fulfilment of the agreement. If the licensor or administrator does not provide a sufficient guarantee, then the agreement is deemed to be rescinded. There are no provisions in Chinese bankruptcy law for automatic termination or reversion of rights, but in practice the parties involved can make relevant arrangements for when the licensor enters into bankruptcy with regard to the reversion of rights.

### 2.2 Powers of administrators, receivers or trustees in the licensor's bankruptcy

In China, the bankruptcy administrator may terminate any kind of licence agreement with other parties when the licensor is accepted for bankruptcy. The law does require the bankruptcy administrator to inform the other parties with a written notice of such action and termination. The other parties involved may make a claim against the licensor for any damages caused by the termination of a license agreement.

In practice, some intellectual rights that have been entrusted by the licensor for other parties to use cannot easily be encumbered without causing significant damages. This is often the issue where the other parties have 'works in progress' that would severely affect its business if it were to be unable to provide services or products. The agreement itself can be cancelled, but the other parties would generally be permitted to finish work that has already started.

The power of the bankruptcy administrator to rescind or continue performance of a contract comes from Article 18 of the Enterprise Bankruptcy Law. More specifically, this is to cover an executory contract that has not been fully performed by the debtor and other parties. As mentioned before, the bankruptcy administrator is required to notify other parties of the executory contract and the decision over whether to continue or to rescind performance of the contract. However, if the administrator does not notify other parties within two months of a bankruptcy case being accepted by the courts, then the contract will be deemed rescinded. Furthermore, if the administrator does not respond to an exhortation made by other parties within 30 days, the contract will be rescinded.

Further powers of the bankruptcy administrator are provided in Article 69 of the Enterprise Bankruptcy Law, which covers rules on the transfer or sale of property and rights. For the sale or transfer of rights (including licences), the bankruptcy administrator is required to report to the creditors' committee in a timely manner. In the event that there is no creditors' committee, then the administrator will need to report to the People's Court on any sale or transfer. Approval is also needed from the People's Court if these actions are taken before the first creditors' meeting. Generally, and in practice, the administrator should terminate the agreement prior to the sale of a debtor's business.

### 2.3 Effects on licence agreements in the licensee's bankruptcy

Similarly to what occurs under a licensor's bankruptcy, a licence agreement in the event of a licensee's bankruptcy will still be valid after the acceptance of the bankruptcy case. The agreement will not be enforceable unless the administrator deems otherwise. If the licensee or administrator wishes to continue the agreement, the licensor may ask the administrator to provide an appropriate security or guarantee for the fulfilment of the agreement.

The main difference from a licensor's bankruptcy is that the administrator in a licensee's bankruptcy will often seek to delay the sale or transfer of the licence agreement or associated intellectual property in order to maintain value in the licensee during the proceedings.

### 2.4 Powers of administrators, receivers or trustees in the licensee's bankruptcy

Although a bankruptcy administrator has the right to terminate a licence agreement, in the event of a licensee's bankruptcy the administrator will in practice normally contact the licensor in order to continue or fulfil the agreement. The licensor may then ask the administrator for appropriate securities or guarantees in exchange.

The difference with a licensor filing for bankruptcy is that the licensor will want to terminate the agreement and transfer the rights in order to obtain as much value from its bankruptcy as possible.

### 2.5 Impact of registration

The registration of a licence agreement does not have an effect on the validity of the agreement. Yet, in accordance with relevant IP rules, it is required to register a licence agreement with certain government agencies. Without this registration, it can be inconvenient or difficult to make claims against infringements or to request assistance from government authorities. In accordance with the Regulations on the Customs Protection of IP Rights, for example, only those that have registered their IP with customs officials can seek immediate action against violators of their IP (including the seizure or confiscation of goods).

## 3. Licence agreements in the phase after declaration of bankruptcy

### 3.1 Treatment of intellectual property rights

There are many issues affecting intellectual property rights in bankruptcy, especially with the involvement of multiple parties, but currently there are no specific articles in the Enterprise Bankruptcy Law on the treatment of IP rights. Article 1 of the second judicial interpretation of the Enterprise Bankruptcy Law specifies clearly that the intellectual property rights belong to the debtor's assets.

In practice, there is a distinction between different kinds of intellectual property rights in terms of how they are treated in the event of bankruptcy. During bankruptcy proceedings, efforts are made to prevent trade secrets from being disclosed. Additionally, the name of a debtor enterprise is not transferrable when the debtor's intellectual property rights are sold or transferred: although the new owner has the right to use the intellectual property, the debtor maintains the right of authorship.

### 3.2 Effects on licence agreements in the licensor's bankruptcy

Effects on the licence agreement during bankruptcy proceedings can occur after the acceptance of the case by the People's Court. After the declaration of bankruptcy, the licence agreement is still valid but unenforceable. The licensor also has the power to terminate the agreement, which is generally done by the administrator.

### 3.3 Powers of an administrator, receiver or trustee in the licensor's bankruptcy

The same powers of an administrator upon the acceptance of bankruptcy are in place after a declaration of bankruptcy. In practice, the administrator in a licensor's bankruptcy will normally terminate a licence agreement in order to sell or transfer the rights so as to increase the value of the business during proceedings (and that transfer or sale can occur back to the licensee).Generally speaking, the selling of assets, including IP that has been authorised to be used by the licensee, is normally done after the necessary declaration of assets.

### 3.4 Powers and rights of creditors in a licensor's bankruptcy

In ordinary cases, the creditors or the creditors' meeting will not make a decision to terminate or continue an agreement. According to the Enterprise Bankruptcy Law, this is the right and duty of the bankruptcy administrator and only it can make such a decision. However, in certain cases where the continuation (or not) of the agreement has a direct relationship to continued operation of the licensor, it will fall upon the creditors' meeting to make a resolution on whether to continue an agreement.

Article 64 of the Enterprise Bankruptcy Law provides the two requirements that must be met in order to pass a resolution. The first requirement is for majority (more than half) approval of the resolution by the creditors that attend the meeting and that have a right to vote. The other requirement is that the creditors represent a majority (50% or more) of the unsecured claims (two-thirds in a reconciliation or reorganisation). All creditors will be bound to the resolution once it has been adopted by the creditors' meeting.

Creditors that disagree with an adopted resolution, under the argument that it goes against the provisions of law or goes against their own interests, may petition the People's Court within 15 days to revoke the resolution.

### 3.5 Effects on licence agreements in the licensee's bankruptcy

After a declaration of bankruptcy, a licence agreement is generally cancelled and any damages claimed by the licensor will be considered an unsecured claim.

### 3.6 Powers of an administrator, receiver or trustee in the licensee's bankruptcy

The bankruptcy administrator has the right to continue or cancel agreements after the acceptance of a bankruptcy case, and this right is also available after the declaration of bankruptcy. For the licensee's bankruptcy, it is the administrator that will generally cancel an agreement and respond to claims by the licensor.

### 3.7 Powers and rights of creditors in a licensee's bankruptcy

As with rights under a licensor's bankruptcy, creditors generally do not have a right to continue or terminate licence agreements during bankruptcy. Yet, if a decision has a direct effect on the continuation (or otherwise) of a licensee's operations, then it will ultimately be decided by the creditors' meeting.

### 3.8 Exclusive and non-exclusive licences

The Enterprise Bankruptcy Law does not have any provisions relating to the different treatment of exclusive and non-exclusive licences in bankruptcy.

### 3.9 Perpetual and non-perpetual licences

The Enterprise Bankruptcy Law does not have any provisions relating to perpetual and non-perpetual licences. Even so, in practice the People's Court will normally support the priority of the licensee to purchase the entrusted IP rights under the same terms and conditions.

### 3.10 Effects on a sub-licence in a licensor's bankruptcy

If the licensor or bankruptcy administrator terminates a licence agreement, then any sub-licensee can contact the licensor directly in order to arrange for the continuation of the agreement. Otherwise, the sub-licence agreement will end. This is within the scope of the licence agreement with a licensee and will generally be supported by the court.

### 3.11 Effects on a sub-licence in a licensee's bankruptcy

Similar to the situation in which the licensor enters bankruptcy, a sub-licensee can make arrangements with the licensor directly to continue or arrange a new licence agreement.

### 3.12 Impact of registration

Registration is generally a procedural arrangement under the relevant IP laws and regulations. Registration does not have a substantial effect on the validity of a licence agreement. In practice, however, appropriate registration before relevant government agencies will encourage government agencies to take some immediate measures in the event of serious licensing infringements. These measures are taken by relevant government agencies and may include an order to have the alleged violator cease its actions immediately, with the possibility of seizure or confiscation of its goods as mentioned above

## 4. Contractual arrangements in deviation from the law

### 4.1 Exceptions

The Enterprise Bankruptcy Law does not have any provisions that cover exceptions to contractual arrangements or any deviation from the prescribed legislation. Moreover, there are no different regimes from normal licence agreements relating to intellectual property.

### 4.2 Scope to alter statutory mechanisms

In accordance with the Enterprise Bankruptcy Law, there are no means to validly agree in a contract to alter statutory mechanisms. The administrator has the right to terminate any agreement that includes articles that may favour one party over another.

### 4.3 Termination rights and automatic reversions

In accordance with the PRC's Contract Law, parties can agree on a termination right of an agreement in the event of a licensee's or licensor's bankruptcy. However, if parties make relevant arrangements to require continuing performance of the licence agreement in the event of the other party's bankruptcy, such arrangements, in practice, are generally treated as invalid for the violation of relevant articles of the Enterprise Bankruptcy Law.

## 5. Cross-border aspects

### 5.1 Foreign law

When dealing with cross-border issues and the use of foreign law, it is important to distinguish between procedural matters and other specific issues in a bankruptcy case.

For procedural matters, it is mandatory to use Chinese law. For some other issues (especially for certain rights), the company laws where the company is registered, or where the main interests are located, should be used.

In China, it is possible to use foreign laws to deal with some specific issues, but as it is essential for certain procedural issues to be undertaken in order to move bankruptcy proceedings along, it is necessary in practice to use Chinese law for issues related to bankruptcy. Nonetheless, China's Civil Procedure Law allows for a choice of foreign law to be applied within China if it is deemed to be more relevant to a particular issue.

Generally, all the rights of the bankruptcy administrator come from the Enterprise Bankruptcy Law and those rights are not subject to foreign law. However, if some assets of the debtor are located outside the PRC, then the administrator is obliged to fulfil some rights arising from the foreign jurisdiction, and this will be considered a cross-border insolvency issue.

### 5.2 Foreign jurisdiction

An article was included in the Enterprise Bankruptcy Law (Article 5) to cover the recognition and acceptance of foreign judgments in bankruptcy proceedings. Article 5 also deals with any debtor's property outside the PRC.

A foreign judgment is reviewed to ensure it does not violate the basic principles of PRC law, does not violate public interest or the sovereignty and security of China, and does not deteriorate the rights and interests of creditors within China. For recognition of foreign judgments, Article 224(2) and 281 of the PRC's Civil Procedure Law (promulgated on August 31 2012) states that proceedings must take place before the intermediate people's court where the debtor is domiciled or where its property is located.

Although Article 5 has introduced the basic principles of cross-border insolvency issues, there are still concerns that need to be addressed over the lengthy procedures associated with foreign judgment recognition. Challenges have risen since China has not established specific and practical rules for procedures in order to ensure eligible applications will be respected and dealt with efficiently. The next step is for the Supreme People's Court to address cross-border insolvency by drafting further judicial interpretations while taking account of the UNCITRAL (UN Commission on International Trade Law) Model Law.

# Denmark

**Arly Carlquist**
**Carsten Ceutz**
Bech-Bruun

## 1. Overview

### 1.1 Relevant legislation governing bankruptcy

The relevant legislation governing bankruptcy is Denmark's Bankruptcy Act, Act 217 of March 15 2011, which consists of 265 sections governing bankruptcies, the restructuring of insolvent companies and debt rescheduling. Further, certain provisions of the Danish intellectual property acts – in particular, Denmark's Copyright Act, Act 202 of February 27 2010 – should be taken into consideration when it comes to dealing with intellectual property rights in connection with bankruptcy and restructuring proceedings.

In this chapter it is assumed that the term 'licensor' refers to a legal or natural person that is the owner of specific intellectual property rights, and that the licence agreement concerns the licensing of such intellectual property rights to a licensee.

### 1.2 Types of insolvency procedure

Bankruptcy is the main procedure in insolvency proceedings and applies to legal and natural persons – limited companies, businesses in broad terms, partnerships and individuals.

In the event of bankruptcy, a limited company, business, partnership or individual is wound up by a trustee appointed by the bankruptcy court or elected by the creditors in a voting process, taking into account the size and priority of the creditors' claims. All powers are transferred to the trustee to act for the benefit of the creditors. The assets are distributed to the creditors according to the priority of their claims, pursuant to Part 10 of the Bankruptcy Act. In the bankruptcy of individuals and some partnerships, the creditors will retain their claims against the debtor for the uncovered part if the assets do not fully cover their claims.

The alternative to bankruptcy is a restructuring of the insolvent business. The debtor or any creditor can file for restructuring. Once the in-court restructuring proceedings have commenced, there is no turning back: either the restructuring proceedings are completed successfully or the business is declared bankrupt.

A restructuring administrator is appointed by the bankruptcy court just as in bankruptcy proceedings. Since the debtor during a restructuring proceeding as a general rule stays in position, the functions of an administrator are more of a monitoring and confirming kind. The restructuring administrator must, within the specific deadlines set out in Part 2 of the Bankruptcy Act, draft a restructuring plan for the business, which must contain a proposal for a so-called 'compulsory composition' and/or a business transfer within the restructuring proceedings.

The effect of a 'compulsory composition' is that the debtor is relieved of that part of the debt not taken over in the composition. The compulsory composition is furthermore binding on known as well as unknown creditors at the time when the compulsory composition is adopted.

If the restructuring proceedings are conducted as a business transfer, bankruptcy proceedings must be commenced against the debtor's estate in connection with the termination of the restructuring proceedings, as set out in Section 15(3) of the Bankruptcy Act. This means that a petition for bankruptcy is not necessary.

According to the principles mentioned above, the creditors of the business that is in difficulties will then vote for or against the restructuring plan at a court hearing. If the restructuring plan set out by the restructuring administrator is rejected by the creditors, the business will be declared bankrupt by the court. Bankruptcy proceedings will then be commenced and a trustee will be appointed.

Heavily indebted individuals can submit an application for debt rescheduling pursuant to Part 25 of the Bankruptcy Act. Debt rescheduling is not possible for limited companies, businesses and partnerships and will not be described in the remainder of this chapter.

### 1.3 Grounds of bankruptcy

A company, business, partnership or individual (a debtor) may be declared bankrupt if insolvent. A debtor is insolvent when it is incapable of paying its debts as they fall due unless such inability to pay is deemed to be of a temporary nature only.

Insolvency is presumed to exist if:

- the debtor admits to being insolvent;
- restructuring proceedings have been commenced against the debtor;
- the debtor has suspended its payments; and
- it has not been possible, by a levying of execution in the course of the last three months prior to the bankruptcy court's receipt of the petition for bankruptcy, to obtain coverage from the debtor.

### 1.4 Filing for bankruptcy

Both a creditor and the debtor can file for bankruptcy. The burden of proof as to whether a debtor is insolvent is on the creditor if the creditor files the petition. When a petition for restructuring proceedings is filed, it is a requirement that insolvency can be proved.

Any creditor with a legal interest may submit a bankruptcy petition. A 'legal interest' means that the creditor's claim is unsecured, but not necessarily that the payment from the debtor has fallen due, and furthermore that there must be at least a slight possibility of partial coverage (called a dividend) of the claim.

A petitioning creditor must be aware of the risk that it may be liable for the costs of the bankruptcy proceedings if it turns out that the assets of the debtor are insufficient to cover the costs.

The debtor may also file for bankruptcy and, to avoid management liability, the management should do so if the point of no return has passed. There is, however, no explicit obligation to do so.

The above-mentioned principles also apply to restructuring.

As a general rule, petitions for restructuring proceedings or bankruptcy, or an application for debt rescheduling, must be filed with the bankruptcy court situated in the district where the debtor engages in commercial activity.

### 1.5 Administrators and other appointed persons

A trustee is appointed by the bankruptcy court at the time of the bankruptcy order. The trustee's position in, and administration of, the bankruptcy estate is similar to those of the business's management, and the transactions and arrangements made by the trustee will be binding on the bankruptcy estate.

A trustee is not appointed at the time of filing for bankruptcy and the estate is therefore not under any specific administration at that time. However, transactions or other arrangements made after the date of filing are of particular relevance to the subsequently appointed trustee.

In restructuring proceedings, a restructuring administrator and a restructuring accountant are appointed by way of a bankruptcy order made on the basis of a petition submitted by a creditor or a debtor. The petition must contain a proposal for a restructuring administrator and a restructuring accountant. Where the restructuring proceedings of a limited company commence without consent from the debtor, the management of the business up until the bankruptcy order will be replaced by the restructuring administrator.

## 2. Licence agreements in the phase between filing and declaration of bankruptcy

### 2.1 Effects on licence agreements in the licensor's bankruptcy

A trustee of a bankruptcy estate is only appointed by the court once the bankruptcy order is issued. Until the bankruptcy order has been issued, the estate is under no specific administration. Accordingly, there is no immediate effect on a licence agreement in the period between the date of filing for bankruptcy and the date of a bankruptcy order.

If, according to the terms of the licence agreement or other circumstances, a valid cause for altering or terminating the licence agreement exists, the contracting parties are free to act in accordance therewith. However, the licensee must be aware of the substantial risk of invalidation (or avoidance), just as the licensee must be aware of the fact that a bankruptcy order in itself is not a valid cause for termination of a licence agreement and that such termination based on the bankruptcy only is not binding on the bankruptcy estate.

The above-mentioned principles also apply to restructuring.

### 2.2 Powers of administrators, receivers or trustees in the licensor's bankruptcy

A trustee is not appointed by the bankruptcy court until the time of the bankruptcy order. Until the bankruptcy order, the exercise of management and control will continue without any immediate effect, meaning that the management remains in place. However, the debtors (eg, the management) have to bear in mind the strict liability for damages incurred in the period after the filing of a bankruptcy petition. The management and the creditors should also be aware of the substantial risk of invalidation (or avoidance) of arrangements made in this period, as well as of the risk of management liability, and as a general rule they may only take cautious decisions and enter into transactions only in order to safeguard the assets of the business.

Consequently, a licence agreement is not immediately affected by the filing of a petition for bankruptcy and will continue unaffected in the period between the filing of the bankruptcy petition and the issue of the bankruptcy order.

The above-mentioned principles also apply to restructuring.

### 2.3 Effects on licence agreements in the licensee's bankruptcy

See section 2.1 above.

### 2.4 Powers of administrators, receivers or trustees in the licensee's bankruptcy

See section 2.2 above.

### 2.5 Impact of registration

Registration of a licence at the Danish Patent and Trademark Office is to be considered as an informative disposition only when performed by the licensor or licensee and is not of practical relevance when a licensor or licensee is declared bankrupt (ie, such registration does not serve as perfection procedure).

A creditor performing debt enforcement towards a licensor or licensee should be aware that the correct perfection procedure is registration of the execution or pledge in accordance with the rules set out in the Registration of Property Act, meaning registration within the register of persons.

## 3. Licence agreements in the phase after declaration of bankruptcy

### 3.1 Treatment of intellectual property rights

Intellectual property rights are protected pursuant to separate acts governing the specifics of each category of intellectual property rights. For instance, copyrighted works are protected under the Copyright Act, trademarks under the Trademarks Act and patents under the Patents Act. Copyrighted items, patented material, utility models (known as 'small patents'), trademarks, designs and other forms of intellectual property are all protected.

Although governed by separate intellectual property acts, the principles relevant to bankruptcy and restructuring proceedings are generally alike, regardless of the specific type of intellectual property right involved. It should be noted, however, that Part 3 of the Copyright Act (as opposed to other Danish intellectual property rights acts) sets out certain principles concerning the assignment of copyrights and the interpretation of licence agreements, including a specific provision concerning debt collection. Also, the copyright protection differs from the protection of other intellectual property rights, in that the Copyright Act protects not only economic rights but also moral rights of a non-economic nature – which may be relevant, depending on the specific circumstances.

In summary, all intellectual property rights will generally be treated in the same manner in the event of bankruptcy.

In the event of the bankruptcy of the owner of intellectual property rights (ie, the licensor), such intellectual property rights will generally form part of the assets of the bankruptcy estate (with some exceptions regarding copyrights) and the trustee will eventually have to sell such rights if possible.

### 3.2 Effects on licence agreements in the licensor's bankruptcy

As a fundamental principle, no contracting party should accept that the rights and obligations of the other contracting party to a bilateral agreement are transferred to a third party without the consent of the contracting party in question.

However, the essence of the rules set out in Part 7 of the Bankruptcy Act is that the bankruptcy estate may – although the estate is not obliged to do so – take the place of the debtor in a bilateral agreement in the absence of statutory provisions to the contrary or where the nature of the legal relationship involved so dictates. The transformation from an ongoing business to a bankruptcy estate or a business in restructuring is not to be considered as a breach of contract or as a transfer to a third party of the rights and obligations under (for example) a licence agreement.

A licensee would, in the absence of the above-mentioned exemptions, have to accept the situation if the bankruptcy estate wishes to adopt and continue the licence agreement.

The circumstances under which a licence agreement may be exempted from the bankruptcy estate's adoption of the licence agreement, as a result of the nature of the legal relationship in question, are subject to a case-by-case assessment. However, as a general rule and to safeguard the interests and ensure the equal treatment of all creditors, the grounds for barring the right of the bankruptcy estate must be quite substantial.

In accordance with the above, there is no immediate effect on a licence agreement in the event of the licensor's bankruptcy if the contract is adopted by the trustee of the bankruptcy estate. The bankruptcy estate will assume the rights and obligations, including liabilities, under the terms of the agreement. However, the bankruptcy estate is entitled to release itself from an agreement relating to a continuously provided service by giving one month's notice irrespective of any agreed notice period. The licence agreement will be regarded as entered into by the bankruptcy estate itself and any claim of payment, damages etc of the licensee under the licence agreement will be given preferential status.

The contracting parties must be aware of the fact that a contractual term in the licence agreement stating that the licence agreement is automatically terminated in the event of bankruptcy is not binding on the bankruptcy estate.

The licensee may terminate the licence agreement if the bankruptcy estate does not wish to adopt the licence agreement and may, in accordance with the rules set out in Part 7 of the Bankruptcy Act, claim damages for the loss incurred that is due to such non-performance. However, a claim for damages may be partly diminished against the bankruptcy estate pursuant to Section 61 of the Bankruptcy Act, in which it is stated that the estate is entitled to terminate an agreement on a continuing legal relationship at the usual or a reasonable period of notice, notwithstanding that a longer period of notice or non-terminability has been agreed: an estate is entitled to shorten a notice period in the event of a licensee's termination, and the licensee's claim of damages based on the notice period will as a result thereof be diminished.

It should be noted that, under Section 58(2) of the Bankruptcy Act, a licensee may at any time terminate a licence agreement for convenience where it would have been entitled to do so had bankruptcy proceedings not been commenced. The licensee may also terminate the relevant licence agreement for cause following the adoption of the licence agreement by the bankruptcy estate if the bankruptcy estate acts in such a manner as to entitle the licensee to terminate the licence agreement for cause.

The above-mentioned principles also apply to restructuring, and with the consent of the restructuring administrator a licensor may continue a bilateral agreement unless this is excluded due to the nature of the legal relationship.

### 3.3 Powers of an administrator, receiver or trustee in the licensor's bankruptcy

The management and administration of a bankruptcy estate is performed by the appointed trustee, whose powers can be compared with the powers of the business's management. The former management of the bankruptcy estate will resign at the time of the bankruptcy order and their powers will be transferred to the appointed trustee. This means that the trustee is authorised to enter into agreements or make other similar arrangements on behalf of the bankruptcy estate to the effect that such agreements or arrangements will be binding on the estate.

In performing its duties, the trustee must manage the interests of the estate and in this connection safeguard the assets of the estate, take the measures necessary to prevent unauthorised transactions involving the assets, and represent the estate in all respects.

The task defined in the preceding paragraph means that the overall function of the trustee is to wind up the bankruptcy estate by achieving the best possible result for the creditors of the debtor – ie, the highest possible dividend. This result might be achieved by continuing the operation of the estate's activities for a certain period. Any transactions made by the trustee, such as the adoption of an agreement on behalf of the bankruptcy estate, may affect the ranking of individual claims in terms of their order of priority.

Where restructuring proceedings have been commenced against a limited company with the consent of the debtor, the debtor will in principle continue to have the assets at its disposal and will be entitled to deal with them. However, the debtor is not entitled to enter into transactions of material significance without the consent of the appointed restructuring administrator. In this situation, the powers of the restructuring administrator will be to supervise the administration.

If the restructuring proceedings against a limited company are commenced without the consent of the debtor, or if creditors, representing in the aggregate at least 25% of the total known amount entitling the holder represented to vote, request the restructuring administrator to take over the management and control of the debtor's business and replace the board of management and board of directors, the powers of the appointed restructuring administrator are very similar to the powers of an appointed trustee in bankruptcy proceeding – although there are some notable differences (see especially section 3.5 below).

### 3.4 Powers and rights of creditors in a licensor's bankruptcy

In general, individual creditors have no powers in respect of the transactions made by the appointed trustee, and the trustee's transactions will bind the bankruptcy estate. There is no specific definition of the powers of the trustee in administering an estate, apart from the description given above – but see, in particular, Section 110 of the Bankruptcy Act.

Notwithstanding the above, the bankruptcy court may set up a creditors' committee, which will consist of elected creditors. This committee is not capable of making binding decisions or of requiring the trustee in any other way to make any transactions. The main focus of the committee is to exercise some control of the work of the trustee, and therefore the trustee is legally obliged to inform the committee of all important transactions and of any contemplated transactions of material significance unless such transactions cannot be postponed without detriment to the estate.

The sanctions available to the committee are subsequently to request that a creditors' meeting be convened for the purpose of requesting the bankruptcy court to exercise its right to remove the appointed trustee. If the request is granted, a new trustee will be appointed in accordance with the rules for voting mentioned in section 1.2.

### 3.5 Effects on licence agreements in the licensee's bankruptcy

With reference to section 3.2 and in accordance therewith, there is no immediate effect on the licence agreement in the event of the licensee's bankruptcy if the licence agreement is adopted by the trustee of the bankruptcy estate. The bankruptcy estate will assume the rights and obligations, including liabilities, under the terms of the licence agreement.

Accordingly, the licence agreement will be regarded as entered into by the licensee's bankruptcy estate itself and the claims of the licensor will consequently be given preferential status. Thus, where a licence is granted to the licensee on an ongoing basis under a licence agreement, the licensee's bankruptcy estate will be obliged, when adopting the agreement, to pay the amount payable for the time after the date of the bankruptcy order as a pre-preferential claim (see Section 56(2) of the Bankruptcy Act).

In accordance with the foregoing, the trustee of the bankruptcy estate is generally not permitted to transfer the rights and obligations under the licence agreement (or the licence agreement itself) to a third party unless such transfer is explicitly permitted within the terms of the agreement or explicitly accepted by the licensor.

Another issue is what the legal position of the licensee will be if the bankruptcy estate does not adopt the licence agreement. As described in section 3.2 above, if the licensee's bankruptcy estate does not adopt the licence agreement, the licence agreement will in practice be terminated and, consequently, the licensee's bankruptcy estate cannot rely on the licence agreement to dispose of intellectual property rights licensed pursuant to the licence agreement. However, the question may arise as to whether the licensee may dispose of goods manufactured by the licensee under the licence agreement prior to termination if the distribution takes place following termination of the licence agreement. For instance, is a licensee allowed to sell stocks following termination of the licence agreement? This question must be assessed on a case-by-case basis, taking into consideration the terms and conditions of the licence agreement and the general 'principle of exhaustion' applicable under the respective intellectual property acts.

A licensor may terminate the licence agreement if the bankruptcy estate does not wish to adopt the licence agreement and, in accordance with the rules set out in Part 7 of the Bankruptcy Act, claim damages for the loss incurred as a result of the non-performance. However, the claim may – as mentioned in section 3.2 – be partly unenforceable against the licensee's bankruptcy estate, pursuant to Section 61 of the Bankruptcy Act.

If restructuring proceedings are commenced against a licensee, the licensor should be aware of some notable differences compared with a situation where a licensee is declared bankrupt. As mentioned in section 3.2 above, a licensee may also, with the consent of the restructuring administrator, continue a bilateral agreement unless this is excluded owing to the nature of the legal relationship.

The right to continue bilateral agreements is available, not only in relation to licence agreements that are in force, but also in relation to licence agreements which the licensor had terminated due to a licensee's default on its payment obligations less than four weeks prior to the licensee's declaration that it intended to continue the agreement. However, if the licensor had already entered into transactions on the basis of the termination, the licence agreement cannot be revived.

As a general rule, following a decision to continue a licence agreement, a licensee is bound by the licence agreement as if it had not been terminated. However, as is the case in bankruptcy proceedings, the licensee has the possibility of reducing unusual or unreasonably long notice periods for termination for convenience. If the contract is related to a continuously provided service to the licensee, the licensee may, as in bankruptcy proceedings – and irrespective of the notice of termination agreed – always release itself from a preferential claim arising from the estate's use by giving one month's notice only. Regarding a business transfer, see section 1.2 above.

Finally, in restructuring proceedings it is not only possible for a licensee in restructuring to adopt a licence agreement. The licensor is also forced to accept a transfer of the licence agreement in connection with a business transfer irrespective of any terms to the contrary in the licence agreement and irrespective of whether the above-mentioned requirements are met.

### 3.6 Powers of an administrator, receiver or trustee in the licensee's bankruptcy

See section 3.3 above.

### 3.7 Powers and rights of creditors in a licensee's bankruptcy

See section 3.4 above.

### 3.8 Exclusive and non-exclusive licenses

There is no distinction between exclusive and non-exclusive licences in the event of bankruptcy.

### 3.9 Perpetual and non-perpetual licenses

The term 'perpetual' may be interpreted as meaning that a licence fee is paid as a single upfront payment and the licence agreement then remains in force in perpetuity; this means that a perpetual licence agreement is not up for examination of a bankruptcy trustee.

A perpetual licence is an asset that may be subject to realisation, taking the restrictions set out in section 3.5 into account.

However, bankruptcy claims arising from a perpetual or non-perpetual agreement with ongoing mutual obligations are always subject to examination, in order to take account of ordinary conventional claims with an acceptable normal notice period in the estate's distribution of assets.

Thus, in the event of either the licensor's or licensee's bankruptcy, the bankruptcy trustee must take this into account if it chooses not to continue the agreement after the date of the adjudication order.

### 3.10 Effects on sub-licence in a licensor's bankruptcy

There is no practical distinction between a licence and a sub-licence in the event of a licensor's bankruptcy. Thus, if the trustee terminates the licence, the right of the sub-licensee will terminate as well.

### 3.11 Effects on sub-licence in a licensee's bankruptcy

There is no practical distinction between a licence and a sub-licence in the event of a licensor's bankruptcy.

### 3.12 Impact of registration

See 2.5.

## 4. Contractual arrangements in deviation from the law

### 4.1 Exceptions

Generally, licence agreements concerning intellectual property rights are treated in the same manner as any other agreements. Neither the Bankruptcy Act nor any of the intellectual property laws generally include special provisions governing licence agreements in terms of bankruptcy proceedings (save that Section 62 of the Copyright Act entails certain limited exceptions in terms of non-published copyrighted works).

### 4.2 Scope to alter statutory mechanisms

The appointed trustee of the bankruptcy estate is authorised to terminate or to adopt a licence agreement on behalf of the bankruptcy estate even if the licence agreement contains any terms to the contrary, as set out in Part 7 of the Bankruptcy Act. Accordingly, the contracting parties cannot validly agree on, for example, a 'no reversion of rights' clause in the event of bankruptcy, because such an arrangement would be a circumvention of the mandatory rules set out in Part 7 of the Bankruptcy Act.

### 4.3 Termination rights and automatic reversions

Bilateral agreements are governed by the provisions of Part 7 of the Bankruptcy Act, which are mandatory to the extent that it cannot validly be agreed that bankruptcy is a cause for termination of the licence agreement. Such a contractual term would be invalid and not binding on the bankruptcy estate.

However, the contracting party to a bilateral agreement is entitled to demand that the trustee of the bankruptcy estate decides, without undue delay, whether the bankruptcy estate is willing to adopt the licence agreement or not. The contracting parties may agree on a defined notice period in the event of bankruptcy – as long as the term is not a circumvention of Section 55(2) of the Bankruptcy Act, which provides that a contracting party to a bilateral agreement is entitled to demand that the estate decides, without undue delay, whether to adopt the contract. This means that a defined notice period agreed between the parties cannot be so short that it deprives the estate of the opportunity of adopting the licence agreement.

## 5. Cross-border aspects

### 5.1 Foreign law and foreign jurisdiction

As a consequence of Denmark's opt-out from EU justice and home affairs requirements, the bankruptcy regulations set down by the European Union do not apply in Denmark. As a general rule, any dispute relating to bankruptcy and restructuring proceedings are therefore governed by and settled in accordance with Danish law, including in accordance with the Danish rules on private international law.

The provisions of (among others) the Danish law of property and the Danish law of bankruptcy are mandatory, and a Danish court will always settle disputes regarding these laws in accordance with Danish law even if venue and choice of law has been agreed otherwise.

However, if a dispute arises and the contractual term regarding choice of law or jurisdiction appears to be a customary term in similar contractual relationships, and provided that the dispute does not concern any of the mandatory rules mentioned above, a Danish court might settle the dispute in accordance therewith.

An example can be given. Up until the date of the bankruptcy order or commencement of restructuring proceedings, the parties can agree that a German supplier has retention of title in goods delivered to a Danish business according to German law. The Danish court will be obliged to follow the requirements of German law for enforcing the retention-of-title clause. Immediately upon the date of a bankruptcy order and commencement of restructuring proceedings, only Danish law will apply and, since the requirements of Danish law for retention of title are more demanding than in German law, the retention of title may be rejected.

# England and Wales

**Peter Armstrong**
**Rhys Llewellyn**
Harbottle & Lewis LLP

---

## 1. Overview

This chapter considers the impact of insolvency on licence arrangements involving one or more parties incorporated in England and Wales.

### 1.1 Relevant legislation governing intellectual property and bankruptcy

#### (a) *Insolvency laws*

English insolvency laws derive from a number of different statutes and a significant body of case law. The primary legislation comprises the Insolvency Act 1986 (hereinafter the Insolvency Act), as amended by the Enterprise Act 2002 and the Insolvency Act 2000, and the Companies Act 2006. The legislation is supplemented by secondary and EU legislation, including the Insolvency Rules 1986. There is no specific legislation which deals with intellectual property rights (IPRs) separately from other asset classes in the event of insolvency.

#### (b) *Intellectual property*

The key pieces of legislation governing IPRs are the Trade Marks Act 1994, the Copyright, Designs and Patents Act 1988 and the Patent Act 1977. Whilst none of these acts address insolvency issues specifically, they do set out the legal mechanisms by which ownership of certain IPRs arises and can be determined.

### 1.2 Types of insolvency procedure

English law provides for a number of different insolvency procedures but the most commonly used are liquidation and administration.

#### (a) *Liquidation*

The objective of liquidation (or winding-up) is to realise the assets of a company and distribute them to its creditors in a prescribed order. Liquidation is also available to solvent companies – although this chapter will focus on the two procedures relevant to insolvent companies, namely compulsory liquidation and creditors' voluntary liquidation:

- *Compulsory liquidation* A compulsory liquidation procedure is commenced by the making of a petition to the court (usually the High Court, either in the Companies Court in London or a District Registry) for the company to be wound up.[1] A court hearing is held at which the court will consider the facts and make a winding-up order if satisfied that one or more grounds for winding up apply. If a winding-up order is made, then the winding-up is treated as having commenced when the petition was first presented (unless a voluntary winding-up was then already in progress). The official receiver usually becomes the first liquidator although the court may appoint another person (for example where the winding up follows the discharge of an administration order).

- *Creditors' voluntary liquidation (CVL)* CVL is a voluntary process commenced by the company's members passing a resolution to approve the company's winding-up. Within 14 days a meeting of creditors is convened at which a statement of the company's affairs is presented by the directors and the identity of the liquidator must be approved. The winding-up will be treated as having commenced on the date on which the members' resolution was passed. Once a liquidator is appointed, he takes control of the company and the directors lose their powers. The liquidator will realise the company's assets in order to make payments to creditors, and the company's business will be terminated. Once the process is complete, the company will be dissolved and cease to exist as a legal entity.

Liquidators have extensive powers to carry out their functions, some exercisable in their own discretion (including power to sell company property) and some exercisable only with the sanction of the court (in a compulsory liquidation) or creditors (in a CVL). Liquidators can carry on a company's business to the extent needed for its beneficial winding-up without sanction in a CVL or with court approval in a compulsory liquidation.

### *(b)* ***Administration***

Administration is most commonly used where a company has a sound underlying business which has run into difficulties. Its primary objective is to rescue the company so it can continue trading as a going concern. Where this is not possible, the objective is to achieve a better result for creditors as a whole than would be likely if the company were simply placed into liquidation. Where neither of these is achievable, the purpose must be to realise the company's property to make a distribution to the company's secured or preferential creditors.

There are two ways that a company can be put into administration:

- *Court order* Amongst others a company itself, its directors or any of its creditors can apply to court for an administration order. If granted, an administrator is appointed under that order and a moratorium comes into effect.
- *Out-of-court process* The company itself, its directors or the holder of a qualifying floating charge can appoint an administrator through an out-of-court process which involves the filing of various forms at court and the service of notices on certain interested parties.

---

1 Various parties can bring a winding-up petition although they are usually made by creditors owed more than £750.

Administration creates a moratorium during which:

- no winding up order can be made in respect of the company;
- no resolution can be passed for the company's winding up; and
- certain actions require the approval of either the administrator or court, including any enforcement of security held over the company's property and the institution or continuation of any legal proceedings against the company.

An interim moratorium comes into effect upon an application being made for an administration order or upon notice of intention to appoint an administrator being filed at court. Once an administrator is appointed, the moratorium is extended until the expiry of the administration (which will occur 12 months after it began unless extended).

Once appointed, an administrator takes over control of a company from its directors and acts as the company's agent when exercising his powers. Administrators can do anything necessary or expedient for the management of the company's affairs, business and property. This usually includes taking control and possession or selling or disposing of the company's property, bringing or defending legal proceedings on the company's behalf and/or carrying on the company's business.

If administration succeeds in rescuing a company as a going concern, control will revert to the directors once administration ends. Otherwise, proceeds realised from the sale of the company's business or assets will be distributed to creditors by the administrator or any subsequently appointed liquidator and the company may never trade again.

### *(c) Other procedures*

Administration and liquidation are by far the most common English corporate insolvency procedures and the remainder of this chapter will focus on them. However, other insolvency procedures exist, of which company voluntary arrangements (CVAs) and schemes of arrangement are most widely used.

## 1.3 Grounds of insolvency

Administration and CVL are only available to insolvent companies. In determining insolvency, the courts apply two main tests in order to determine whether a company is able to pay its debts:

- *Cash flow test* The court will determine on the evidence whether the company is able to pay its debts as they fall due. If the company is judged not to be able then, regardless of whether its assets exceed its liabilities, it will be insolvent.
- *Balance sheet test* A company will be treated as unable to pay its debts if the amount of its assets is less than the amount of its liabilities taking into account all contingent and prospective liabilities.

In addition, a company will be presumed unable to pay its debts if it fails to satisfy a creditor's statutory demand for a debt exceeding £750 or to satisfy in full a judgment debt or similar court order.

## 2. Impact of insolvency on licence agreements

### 2.1 Treatment of intellectual property rights on insolvency

Neither the administration nor liquidation of a company (nor any steps being taken for the administration or liquidation of a company such as the filing of any notice of intention to appoint an administrator with the court in an administration) in themselves have any effect on the ownership of IPRs owned by that company before the procedure was instituted – although, as discussed below, a licensee may lose the right to use IPRs licensed to it if the licence governing such use allows termination on insolvency. However, if a company continues to own any IPRs at the time it is dissolved, then, upon dissolution, such right or title as the company holds in those IPRs will pass *bona vacantia* to the Crown.[2]

### 2.2 Impact of a licensor's insolvency

A licence will not as a matter of law automatically terminate upon a licensor's insolvency. It will therefore remain in force and the parties will continue to be bound by its terms, albeit if an insolvent licensor has ongoing obligations then it may not be able to comply with them. The terms of the licence itself will determine the extent to which it is terminable following the insolvency of any party.

Whether a licensee would terminate a licence following a licensor's insolvency if it had the right to do so would depend on the circumstances. If the licence granted the right to use valuable IPRs which a licensee relied on for its business, termination by the licensee is unlikely. However, if the licence was of lesser importance and/or contained onerous terms, a licensee could use the licensor's insolvency as an opportunity to terminate the agreement and escape ongoing obligations.

If a licensor can terminate following its own insolvency, the administrator or liquidator will consider any benefits of retaining the licence (such as ongoing royalties or fees) against any benefits of terminating it (eg, the ability to sell the licensed IPRs free from the terms of the licence).

### 2.3 Powers of administrators and liquidators of a licensor

As mentioned above, administrators and liquidators have wide-reaching powers in relation to a company's business and assets to allow them to perform their duties. Amongst other things, they can sell IPRs and other assets to generate funds, and they have statutory powers to disclaim certain property and challenge certain transactions entered into before their appointment.

#### *(a) Disposal of IPRs and other property*

The simplest transaction for an administrator or liquidator to effect in order to generate monies to pay creditors will be to sell the business and assets of the company as a going concern, although individual assets could be sold off on a piecemeal basis. The assets could include IPRs licensed to a licensee under a licence agreement or even the licensor's rights under the licence agreement itself.

---

2 Section 1012 of the Companies Act 2006.

A substantial risk arises for licensees where a licensor becomes insolvent, because under English law a purchaser of IPRs in good faith for valuable consideration without actual or constructive knowledge of a licence will take those IPRs free of the licence.

Administrators and liquidators often want to sell the business or assets of a company promptly following their appointment, in order to limit damage to goodwill and reduce any period during which the company trades under their control. Indeed, administrators often agree the terms of sale transactions with purchasers before their appointment and then implement those transactions immediately after appointment in what are known as 'pre-pack' sales.

Owing to the risk involved in IPRs being sold to a third party who has no knowledge of a licence and the timescales within which sale transactions are effected in insolvency scenarios, it is imperative that licensees act swiftly if they suspect or become aware that an administrator or liquidator may be, or has been, appointed. At the very least, licensees should make the administrator or liquidator (or even known prospective purchasers) aware of the existence of their licence, particularly if it is not, or is incapable of being, registered (see further below). Licensees may also want to express an interest in acquiring the IPRs themselves, particularly if their business is dependent on their ongoing use.

***(b) Disposition of property after commencement of winding-up***

By virtue of section 127 of the Insolvency Act, any disposition (including a sale or transfer) of a company's property after the presentation of a winding-up petition other than by a liquidator will be void unless otherwise ordered by the court. Accordingly, where a licensee is aware that IPRs it wishes to license have been acquired by a licensor from a third party, it should check (and/or ask the licensor to warrant) that the disposal by the third party does not contravene this section.

***(c) Disclaimer of onerous property and contracts***

Liquidators (but not administrators) can apply to court to disclaim unprofitable contracts or property of a company which are unsaleable or not readily saleable or which may give rise to a liability to pay money or perform any other onerous act.[3] For example, if a licence required a licensor to pay expensive ongoing registration fees or actively pursue third parties infringing the licensed IPRs, a liquidator may argue that these are onerous obligations.

If granted, the effect of a disclaimer is to determine the rights, interests and liabilities of a company in or in respect of the property disclaimed; but it does not, except to the extent necessary for the purpose of releasing the company from any liability, affect the rights or liabilities of any other person. The court will usually attempt to minimise the impact of a disclaimer on licensees – for example, by allowing a licence to continue with only more onerous obligations disclaimed, which may allow the licensee to continue using the IPRs subject to ongoing compliance with its obligations under the licence.

If a licensee suffers loss as a result of a disclaimer, it can prove for that loss in the

3 Section 178 of the Insolvency Act 1986.

licensor's winding-up – although this is unlikely to result in full recovery of that loss.

Of more concern to a licensee may be any attempt to disclaim the underlying IPRs themselves, particularly in the case of registered IPRs such as trademarks or patents. If registrations were allowed to lapse, this could expose licensees (and, particularly, exclusive licensees) to unwanted third-party competition in what may formerly have been an exclusive market for them.

Where licensed IPRs are disclaimed, a licensee may be able to apply to the court to have those disclaimed IPRs vested in it on the basis that it has an interest in those IPRs as a licensee.[4]

***(d) Undervalue transactions***

Liquidators and administrators can apply to court to challenge certain so-called 'undervalue' transactions involving a company that have been effected within six months of the onset of its insolvency in the case of unconnected parties, or within two years of the onset of its insolvency in the case of connected parties if the company was insolvent at the time of the transaction or became insolvent as a result.[5] The court can make whatever order it thinks fit for restoring the position that would have existed had the company not entered into the transaction.

Undervalue transactions arise where a company makes a gift to or otherwise enters into a transaction with a person on terms that provide for the company to receive no consideration or consideration which is significantly less than the value of the consideration provided by the company (unless it is established that the transaction was entered into in good faith for the purpose of carrying on the company's business and at the time there were reasonable grounds for believing the transaction would benefit the company).

An undervalue transaction could include, for example, a company granting an exclusive licence to use valuable IPRs for a nominal sum to a connected company shortly before it entered into administration. The existence of the licence could have an impact on the value the administrator could realise from the IPRs on a sale and so would be at risk of being challenged.

Liquidators and administrators have a similar power to challenge undervalue transactions undertaken at any time where it can be shown there is an intent to defraud creditors by putting assets outside their reach or to prejudice their interests.[6]

***(e) Preferences***

Liquidators and administrators can apply to court to challenge certain actions taken by a company, known as 'preferences', which have the effect of putting any person in a position that, in the event of the company going into insolvent liquidation, would be better than the position he would have been in otherwise, and the court is satisfied that, when entering into the transaction, the company was influenced by a desire to give the person concerned a preference.[7] An example of a preference would

4 Section 181 of the Insolvency Act 1986.
5 Section 238 of the Insolvency Act 1986.
6 Section 423 of the Insolvency Act 1986.
7 Section 239 of the Insolvency Act 1986.

be a decision by a licensee to pay licence fees to a licensor under common ownership in priority to other creditors in circumstances where there was no real commercial justification for doing so.

### 2.4 Impact of a licensee's insolvency

As discussed in section 2.2 above, a licence will not as a matter of law automatically terminate upon one of the contracting parties becoming insolvent, although most well-drafted licences will include provisions allowing the licensor to terminate in certain circumstances – typically including the licensee's insolvency.

### 2.5 Powers of administrators and liquidators of a licensee

The same issues arise upon a licensee entering into insolvency as apply to licensors, as explained in section 2.3 above.

If the terms of any licence were particularly onerous on the licensee, the agreement could be challenged under one or more of the powers mentioned in section 2.3 above. For example, if a licensee had to pay substantial licence fees for using IPRs which generated little income, a liquidator may apply to court to disclaim the licence.

If a licensee continues to pay royalties or fees to a licensor in priority to other creditors, there is a risk that a liquidator or administrator could apply to have those payments unravelled if it could show that they amounted to a preference (see section 2.3(e) above).

If a licensor does not or cannot terminate a licence on the licensee's insolvency, the licence will remain in force and form part of the licensee's assets that any administrator or liquidator will seek to realise to raise funds for creditors. The extent to which value can be realised from the sale of a licence will depend on any restrictions on assignment or transfer in the licence itself, and so licensors are advised to insist on non-assignment provisions. In the absence of a restriction on assignment or similar restrictions on the licensee's ability to permit third parties to use licensed rights, the rights of a licensee under a licence governed by English law would usually be assignable to a third party.

### 2.6 Impact of registration

Licences pertaining to patents, registered trademarks and registered designs can be registered in England and Wales. The UK Intellectual Property Office (IPO) maintains registers on which details of such licences can be recorded (although where a licence relates to IPRs registered on an EU community-wide basis, the licence should be recorded on the registers maintained by the Office for Harmonization in the Internal Market (OHIM)). It is not currently possible to register in England and Wales licences in respect of copyright, unregistered designs, confidential information or unregistered trademarks.

Although registration of a licence will not in itself limit the powers available to any administrator or liquidator of the licensor to deal with those IPRs, as outlined earlier in this chapter, it will have a significant impact on the licensee's rights if the IPRs are sold as part of the administration or liquidation. As described in section 2.3(a) above, a purchaser of IPRs in good faith for valuable consideration without actual or constructive knowledge of a licence will take those IPRs free of that licence. However, a purchaser will be treated as having knowledge of any registered licences and so should carefully check relevant registries before acquiring IPRs in an insolvency scenario.

**2.7 Powers and rights of creditors**

Once appointed, an administrator or liquidator will assume responsibility for a company's affairs and individual creditors have limited powers to direct how they should act (albeit creditors do have input on the appointment of liquidators and the exercise of certain powers by them). Administrators and liquidators must act in good faith and be independent and impartial in their management of a company's affairs and property and act with regard to the interests of creditors as a whole.

**2.8 Exclusive and non-exclusive licences**

Both exclusive and non-exclusive licences are subject to the same potential challenges and issues on insolvency. An exclusive licence will not be treated as transferring any right of ownership in the underlying IPRs to a licensee, but merely to create a right for the licensee to use those rights subject to the terms of the licence.

On a licensee's insolvency, it is more likely that a licensor would take steps to terminate an exclusive licence rather than a non-exclusive licence if the insolvency means no value is being realised by the licensor from the licensed IPRs.

On a licensor's insolvency, an exclusive licensee is likely to be best placed to gain a vesting order in the event that the licensor disclaimed the IPRs which were the subject of a licence.[8] However, a non-exclusive licence is less likely to be disclaimed because additional non-exclusive licences could be granted to generate funds.

**2.9 Perpetual and non-perpetual licences**

Where a licence is granted on a 'perpetual' basis, the use of the word 'perpetual' will not in itself guarantee that the licence will survive the insolvency of the licensee or licensor if the licence contains other provisions that could lead to termination in the event of one party's insolvency or any other circumstances.

In *BMS Computer Solutions Ltd v AB Agri Ltd*,[9] the High Court granted summary judgment to a licensor upholding its termination of a licence that was expressed to be perpetual. The court held the phrase 'perpetual' can have "different shades of meaning" and that whilst in some instances it can mean "never ending" it can also mean "of indefinite duration but subject to any contractual provisions governing termination". The court upheld the latter interpretation in this case on the basis that the termination provisions in the licence were of fundamental importance. Accordingly, where a licence is not intended to be capable of termination in any circumstances, the licence should expressly state that is the parties' intention and any termination or other provisions that would be inconsistent with an irrevocable licence should be removed or amended as appropriate.

---

8 See paragraph 2.3(c) of this chapter.

9 [2010] EWHC 464 (Ch).

## 2.10 Impact of insolvency on sub-licences

The impact that a licensor or licensee's insolvency may have on any sub-licences will vary from case to case and depend on a number of factors, including the relationship between the head licensor and a licensee and the terms of the licences between them, as well as between a licensee and sub-licensee. It is generally accepted that if a head licence between a licensor and licensee is terminated, this will lead to the termination of sub-licences; however, there are limited exceptions to this.

### (a) *Impact of licensor's insolvency on sub-licences*

A sub-licensee's position on the insolvency of a head licensor will be influenced by the impact of the insolvency on the head licensee. The insolvency could result in the head licensee losing the right to use the IPRs licensed to it on the same basis as before – eg, where the IPRs are sold to a purchaser who had no knowledge of the licence or sub-licence arrangements, or where the head-licence is disclaimed. If the head licensee loses its rights in respect of the IPRs, the sub-licensee itself is likely to lose its rights as well.

### (b) *Impact of licensee's insolvency on sub-licences*

If a sub-licence was not terminated on a licensee's insolvency, then a sub-licensee could be at risk if it continued to use licensed IPRs in circumstances where the head licence has been terminated, because such use could breach the head licensor's rights. However, the English courts will determine each case on its facts; and if a licensee can establish this the parties intended that a sub-licence should survive termination of a head licence, then the courts may allow the sub-licence, or at least the sub-licensee's right to continue using the licensed IPRs, to survive.[10]

A head licensor wishing to ensure that a sub-licence terminates on a licensee's insolvency or on termination of any head licence should ensure that express termination provisions to this effect are included in both the head licence and any sub-licence. It should also insist that the head licence provides that no agency relationship exists or should be implied between the parties, and require the licensee to obtain the head licensor's prior approval before any sub-licences are granted. The head licensor could also dictate the form that sub-licences must take (incorporating appropriate termination provisions) and ensure each licensee notifies sub-licensees of its rights.

A sub-licensee seeking to protect its position should verify who the underlying owner of the IPRs being licensed is and how its sub-licensor has obtained its rights. A sub-licensee could request a covenant from a head licensor that its sub-licence will survive any termination of the head licence (perhaps structured so that, following termination of the head licence, sums payable under the sub-licence would be paid

---

10 See *VLM v Ravensworth* [2013] EWHC 228 (Ch), where a company granted an informal licence to a subsidiary which granted a sub-licence to an unrelated party. The court held the head licence amounted to little more than a right to grant sub-licences and that the sub-licence had effectively been granted on an agency basis on behalf of the head licensor and it did not follow that termination of the right to grant sub-licences would affect sub-licences already granted. In spite of the fact that the licensee was liquidated, the court held that the sub-licensee retained the right to use the IPRs as, effectively, the permission for use had been granted by the head licensor.

instead to the head licensor, thus effectively creating a new contractual relationship between head licensor and sub-licensee). Clearly the extent to which any of these protections can be negotiated will depend on the bargaining power of the parties.

## 3. Contractual arrangements in deviation from the law

### 3.1 Exceptions

English law does not distinguish between licences dealing with different types of IPRs on insolvency and so all licences are subject to the same basic laws and principles.

### 3.2 Scope to alter statutory mechanisms

The English courts have consistently held that it is against public policy to uphold any contractual provision which seeks to disapply the operation of UK insolvency laws, and this is commonly known as the 'anti-deprivation principle'.

The structuring of arrangements under which a person wishes to use IPRs owned by another person therefore needs careful consideration as this could have a significant impact if one of those persons later becomes insolvent. In practice the structuring of any such arrangements will depend on the bargaining power of the parties.

An owner of IPRs wanting to protect itself against a licensee's insolvency will resist any attempt to implement complicated structures proposed by the licensee and will look to retain ownership and grant a simple licence capable of termination on the licensee's insolvency or other trigger events. It may also demand that royalties or fees be paid in advance rather than in arrears and that payments be made regularly to avoid substantial gaps between payment dates. It could also demand a charge over items created using the IPRs to provide security against failure to pay royalties or fees.

Conversely, a licensee whose business depends on the use of IPRs owned by a licensor may not feel secure if a simple licence is granted and may wish to consider more complex structures or taking certain steps to guard against the licensor's insolvency, which could include:

- acquiring ownership of the IPRs instead of taking an exclusive licence – if the owner needs to use the IPRs, a licence back could be granted to the extent necessary;
- the owner transferring ownership of the IPRs to a newly incorporated non-trading subsidiary which could then grant the licence as licensor to the licensee and undertake not to carry on any other business or activities, thereby reducing the risk of the licensor entity becoming insolvent;
- a conditional assignment under which ownership of the IPRs is vested in the licensee, subject to a condition that it would be transferred back to the licensor at a later date;
- ownership of the IPRs being transferred to independent trustees to hold on trust on terms that on the licensor's insolvency the trustees would vest ownership in the licensee;
- the licensee being granted an option to purchase the IPRs from the licensor if certain events occur. The timing of the exercise and the price payable

would need careful thought to avoid any exercise of the option being set aside in any administration or liquidation of the licensor (for example, it could be set aside as an undervalue transaction unless market value consideration was payable on exercise);

- the licensee being granted a fixed charge over the licensed IPRs, which in the event of the licensor's insolvency would restrict the ability of any administrator or liquidator to deal with the IPRs and allow the licensee to appoint its own receiver – whether this is feasible will depend on the extent of any obligations or liabilities of the licensor that could actually be secured;
- reducing the risk of a licence being disclaimed by, for example: including onerous obligations in an ancillary agreement entered into contemporaneously with the main licence (allowing any disclaimer to apply only to the ancillary agreement); giving the licensee the right to step in and perform obligations in lieu of the licensor (for example, an obligation to pay registration or renewal fees) or to waive the performance of certain obligations; or providing for royalties or fees to be paid in equal instalments over the term of the licence; and
- where appropriate, registering its licence at applicable registries.

### 3.3 Termination rights and automatic reversions

Licences can provide for termination by a licensor in the event of the licensee's insolvency and consequent reversion of rights. Indeed, most well-drafted licence agreements will contain such a provision. The English courts have traditionally upheld a licensor's right to terminate a licence in these circumstances on the basis that termination brings to an end a limited interest held by the licensee in the property of the licensor.[11]

The licensor will need to consider whether termination occurs automatically or becomes effective following notice. In many cases it will be preferable for termination to require notice so that the licensor can assess the best course of action at the relevant time.

Licensors will not usually want to wait until a licensee's administration or liquidation before terminating a licence, because administration or liquidation may occur some time after problems have emerged. Licensors may therefore prefer earlier termination triggers such as failure to pay royalties or fees when due, failure to meet performance targets, or other breaches of the licence. Terminating earlier may reduce a licensor's losses where it has costly ongoing obligations under the licence agreement or where the rights could be granted to another licensee on the same or more favourable terms.

It is possible for rights to revert to a licensor on a licensee's insolvency, provided that underlying ownership of the rights that are to revert has not been vested in the licensee and the licensee has only been using those rights under licence.

---

11 See *Perpetual Trustee Co Ltd v BNY Corporate Trustee Services Ltd* [2009] EWCA Civ 1160 and *Butters (joint administrators of WW Realisation 8 Ltd) v BBC Worldwide Ltd* [2009] WLR (D) 322.

## 4. Cross-border aspects

### 4.1 Foreign law

The administration or liquidation of an English party to a licence agreement will not in itself have an impact on the choice of law chosen to govern that agreement. Therefore if a licence agreement provides for the laws of a foreign jurisdiction to govern it, that law will continue to apply.

However, even if a foreign law governs the terms of a licence to which an English company is a party, English insolvency laws will still be relevant if that company becomes insolvent as it is not possible for an English company to contract out of the operation of those laws. For example, if a licensor granted a licence governed by foreign law but an administrator or liquidator considered the terms of the licence amounted to an undervalue transaction, the administrator or liquidator could take steps to challenge the transaction in the English courts notwithstanding that the agreement itself is governed by foreign law. The choice of foreign law as the governing law of a contract cannot therefore as a matter of English law be used to avoid the application of English insolvency laws.

### 4.2 Foreign jurisdiction

Similarly, the administration or liquidation of an English party to a licence will not in itself impact on the choice of jurisdiction that the parties have chosen for the licence. So if the courts of a foreign jurisdiction had jurisdiction in respect of disputes arising under the contract pre-insolvency, they would continue to do so post-insolvency.

However, the moratorium created by the administration process would have an impact on any pending or continuing overseas legal proceedings, because under English law the commencement or continuation of those proceedings would need to be approved by the administrator or court (in the case of administration). This may lead to complex legal disputes arising regarding jurisdictional and choice-of-law issues, which would need to be determined based on the facts of the specific case.

# Finland

**Pekka Jaatinen**
**Elina Pesonen**
Castrén & Snellman Attorneys Ltd

---

## 1. Overview

### 1.1 Relevant legislation governing intellectual property and bankruptcy

The most important legislation governing bankruptcy in all of its forms is Finland's Bankruptcy Act (20.2.2004/120). The provisions of the Bankruptcy Act apply to the extent not otherwise provided in another act or agreed with a foreign state.

With regard to intellectual property, the most important statutes are the Patents Act (15.12.1967/550), the Copyright Act (8.7.1961/404) and the Trade Marks Act (12.3.1971/221). There are, of course, a number of other statutes but those just listed tend to be the most important in practice.

### 1.2 Types of insolvency procedure

In Finland, the law provides for two types of corporate insolvency procedure. First, there is the bankruptcy proceeding, which concentrates on the liquidation of a debtor's assets and which is governed by the Bankruptcy Act. Secondly, there is the restructuring proceeding, concentrating on the rehabilitation of the debtor's viable business, which is governed by the Restructuring of Enterprises Act (25.1.1993/47). Normally the debtor or the company itself may select the more appropriate proceeding, but the court will finally decide on the commencement of such proceedings.

Bankruptcy is a form of insolvency proceedings covering all the liabilities of the debtor, where the assets of the debtor are used in the payment of the claims in bankruptcy. In order to achieve the objective of the bankruptcy, at the beginning of bankruptcy the assets of the debtor must become subject to the authority of the creditors. An estate administrator appointed by the court sees to the management and liquidation of the assets of the debtor and to the other administration of the bankruptcy estate. In other words, the estate administrator takes over the management and control of the debtor's business and the debtor (whether managing director, board of directors or shareholders' meeting) loses authority over the assets of the bankruptcy estate.

The restructuring proceedings are commenced in order to rehabilitate a distressed debtor's viable business, to ensure its continued viability and to achieve debt arrangements. Commencement of the proceedings leads to a standstill. Once the proceedings have commenced, the debtor must not repay restructuring debts or provide security for such debts.

After the commencement of the proceedings, no measures should be directed at the debtor in order to collect on a restructuring debt (ie, all of the debtor's debts that have arisen before the filing of the application), debt subject to the interdiction of repayment or in order to ensure the payment of the debt. Measures that have already been initiated must not be continued. Moreover, no sanctions for default should be directed at the debtor in respect of such debt – for example, the termination of a debt and the termination or cancellation of the contract underlying such a debt as a result of a default will fall within the sphere of an interdiction.

### 1.3 Grounds of bankruptcy

A prerequisite for bankruptcy is that the debtor is insolvent – ie, unable to repay its debts as they fall due other than on a temporary basis.

### 1.4 Filing for bankruptcy

Bankruptcy proceedings can be initiated by the debtor itself or by its creditors with a written petition. If the debtor itself files for bankruptcy, insolvency assumptions will apply. This means that the debtor will be deemed insolvent if the debtor declares its insolvency and there are no special reasons for not accepting this declaration.

Where a creditor files for bankruptcy of a company, more information on the company's insolvency is needed. However, the creditors are able to invoke insolvency assumptions: unless proven otherwise, insolvency is presumed if:

- the company has discontinued its payments;
- enforcement proceedings have taken place in the preceding six months and by those proceedings it has been determined that the company's assets do not cover its outstanding debts in full; or
- having received the creditor's request for payment, the company has not paid a clear-and-due debt within one week.

In practice, it is quite often the creditor's candidate for estate administrator that drafts the petition for bankruptcy of the company to be declared bankrupt. The petition usually includes a proposal for the estate administrator to be appointed by the court. The bankruptcy petition contains, in short, the request of the petitioner, the grounds thereof and the basic information of the debtor and of the petitioner.

The debtor cannot be declared bankrupt on the petition of a creditor if:

- the creditor holds adequate collateral or another comparable security;
- the creditor holds an adequate security given by a third party for the repayment of a claim that has fallen due and a petition for bankruptcy is contrary to the terms that the creditor is deemed to have consented to when accepting the security; or
- the creditor's claim has not fallen due and the creditor holds an adequate security given by a third party, or a third party is offering to provide such security. A personal guarantee is also considered a form of security.

#### *(a) Competent authority for receiving petitions of bankruptcy*

A matter pertaining to an order of bankruptcy is heard by the court in whose district the general legal seat of the debtor is located. However, a matter pertaining to a corporation, foundation or other legal person must in Finland be heard by the court in whose district the effective management of the corporation, foundation or legal person is located. If there is no court with jurisdiction by virtue of the preceding provisions, the matter is heard by the court in whose district the main operations of the debtor have been pursued, where the debtor has assets or where the hearing of the matter is otherwise deemed expedient in the given circumstances.

If the debtor is a part of a group of companies and it is more expedient to do so, a matter pertaining to an order of bankruptcy may be heard by another court – but this court must have jurisdiction over the bankruptcy matter of another debtor in the same group of companies.

### 1.4 Administrators and other appointed persons

The court appoints an estate administrator at the beginning of the bankruptcy (upon declaration of bankruptcy by the court). Several administrators may be appointed if this is necessary because of the extent of the duties involved, or for some other reason.

Before the appointment of an estate administrator, the court must reserve an opportunity to be heard for the main creditors, the nominee and, at the court's discretion, the debtor and the other creditors. Usually, the administrator is a well-known attorney who is supported by the major creditors.

## 2. Licence agreements in the phase between filing and declaration of bankruptcy

### 2.1 Effects on licence agreements in the licensor's bankruptcy

Bankruptcy proceedings, and any legal effects that the proceedings may have, commence when the court makes a decision to declare bankruptcy. In addition, if the bankruptcy petition is justified, the court may order that some precautions are taken, as set out in the next paragraph, before an order of bankruptcy.

The court may order the seizure of the debtor's assets or make another precautionary order so as to safeguard the disbursements to the creditors out of the assets of the debtor should there be a danger of the debtor hiding, destroying or conveying assets to the detriment of the creditors, or otherwise acting in a manner compromising their interests. The court may also order the seizure of the debtor's books, receipts and other accounting materials, as well as documents on the debtor's administration and other business papers and records of the debtor, as necessary, if there is a danger of the debtor hiding, destroying or damaging the said materials or otherwise acting in a manner compromising the interests of the creditors and thus hampering the scrutiny of the estate. Furthermore, the court may prohibit the debtor from leaving the country if there are probable reasons to believe that the debtor will abscond and thus fail to discharge its duty of cooperation and information.

There are no specific effects on licence agreement that differ from these general principles.

### 2.2 Powers of administrators, receivers or trustees in the licensor's bankruptcy

An estate administrator is appointed when the bankruptcy proceedings are commenced. Therefore, the administrator has no powers before the declaration.

### 2.3 Effects on licence agreements in the licensee's bankruptcy

See section 2.1 above.

### 2.4 Powers of administrators, receivers or trustees in the licensee's bankruptcy

See section 2.2 above.

### 2.5 Impact of registration

Finnish law does not require any registration of any licence agreements. However, with the exception of copyright (which cannot be registered) all other intellectual property right licence agreements can be registered. Registration of a licence agreement will provide protection against all third parties acting in good faith.

A licence agreement registered after a bankruptcy filing would likely not be given the same effect as a licence agreement registered prior to filing. A licence agreement registered after the filing may not be given *erga omnes* or *in rem* effect.

## 3. Licence agreements in the phase after declaration of bankruptcy

### 3.1 Treatment of intellectual property rights

While there is little or no relevant case law in Finland, we believe licences may be treated differently in bankruptcy proceedings depending on the nature of the underlying intellectual property right.

### 3.2 Effects on licence agreements in the licensor's bankruptcy

Under Finnish law, it is unclear to what extent licences survive the insolvency of the licensor and what the exact criteria for this are. The Bankruptcy Act does not contain separate provisions regarding licence agreements, nor do any of the *travaux préparatoires* (the official record of a negotiation) address the issue. Furthermore, there is no Finnish Supreme Court decision to be found regarding licence agreements in bankruptcy proceedings.

As a main rule, bankruptcy in itself does not constitute grounds for the administrator of the bankruptcy estate to terminate or cancel an agreement; in principle, licence agreements do not form an exception to this rule. As such, a licence agreement will stay in force despite the commencement of bankruptcy proceedings. The fact that the licence agreement stays in force means that it will not automatically be cancelled due to bankruptcy.

It is also, however, widely recognised that a bankruptcy estate may withdraw from contracts. This means that if, at the start of bankruptcy proceedings, the debtor has not performed a contract to which it is a party, the other contracting party can request a declaration of whether the bankruptcy estate commits to the contract. If the estate declares, within a reasonable time, that it commits to the contract, the contract cannot be terminated for cause. However, the other contracting party may terminate the contract for cause if the contract is of a personal nature or there is another special reason for which it cannot be required that the other party stay under contract with the bankruptcy estate. The granting of rights would not, for example, be considered of a personal nature. If the bankruptcy estate can fulfil its part of the contract with money, the termination is not possible. This principle has been codified in the Bankruptcy Act.

The general opinion among legal writers also supports an interpretation according to which a patent licence survives the licensor's insolvency. Some uncertainty remains as to whether registration is required for a licence to survive. Certain writers have cautiously emphasised registration and concluded that at least registered licences should survive in the bankruptcy. However, as a general rule Finnish law applies the principle of time priority where, according to this principle, the prior transferee's right will prevail in a collision of rights.

### 3.3 Powers of an administrator, receiver or trustee in the licensor's bankruptcy

According to the Bankruptcy Act, the estate administrator's main duties are to take possession of the assets of the estate, see to the management and maintenance of the assets and arrange for the sale of the owned assets. This necessarily includes the process of going through the debtor's contracts. The administrator needs also to draw up the necessary documentation in the bankruptcy, such as an estate inventory and disbursement list.

To the extent the estate may withdraw from an existing licence agreement (see section 3.2 above), the administrator has the authority to do so.

The administrator is obliged to report annually on the administration of the bankruptcy estate.

### 3.4 Powers and rights of creditors in a licensor's bankruptcy

As described in section 3.2 above, licence agreements are not automatically cancelled due to bankruptcy. However, it is widely recognised that a bankruptcy estate (as represented by the administrator and creditors) may withdraw from contracts. This principle has been codified in the Bankruptcy Act.

With regard to licences it should be noted that, because liquidation is the final objective of the bankruptcy proceedings, the administrator will seek to sell the patents and other intellectual property (IP) rights. To our understanding, there should first be an attempt to sell any patents with any associated licence in force.

The right to exercise the creditors' authority belongs to those creditors who have a claim in bankruptcy against the debtor. After the lodgement date, the right belongs only to those creditors who have lodged their claim or whose claim can otherwise be taken into consideration in the disbursement list, as well as to the creditors protected by collateral who have presented an account of their claim. The creditors normally exercise their authority in the creditors' meeting, and the creditors retain decision-making power in the bankruptcy proceedings thereby.

### 3.5 Effects on licence agreements in the licensee's bankruptcy

As described in section 3.2 above, licence agreements are not automatically cancelled due to bankruptcy. However, it is widely recognised that a bankruptcy estate (as represented by the administrator and creditors) may withdraw from contracts. This principle has been codified in the Bankruptcy Act. Even so, it should be noted that the estate may not have a right to transfer to third parties any licence agreements associated with a bankrupt licensee.

### 3.6 Powers of an administrator, receiver or trustee in the licensee's bankruptcy

See section 3.3 above.

### 3.7 Powers and rights of creditors in a licensee's bankruptcy

See section 3.4 above.

### 3.8 Exclusive and non-exclusive licences

Finnish bankruptcy law does not separate licences by exclusivity.

### 3.9 Perpetual and non-perpetual licences

There is no clear case law on whether there is a distinction between perpetual and non-perpetual licences in the event of bankruptcy. Nonetheless, some commentators hold the view that the court would be more likely to hold perpetual licences (especially if they are essentially executory in nature) to be binding against the bankruptcy estate.

### 3.10 Effects on a sub-licence in a licensor's bankruptcy

See section 3.2 above. To date, there is no case law or other legal authority on the topic of sub-licences and their exact relationship with the primary licence.

### 3.11 Effects on a sub-licence in a licensee's bankruptcy

See section 3.5 above. To date, there is no case law or other legal authority on the topic of sub-licences and their exact relationship with the primary licence.

### 3.12 Impact of registration

The question of the criteria applicable for when a licence agreement becomes binding on the bankruptcy estate is very unclear under Finnish law. Legal writers have argued that the registration of the licence agreement may provide perfection of the licence in terms of making it binding *erga omnes* or as an *in rem* right and therefore also against the bankruptcy estate itself. It is conceivable, however, that IP licences may become binding even without registration in some cases.

Despite the uncertainty of Finnish law on the relevant criteria, the general consensus is that licensees should always seek to register licence agreements in order to ensure maximum rights in the event of the licensor's bankruptcy.

## 4. Contractual arrangements in deviation from the law

### 4.1 Exceptions

Certain types of licence agreements have specific rules applicable only to them (such as publishing agreements). There is no case law, however, to suggest that these differences are relevant in an insolvency context.

### 4.2 Scope to alter statutory mechanisms

There might be special conditions in the licence agreement concerning the event of bankruptcy. The most typical form of these bankruptcy conditions is a clause that guarantees to the one party a right to terminate the agreement if the other party becomes insolvent. This kind of a bankruptcy clause in considered null and void under Finnish bankruptcy legislation.

Generally speaking the parties cannot, as a matter of principle, contract around the relevant rules. In practice, parties can agree that the licence will be registered and this might have some effect in insolvency proceedings.

### 4.3 Termination rights and automatic reversions

Parties cannot agree on a termination right or an automatic reversion of the rights to the licensor if the licensee becomes bankrupt, since such provisions and agreements are considered null and void under Finnish bankruptcy legislation.

## 5. Cross-border aspects

### 5.1 Foreign law and foreign jurisdiction

If the administrator of a bankruptcy estate chooses to commit to a licence agreement, the agreement remains in force as it stands, including the choice of law. In that respect the estate does not have the power of cherry-picking clauses it wishes to retain.

In terms of the *in rem* effects of licences, it is generally assumed that the property law of the country where the IP right is in force may be relevant, in accordance with the *lex loci protectionis* principle. There is, however, no case law on this in Finland.

# France

**Amélie Dorst**
**Anja Droege Gagnier**
BMH AVOCATS

## 1. Overview

### 1.1 Relevant legislation governing intellectual property and insolvency

The French intellectual property regime is governed by the Intellectual Property Code, established by Act 92-597 of July 1 1992, as well as the relevant European laws and international treaties.

The French insolvency regime is governed by provisions comprised in the sixth book of France's Commercial Code, as reformed and amended from time to time – in 2005 (Law 2005-845 of July 26 2005), in 2008 (Order 2008-1345 of December 18 2008), in 2010 (Law 2010-1249 of October 22 2010) and, more recently, in March 2014 (Order 2014-326 of March 12 2014;[1] hereinafter the '2014 Reform').

### 1.2 Types of insolvency procedure

French insolvency proceedings are court-controlled procedures, comprising different tools used according to the difficulties faced by the debtor. They can take various forms:

- the safeguard procedure[2] and the accelerated safeguard procedure, including the accelerated financial safeguard procedure – to be opened while the debtor is not yet insolvent;
- a reorganisation; and
- judicial liquidation procedures, both to be opened as from the moment of insolvency of the debtor.

French law also provides for two consensual pre-insolvency proceedings which do not trigger a stay of payments/actions: the '*mandat ad hoc*' procedure and the so-called 'conciliation' procedure. Both are aiming to reach an amicable debt rescheduling under the supervision of a mediator[3] appointed at an early stage in order to avoid insolvency.

---

1 Order 2014-326 entered into force on July 1 2014.

2 We have chosen to classify the safeguard procedure under the insolvency proceedings even though the debtor is not yet insolvent while starting such proceedings, but only in financial difficulties that it might not overcome.

3 Respectively, a *mandataire ad hoc* or a conciliator, chosen from among insolvency practitioners and very often an administrator (receiver).

### *(a) Consensual pre-insolvency proceedings*

As mentioned in the previous paragraph, there are two types of pre-insolvency proceedings, each of which is described further next.

***Mandat ad hoc* procedure:**[4] A debtor[5] facing financial difficulties without being insolvent[6] can file a petition at the competent commercial court to obtain an order appointing an insolvency practitioner[7] as *mandataire ad hoc*. The *mandataire ad hoc* assists the debtor in negotiating a solution to the debtor's difficulties with its creditors. One of the keys of success of the *mandat ad hoc* procedure is confidentiality in the negotiations,[8] which can be limited to only some creditors (eg, financial creditors). Ordinary business continues, and no specific rules apply to ongoing contracts which are not affected by the negotiations.

The *mandataire ad hoc* does not have any management responsibilities, which remain in the debtor's hands; the mediator's mission is limited to monitoring negotiations and trying to reach settlement between the debtor and the creditors involved, for example via a debt rescheduling. Although the negotiations are not subject to any rules and are freely conducted between the parties, in practice the *mandataire ad hoc* exercises a substantial influence on the outcome of the discussions. The settlement agreement is only binding upon the parties thereto and remains confidential.

At any moment, the *mandat ad hoc* procedure – which is not limited to a certain time frame – may be converted into conciliation proceedings – for instance, if the parties are seeking a court homologation (see below). If the debtor becomes insolvent in the meantime, it must file a petition for insolvency proceedings (see below).

**Conciliation procedure:**[9] The conciliation procedure is similar to the *mandat ad hoc* procedure since it is also aiming to reach an amicable settlement between a debtor and its main creditors at an early stage of the difficulties, and to do so under the supervision of a mediator, in this instance called the 'conciliator'.[10]

The conciliation procedure is limited to a period of four months[11] and the debtor must not be insolvent[12] for more than 45 days at the moment of filing. Upon petition of the debtor explaining its (actual or potential) economic, social or financial

4 See Article L 611-3 of the Commercial Code.

5 Insolvency proceedings set out in the French Commercial Code apply to self-employed individuals, corporate entities, merchants, farmers and craftsmen. However, *mandat ad hoc* and conciliation proceedings are not applicable to farmers and self-employed individuals, who are subject to specific preventive measures.

6 'Insolvent' means unable to meet its payment obligations when they fall due. There is a cash-flow insolvency test (see section 1.3 following).

7 See footnote 3 above: the insolvency practitioner chosen is often an administrator. The debtor can propose one to the court.

8 See Article L 611-15 of the Commercial Code. Listed companies on the stock exchange must disclose to the public as soon as possible any 'privileged' information (Article 223-2 of the general regulation of the Autorité des Marchés Financiers (AMF)), meaning any information having a significant effect on the prices of financial instruments.

9 See Article L 611-4 of the Commercial Code.

10 See footnote 7 above; see also Article L 611-7 of the Commercial Code.

11 The conciliator can be appointed for a maximum period of four months, which may be extended to five months upon the request of the conciliator.

12 See footnote 6 above.

difficulties, the president of the competent commercial court can appoint a conciliator. In practice, very often only the main creditors (eg, financial creditors) are involved in the conciliation procedure; the suppliers are not informed about it, in order to avoid any disturbing of the business. Thus, the procedure is confidential. The debtor and its management remain in charge of running the ordinary business.

The 2014 Reform extended the conciliator's mission of negotiating an amicable settlement between the main creditors and the debtor: as from July 1 2014[13] the conciliator can, at the request of the debtor, seek a partial or total disposal of assets of the debtor. In the conciliation procedure, no 'haircut' can be imposed on the creditors who can hinder a sale where the proceeds are not sufficient to cover their claims. But in practice this obstacle can be circumvented by filing a petition for the opening of 'accelerated safeguard proceedings', during which the planned disposal may be enforced against the dissenting creditors[14] in a case of partial disposal.[15]

As in the *mandat ad hoc* procedure, the settlement agreement obtained in the conciliation procedure is only binding upon the parties to it. The settlement agreement can either be acknowledged by an order of the president of the court[16] or approved by a formal judgment of court homologation.[17]

The advantage of court homologation is to confer legal comfort to the debt rescheduling – eg, a new-money privilege for lenders injecting fresh money, or certainty about the date of insolvency in a case of a further insolvency.[18] By acknowledging or approving the settlement agreement, the court can appoint the conciliator[19] to act as a representative entrusted with implementing the settlement agreement. In the event that a creditor tries to enforce a claim against the debtor during the implementation of the settlement agreement, the debtor can request the court to order postponements of enforcement to that creditor.[20]

If the debtor becomes insolvent during the implementation of the settlement agreement, it must file for insolvency proceedings.

### *(b) Insolvency proceedings*

There are four types of insolvency proceedings, as described next.

**Safeguard proceedings:** The Law of July 26 2005 introduced in the French legal system a new restructuring tool called 'safeguard' proceedings, which can be opened by the commercial court upon request by the debtor only.

The debtor must not be in a secure financial position; rather, it must be facing

13 The date of entering into force of the 2014 Reform.
14 This arrangement is known as a 'pre-pack', See section 1.2(b) below in relation to a 'cram-down' via a two-thirds majority in a creditor committee.
15 Safeguard proceedings do not permit a total disposal – see Article L 626-1 of the Commercial Code.
16 This order is recorded by the president of the court at the request of all parties to the conciliation agreement, granting enforceability of a judgment but remaining confidential.
17 The court homologation is approved at the debtor's request.
18 While defining the moment of insolvency (ie, the moment when the debtor in unable to pay its debts when they fall due), which is relevant for avoidance/clawback actions, the insolvency court could not go beyond the date of judgment homologating the settlement agreement.
19 Called in French a *mandataire à l'exécution de l'accord*, under Article L 611-8 of the Commercial Code (newly introduced by the 2014 Reform).
20 Article L 611-10-1 of the Commercial Code.

difficulties which it does not believe it is able to overcome.[21] The aim is to facilitate reorganisation of the debtor at an early stage, in order to continue the business, to rescue jobs and to pay off the creditors.

Although no insolvency status should be reached, safeguard proceedings trigger a general stay of payments and actions, including those applicable to secured creditors. Collateral is not enforceable during the entire 'observation' period. The court orders the opening of an observation period for a maximum period of 12 months,[22] during which the business is continued by the debtor, assisted by an administrator where certain thresholds are met.[23]

During the observation period, the debtor has to establish a 'safeguard plan', to be approved or rejected by the creditor committees[24] and the bondholder assembly (if any). The 2014 Reform introduced the creditors' ability to submit a plan competing with the one proposed by the debtor.[25] The last word for approval or rejection of a safeguard plan (for recovery or transfer) is reserved to the court.

Safeguard proceedings can be converted into reorganisation or liquidation proceedings.

**Accelerated safeguard proceedings:** The 2014 Reform extended the concept of accelerated proceedings to all pre-existing creditors (excluding employees and landlords) that have made a claim for outstanding debts owed to them. These new arrangements were called 'accelerated safeguard proceedings'.[26] The time frame for approval of a safeguard plan is three months, without possibility for an extension: where the plan is not approved within the three-month time frame, the procedure is closed with no possibility of conversion in an 'ordinary' safeguard, only reorganisation or liquidation proceedings are operated. It is interesting to note that some provisions with respect to the continuation of ongoing contracts[27] are not applicable to the accelerated safeguard procedure: such contracts continue to stay in force even if the administrator does not notify parties of a decision to maintain them and even if the debtor does not pay the consideration.

The opening of an accelerated safeguard procedure does not trigger the termination of ongoing contracts, which is the general rule in French insolvency law.

The 'accelerated financial safeguard procedure' was introduced into French law in 2010,[28] enabling the implementation of pre-packed plans designed during conciliation proceedings and approved during the safeguard procedure commenced immediately upon the request of the debtor for a very limited period of time.[29] The

---

21 See Article L 620-1 of the Commercial Code.

22 With a possible extension up to 18 months.

23 The court can, but does not have to appoint an administrator when the debtor has less than 20 employees and a turnover below €3 million (excl. VAT). – see Article L 621-4 of the Commercial Code and Article R. 621-11 of the Commercial Code.

24 There are two creditor committees: the committee comprising the financial creditors and the committee composed of suppliers, each voting where motions have to be passed with a two-thirds majority of the amount of the receivables held by the voting members.

25 Article L 626-30-2 of the Commercial Code.

26 See Article L 628-1 of the Commercial Code.

27 Article L 622-13 of the Commercial Code.

28 Completed, in terms of eligibility requirements, by the Law of March 22 2012.

29 One month, with a possibility of a one-month extension.

accelerated financial safeguard procedure affects only creditors that are members of credit institutions or bondholders; suppliers remain outside this procedure and do not suffer a standstill.

**Reorganisation proceedings:**[30] A debtor is required to file a petition at the commercial court for the opening of reorganisation proceedings within 45 days of the occurrence of insolvency.[31] Reorganisation proceedings are opened if there is a prospect that the business can recover;[32] in contrast, the court will order the commencement of liquidation proceedings if that does not seem possible. Reorganisation proceedings generate a general stay of actions and payments to all secured and unsecured creditors.

The court appoints an administrator,[33] in general assisting the debtor in running the business during the observation period,[34] investigating the business and making proposals for a reorganisation of the business. At the commencement of proceedings, the court also appoints a creditors' representative[35] entrusted with the listing of claims and with communication with the creditors.

At the end of the observation period, the court orders:

- the continuation of business by way of an agreed reorganisation plan[36] which provides for the partial or total payment of debts over a number of years (generally up to 10); or
- if a reorganisation is not possible, the disposal of assets as a going concern to a third party, in accordance with a 'sale plan';[37] or
- failing both of the above, the liquidation of the debtor.

**Judicial liquidation proceedings:** Judicial liquidation proceedings are the ultimate tool in insolvencies, where all the assets of the debtor are disposed of either through a sale as a going concern (ie, a sale plan including assets, contracts, 'jobs' etc)[38] or on a piecemeal basis either at a public auction or by mutual agreement. The role of the court appointed liquidator is to liquidate all the assets of the debtor with the view of maximising proceeds and the reimbursement of creditors.

### 1.3 Grounds of bankruptcy

Safeguard proceedings are available to a debtor who is not insolvent but is facing difficulties that he cannot overcome.[39] A debtor that is insolvent but whose business

30 In French, the *procédure de redressement judiciaire*.
31 Article L 631-1 of the Commercial Code.
32 And in practice in any case when the debtor has employees; see footnote 23 above.
33 When the thresholds of Rule 621-11 of the Commercial Code are met (see footnote 23 above).
34 In general for two or three months, extended to 18 months at a maximum.
35 In French, a *mandataire judiciaire*.
36 Which has been discussed and approved in the creditor committees and by the bondholders (if any), or submitted to creditors on an individual consultation if no committees are set up. Since the 2014 Reform, creditors can propose a competing plan.
37 In French, a *plan de cession*.
38 If possible, the court opens the liquidation proceedings by ordering the continuation of business (for a maximum period of six months), when it is favourable towards selling the business as a going concern and to save jobs. In that case, and in addition to the liquidator, an administrator is appointed for such period.
39 See Article L 620-1 of the Commercial Code.

appears to be viable must apply for the opening of reorganisation proceedings within 45 days of the occurrence of insolvency.[40] Where the court considers there are prospects for the company to recover, it may order the opening of reorganisation proceedings. If this condition is not met, the court will open liquidation proceedings.

Where during the observation period a reorganisation plan appears to the court as totally infeasible, the court will either order the disposal of assets (via a sale plan – see section 1.2(b) above), or open judicial liquidation proceedings (see section 1.2(b) above).

### 1.4 Filing for insolvency

Safeguard proceedings can only be filed by the debtor, which, without being insolvent, must give evidence to the court that it is facing difficulties.[41]

Concerning reorganisation or liquidation proceedings, the debtor (ie, managing director(s) if the debtor is a company) is required to file a petition no later than 45 days after the date the company became insolvent.[42] Furthermore, any unpaid creditor (secured or unsecured) or the public prosecutor's office may file a petition for insolvency against the debtor.

The authority lawfully empowered to receive petitions of insolvency is the president of the commercial court at the place where the debtor has its registered office.

The court appoints one or more insolvency judge(s)[43] in order to monitor the proceedings. Regarding the sale of business as a going concern pursuant to a sale plan or over substantial decisions in the proceedings, the court remains the only authority empowered to allow them. The insolvency judge will request the opinion of the public prosecutor before taking such decisions.

## 2. Licence agreements in the phase between filing and declaration of bankruptcy

### 2.1 Effects on licence agreements in the event of licensor's bankruptcy

Under French insolvency law (unlike laws of other jurisdictions – eg, Germany), the opening of insolvency proceedings, whether reorganisation or judicial liquidation, follows immediately[44] the filing of the petition at court. Insolvency rules are applicable as of the date of the opening judgment so that, in the phase between filing and opening proceedings, the debtor is not governed by insolvency law apart from rules with respect to clawback actions for operations done in the 'twilight' period.[45] The 'twilight' period is defined as the period between the day of occurrence of

---

40 Unless conciliation proceedings are running.

41 See Article L 620-1 of the Commercial Code.

42 Unless conciliation proceedings are pending. The legal representative of the debtor who failed to request the opening of reorganisation or liquidation proceedings within the 45-day period is potentially facing different types of sanctions: financial (liability for all or part of the shortfall of assets, under Article. L 651-2 of the Commercial Code), professional (under Article L 653-8 of the Commercial Code) and criminal (imprisonment for a period of up to five years and a fine of up to €75,000, under Article L 654-2 of the Commercial Code).

43 In French, *juge commissaire*.

44 Ie, within a couple of days and, in important files, the day after.

45 See Articles L 632-1 and L 632-2 of the Commercial Code.

insolvency and the formal opening judgment of insolvency. The date of occurrence of insolvency, called the 'date of cessation of payments', is set by the court in the opening judgment. It can retroactively be set to 18 months prior to the opening judgment, apart from when transactions are passed without consideration, in which case the court can set a retroactive period up to 24 months.[46] During the twilight period, various transactions are *per se* null and void[47] and some acts may be declared by court as null and void.[48]

A pledge on patents registered during this period in order to secure a previous debt is null and void.[49] If a pledge on patents is registered to secure a concomitant debt or a future claim, the transaction can be declared by court null and void if the co-contractor knew about the state of insolvency of the debtor at the time the transaction was concluded.[50]

A debtor (eg, a licensor) facing difficulties before having filed for insolvency may contemplate securing its intellectual property (IP) rights by placing them into a trust. The IP rights become the property of the trustee and are managed by it during the time of trust. The opening of insolvency proceedings would not affect the IP rights placed into the trust, which will not contain the estate and thus escape the licensor's creditors. Upon termination of the trust, and in accordance with the trust agreement, the assets would then return to the debtor or become the property of a beneficiary contractually defined in the trust agreement.

However, the placement of assets into a trust in this way during the twilight period is *per se* null and void unless the assets are affected as collateral to a debt contracted at the same time as such placement.[51] Therefore, in practice, a restructuring of assets should be operated under the control of a conciliator and fixed in a conciliation agreement, which should then be homologated by a court (see section 1.2.(b) above).

## 2.2 Effects on licence agreements in the licensee's bankruptcy

There is nothing to specify in regard to a licensee's insolvency during the period between filing and a declaration of insolvency.

## 2.3 Impact of registration

There is no impact on registration under French law.

---

46 There is no twilight period before the opening of safeguard proceedings since the debtor is not insolvent.

47 Article L 632-1 of the Commercial Code states that transactions are *per se* null and void if they are: (i) transactions made without consideration; (ii) unbalanced transactions (ie, if the obligations of the debtor exceed significantly the obligations of the other party); (iii) prepayments; (iv) payments made otherwise than in a manner commonly accepted; (v) deposits or escrows of money without a final court decision; (vi) securities in relation to pre-existing debt; (vii) attachments or other remedial measures in favour of a creditor; (viii) authorisations or exercisings of stock options; (ix) any transfers of goods or rights into a trust fund, (x) goods or rights already transferred into the trust property that are affected by an amendment to the trust deed; (xi) where the debtor is an individual businessman with limited liability, any allocation or modification in the allocation of an asset resulting in a decrease in the assets of the estate of the insolvent business for the benefit of the businessman's personal assets and (xii) statements of unseizability by the debtor.

48 See Article L 632-2 of the Commercial Code.

49 See Article L 632-1-I-6 of the Commercial Code.

50 See Article L 632-2-1 of the Commercial Code.

51 Article L 632-1-I-9 of the Commercial Code.

## 3. Licence agreements in the phase following declaration of bankruptcy

### 3.1 Treatment of intellectual property rights

The provisions of insolvency law are matters of public policy: following the opening judgment, IP rights are governed by the provisions of insolvency law.

Nevertheless, the French Intellectual Property Code contains special rules regarding publishing and audiovisual production contracts, in that certain aspects of insolvency law have a bearing on such agreements.[52] The aim is to protect the author's rights and in particular its moral and financial interests.

### 3.2 Effects on licence agreements in the licensor's bankruptcy

As a general rule, the opening of insolvency proceedings[53] triggers a stay of actions, including the termination of 'ongoing contracts',[54] which is not permitted. As a result, ongoing contracts stay in force and the co-contractor must perform its contractual commitments.[55] Licence agreements are qualified as 'ongoing contracts' as long as the licence fees are periodically due.[56]

Contractual clauses providing for an automatic termination of the ongoing licence agreement in the event of the opening of insolvency proceedings (of whatever kind) relating to the licensee are frequent in practice, but according to Article L 622-13-I of the Commercial Code such clauses have no effect on the 'ongoing contract', which stays in force. As for the licensor's insolvency, such clauses are less frequently contained in contracts: if the licensor can still perform its contractual obligations despite its insolvency and its business can be rescued, the licensee might want to keep this position.

### 3.3 Powers of an administrator, receiver or trustee in the licensor's bankruptcy

The judicial administrator is in general either overseeing or assisting the debtor in running the business during the observation period, supervising the drawing-up of the safeguard or reorganisation plan and helping in the search for a possible purchaser. Unlike other jurisdictions, the French judicial administrator is not authorised to sell any assets (eg, IP rights); the commercial court is the only lawful authority empowered to take a decision with respect to the disposal of assets, in part or in full.

The judicial administrator can force the co-contractor (eg, the licensee) to continue to perform its contractual obligations (eg, the payment of royalties) during the observation period – provided, however, that the administrator ascertains the relevant consideration.[57]

Moreover, pursuant to Article L 622-13-IV of the Commercial Code, the judicial

---

52 Articles L 132-15 and L 132-30 of the Intellectual Property Code. See also section 4.1 below.
53 Whether safeguard, reorganisation or liquidation proceedings.
54 In French, *contrats à execution successive*.
55 See Articles L 622-13 (safeguard proceedings), L 631-14 (reorganisation proceedings) and L 641-11-1 (liquidation proceedings) of the Commercial Code.
56 The licence agreement is in general not qualified as 'ongoing' if an upfront payment is made upon signing.
57 Article L 622-13-II of the Commercial Code.

administrator is entitled to file a request to the insolvency judge seeking termination of the agreement if such termination is necessary for the safeguarding of the debtor's business and does not excessively harm the interests of the co-contractor. In the present hypothesis – ie, licensor insolvency – it is difficult to see how the termination of the licence agreement would not excessively harm the licensee, whose business might be quasi-dependent on the licence. In this case the licensee could, at a minimum, request adequate compensation.

### 3.4 Powers and rights of creditors in a licensor's bankruptcy

In French insolvency proceedings, where the principal aim is to rescue the debtor's business and thus to save jobs, creditors have limited rights. First of all, as a consequence of the general rule of stay of actions and payments, creditors cannot claim from their debtor the payment of any alleged unpaid consideration.[58] The question of whether the creditor is secured or unsecured is irrelevant, since no security or collateral may be enforced once the proceedings are opened.[59]

All the same, the opening of insolvency proceedings is stopping any legal action being brought by a creditor for a claim incurred prior to the opening judgment.

Legal claims based on the infringement of IP rights do not fall under the scope of Article L 622-21 of the Commercial Code, even though they are based on facts occurred prior to insolvency, provided that the claim is aimed at determining the amount of damages[60] and obtaining termination of the infringement even under penalty,[61] as well as the seizure of the product in infringement. Once the amount of damages determined by the court cannot be paid by the debtor in insolvency, they must be declared by the creditor to the estate in order to benefit from any further dividend distribution, like any other unsecured creditor.

All claims incurred prior to the opening of insolvency proceedings must be declared to the insolvency estate by bringing the situation to the attention of the creditors' representative within two months of the publication of the insolvency judgment in the *BODACC*. Creditors located abroad benefit from two additional months.[62] Since the 2014 Reform, the claims are deemed to be declared to the estate with the simple transmission of the list of debts to the creditors' representative by the debtor who is presumed to act on behalf of the relevant creditor. In parallel, the creditor is still able to file himself a declaration of claim, stating the amount due according to him and informing the creditors' representative about the relevant collateral.[63]

Creditors' claims may be privileged if incurred after the opening of insolvency

---

58 Article L 622-21 of the Commercial Code.

59 As an exception, a creditor may enforce its rights on assets secured in a trust – eg, IP rights (see section 2.1 above) – save in the case of a lease agreement (or a supply agreement) relating to the relevant asset to the benefit of the debtor.

60 Pursuant to Article L 622-24 and Rule 622-24 of the Commercial Code, the claim must be lodged within two months of the opening judgment being published in the *BODACC* (French official bulletin for civil and commercial announcements).

61 TGI Paris, 3 Ch, December 17 2008 (case RG06/00419); and CA Paris, December 17 2010 Case 2010-026096).

62 Article L 622-24 and Rule 622-24 of the Commercial Code.

63 See Article L 622-24 §3 of the Commercial Code.

proceedings and if corresponding to an agreement which has been continued by the express or tacit consent of the administrator after the opening of the proceedings (eg, rental claims).[64]

Moreover, creditors benefiting from property rights on assets stored, deposited in the debtor's hands or sold to the latter under a retention-of-title clause may claim their rights to extract the asset out of the estate. They should direct their claim towards the administrator or liquidator within three months of the publication of the opening judgment.[65] In practice, such a claim is only worthwhile if the said asset has not been transformed or incorporated into other goods and if it has not been sold to a third party which has paid the purchase price.

Another consequence of the general rule of stay of actions is the continuation of ongoing contractual relationships (eg, licence agreements and lease agreements). They cannot be terminated by the creditor on the grounds of the opening of insolvency proceedings (see section 3.2 above).

Instead, licensor's creditors may file a request to the judicial administrator[66] to formally take a position on whether the agreement (representing an ongoing contractual relationship) has to be continued.[67] If the administrator does not respond within one month, the request of the creditor to terminate the agreement is deemed to be accepted and the agreement is terminated.[68]

In addition, a creditor may request the appointment by the court of a 'controller'. The mission of a controller is to ensure that the creditors' representative appointed by the court is acting in the interests of the creditors, failing which a controller is entitled to initiate legal action on behalf of the creditors. Up to five creditors can be appointed as controllers.

### 3.5 Effects on licence agreements in the licensee's bankruptcy

In the event that a licensee must file for insolvency,[69] the general rule as set forth in Article L 622-13 of the Commercial Code applies: no automatic termination of the licence agreement occurs upon the opening of insolvency proceedings despite any contractual clause providing for termination or alteration of rights (see also section 4.2 below). Regarding the special cases of publishing and audiovisual production contracts, refer further to section 4.1 below.

At the choice of the judicial administrator, the licence agreement may be continued by the licensee during the observation period of the insolvency proceedings – provided, however, that consideration to the licensor is duly satisfied.[70] In contrast, the licensor is entitled to terminate the licence agreement with immediate effect. The administrator is personally liable for execution of the

---

64 See Article L 622-17 of the Commercial Code: basically, they are only superseded by tax, employees' claims and the new-money privilege.

65 Article L 624-9 of the Commercial Code.

66 By sending him a registered letter with acknowledgement of receipt.

67 Article L 622-13-III-1 of the Commercial Code.

68 The administrator may, however, ask the insolvency judge to grant an extension to the contract period (up to a maximum of two months). The co-contractor may also ask the insolvency judge to order a response in a shorter time frame.

69 Whether safeguard, reorganisation or liquidation proceedings.

70 Article L 622-13-II of the Commercial Code.

consideration; so the administrator must ascertain that the debtor has enough cash for continuation of the agreement according to the contractual terms.[71] If it appears that the debtor is facing a cash shortfall for the next payment term, the administrator must terminate the agreement. Once the agreement is terminated (ie, due to default of payment of licence fees or when the termination date has been reached), the debtor is no longer entitled to use the licence.

Licensor's claims incurred from non-payment of licence fees would have to be declared to the insolvency estate by bringing them to the attention of the creditors' representative.[72] Such claims are privileged if incurred after the opening of insolvency proceedings.[73]

### 3.6 Powers of an administrator, receiver or trustee in the licensee's bankruptcy

The judicial administrator can force the co-contractor (ie, the licensor) to continue to perform its contractual obligations (ie, maintain the rights giving rise to the licence agreement) during the observation period – provided, however, the administrator ascertains the relevant consideration (ie, payment of royalties).[74] Particular rights apply for the benefit of authors in publishing and audiovisual production agreements – see further section 4.1 below.

Pursuant to Article L 622-13-IV of the Commercial Code, the judicial administrator is entitled to file a request to the insolvency judge, seeking termination of the agreement, if such termination is necessary for the safeguarding of the debtor's business and does not excessively harm the interests of the co-contractor.

### 3.7 Powers and rights of creditors in a licensee's bankruptcy

See section 3.4 above.

### 3.8 Exclusive and non-exclusive licences

As a general rule, French insolvency law does not provide for a different treatment of exclusive and non-exclusive licence agreements.

However, the insolvency of a licensee under an exclusive licence might cause difficulties in practice. The licensee in insolvency may be in a situation whereby it is no longer able to market the products or use the trademarks, whereas the licensor and owner of the IP rights must, contractually, refrain from marketing the products or using the trademarks under an exclusive licence in the territory. As a result, the

---

71 As a principle, the payment is to be made immediately, unless the co-contractor consents to different payment terms (Article L 631-14 of the Commercial Code).

72 Article L 622-24 and Rule 622-24 of the Commercial Code state that the filing of a claim must be lodged within two months for domestic creditors, and within four months (as from the publication in the BODACC) for creditors located abroad, when the claim was incurred prior to the opening of insolvency proceedings. As for claims incurred after the opening of insolvency proceedings (Article L 622-17-I of the Commercial Code on privileged claims relating to expenses necessary for the business of ordinary activities or those required by the procedure), the declaration is to be made immediately as from the due date, within one year after the end of the observation period or after the judgment approving the sale plan and within six months of the publication of the judgment ordering the liquidation (Article L 641-13 of the Commercial Code).

73 Article L 622-17 of the Commercial Code: basically, such claims are only superseded by tax, employees' claims and the new-money privilege.

74 Article L 622-13-II of the Commercial Code.

general rule according to which the holder of IP rights must exploit them in the given territory can no longer be followed. This situation can lead to the granting of compulsory licences for patented products[75] or to an action of a competitor seeking the revocation of the trademark rights for lack of use in the territory. Furthermore, a 'weak' use might not be considered as sufficient in that respect.

### 3.9 Perpetual and non-perpetual licences

As a general rule, French insolvency law does not provide for a different treatment of perpetual and non-perpetual licence agreements.

However, assuming that a licence is non-perpetual and its contractual term is reached in the course of the observation period of insolvency proceedings, the licence will be terminated as contractually agreed. The judicial administrator of a licensee facing insolvency proceedings may, though, request the licensor to renew the licence agreement, in which case the latter is free to accept (eg, under such conditions as an upfront payment of royalties) or not.

In practice and depending on the weight that the IP right represents in the business of the debtor, the non-renewal of the licence agreement might jeopardise the contemplated continuation plan and thus the reorganisation of the business. Moreover, according to general commercial law as set out in Article L 442-6-I-5 of the Commercial Code, a refusal by the licensor to renew a licence agreement may be qualified as abrupt termination of business relationships and, thereby, trigger damages for the licensee on the basis of the law of torts. In assessing damages for an abrupt termination, courts are particularly attentive to the duration of the business relationship.[76] Another element in the assessment of damages suffered by a licensee is a possible economic dependence of the latter on the licensor.

### 3.10 Effects on a sub-licence in a licensor's bankruptcy

Sub-licences are handled in the same way as licences when a licensor is insolvent, and no contractual deviation is allowed.

### 3.11 Effects on a sub-licence in a licensee's bankruptcy

Sub-licences are in general handled in the same way as licences when a licensee is insolvent. However, it is possible to foresee contractual clauses providing otherwise (eg, in a licence relationship between the licensor and the sub-licensee directly, the latter taking the place of the licensee which had become insolvent). In practice, such contractual clauses are rather rare.

### 3.12 Impact of registration

The registration of licences does not have any impact on insolvency situations.

It has to be noted that the sole purpose of the registration of a licence is to inform third parties of the existence of the licence (and it is therefore only useful for

---

75 Article L 613-11 of the Intellectual Property Code.

76 In general, courts are tending to consider six weeks to two months per year of existence of the business relationship as a decent notice period.

exclusive licences). This publicity allows scope for an exclusive licensee to sue any counterfeiter in court without requiring the IP owner to be part of the proceedings.

## 4. Contractual arrangements in deviation from the law

### 4.1 Exceptions

French insolvency law does not contain special provisions with respect to intellectual property rights in general. However, the Intellectual Property Code contains some additional rules with respect to publishing agreements and audiovisual production agreements,[77] aiming to give authors extra protection.

As a principle, the opening of reorganisation proceedings for the benefit of a publisher (or producer) should not induce the termination of the licence agreement granted by the author. If the business of the publisher is continued during the observation period, all commitments contained in the ongoing licence agreement must be fulfilled towards the author. A similar rule exists for audiovisual production contracts where the making or exploitation of the work is continued during the observation period: all existing commitments are to be fulfilled by the debtor (ie, the producer) towards the author(s).

The Intellectual Property Code is silent with respect to sanctions when consideration is not paid by the licensee to the author. In this situation, the rules as set forth in the Commercial Code for insolvency situations, and in particular the provisions in Article L 622-13 (which are rather detailed), apply. Indeed, the principle of continuation of the licence agreement in the event of the insolvency of the producer/publisher (ie, the licensee) is not a deviation from the general rule of continuation of ongoing contracts set forth in the Commercial Code,[78] which remains applicable to publishing and audiovisual production contracts.

The author can request the termination of the publishing agreement (or audiovisual production agreement) in the event that the business activities of the publisher (or producer) have ceased for more than three months, or in the event that judicial liquidation is pronounced.[79]

In the event of the partial or total disposal of the assets of the producer, case law has indicated with respect to audiovisual production agreements that the author benefits from a termination right which cannot be affected by the pre-emption right of the co-producer (see below). As a result, any licence agreement with respect to exploitation rights granted by the producer to a licensee will equally be terminating.[80]

Moreover, in the event of sale of all or a part of the business of the producer in insolvency (or the publisher in insolvency),the authors and co-producers of the work benefit from a pre-emption right with respect to the assets concerning their respective IP rights. The co-producer's pre-emption right prevails over the author's pre-emption right.

77 Articles L 132-15 and L 132-30 of the Intellectual Property Code. See also section 3.1 above.
78 Article L 622-13 of the Commercial Code; see also section 3.5 above.
79 Articles L 132-15 (publishing agreements), L 132-30 (audiovisual production agreements) of the Intellectual Property Code.
80 Judgment dated September 6 2001, Court of Appeal, Versailles, case 2000-3656.

To implement the process of exercising pre-emption rights, the first step by the administrator or the liquidator (as the case may be) is to establish a separate lot for each audiovisual work that may be subject to assignment or auction. Then, in a second step, the administrator or liquidator informs each co-producer or author of an audiovisual work of its pre-emption rights.[81] If in the pre-emption process the parties do not agree on a purchase price, an appointed expert's valuation shall prevail.

In the event of disposal to a third party of the assets of the producer's (or publisher's) business containing IP rights, the purchaser is bound to all obligations and commitments that the seller had in the transferred agreement. Moreover, in the event of a total or partial disposal of assets,[82] authors, compositors and artists benefit from a privileged ranking for the payment of royalties and remunerations incurred in the last three years.[83]

On all other aspects, publishing agreements and agreements on know-how are subject to the same provisions as licence agreements in the context of insolvency – eg, to the general rules of Article L 622-13 of the Commercial Code concerning the continuation of ongoing contracts and Article L 622-21 of the Commercial Code concerning the stay of actions and payments. The co-contractor to an agreement on know-how is treated in the same way as other creditors, which in this context are often unsecured creditors (see section 3.4 above).

## 4.2 Scope to alter statutory mechanisms

French insolvency law provisions qualify as public policy rules and are therefore compulsory in all respects. Any means in a contract of agreeing to alter the statutory mechanism – for instance, a clause providing for the automatic termination of a contract (licence agreement) in the event of insolvency – is invalid.

As set out in section 1.2(a) above, the 2014 Reform introduced a further protection for a debtor under pre-insolvency proceedings without being insolvent (or being insolvent for less than 45 days as far as conciliation proceedings are concerned).. Any clause altering the conditions for a debtor set forth in an ongoing contract in the event of a request for the opening of *mandat ad hoc* or conciliation proceedings is null and void.[84] Here, 'altering' means limiting the rights or increasing the obligations of the debtor.

## 4.3 Termination rights and automatic reversions

Contractual clauses providing for an automatic termination of an ongoing licence agreement in the event of the opening of licensee insolvency proceedings (of

81 Notification is by registered letter with acknowledgment of receipt, at least one month (or 15 days with respect to publishing agreements) before any decision on assignment or disposal or any procedure for sale by auction of the assets is conducted by the court. Failing such notification, the sale of assets is null and void.

82 When either insolvent or solvent.

83 Article L 131-8 of the Intellectual Property Code.

84 Article L 611-16 of the Commercial Code makes clear that, despite a general rule having been specified, the contracts mainly concerned with these new provisions are likely to be financial documentation stipulating in general the opening of pre-insolvency proceedings as a default position.

whatever kind) are frequent in practice. According to Article L 622-13–I of the Commercial Code, such clauses have no effect on the 'ongoing contract' (ie, the relevant licence agreement), which stays in force. As for what happens under the licensor's insolvency, such clauses are less frequently contained in contracts: if the licensor can still perform its obligations under the contract despite its insolvency and its business can be rescued, the licensee might want to retain the status quo.

Under French law, there is no need for contractual clauses providing for an automatic reversion in the event of insolvency of the licensee, because the licensor does not lose its IP rights within the frame of the licence agreement – ie, the licensor is only granting IP rights on a temporary basis to a licensee and therefore remains the owner of the IP rights.

## 5. Cross-border aspects

### 5.1 Foreign law

According to the general rules of French private international law, parties to an agreement containing a 'foreign element' – for example, a territory clause in a licence agreement that is not limited to the territory of the respective jurisdiction of the parties A and B, but also includes the territory of a third jurisdiction C – may freely and validly choose a law which should govern the agreement. The law chosen might be the law of country A or country B or of another country (C or even D), except that public policy rules are compulsory and cannot be validly circumvented. Moreover, a clause stipulating that UNIDROIT principles are applicable to the licence agreement can also be contemplated.

The parties and (as representative of the debtor) the judicial administrator are bound by the law governing the licence agreement, as chosen by the parties, or as applicable according to private international law. Nonetheless, to the extent that the rules of such law violate French public policy rules, they are void or disregarded in France. As already stated, insolvency law is deemed to be public policy and consequently mandatory in all aspects.

### 5.2 Foreign jurisdiction

In international licence agreements,[85] parties may elect a foreign jurisdiction for any disputes.

Moreover, concerning domestic licence agreements,[86] Article 48 of the French Civil Procedure Code considers those concluded between merchants to be valid jurisdiction clauses waiving the mandatory rules. Thus, it is possible for two merchants (in our context, a licensor and a licensee) of country A to submit their contract to the jurisdiction of the courts of country B. In practice, such a possibility might only make sense if the parties also elect to be bound by the law of country B – although the question of election of law is treated separately from the question of election of jurisdiction.

---

85 Meaning, according to French private international law, agreements containing a 'foreign element'.
86 Meaning, according to French private international law, agreements without any 'foreign element'.

As to whether a jurisdiction clause is valid according to the applicable rules of French domestic or French private international law, a judicial administrator – as representative of the debtor[87] – is bound to it in the same way as the original parties, always within the limits of public policy (including, of course, French insolvency law).

All the same, arbitration clauses contained in a licence agreement are binding on the judicial administrator, as representative of the debtor,[88] to the extent that they are valid according to French law. Pursuant to Article L 615-17 of the Intellectual Property Code, an arbitration clause is valid under the conditions set forth in Articles 2059 and 2060 of the French Civil Code – ie, when referring to disputes falling in the purely contractual area, such as warranty obligations or the payment of royalties. However, conflicts involving a matter of public policy (eg, the validity of French patents[89]) are excluded from arbitration and must be settled by courts.[90]

*The authors are grateful for the kind assistance of Anne-Cécile Khouri-Raphael and Stéphane-Alexandre Dassonville in the preparation of this chapter.*

87 Or assistant to the debtor, if appointed to these functions by a court.
88 *Id.*
89 Except the contractual exploitation of patents.
90 In these circumstances, the Court of Justice (in French, the *tribunal de grande instance*).

# Germany

**Matthias Nordmann**
**Ulrich Reber**
SKW Schwarz

---

## 1. Overview

### 1.1 Relevant legislation governing intellectual property and bankruptcy

Intellectual property rights are governed by the applicable federal statutes in Germany, of which the most relevant are the Patents Act, the Trademark Act, the Copyright Act, the Publishing Act, the Utility Patent Act and the Designs Act.

The Insolvency Act is the main statute for insolvency proceedings in Germany. There is no express codification of intellectual property rights or licence agreements in the case of insolvency, with the exception of very limited provisions in the Publishing Act (see further section 4.1 below). Attempts at codifying the fate of licence agreements in an insolvency recently failed during the legislative process and did not become law, so that the rules developed by courts are still relevant.

### 1.2 Types of insolvency procedure

Germany has consolidated several procedures that existed before and now recognises one unified insolvency procedure. Several variants of this procedure exist, most notably a personal management procedure (which allows more liberty in the administration of the insolvent company by the existing management but under the surveillance of a custodian). Furthermore, in order to promote early restructuring efforts a court may order, upon petition of the debtor who has filed for insolvency due to imminent illiquidity or over-indebtedness, that a restructuring plan is presented within a period not exceeding three months. Only if this attempt fails will insolvency proceedings be opened.

### 1.3 Grounds of bankruptcy

General grounds of bankruptcy are:

- illiquidity – ie, the inability of the debtor to make payments as they become due, and in particular the cessation of payments; and
- over-indebtedness – ie, where the debtor's assets fall short of covering the existing liabilities unless the continuance of operations of the company is significantly likely.

A debtor (but not a creditor) may also file for insolvency in the case of imminent illiquidity. Illiquidity is 'imminent' if the debtor is likely to be in a position where it will not be able to make payments when they become due.

### 1.4 Filing for bankruptcy

If the debtor is a company, the management of the company must file for insolvency without undue delay from the time that insolvency has occurred but no more than three weeks from occurrence of illiquidity or over-indebtedness. A creditor is entitled to file for insolvency if it has a legal interest in the opening of insolvency proceedings and establishes having a claim against the debtor on a prima facie basis.

The competent court for receiving petitions of insolvency is the insolvency court (at the local court level) where the debtor has its business seat, unless the centre of its business activity is in another precinct in which case the insolvency court in that precinct is competent. International jurisdiction of an insolvency court is subject to European Council Regulation 1346/2000 on Insolvency Proceedings, according to which the court of the EU member state has jurisdiction within the territory in which the centre of a debtor's main interests is situated.

### 1.5 Administrators and other appointed persons

Upon receiving a filing for insolvency, the insolvency court will order all measures which are deemed necessary for preventing any loss of assets in the debtor's estate. This usually entails the appointment of a preliminary insolvency administrator. The powers of the preliminary insolvency administrator are determined by the insolvency court and may even include an approval right of the preliminary insolvency administrator in relation to any transactions envisaged by the debtor.

Upon opening the insolvency proceedings – ie, on a declaration of insolvency by the insolvency court – an insolvency administrator is appointed by the court. Usually, the insolvency administrator is the same person as the preliminary insolvency administrator. From that time on, the insolvency administrator exclusively manages the debtor's estate, secures the assets and either seeks a restructuring of the business or liquidation of the company.

## 2. Licence agreements in the phase between filing and declaration of bankruptcy

### 2.1 Effects on licence agreements in the licensor's bankruptcy

The filing for insolvency does not have a direct impact on the licence agreement; the agreement is still enforceable. The grant of rights stays in place and the licensee continues to be obligated to pay the agreed licence fee. Neither a termination nor a reversion of rights occurs. Should the licensee wish to terminate the licence agreement as a result of the filing for insolvency, such a declaration may be held to be invalid (irrespective of such termination being also subject to being contested – see section 2.2 below).

### 2.2 Powers of administrators, receivers or trustees in the licensor's bankruptcy

Although the insolvency administrator has the power to contest any transactions that are harmful to the estate after the filing for insolvency (and even for a limited time before such time, pursuant to rules on the contestation of transactions to the detriment of the debtor's estate), the preliminary insolvency administrator does not have that power.

Furthermore, in a licensor insolvency there is usually no need for contesting the grant of rights as the debtor's estate is likely to receive licence fees in return, which would benefit the estate. This may be different if the rights are granted against a licence fee that is unusually low, so that an insolvency administrator may be interested in licensing the rights to a third party for a higher licence fee.

### 2.3 Effects on licence agreements in the licensee's bankruptcy

The filing for insolvency does not have a direct impact on the licence agreement; the agreement is still enforceable. The grant of rights stays in place and the licensee continues to be obligated to pay the licence fee. Neither a termination nor a reversion of rights occurs.

Should the licensor wish to terminate the licence agreement, such a declaration is invalid if it is based on the licensee's default of payment or on a deterioration in the licensee's financial status.

### 2.4 Powers of administrators, receivers or trustees in the licensee's bankruptcy

The preliminary insolvency administrator (when ordered by the relevant insolvency court) may have control over whether the licensee pays the licence fee to the licensor. Such payments are often subject to being challenged if they are likely to have a negative impact on the debtor's estate. This means that, frequently, licence fee payments which were due to the licensor before the filing for insolvency and during the time of the preliminary proceedings are stopped. As explained in section 2.3, this does not justify the exercise of any termination right by the licensor.

As a result, the licence is 'frozen' during the time between filing and declaration of insolvency – ie, the licensor does not receive any more licence fee payments, and on the other hand it may not claim back any of the rights granted. The reason for this is that the law protects the estate during the phase of preliminary insolvency and prevents any loss of assets during this phase.

### 2.5 Impact of registration

While licence agreements for some intellectual property (IP) rights (particularly patents, community trademarks, community patents etc) are susceptible to registration under German or EU law, this has no effect on how they are treated in the phase between filing and the opening of insolvency proceedings.

## 3. Licence agreements in the phase after declaration of bankruptcy

### 3.1 Treatment of intellectual property rights

There is no distinction between different intellectual property rights in terms of how they are treated in an insolvency event.

### 3.2 Effects on licence agreements in the licensor's bankruptcy

If the contract is executory – ie, it has not been completely performed by either of the parties (so, for instance, the licence term is still continuing and licence fee payments are still due) – all rights and obligations by either party under the licence agreement become suspended from the time that licensor insolvency proceedings are opened. This means that a licensee no longer has a claim against the licensor for the grant of rights, and the licensor may not ask for payment. This unenforceability remains until the insolvency administrator chooses to reconfirm or reject the licence agreement.

The situation is different with licence agreements where at least one contracting party has entirely performed its obligations (a 'unilaterally executed' contract) – a licence agreement is not deemed executory if at least one party has fully performed its obligations. While it is generally held that the granting of a licence occurs over time and therefore is fully performed by the licensor only at the time that the licence period ends, the licensee may have fully performed the licence agreement by full payment of a (lump sum) licence fee before the opening of insolvency proceedings. In this case, the licence agreement is treated more like a purchase agreement: the licensor can keep the consideration that it has received from the licensee. However, the licensee can generally no longer use the right (though see section 3.9 below for possible exceptions). The licensee then has a damages claim against the estate, which is satisfied out of the quota attributed to each creditor.

The line between executory and unilaterally executed contracts is sometimes blurry as there are many cases where it is not clear whether licensor or licensee has fully performed its side of the transaction. This is particularly so when ancillary obligations continue to exist even after one party has essentially fulfilled the contract (eg, obligations to maintain the intellectual property, delivery of physical material, etc).

### 3.3 Powers of an administrator, receiver or trustee in the licensor's bankruptcy

If the licence agreement is executory – ie, it has not been entirely performed by either the licensor or the licensee, the insolvency administrator may elect to perform the licence agreement and thus ask for the payment of the licence fee from the licensee. Otherwise, the licence agreement remains suspended and the licensee can only seek damages from the estate (which have the same rank as other insolvency obligations that are satisfied in proportion to the remaining assets of the debtor – ie, usually to a small degree).

The licensee may require the insolvency administrator to exercise the right to confirm or reject the licence agreement. The insolvency administrator must respond without undue delay. If the insolvency administrator fails to respond in a timely fashion, the contract is deemed rejected and no longer has any effect.

If the insolvency administrator elects performance of the licence agreement, the agreement must be performed. The insolvency administrator may claim from the licensee the full consideration, including licence fees that were due before the opening of insolvency proceedings.

### 3.4 Powers and rights of creditors in a licensor's bankruptcy

The creditors do not have a direct say in the fate of a licence agreement. Although the creditors are organised in a creditor assembly and creditor committee, the insolvency administrator is free to determine whether to confirm or reject a licence agreement after the opening of insolvency proceedings.

### 3.5 Effects on licence agreements in the licensee's bankruptcy

As explained in section 3.2 above, executory agreements become suspended upon the opening of insolvency proceedings. This means that the licensor's and the licensee's obligations become unenforceable. This continues until the insolvency administrator decides whether the contract shall be continued or terminated.

Contracts that have been performed by at least one contracting party do not have that effect. If, for example, the licensee has prepaid the total licence fee before insolvency, it continues to be able to make use of the right granted by the licensor. So while the advance that is paid by the licensee to an insolvent licensor is lost, an insolvent licensee can still make use of the right licensed by the licensor.

### 3.6 Powers of an administrator, receiver or trustee in the licensee's bankruptcy

As explained in section 3.3 above, the performance of executory agreements is subject to the insolvency administrator's right of confirmation or rejection. This applies to licence agreements where the licensee has not fully paid the licence fee owed over the duration of the contract.

An insolvency administrator seeking to liquidate the company will attempt to liberate the estate from further money obligations and thus will choose rejection of the licence agreement. In that case, the licensor must file its claim with the insolvency administrator for it to be included in the schedule of claims. The rights revert to the licensor upon rejection of the contract. In the case that the licensee has partially prepaid the use of the right before insolvency, the licensee is entitled to make use of the right for the whole period for which the prepayment relates.

If the insolvency administrator, in contrast, confirms the licence agreement, the licence fee must be paid out of the estate and the insolvency administrator is personally liable for performance thereof. The insolvency administrator will choose this option if the licensed right is vital for the operation of the business that the insolvency administrator intends to maintain. The insolvency administrator's obligation to pay the licence fee does not, however, extend to payments that became due before the opening of insolvency proceedings. If the licensor was entitled to licence fees that predated the insolvency proceedings and which were not paid, these need to be registered as ordinary insolvency claims against the estate.

In scenarios of at least unilateral performance in full by one party, the insolvency administrator has no powers over the licence agreement. This happens, for example, in situations where the licensee has fully prepaid the licence fee before the opening of insolvency proceedings. Then, the rights continue to be granted for the full duration of the contract, and the licensor may not revoke the rights or terminate the agreement.

### 3.7 Powers and rights of creditors in a licensee's bankruptcy

As explained in section 3.4 above, the creditors have no direct influence on the fate of the licence agreement. Usually, however, the insolvency administrator will consult with the creditors' representative(s) before exercising the right of upholding or rejecting a licence agreement that is vital to the debtor's business.

### 3.8 Exclusive and non-exclusive licences

Germany's insolvency law does not draw a distinction between exclusive and non-exclusive licences in insolvency scenarios.

### 3.9 Perpetual and non-perpetual licences

Whether the licence granted is perpetual or non-perpetual may make a difference for the qualification of executory versus executed licence agreements. If the licence is perpetual, the agreement is more likely to be deemed as executed, similar to a sales agreement. This means that a licensor may have fully performed its obligation under the licence agreement when granting a perpetual licence.

If this has occurred before the insolvency but the licensee has failed to pay the licence fee, in a licensor's insolvency the insolvency administrator would be able to recover the full licence fee; in a licensee's insolvency, the licensor's claim for the payment of the licence fee is a mere claim against the estate. If the licensee has already paid before insolvency for a perpetual licence, the contract is deemed fully executed and thus the insolvency has no impact on the contract.

### 3.10 Effects on a sub-licence in a licensor's bankruptcy

A licensor's bankruptcy can have an effect on a sub-licence. A licence agreement may tie the granting of the sub-licence to the main agreement, so that the sub-licence is either extinguished or upheld when the main licence agreement is terminated, depending on what was stipulated in the licence agreement. If there is no provision in the agreement, case law suggests that the sub-licence is more likely to survive the licensor's bankruptcy.

### 3.11 Effects on a sub-licence in a licensee's bankruptcy

The position set out in section 3.10 above would also be the case in a licensee's bankruptcy. Subject to the interpretation of the relevant provisions in the licence agreement, the sub-licence is more likely to survive the licensee's insolvency.

For executory contracts which the insolvency administrator rejects, the sub-licensee then becomes a direct licensee of the licensor and the licensor steps into the licensee's contractual position. The licence agreement then continues to be enforceable between these two parties.

### 3.12 Impact of registration

While licence agreements for some IP rights (particularly patents, community trademarks, community patents, etc) are susceptible to registration under German or EU law, this has no effect on how they are treated in an insolvency scenario. The registration only serves as a means of creating publicity for the licence holder but has no impact on the rights of the parties in an insolvency.

## 4. Contractual arrangements in deviation from the law

### 4.1 Exceptions

Special rules apply for publishing agreements between authors and publishers. The

Publishing Act accords to the author, if the publisher becomes insolvent, a right of revocation until the publisher has commenced reproduction (ie, printing) of the work. The Publishing Act also provides protection to the author if the publishing rights are sold by the insolvency administrator to another company. In that case, not only is the estate liable for the author's remuneration but also the entity to which the publishing agreements have been transferred.

### 4.2 Scope to alter statutory mechanisms

The extent to which statutory mechanisms can be altered by contractual agreement is heavily disputed in Germany. The majority opinion is that the possibilities of altering the statutory mechanisms are extremely limited, arguing mainly that the interests of the creditors deserve priority over the interests of a single contracting party. The insolvency administrator's right to choose between performance and non-performance of an executory contract cannot be restricted by contractual arrangement.

### 4.3 Termination rights and automatic reversions

Although the topic of termination rights and automatic reversions is heavily disputed under German law, the majority opinion treats the statutory rules as mandatory. Termination rights or automatic reversions in the event that insolvency is filed or declared with respect to the other contracting party are normally deemed invalid because they interfere with the insolvency administrator's right to administer the estate.

Some quite complex work-arounds have, nevertheless, meanwhile been accepted by the courts, particularly in relation to the protection of licensees' interests. The general rule is, however, that in a licensor's insolvency the licensee is at the insolvency administrator's mercy if the administrator intends to keep the licence that it has obtained.

## 5. Cross-border aspects

### 5.1 Foreign law

An insolvency administrator is generally bound by the election of a foreign law in the licence agreement when seeking to enforce rights under the contract. This, however, has no effect on the rights or mechanisms of the German insolvency laws, which are mandatory and apply to all insolvencies that are opened in Germany (ie, where the insolvent party is located in Germany). The insolvency administrator's choice between upholding or cancelling an agreement is thus mandatory and cannot be ruled out by electing a foreign law.

### 5.2 Foreign jurisdiction

An insolvency administrator is generally bound by the choice of a foreign forum. However, EU Regulation 1346/2000 on Insolvency Proceedings specifies certain exceptions – for instance, the enforcement of clawback provisions against a party. These can be initiated in the court of the place where the insolvency proceedings have been opened. In general, however, the insolvency administrator can only enforce rights under the licence agreements at the place that is specified in the contract. The insolvency administrator is also bound by any arbitration clauses.

# Hong Kong

**Mark Bedford**
**Kevin Lee**
Boughton Peterson Yang Anderson in association with Zhong Lun Law Firm

## 1. Overview

### 1.1 Relevant legislation governing intellectual property and bankruptcy

In Hong Kong, the legislation governing intellectual property is found in several ordinances, the principal ones being the Trade Marks Ordinance, the Patents Ordinance, the Copyright Ordinance and the Registered Designs Ordinance.

Two government agencies, the Intellectual Property Department and the Customs and Excise Department, administer intellectual property law in Hong Kong. Trademarks, patents and designs may be registered with the Intellectual Property Department to obtain protection against infringement. The Customs and Excise Department enforces criminal sanctions against copyright and trademark infringement.

The term 'bankruptcy' is generally used in Hong Kong in relation to insolvent individuals, including sole proprietors and partners of firms, but not in the context of corporate insolvency. When a limited company is insolvent, an application may be made to 'wind up' the company. This is also referred to as putting the company into liquidation.

The main legislation governing bankruptcy is the Bankruptcy Ordinance, and for corporate insolvency it is the Companies (Winding Up and Miscellaneous Provisions) Ordinance[1] and the Companies (Winding-up) Rules. Save for a brief explanation in section 1.2 below of the different bankruptcy procedures, this chapter will focus on corporate insolvency.

Hong Kong's insolvency legislation does not contain provisions which address specifically the insolvency of a licensor or a licensee.

### 1.2 Types of insolvency procedure

#### *(a) Bankruptcy (individuals)*

Under the Bankruptcy Ordinance, a bankruptcy order can be made after a

1 Corporate insolvency was previously dealt with in the Companies Ordinance, but this has been replaced by a new Companies Ordinance which came into operation in March 2014. This new Companies Ordinance does not deal with the winding-up of companies, which is still covered by the existing Companies Ordinance, now renamed the Companies (Winding up and Miscellaneous Provisions) Ordinance. It is expected that proposed new legislation regarding the winding-up of companies will be enacted by Hong Kong's Legislative Council before July 2016, which is when the Legislative Council's current term ends.

bankruptcy petition is filed with the court either by a creditor or by the debtor himself. There is also a procedure called an Individual Voluntary Arrangement (IVA), which provides an alternative to bankruptcy for an individual debtor.

A creditor may file a petition for a bankruptcy order to be made against an individual, a firm or a partnership, in respect of a debt of HK$10,000 (around US$1,300) or more, which the debtor either appears to be unable to pay or to have no reasonable prospect of being able to pay.[2]

A debtor may himself file a petition for bankruptcy if he is unable to pay his debts, whether his indebtedness is greater or smaller than HK$10,000. A debtor's petition must be accompanied by a sworn statement of affairs containing particulars of his creditors, his debts and other liabilities, and his assets.[3]

Upon hearing either a creditor's or debtor's petition, if the court makes a bankruptcy order against the debtor, the Official Receiver (the civil service official responsible for administering court insolvencies for both bankruptcies and the compulsory liquidation of companies) will become the provisional trustee of the bankrupt's assets.[4] The trustee will realise the bankrupt's assets and if, after the deduction of fees and expenses, there are funds remaining in the bankrupt's estate, the trustee will pay a dividend to the bankrupt's creditors.

An IVA enables a debtor to make a repayment proposal to the court and his creditors, which, if approved by 75% (in value) of the creditors, will become legally binding on all of them.

### *(b) Insolvency (companies)*

There are five main 'insolvency' procedures for companies in Hong Kong, although it is not necessary for a company to be insolvent for some of the procedures to be implemented. The main procedures (further outlined below) are:

- compulsory liquidation;
- a creditors' voluntary liquidation;
- a members' voluntary liquidation;
- a scheme of arrangement; and
- appointment of a receiver.

There are several grounds upon which the court can order the winding-up of a company in a compulsory liquidation, including that the company is unable to pay its debts (ie, it is insolvent).[5] Similarly, in a creditors' voluntary liquidation a company elects to put itself into liquidation because it is insolvent or in financial difficulties. However, in a members' voluntary liquidation, the shareholders decide to put the company into liquidation while the company is still solvent – for example, a members' voluntary winding-up may be implemented as part of a group restructuring.

A company that is liable to be wound up under the Companies (Winding Up and Miscellaneous Provisions) Ordinance can enter into a scheme of arrangement with

2 Section 6 of the Bankruptcy Ordinance.
3 Section 10 of the Bankruptcy Ordinance.
4 Section 12 of the Bankruptcy Ordinance.
5 Section 177(1)(d) of the Companies (Winding Up and Miscellaneous Provisions) Ordinance.

its creditors. On application by the company, by its creditors or (if a winding-up procedure has already started) by the liquidator, the court may order that a meeting of the creditors be held; and if a majority in number representing at least 75% (in value) of the creditors present and voting agree to the proposal, and the court sanctions it, the scheme of arrangement will be binding on all the creditors.[6]

A receiver is usually appointed under a debenture holder's security document, but may also be appointed by the court in all cases in which it appears to the court to be just and convenient to do so.[7] The extent of the receiver's powers is determined by the security document or the court order pursuant to which the receiver is appointed; but if the receiver is appointed under a security document following an event of default, the role is likely to be to collect and realise the assets which comprise the security in order to pay the security holder. If it is still able to, the company might then continue trading; but if it is insolvent, a creditor of the company itself may apply to wind up the company.

Hong Kong does not have an equivalent to the US Bankruptcy Code Chapter 11 reorganisation procedure for businesses, nor to the 'administration' procedure in England and Wales. The scheme of arrangement is the only procedure that Hong Kong has which aims to rescue companies.

### 1.3 Grounds for winding up a company

Note that this section and section 1.5 do not deal with a members' voluntary liquidation, as this type of liquidation is not based on a company being insolvent.

#### *(a) Compulsory liquidation*

Section 177(1) of the Companies (Winding Up and Miscellaneous Provisions) Ordinance specifies six grounds for winding up a company in a compulsory liquidation, including (Section 177(1)(d)) that the company is unable to pay its debts. In this context a company will be deemed to be unable to pay its debts if:

- a creditor to whom the company is indebted in a sum of HK$10,000 or more has served a statutory demand on the company requiring it to pay the debt and the company has for three weeks thereafter neglected to pay the sum, or to secure or compound for it to the reasonable satisfaction of the creditor;
- execution or other process issued on a judgment, decree or order of any court in favour of a creditor of the company is returned unsatisfied (in whole or in part); or
- it is proved to the satisfaction of the court that the company is unable to pay its debts, taking into account the contingent and prospective liabilities of the company.[8]

However, the court will not make a winding-up order if the debt is the subject of a *bona fide* dispute on substantial grounds.

---

6 Sections 673 and 674 of the Companies Ordinance.
7 Section 21L of the High Court Ordinance.
8 Section 178(1) of the Companies (Winding Up and Miscellaneous Provisions) Ordinance.

### (b) *Creditors' voluntary liquidation*

A company can put itself into voluntary liquidation by the company's shareholders passing (by not less than 75% of the votes cast) a special resolution to wind up the company.[9] The directors of the company may propose this course to the shareholders if they do not think the company will be able to trade out of its financial difficulties.

Further, under section 228A of the Companies (Winding Up and Miscellaneous Provisions) Ordinance the directors can themselves start a voluntary liquidation and appoint a provisional liquidator without consulting the shareholders if they resolve at a directors' meeting and deliver to the Registrar of Companies a statement, signed by one of the directors, certifying that a resolution has been passed to the effect that:

- the company cannot by reason of its liabilities continue its business;
- the directors consider that it is not reasonably practicable for the company to be wound up under another section of the Companies (Winding Up and Miscellaneous Provisions) Ordinance; and
- meetings of the shareholders and the company's creditors will be held within 28 days after the delivery of the winding-up statement to the registrar.[10]

## 1.4 Filing for the winding-up of a company

A winding-up petition may be presented to the court by the company, a creditor or, in certain circumstances, a contributory (ie, a person liable to contribute to the assets of a company in the event of its being wound up, which normally includes all shareholders if the company has standard share capital), the Financial Secretary of Hong Kong, the Registrar of Companies or the Official Receiver.[11] In most cases a winding-up application will be made by a creditor or the company.

Winding-up petitions are filed with and heard by Hong Kong's Court of First Instance.

In a creditors' voluntary liquidation (or a members' voluntary liquidation), the shareholders of the company make the decision to wind up the company, although in certain circumstances a creditors' voluntary liquidation can be commenced by the company's directors.

## 1.5 Administrators and other appointed persons

### (a) *Compulsory liquidation*

If a court, on hearing a winding-up petition, is satisfied that one of the grounds specified in Section 177(1) of the Companies (Winding Up and Miscellaneous Provisions) Ordinance applies, and makes a winding-up order, the Official Receiver is then automatically appointed as the provisional liquidator of the company, and continues in that role until he or another person is appointed as the liquidator.[12]

However, if a creditor is concerned that the assets of the company might be misappropriated or wasted before the hearing of the petition, that creditor can ask

9 Section 228 of the Companies (Winding Up and Miscellaneous Provisions) Ordinance.
10 Section 228A of the Companies (Winding Up and Miscellaneous Provisions) Ordinance.
11 Section 179 of the Companies (Winding Up and Miscellaneous Provisions) Ordinance.
12 Section 194(1) of the Companies (Winding Up and Miscellaneous Provisions) Ordinance.

the court to appoint a provisional liquidator at any time after the presentation of the petition, in order to protect the company's assets until the petition has been heard by the court.[13]

The liquidator's role is to take possession of the company's assets, investigate the company's affairs, realise the assets and, where possible, pay a dividend to creditors.

### *(b) Creditors' voluntary winding-up*

If the directors of a company start a creditors' winding-up pursuant to section 228A of the Companies (Winding Up and Miscellaneous Provisions) Ordinance, the winding-up of the company commences from their delivery of the winding-up statement to the registrar, and the directors are then empowered to appoint a person to be the provisional liquidator.[14]

Otherwise, at the meeting where the shareholders resolve to wind up the company, the shareholders will nominate a liquidator. However, a meeting of the company's creditors must be held on the same day as the shareholders' meeting (or on the following day) and the creditors may agree to the appointment of the shareholders' nominee as liquidator, or nominate a different person to act as liquidator.[15] In the event of the shareholders and creditors nominating different people to be the liquidator, the creditors' nominee will be appointed.

The role of the liquidator is essentially the same as in a compulsory liquidation, ie to realise the company's assets and, where possible, pay a dividend to creditors, and to investigate the company's affairs.

## 2. Licence agreements in the phase between filing a winding-up petition and the making of a winding-up order

### 2.1 Effects on licence agreements in the licensor's winding-up

Between the filing of a winding-up petition and the making of a winding-up order, a licence agreement will remain valid and enforceable, unless the licence agreement provides that it shall be automatically terminated upon the presentation of a winding-up petition.

However, any disposition of the property of the company, including contractual rights, made after the commencement of the winding-up (which is deemed to be at the time of the filing of the winding-up petition[16]) will, unless the court otherwise orders, be void.[17] Accordingly, a licensor would not, without the court's approval, be able to assign a licence after a winding-up petition had been filed against it.

### 2.2 Powers of a liquidator in the licensor's winding-up

A liquidator will usually be appointed only once a winding-up order has been made, upon the hearing of a winding-up petition.

---

13 Section 193 of the Companies (Winding Up and Miscellaneous Provisions) Ordinance.
14 Section 228A(5)(a) of the Companies (Winding Up and Miscellaneous Provisions) Ordinance.
15 Section 241 of the Companies (Winding Up and Miscellaneous Provisions) Ordinance.
16 Section 184 of the Companies (Winding Up and Miscellaneous Provisions) Ordinance.
17 Section 182 of the Companies (Winding Up and Miscellaneous Provisions) Ordinance.

However, a provisional liquidator can be appointed by the court at any time after the presentation of a winding-up petition, and will usually be appointed if a creditor is concerned that the company's assets may be dissipated or wasted before the hearing.[18] A provisional liquidator's powers are, though, limited to those set out in the order under which he is appointed.

A provisional liquidator's main objective is to preserve the value of the company's assets, and his powers will typically not include the power to dispose of the company's assets. If a provisional liquidator wished to sell the rights granted under the licence, he would normally have to make an application to the court for approval to do so.

If the provisional liquidator wished to terminate a licence – for example, when the licensee has failed to pay the licence fee – the provisional liquidator's power to do so would depend on the terms of the licence agreement.

### 2.3 Effects on licence agreements in the licensee's winding-up

Between the filing of a winding-up petition and the making of a winding-up order, a licence agreement will remain valid and enforceable, unless the licence agreement provides that it shall be automatically terminated upon the presentation of a winding-up petition.

However, any disposition of the property of the company, including contractual rights, made after the commencement of the winding-up (which is deemed to be at the time of the filing of the winding-up petition[19]) will, unless the court otherwise orders, be void.[20]

### 2.4 Powers of a liquidator in the licensee's winding-up

A liquidator will usually be appointed only once a winding-up order has been made upon the hearing of a winding-up petition.

However, a provisional liquidator can be appointed by the court at any time after the presentation of a winding-up petition, and would usually be appointed if a creditor is concerned that the company's assets may be dissipated or wasted before the hearing of the winding-up petition.[21] The provisional liquidator's powers are, though, limited to those set out in the order under which he is appointed.

A provisional liquidator's main objective is to preserve the value of the company's assets, and his powers will typically not include the power to dispose of the company's assets. If a provisional liquidator wishes to sell a licence (assuming the terms of the licence permit this), he must normally have to make an application to the court for approval to do so.

### 2.5 Impact of registration

In the case of a licence to use a registered trademark, the grant of such a licence is a registrable transaction under the Trade Marks Ordinance, and until an application has been made for registration of the grant of the licence, the licence is ineffective

---

18 Section 193 of the Companies (Winding Up and Miscellaneous Provisions) Ordinance.
19 Section 184 of the Companies (Winding Up and Miscellaneous Provisions) Ordinance.
20 Section 182 of the Companies (Winding Up and Miscellaneous Provisions) Ordinance.
21 Section 193 of the Companies (Winding Up and Miscellaneous Provisions) Ordinance.

against a person acquiring a conflicting interest in or under the registered trademark in ignorance of the licence.[22] Accordingly, if a licensee fails to register its licence, and a provisional liquidator sells the trademark to a third party, the rights granted by the licence would be ineffective against the third party.

There are similar provisions in the Registered Designs Ordinance[23] and the Patents Ordinance[24] regarding the registration of a grant of a licence under a registered design or under a patent.

## 3. Licence agreements in the phase after a winding-up order is made

### 3.1 Treatment of intellectual property rights

There is no distinction between different intellectual property rights in terms of how they are treated in the event of the winding-up of a company.

### 3.2 Effects on licence agreements in the licensor's winding-up

Once a winding-up order has been made (or where a provisional liquidator has been appointed), the liquidator or the provisional liquidator takes into his custody, or under his control, all the property and things in action to which the company is, or appears to be, entitled,[25] which includes a licensor's rights and obligations under a licence agreement.

A licence agreement will not by law automatically terminate upon a winding-up order being made unless there is express provision in the licence agreement that it should do so.

### 3.3 Powers of a liquidator in the licensor's winding-up

Assuming the licence agreement does not provide for it to be terminated upon a winding-up order being made against the licensor, a liquidator of a licensor may elect to continue to enforce the licence agreement, but his ultimate aim will usually be to sell the rights which are the subject of the licence.

Nonetheless, a liquidator also has the right, with the leave of the court, to disclaim 'onerous property', including unprofitable contracts and any property that is unsaleable, or not readily saleable, by reason of it binding the possessor to the performance of any onerous act or to the payment of any sum of money.[26] And an intellectual property licence could be regarded as 'onerous property' if, for example, the licensor was required to pay renewal fees in respect of the intellectual property right.

Such a disclaimer by the liquidator will determine the rights, interest and liabilities of the company in respect of the onerous property, but will not affect the rights or liabilities of any other person except in so far as is necessary to release the company and its property from liability.[27]

---

22 Section 29(3)(a) of the Trade Marks Ordinance.
23 See Section 34 of the Registered Designs Ordinance.
24 See Section 52 of the Patents Ordinance.
25 Section 197 of the Companies (Winding Up and Miscellaneous Provisions) Ordinance.
26 Section 268 of the Companies (Winding Up and Miscellaneous Provisions) Ordinance.
27 Section 268(2) of the Companies (Winding Up and Miscellaneous Provisions) Ordinance.

Any person injured by the operation of a disclaimer (including, potentially, a licensee) is deemed to be a creditor of the company to the amount of the injury, and he may prove such amount as a debt in the winding-up of the company.[28]

Further, a person who either claims an interest in any disclaimed property, or is under any liability not discharged by the Companies (Winding Up and Miscellaneous Provisions) Ordinance in respect of any disclaimed property, can apply to the court for an order that the property be transferred to it on such terms as the court thinks fit.[29] Consequently, a licensee of an intellectual property licence disclaimed by the liquidator could apply to the court for an order that the ownership of the intellectual property rights be transferred to that licensee.

### 3.4 Powers and rights of creditors in a licensor's winding-up

A licensor's creditors do not have powers or rights with regard to the licence agreement. However, creditors may, through a 'committee of inspection', influence certain decisions that a liquidator might take in relation to a licence agreement. When a winding-up order has been made, one of the matters to be decided at the meeting of creditors is whether to appoint a committee of inspection,[30] made up of five or six creditors (and possibly shareholders) to help and guide the liquidator in the exercise of his duties.

If a committee of inspection was appointed and the committee suggested, for example, that the liquidator should (or should not) sell intellectual property rights that were the subject of a licence, then even though a liquidator is not bound to follow the committee's wishes, it would be unusual for the liquidator to act against such wishes.

### 3.5 Effects on licence agreements in the licensee's winding-up

Once a winding-up order has been made (or where a provisional liquidator has been appointed), the liquidator or the provisional liquidator takes into his custody or control all the property and things in action to which the company is, or appears to be, entitled,[31] which includes a licensee's rights and obligations under a licence agreement.

A licence agreement will not automatically terminate unless there is express provision in the licence agreement that it should do so – although a licensor will usually have such a right upon a winding-up order being made against a licensee.

### 3.6 Powers of a liquidator in the licensee's winding-up

In the unlikely event that the licence agreement does not provide for it to be terminated upon a winding-up order being made against the licensee, and does not prohibit the licensee from using the rights granted by the licence when the licensee is being wound up, the liquidator could continue to use the rights granted by the licence during the winding-up of the licensee.

---

28 Section 268(7) of the Companies (Winding Up and Miscellaneous Provisions) Ordinance.
29 Section 268(6) of the Companies (Winding Up and Miscellaneous Provisions) Ordinance.
30 See Section 206(1) of the Companies (Winding Up and Miscellaneous Provisions) Ordinance.
31 Section 197 of the Companies (Winding Up and Miscellaneous Provisions) Ordinance.

A liquidator also has the right, with the leave of the court, to disclaim 'onerous property under Section 268 of the Companies (Winding Up and Miscellaneous Provisions) Ordinance (see section 3.3 above). An intellectual property licence could be regarded as 'onerous property' if the licensee is required to pay royalties to use the rights granted under the licence. Such a disclaimer by the liquidator will determine the rights, interest and liabilities of the company in respect of the onerous property, but will not affect the rights or liabilities of any other person except in so far as is necessary to release the company and its property from liability.[32]

Any person injured by the operation of a disclaimer (eg, a sub-licensee or a licensor) is deemed to be a creditor of the company to the amount of the injury, and he may prove such amount as a debt in the winding-up of the company.[33]

### 3.7 Powers and rights of creditors in a licensee's winding-up

A licensee's creditors do not have powers or rights with regard to the licence agreement. However, creditors may, through a 'committee of inspection', influence certain decisions which a liquidator might take in relation to a licence agreement – see section 3.4 above.

### 3.8 Exclusive and non-exclusive licences

There is no distinction in Hong Kong between exclusive and non-exclusive licences in the event of the winding-up of a licensor or a licensee.

### 3.9 Perpetual and non-perpetual licences

There is no distinction in Hong Kong between a perpetual licence (where the whole of the licence fee is paid upfront) and a non-perpetual licence in the event of the winding-up of a licensor or a licensee.

Where the whole licence fee has been paid upfront, whether the licence could be terminated or whether any part of the fee could be recoverable by the licensee will depend on the terms of the licence agreement.

### 3.10 Effects on a sub-licence in a licensor's winding-up

In the event of a winding-up order being made against a licensor, the effect on a sub-licence will depend on the terms of the licence agreement between the licensor and the licensee, the terms of the sub-licence and what the liquidator decides to do with the licence and/or the rights granted under it (eg, disclaim the licence as 'onerous property').

The sub-licence would not automatically be terminated in these circumstances unless there was a provision in the licence or sub-licence to that effect.

### 3.11 Effects on a sub-licence in a licensee's winding-up

In the winding-up of a licensee, the effect on a sub-licence would depend on the terms of the licence and the sub-licence, and whether the licensee disclaimed the licence as 'onerous property'.

---

32 Section 268(2) of the Companies (Winding Up and Miscellaneous Provisions) Ordinance.
33 Section 268(7) of the Companies (Winding Up and Miscellaneous Provisions) Ordinance.

A licensor will usually have the right to terminate a licence if a winding-up order is made against a licensee, and the licence may further provide that the sub-licence is automatically terminated if the licence is terminated.

### 3.12 Impact of registration

In the case of a licence to use a registered trademark, the grant of such a licence is a registrable transaction under the Trade Marks Ordinance; until an application has been made for registration of the grant of the licence, the licence is ineffective against a person acquiring a conflicting interest in or under the registered trademark in ignorance of the licence.[34] Accordingly, if a licensee fails to register its licence and a liquidator sells the trademark to a third party, the rights granted by the licence would be ineffective against the third party.

In the Trade Marks Ordinance, a 'licence' includes a 'sub-licence', and failure to register a sub-licence will have the same consequences as for a licence.

There are similar provisions in the Registered Designs Ordinance and the Patents Ordinance, where a 'licence' also includes a 'sub-licence'.

## 4. Contractual arrangements in deviation from the law

### 4.1 Exceptions

There are no types of licence agreement relating to intellectual property that are subject to a different regime from other licence agreements in an insolvency situation.

### 4.2 Scope to alter statutory mechanisms

A Hong Kong company cannot contract out of the provisions of the Companies (Winding Up and Miscellaneous Provisions) Ordinance regarding the winding-up of companies. However, since this ordinance does not address specifically what is to happen to a licence agreement in the event that a winding-up order is made against a licensor or a licensee, as long as the parties to a licence agreement do not contravene the provisions of this ordinance regarding the winding-up of companies, they can stipulate what should happen to the rights granted under the licence if a winding-up order is made against the licensor or licensee.

### 4.3 Termination rights and automatic reversions

A licensor and a licensee can agree that if a winding-up order is made against the licensee, the licensor may terminate the licence agreement. Equally, they can agree that the rights granted under the licence will in those circumstances automatically revert to the licensor.

## 5. Cross-border aspects

### 5.1 Foreign law

The Hong Kong courts will generally respect the parties' express choice of a foreign

---

34 Section 29(3)(a) of the Trade Marks Ordinance.

law to govern a licence agreement – exceptions would be, for example, where the choice of law was a sham or not sufficiently certain to be enforceable. A liquidator would likewise respect such a choice of governing law as it applied to the rights and obligations of the parties. However, if the licensor/licensee is a Hong Kong company and has a winding-up order made against it, that company would still be subject to the provisions of the Companies (Winding Up and Miscellaneous Provisions) Ordinance regarding the winding-up of a company.

### 5.2 Foreign jurisdiction

The Hong Kong courts would respect a choice of foreign jurisdiction in a licence agreement, so that a foreign court would be able to determine disputes between the parties.

However, in an insolvency context, if a licensor/licensee is a Hong Kong company, a foreign court would not be able to wind up the licensor/licensee because the Companies (Winding Up and Miscellaneous Provisions) Ordinance gives the Hong Kong Court of First Instance exclusive jurisdiction to wind up a Hong Kong company.[35]

---

35 Section 176 of the Companies (Winding Up and Miscellaneous Provisions) Ordinance.

# Hungary

**Gusztáv Bacher**
**Gabor Faludi**
**Dávid Kerpel**
Szecskay Attorneys at Law

---

## 1. Overview

### 1.1 Relevant legislation governing intellectual property and bankruptcy

Set out below is a short summary of relevant legislation regarding intellectual property and bankruptcy/liquidation procedures.

#### *(a) Intellectual property*

There are four relevant pieces of primary legislation:

- Copyright: Act LXXVI of 1999 on Copyright (hereinafter the Copyright Act);
- Patents: Act XXXIII of 1995 on the Patent Protection of Inventions (hereinafter the Patent Act);
- Trademarks: Act XI of 1997 on Trademarks (hereinafter the Trademark Act); and
- Designs: Act LXVIII of 2001 on Designs (hereinafter the Designs Act).

#### *(b) Bankruptcy*

Bankruptcy (reorganisation) and liquidation procedures are governed by Act XLIX of 1991 on Bankruptcy and Liquidation Proceedings (hereinafter the Bankruptcy Act) and European Council Regulation 1346/2000 of May 29 2000 on Insolvency Proceedings. In addition, special rules having a bearing in this context are included in Act CXXXII of 1997 on Hungarian Branch Offices and Commercial Representative Offices of Foreign-Registered Companies.

### 1.2 Types of insolvency procedure

The two main types of insolvency procedure in Hungary are, as stated above, bankruptcy procedures and liquidation procedures. For the purposes of this chapter we will only examine these two main types of insolvency procedure.

Bankruptcy procedures are generally aimed at the reorganisation of the debtor, whereby the court will grant a temporary moratorium for the debtor during which it shall attempt to reach a settlement with its creditors. If the reorganisation is successful and the claim of the creditors can be satisfied, the debtor may continue to operate.

Liquidation procedures are aimed at the dissolution of an insolvent debtor as its debts exceed its assets. In the case of liquidation, all the assets of the debtor are sold and the income deriving from this process is divided among the creditors. The debtor is subsequently dissolved.

## 1.3 Grounds of bankruptcy

### (a) *Bankruptcy*

Upon formal analysis of a debtor's request, the court automatically orders a temporary moratorium. The quota holders or shareholders (as appropriate) of the company must give their prior approval to the application.

The debtor may not file a petition for bankruptcy if it is already under bankruptcy, or if a request for its liquidation has been submitted and a decision has already been adopted in the first instance for the debtor's liquidation. The debtor may not file another petition for bankruptcy:

- before the satisfaction of any creditor's claim that existed at the time of ordering the previous bankruptcy proceedings or that was established by such proceedings; and
- inside a period of two years following the time of publication of the final and definitive conclusion of the previous bankruptcy proceedings; or
- if the court *ex officio* refused the debtor's request for the previous bankruptcy proceedings, and if it is inside the one-year period following the time of publication of the final ruling thereof.

### (b) *Liquidation*

The court has the power to order a liquidation procedure if a debtor is insolvent. The court will declare a debtor insolvent if at least one of the following holds:

- The debtor fails to settle or contest its previously uncontested and acknowledged contractual debts within 20 days of the due date, and fails to satisfy such debt upon receipt of the creditor's written payment notice.
- The debtor fails to settle its debt within the deadline specified in a final court decision or order for payment.
- An enforcement procedure against the debtor has been unsuccessful.
- The debtor did not fulfil its payment obligation as stipulated in a settlement agreement concluded in bankruptcy or liquidation proceedings.
- The debtor has declared the previous bankruptcy proceedings terminated.
- The debtor's liabilities in proceedings initiated by the debtor or by the receiver exceed the debtor's assets, or the debtor is unable and is presumed not to be able to settle its debts on the date when they are due, and in proceedings opened by the receiver the members (shareholders) of the debtor (as an economic operator) fail to provide a statement of commitment – following due notice – to guarantee the funds necessary to cover such debts when due.

In the first two sets of circumstances listed above, a request for the debtor's liquidation may be submitted if the amount of the claim (not including interest and similar charges) is more than HUF200,000 (approximately €640).

## 1.4 Filing for bankruptcy

Bankruptcy proceedings may be launched by the debtor's executive officer with the approval of the quota holders or shareholders (as appropriate) of the debtor.

A liquidation proceeding may be launched:

- by a court, upon an unsuccessful bankruptcy proceeding;
- by a creditor or the receiver, upon request of the debtor;
- upon receipt of notice from the court of registry, if the court of registry has ordered the liquidation of the company; or
- upon receipt of notice from a criminal court (if the enforcement procedure aiming for the collection of a fine imposed upon a legal person has failed).

Bankruptcy and liquidation proceedings are non-contentious proceedings conducted by the county courts, which possess jurisdiction by reference to the debtor's registered office.

### 1.5 Administrators and other appointed persons

The receiver (in a case of bankruptcy) or the liquidator (in a case of liquidation) is appointed by the court in its order on the commencement of the respective procedure. However, in the case of liquidation procedures and according to the Bankruptcy Act, simultaneously with lodging a request for the opening of liquidation proceedings, or subsequently before the time of the opening of liquidation proceedings, creditors may request the court to appoint a temporary administrator as well.

In the event of bankruptcy, the receiver monitors the debtor's business activities with a view to protecting the creditors' interests and making preparations for a 'composition' with creditors. Accordingly, the receiver will, among other things:

- review the debtor's financial standing;
- carry out – assisted by the debtor itself – tasks relating to the registration and categorisation of claims; and
- approve and endorse any financial commitment of the debtor after the time of the opening of bankruptcy proceedings.

In the event of a liquidation, the liquidator will, among other things:

- analyse the financial standing of the economic operator and the claims against it;
- prepare an opening liquidation account, estimate the costs of liquidation and set up a timetable for its implementation; and
- register and categorise the creditor's claims.

## 2. Licence agreements in the phase between filing and declaration of bankruptcy

### 2.1 Effects on licence agreements in the licensor's bankruptcy

As the bankruptcy or liquidation procedure is ordered by the court, the simple filing as part of such a procedure generally does not affect the validity of a licence agreement or its enforceability. It is possible, nonetheless, that the parties will have in their agreement a provision whereby the mere filing may be a cause for unilateral termination.

### 2.2 Powers of administrators, receivers or trustees in the licensor's bankruptcy

According to the Bankruptcy Act, simultaneously with lodging a request for the opening of liquidation proceedings, or subsequently before the time of the opening of liquidation proceedings, creditors may request the court to appoint a temporary administrator from the register of liquidators to oversee the debtor's financial management.

If such a temporary administrator is appointed, the head of the debtor shall be restricted from entering into any contract considered to be in excess of the scope of normal operations where the economic operator's assets are concerned without the prior consent and endorsement of the temporary administrator, or from entering into any other commitment, including where the debtor is compelled to perform under an existing contract. Thus, the temporary administrator is not entitled independently either to terminate a licence agreement or to sell any assets (including intellectual property rights) of the debtor.

The temporary administrator has authority to monitor the debtor's business activities with a view to protecting creditors' interests, and also to review the debtor's financial situation. To this end, the temporary administrator may inspect the debtor's books, cash holdings, securities holdings and inventories of goods, contracts and current accounts, request information from the directors of the economic operator and even enter any of the debtor's premises and search and inspect any of the debtor's assets. The debtor must comply with any request from the temporary administrator to open locked rooms and areas, objects (furniture and other property of the like) without delay, and must reveal the existence and whereabouts of assets.

### 2.3 Effects on licence agreements in the licensee's bankruptcy

Similarly to section 2.1 above, the simple filing for such a procedure generally does not affect the validity of a licence agreement or its enforceability. It is possible, though, that the parties have in their licence agreement a provision whereby the mere filing for such a procedure may be a cause for unilateral termination.

### 2.4 Powers of administrators, receivers or trustees in the licensee's bankruptcy

See above under section 2.2: the arrangements are the same in a licensee's bankruptcy as they are for a licensor's bankruptcy.

### 2.5 Impact of registration

The fact that a licence of the debtor is registered does not affect the legal analysis described under sections 2.1 to 2.4 above.

## 3. Licence agreements in the phase after declaration of bankruptcy

### 3.1 Treatment of intellectual property rights

There is a distinction between the different intellectual property (IP) rights in terms of how they are treated in the event of bankruptcy. The difference is based on whether such IP rights, or the licences pertaining to such IP rights, are transferable or non-transferable.

Set out in Table 1 is a summary chart on IP rights and their transferability according to Hungarian law (since transferability is the key issue in insolvency proceedings).

**Table 1: IP rights and their transferability under Hungarian law**

| IP right or similar proprietary right | Economic rights are transferable | Economic rights are non-transferable |
|---|---|---|
| Copyrights in general | | Yes |
| Copyrights pertaining to software, databases as a copyright work (as an edited compilation), works ordered for advertisement purposes, synchronisation contracts (except for musical works), employees' work, collective work, and related rights | Yes | |
| Trademarks | Yes | |
| Geographical designations | | Yes |
| Patents, supplementary protection certificates (SPC) | Yes | |
| Designs | Yes | |
| Topography of semiconductor chips | Yes | |
| Know-how (protected knowledge) | Yes | |

As for those copyrights where the economic rights are non-transferable, the holders of such rights are the authors themselves (or their heirs) as private persons. Such rights may only be held by companies (ie, the economic entities which may be subject to an insolvency procedure) if they acquired them as employer from the author as employee on the basis of the Copyright Act, according to which – in the absence of any agreement to the contrary – the employer, as the legal successor to the author, obtains economic rights once a work is handed over if the preparation of the work was the author's obligation within the scope of his employment. The economic rights acquired on the basis of the above are also transferable to third parties.

If an IP right or a licence is transferable, it can be sold by the liquidator in the course of the liquidation. If the IP right or licence is non-transferable, the situation changes as to whether it is the licensor or the licensee under liquidation (see below).

It should also be added that the transferability of an IP licence needs to be considered separately from the licence itself. The parties must agree in their licence agreement (even in case of non-transferable IP rights) regarding the transferability or otherwise of the licence. Under the general rule laid down in all IP acts, no IP licence is transferable unless the parties agree otherwise.

### 3.2 Effects on licence agreements in the licensor's bankruptcy

Should a licensor go into bankruptcy or liquidation, that event would not in itself automatically affect the validity of any licence agreements, nor would it result in an automatic right of termination on the side of the licensee unless the parties otherwise agreed in their respective licence agreements. Since from the starting date of the liquidation procedure it is the liquidator who is entitled to represent the company and sign on behalf of the same, it is in general at the liquidator's discretion to decide whether to sell the transferable IP assets or to terminate the agreements on behalf of the licensor.

### 3.3 Powers of an administrator, receiver or trustee in the licensor's bankruptcy

In a licensor's insolvency, the liquidator has powers to terminate, with immediate effect, contracts concluded by the debtor, or to rescind the contract if neither of the parties has rendered any services. Any creditor's claim may be enforced by notifying the liquidator within 40 days from the date when the rescission or termination was communicated.

The liquidator should also collect the claims of the debtor when due, enforce the claims against the debtor and sell the debtor's assets. If consented to by the creditors, the liquidator may invest the debtor's assets into private limited-liability companies, limited companies or cooperative societies as non-pecuniary assets (contribution) if such an investment promises better results.

On the basis of the foregoing, the liquidator may either decide to sell or to invest, as a piece of the assets, IP rights or licences that are transferable, or to terminate the licence agreements concluded by the licensor. All claims by another party arising from the termination should be reported to the liquidator by that party in the course of the liquidation procedure.

### 3.4 Powers and rights of creditors in a licensor's bankruptcy

In the absence of any specific provision in the relevant agreement between a creditor and the debtor, the creditors do not have any powers or rights pertaining to the licence agreement or the IP rights of the debtor/licensor. However, an aggrieved creditor or group of creditors may challenge any act or omission of the liquidator within eight days of becoming aware of the same.

### 3.5 Effects on licence agreements in the licensee's bankruptcy

Should a licensee go into bankruptcy or liquidation, such a circumstance in itself would not automatically affect the validity of the agreements, nor would it result in an automatic right of termination on the side of the licensor unless the parties have agreed otherwise. Since from the starting date of the liquidation procedure it is the liquidator who is entitled to represent the company and sign on behalf of the same, if the licence is freely transferable the liquidator may decide to sell such a licence. If the licence is not transferable, the liquidator may only choose to terminate the licence agreement when it deems that it is no longer necessary for the remaining operation of the debtor.

### 3.6 Powers of an administrator, receiver or trustee in the licensee's bankruptcy

The general powers of a liquidator that are described above in section 3.3 when a licensor is facing bankruptcy also apply for bankruptcy of a licensee. In this event, it is the liquidator's responsibility to choose when to terminate (if at all) a licence agreement or when to transfer any transferable IP rights.

### 3.7 Powers and rights of creditors in a licensee's bankruptcy

As stated in section 3.4 above, in the absence of any specific provision in a licence agreement between a creditor and the debtor, the creditor does not have any powers or rights pertaining to the licence agreement or the IP rights of the debtor/licensee. However, an aggrieved creditor or group of creditors may challenge any act or omission of the liquidator within eight days of becoming aware of the same.

### 3.8 Exclusive and non-exclusive licences

There is no distinction between exclusive and non-exclusive licences in the event of the bankruptcy of either the licensor or the licensee. (Exclusivity and transferability are separate issues.)

Should the licensor, having earlier provided an exclusive licence to the licensee, go into liquidation, the liquidator still has the same possibilities available, namely sale of the IP right or termination of the licence agreement. Should the licensee, having been earlier provided with an exclusive licence by the licensor, go into liquidation, the liquidator can either sell the licence (if such a licence is transferable) or terminate the licence agreement.

### 3.9 Perpetual and non-perpetual licences

The question as to whether a licence is perpetual or non-perpetual does not alter the analysis set out earlier in this section 3. In the case of the bankruptcy of the licensee, the liquidator will take into consideration the above circumstance and may decide on the timing of the termination of the licence agreement on the basis of the above. For example, if the licence fee were to have been paid upfront such that no further payments are necessary by the bankrupt licensee, the termination of the licence agreement or the sale of the licence (if applicable) is less urgent.

### 3.10 Effects on a sub-licence in a licensor's bankruptcy

Similarly to what is set out in section 3.2 above, the bankruptcy of the licensor would not in itself automatically affect the validity of sub-licence agreements unless the parties otherwise agreed in their respective licence agreements. As stated earlier, it is at the liquidator's discretion to decide whether to sell the transferable IP assets or to terminate on behalf of the licensor the agreements concluded with the licensee (sub-licensor). Should the licensor or the new owner of the transferred IP right terminate the original licence agreement concluded between the licensor and licensee (sub-licensor), it would clearly affect the sub-licence agreement as well, because the sub-licensor would no longer be entitled to sub-license the affected IP right.

### 3.11 Effects on a sub-licence in a licensee's bankruptcy

Similarly to what is set out in section 3.5 above, should a licensee (sub-licensor) go into bankruptcy or liquidation, such a circumstance would not in itself automatically affect the validity of the agreements, nor would it result in an automatic termination right on the side of the licensor or sub-licensee unless the parties have otherwise agreed.

If the licence is freely transferable, the liquidator may decide to sell such a licence. If the licence is not transferable, the liquidator may only choose to terminate the licence agreement when it deems that it is no longer necessary for the remaining operation of the debtor, which would of course also affect the validity of the sub-licence agreement concluded between the licensee (sub-licensor) and the sub-licensee.

Should the sub-licensee go into liquidation, what is set out in section 3.5 above applies.

### 3.12 Impact of registration

The fact as to whether an IP right of the debtor is registered does not affect the legal analysis described in this section 3.

## 4. Contractual arrangements in deviation from the law

### 4.1 Exceptions

Licence agreements in general are governed by the Copyright Act, the Patent Act and the Trademark Act. The Patent Act's provisions on licensing agreements apply to other industrial property subject matter. According to the Copyright Act, authors grant licences for the use of their works on the basis of licence agreements, and the users (licensees) are obliged to pay remuneration in return. The provisions relating to licence agreements apply to contracts for the transfer of authors' economic rights as well as to licence agreements relating to the rights of performers and to the transfer of the economic rights of performers.

As for IP rights other than copyright (relating to trademarks, patents etc), the relevant laws contain specific rules on licence agreements. The general position is that the contents of a licence agreement may be determined by the parties unless otherwise stipulated by law. Unless stipulated otherwise, licences are non-exclusive and non-transferable.

There is no exception in connection with licensing any specific IP rights.

### 4.2 Scope to alter statutory mechanisms

As for licence agreements governed by the Copyright Act, the general rule is that parties may freely determine the content of such agreements. The parties may by mutual consent deviate from the provisions pertaining to licence agreements, unless prohibited by law – for instance, a contract for use in which an author grants a licence for the use of an indefinite number of future works is null and void, since no licence can be validly granted for a means of use that is unknown at the time a contract is concluded. However, if the content of a licence agreement cannot be clearly interpreted, the interpretation that is most favourable for the author must be accepted. The same principle applies to industrial property agreements.

Since there is no provision in the respective laws for the reversion of rights, it would be quite useful for the parties to include such a clause in their agreements in order to safeguard their interests in the case of insolvency.

### 4.3 Termination rights and automatic reversions

Apart from statutory termination rights set by the relevant laws, the parties may rule that any phase in the bankruptcy of the licensee yields a termination right or results in a reversion of right (which is like a type of termination). For termination/reversion, it is advisable to choose a phase of the insolvency proceedings before the granting of the right of an administrator, receiver or trustee to unilaterally terminate the agreements. As advised above, such a provision is advantageous for the licensor because otherwise it would be at the discretion of the liquidator of the licensee to decide what to do about termination of the licence agreement or sale of the licence.

## 5. Cross-border aspects

### 5.1 Foreign law

According to Article 3 of Regulation (EC) 593/2008 of the European Parliament and of the Council of June 17 2008 on the law applicable to contractual obligations (known as 'Rome I'), a contract is governed by the law chosen by the parties. According to Article 9(2) of Rome I, nothing in the regulation restricts the application of the overriding mandatory provisions of the law of the chosen forum.

As for relations with countries outside the European Union, according to Section 25 of Law-Decree 13 of 1979 on International Private Law a contract shall be governed by the law chosen by the parties at the time of the conclusion of the contract, or any time thereafter, for the whole or for only part of the contract. Copyrights shall be judged according to the law of the state in the territory of which protection is required (in practice, usually the territory of the country where the use occurs). As for other IP rights, an inventor and his legal successor are able to receive protection according to the law of the state and in the state in which the patent was granted or where the application was filed. This rule applies to other rights of industrial right protection (including industrial design protection, trademarks etc).

The application of foreign law is, however, disregarded if it conflicts with Hungarian public policy and then Hungarian law applies in place of the disregarded foreign law.

On the basis of the foregoing, we are of the opinion that the Hungarian laws on bankruptcy and liquidation procedure can be regarded as overriding mandatory provisions of the law of the chosen forum, and should be applied irrespective of the law chosen by the parties or the law that is otherwise applicable.

### 5.2 Foreign jurisdiction

From the time of the opening of liquidation proceedings, any claim against an economic operator in connection with any assets realised in liquidation may only be enforced within the framework of liquidation. Because once the bankruptcy or liquidation procedure has begun the creditors can only enforce their claims in the course of such procedures, such claims must be reported to the liquidator in accordance with the Hungarian insolvency procedure rules. The deadline for such a report is 30 days in the case of bankruptcy and 40 days in the case of liquidation procedures. The deadline starts with the publication of the order on the commencement of the procedure in Hungary's Companies Gazette. On this basis, the Hungarian insolvency rules mandatorily apply irrespective of any previous election of foreign jurisdiction.

As for judicial and non-judicial proceedings opened prior to the time of the opening of liquidation, proceedings will continue before the same court. However, creditors are still obliged to report their claims to the liquidator, as advised above.

The liquidator is required to collect the claims of the debtor when due, enforce those claims and sell the debtor's assets. If, on the basis of the foregoing obligation, the liquidator is required to enforce a claim of the debtor on the basis of an existing licence agreement, the liquidator would be bound by the election of foreign jurisdiction in the licence agreement.

# India

**Rahul Goel**
**Sandeep Kumar Gupta**
**Anu Monga**
**Nilesh Sharma**
Dhir & Dhir Associates

## 1. Overview

### 1.1 Relevant legislation governing intellectual property and bankruptcy

The relevant legislation in India that governs intellectual property is as follows:

- the Patents Act 1970, as last amended by Patents (Amendment) Act 2005;
- the Copyright (Amendment) Act 2012;
- the Trade Marks Act 1999, as amended by The Trade Marks (Amendment) Act 2010;
- the Protection of Plant Varieties and Farmers' Rights Act 2001;
- the Semiconductor Integrated Circuits Layout-Design Act 2000;
- the Designs Act 2000; and
- the Geographical Indications of Goods (Registration and Protection) Act 1999.

There is no single comprehensive and integrated corporate insolvency/ bankruptcy law in India that would address the needs of an entity in distress. The insolvency and restructuring framework in India is guided by the following legislation:

- *The Companies Act 1956:*[1] Chapter V of this act lays down the law relating to "arbitration, compromises, arrangements and reconstruction" of companies in India. The said chapter contains the provisions for compromises, arrangements and reconstructions in India between a company and its creditors and shareholders.
- *The Sick Industrial Companies (Special Provisions) Act 1985:*[2] By virtue of this act a bankruptcy tribunal (known as a BIFR (Board for Industrial & Financial Reconstruction)) has been set up to deal with the rehabilitation of viable but sick industrial companies and recommendation of the winding-up of non-

1 The act will soon be scrapped because the Companies Act 2013 has been enacted and 283 sections of the same have already been notified in the *Official Gazette of the Government of India* and are applicable from April 1 2014. The remaining sections (including the provisions relating to arrangement and compromise and winding up) are yet to be notified. They will become effective from the date of notification in the *Official Gazette of the Government of India*.

2 The SICA (Repeal Act) 2002 has already been passed, but it has still not been notified. The act will come into effect from the of notification in the *Official Gazette of the Government of India*; thereafter, the rehabilitation of sick companies will be governed in terms of Chapter XIX of the Companies Act 2013. However, the relevant provisions of Chapter XIX are yet to be notified by the central government.

viable sick industrial companies to the relevant high court. The provisions of the 1985 act do not refer to the terms `insolvency' or `bankruptcy', nor do they conspicuously address the underlying issues. The term 'insolvency' has only been dealt with (but not defined) under Section 433(e) of the Companies Act 1956, which gives the meaning of 'corporate insolvency' as an "inability to pay debts". The provisions of 1985 act deal with 'sickness' of an industrial company and measures for its revival, irrespective of the capability or otherwise of the company to make payment of its debts – ie, it does not necessarily envisage a situation where an entity is unable to pay its debts. The test of sickness relates to a company's net worth rather than its liquidity. If, therefore, an industrial company is facing a cash crunch and is not able to make payment of its debts, but it has not fully eroded its net worth, it is not obligated to file a reference with the BIFR under Section 15(1) of the 1985 act (see further section 1.2(a) below).

## 1.2 Types of insolvency procedure

### *(a) Filing of reference under the existing legislation*

If an industrial company's accumulated losses are equal to or in excess of its net worth as at the end of a financial year on the basis of its audited financial statements for that financial year, the company is under a legal obligation to file a reference with the BIFR in terms of Section 15(1) of the Sick Industrial Companies (Special Provisions) Act 1985. Only medium-scale and large-scale industrial companies under distress fall within the ambit of this act and can approach the BIFR for formulation of a rescue/revival plan. Small and ancillary industrial undertakings have been specifically kept outside the purview of the 1985 act, so that focus remains on rescuing the industries in which larges resources in terms of capital, human resources etc have been deployed.

### *(b) Filing of reference under the impending legislation*

Once the provisions of Chapter XIX of the Companies Act 2013 come into force, all the references/applications for dealing with the sickness of a company will be required to be filed before a National Company Law Tribunal (NCLT), a series of which are to be set up in accordance with the provisions of Chapter XXVII of the 2013 act. Under the 2013 act, the criterion for determination of sickness stands changed from being net worth based presently to being liquidity based – so that if, on demand by secured creditors representing 50% or more of the total secured debt, the company fails to pay, compound or secure the debt, then the secured creditors may file an application for sickness before an appropriate NCLT. The company can also file an application for sickness before an NCLT.

### *(c) Filing of application before the high court (under the existing legislation)*

Under Chapter V of the Companies Act 1956, where a compromise or arrangement is proposed between a company and its creditors or between a company and its members, the commercial court having jurisdiction (ie, the high court of the state where the registered office of the company is situated) may, on application by the company or any creditor or member of the company, or in the case of a company that is being wound up by the liquidator, order a meeting of the creditors or members, as the case may be, to be called, held and conducted in such manner as the court directs. If a majority in number representing three-quarters in value of the creditors or members agree to any compromise or arrangement, the compromise or arrangement shall, if sanctioned by the court, be binding on all the creditors or all the members, as the case may be, and also on the company or, in the case of a company that is being wound up, on the liquidator and contributories of the company.

Under the Companies Act 1956, an application before the high court by the creditors or members of the company may be made for a voluntary winding-up of the company. It may take place on the passing of an ordinary resolution in the general meeting of its shareholders under certain circumstances and on the passing of a special resolution of the shareholders to wind up voluntarily for any reason whatsoever. The court may also compulsorily direct a winding-up of the company if:

- the company has, by a special resolution, resolved that the company be wound up by the court;
- the company commits a default in delivering a statutory report to the registrar or in holding a statutory meeting;
- the company fails to commence its business within one year of its incorporation, or suspends its business for a whole year and the court is convinced that there is no intention to carry on the business;
- the number of members is reduced below the statutory minimum (ie, below seven in the case of a public company and two in the case of a private company);
- the company is unable to pay its debts; or
- the court is of the opinion that it is just and equitable that the company should be wound up.

### *(d) Filing of application under the impending legislation*

Post coming into effect of the relevant provisions of Chapter XV of the Companies Act 2013, all applications for compromise or arrangement between the company and its creditors, or between the company and its members, shall be filed before the NCLT.

## 1.3 Grounds of bankruptcy

### *(a) Under the Sick Industrial Companies (Special Provisions) Act 1985*

A company that is entitled to refer its possible revival to the BIFR is termed a 'sick industrial company' and the test to its being under distress is net worth based – ie, an industrial company that, in addition to fulfilling other prescribed requisites, has at the end of any financial year accumulated losses equal to or exceeding its entire net worth becomes a 'sick industrial company'.

### *(b) Under the Companies Act 1956*

Under the provisions of Sections 391–394 of the Companies Act 1956, any creditor of a company or its members, or the liquidator (in case the company is under winding-up), may approach the court with an application proposing a scheme of compromise or arrangement between the company and its creditors (or any class of them), or between the company and its members (or any class of them). The compromise or arrangement can include the restructuring of debts, a reduction of equity, an amalgamation or a merger/demerger. However, if the court is satisfied that the compromise or arrangement, as sanctioned in Section 391 of the 1956 act, cannot be operated with or without modification, it may make an order for a winding-up of the company.

*(c)* ***Under Chapter XIX of the Companies Act 2013 (impending legislation)***

If, on demand of secured creditors representing 50% or more of the total outstanding secured debt of the company, the company fails to pay, secure or compound that debt, it shall be treated as a sick company and an application may be filed by any of the secured creditors or the company itself, before a NCLT, for declaration of sickness of the company.

*(d)* ***Under Chapter XV of the Companies Act 2013 (impending legislation)***

A scheme of compromise or arrangement (including debt restructuring) between a company and its members or creditors may be filed before an NCLT. The tribunal is empowered to order the holding of meetings of the creditors or the members and to make orders on the scheme for a proposed reconstruction, merger or amalgamation.

A company may be wound up in terms of Chapter XX of the Companies Act 2013 if:

- an application is made in the event of the company being unable to pay its debts;
- the company has itself resolved by special resolution that it should be wound up;
- the company has acted against the interests of the sovereignty and integrity of India;
- the tribunal has ordered a winding-up under Chapter XIX of the 2013 act;
- the tribunal is satisfied that the affairs of the company are being conducted in a fraudulent or unlawful manner;
- the company has defaulted in its filings of financial statements or annual returns for the immediately preceding five consecutive financial years; or
- the tribunal is of the opinion that it is just and equitable that the company should be wound up.

### 1.4 Filing for bankruptcy

As stated in section 1.1 above, India does not have a composite law dealing with the insolvency of companies. While the Sick Industrial Companies (Special Provisions) Act 1985 deals with the revival and rehabilitation of corporate entities, the Companies Act 1956 deals with the compromise, arrangement, reconstruction, liquidation and winding-up of companies. However, the new Companies Act 2013 encompasses provisions that deal with both the revival and rehabilitation of sick companies and also with the reorganisation, arrangement, liquidation and winding-up of companies.

(a) ***Under the Sick Industrial Companies (Special Provisions) Act 1985***

When an industrial company has become a sick industrial company, the board of directors of the said company are required, within 60 days from the date of finalisation of the duly audited accounts of the company for the financial year as at the end of which a company has become a sick industrial company, to make a reference to the BIFR, a quasi-judicial body, for determination of the measures to be adopted with respect to the company for its revival and rehabilitation. However, if the company's board of directors has sufficient reason – even before any finalisation of the accounts – to form the opinion that the company has become a sick industrial company, it shall, within 60 days after it has formed such an opinion, make a reference to the BIFR.

The central government, a state government, the Reserve Bank of India, a public financial institution, a state-level financial institution or a 'scheduled bank'[3] may, if it has sufficient reason to believe that any industrial company has become a sick industrial company under the 1985 act, make a reference to the BIFR in respect of such company.

(b) ***Under the Companies Act 1956***

Under this 1956 act a petition to the court for winding-up may be made by the company itself, a creditor of the company, a contributory or contributories, the Registrar of Companies, the central government or any state government. A creditor of a company can file an application for the winding-up of the debtor company for the latter's inability to pay its debts.

(c) ***Under Chapter XIX of the Companies Act 2013 (impending legislation)***

If a company is unable to pay, secure or compound its debt upon a demand being made by secured creditors representing 50% or more of the total outstanding secured debt of the company, any secured creditor or the company itself may file an application before an NCLT tribunal for a determination that the company may be declared as a sick company.

Without prejudice to the above, if the Reserve Bank of India, a state government, a public financial institution, a state-level institution or a scheduled bank has sufficient reason to believe that a company has become a sick company, it may make a reference of the company to the tribunal for determination of measures for its revival, which may be adopted with respect to such company.

(d) ***Under Chapter XV of the Companies Act 2013 (impending legislation)***

An application for compromise or arrangement, including debt restructuring, between the company and its creditors or members may be made by the company,

---

3 A scheduled bank in India constitutes one of those banks that have been included in the Second Schedule of the Reserve Bank of India Act 1934, wherein are included such banks that satisfy the criteria laid down in Section 42(6)(a) of that 1934 act.

by any creditor or member or (in case of company being wound up) by the liquidator. If an NCLT tribunal is satisfied that such a scheme of compromise or arrangement cannot be implemented satisfactorily with or without modification, and the company is unable to pay its debts as scheduled in the scheme, the tribunal may make an order for the winding-up of the company.

An application for the winding-up of the company may be made before the tribunal by the company, its creditor(s), any contributory(ies), the Registrar of Companies, or (if the company has acted against the interests of the sovereignty and integrity of India) any person authorised by the central government or the central government itself. The creditors of the company include secured creditors, holders of any debentures, trustees for the holders of debentures, and contributories.

## 1.5 Administrators and other appointed persons

### *(a) Under the Sick Industrial Companies (Special Provisions) Act 1985*

Along with a declaration of sickness of an industrial company, if the BIFR is of the opinion that it is not possible for a sick company to make its net worth positive on its own within a reasonable period of time and that it is necessary or expedient in the public interest to revive the company by adoption of various measures for its revival, the BIFR has the power, under the 1985 act, to appoint any one of the secured lenders or an independent bank as an 'operating agency' to formulate a scheme for the revival of a sick company.[4]

The operating agency acts as an extended arm of the BIFR. Generally, the role and responsibility of the operating agency is to prepare (if possible), on the basis of the information furnished by the company and out of its own experience and expertise, a scheme for the rehabilitation of the sick industrial company in accordance with any guidelines set out by the BIFR, and to assist the BIFR in the discharge of its functions. However, control over the assets of the company remains with the debtor company and does not get vested in the operating agency upon its appointment.

The said scheme may provide for the financial reconstruction of the sick industrial company, including as necessary:

- the proper management of the sick industrial company by change in or takeover of its management;
- the company's amalgamation with any other company;
- sale of the industrial undertaking of the sick industrial company, free from all encumbrances and all liabilities of the company or free from specified encumbrances and liabilities to any person (including a cooperative society formed by the employees of such undertaking);
- lease of a part or whole of any of the company's industrial undertaking, including to a cooperative society formed by the employees of such undertaking;

---

4 Generally, one of the existing secured lenders is appointed. However, any other bank or financial institution (which is not a lender to the company involved) may also be appointed as an operating agency.

- the rationalisation of managerial personnel and other workers, in accordance with the law;
- reduction in the interests or rights of the shareholders of the company; and
- such other preventive, ameliorative or remedial measures as may be appropriate.

The scheme prepared by the operating agency is examined by the BIFR and thereafter a Draft Rehabilitation Scheme (DRS) is formulated and published by the BIFR with the aim of seeking suggestions and objections from the all concerned for which a time period of 60 days is allowed, which may further be extended by the BIFR by another 60 days.

The BIFR may, after considering the various responses, sanction a scheme for the revival of the company. The implementation of a sanctioned scheme is monitored by the BIFR, and a monitoring agency is appointed by the BIFR for that purpose. Where the need so arises, the sanctioned scheme may be modified by the BIFR.

***(b) Under Chapter XIX of the Companies Act 2013 (impending legislation)***

Under Chapter XIX of the Companies Act 2013 the NCLT, after determination of a company's sickness (as defined above), shall fix a hearing and appoint an interim administrator to convene a meeting of creditors of the company in order to determine whether the company can be revived and rehabilitated. The interim administrator in turn shall appoint a committee of creditors (representative of all classes of creditor) and hold a meeting of such creditors to decide whether it is possible to revive the sick company or whether the company should be wound up. The interim administrator shall report its findings to the tribunal.

If the company does not file a revival scheme, the tribunal may direct the interim administrator to take over the management of the sick company. Under such a circumstance, the directors and the management of the company are required to extend their full cooperation to the internal administrator to manage the affairs of the company.

If the report of the interim administrator states that it is possible to revive the sick company, the tribunal shall appoint a company administrator to prepare a revival plan for the rehabilitation of the company. The tribunal may also direct the company administrator to take over the assets or the management of the company. The company administrator is also required to convene separate meetings of the secured and unsecured creditors of the sick company for their consent (by at least 25% of the unsecured creditors in value terms and by at least 75% of the secured creditors in value terms) and thereafter present the scheme to the tribunal for its sanction. After sanction of the scheme by the tribunal in the manner specified under the 2013 act, the tribunal may authorise the company administrator to fully implement the sanctioned scheme and require it to furnish periodic reports on the progress of implementation of the sanctioned scheme. However, if the scheme is not approved by the creditors of the company with the requisite ratio, the company administrator has to submit a report to this effect to the tribunal and the tribunal will order the winding-up of the sick company.

*(c) Under the Companies Act 1956*

There is no provision under the 1956 act for appointment of any receiver, administrator or liquidator where an application is filed before the court for a scheme of compromise or arrangement between the company and its creditors or between the company and its members.

However, in the event of a winding-up petition being filed before the court, that court has the power to appoint a provisional liquidator of the company until the making of the winding-up order. The provisional liquidator so appointed takes into its custody or control all the assets, properties, effects and actionable claims to which the company is entitled, and prepares an inventory of the assets of the company. In addition, the company submits a statement of affairs in the prescribed form, under an affidavit, with details of all the assets and liabilities of the company and such other information as the provisional liquidator may desire. The court may restrict the provisional liquidator's powers in any manner it deems fit.

A provisional liquidator is replaced by a liquidator upon a winding-up order being made by the court. The liquidator has the power to institute and/or defend any suit on behalf of the company, to carry on the company's business, to sell the moveable and immovable properties of the company, to sell the entire undertaking of the company, to raise money on security of the assets of the company and to do all such things that might be necessary for the winding-up of the affairs of the company and the distribution of its assets.

*(d) Under Chapter XV of the Companies Act 2013*

There is no provision for the appointment of any receiver, administrator or a liquidator when an application is filed before the NCLT for a scheme of compromise or arrangement between the company and its creditors or between the company and its members.

However in the event of a winding-up petition being filed before the tribunal, the tribunal shall appoint an official liquidator attached to the court as a provisional liquidator of the company until the making of the winding-up order. The provisional liquidator so appointed has the same powers as the official liquidator, subject to restrictions as may be imposed by the tribunal. At the time of making a winding-up order, the tribunal appoints an official liquidator or a company liquidator.[5]

Within three weeks from the making of the winding-up order by the tribunal, the company liquidator must make an application to the tribunal to constitute a winding-up committee – comprising the official liquidator, a nominee of the secured creditors, and a professional nominated by the tribunal – to assist and monitor the liquidation proceedings. A meeting of the winding-up committee must be convened by the company liquidator, and the committee must assist and monitor the liquidation proceedings in the areas of:

- taking over the company's assets;

---

5 An official liquidator is the one attached to the court, while a company liquidator is an outside agency appointed from a panel of professional individuals, firms or bodies corporate that is maintained by the tribunal.

- examining the statement of affairs;
- sale of the assets;
- finalisation of a list of creditors and contributories;
- compromise and the settlement of claims; and
- any other function that the tribunal may direct it to do from time to time.

The company liquidator is obliged to place a report of the meetings of the winding-up committee before the tribunal on a monthly basis, until the time comes for submission of a final report on dissolution of the company after completion of the winding-up procedures.

## 2. Licence agreements in the phase between filing and declaration of bankruptcy

### 2.1 Effects on licence agreements in the licensor's bankruptcy

In the absence of any specific provisions relating to insolvency or bankruptcy in relevant intellectual property legislation, licence agreements are generally governed by the provisions of contract law (see the Indian Contract Act 1872) in relation to the terms of an agreement. However, in the absence of any clause relating to a termination of a licence agreement in the event of filing for bankruptcy, the agreement continues to remain in force and may get assigned to the acquirer of the licensor. In other words, if a licence is in the name of a company, then the licence rights will move with the company. The acquirer may then exercise the option of renegotiating the terms of the licence agreement and/or terminating the licence agreement. In the event of termination of the licence agreement by the acquirer, the acquirer is obligated to fulfil all commitments under the licence agreement as it may contractually be liable to honour. Those commitments might include the payment of damages if contractually agreed.

Under the provisions of Section 22(3) of Sick Industrial Companies (Special Provisions) Act 1985, the BIFR has the power to suspend or modify the operation of all or any of the contracts, assurances of property, agreements, settlements, awards, standing orders or other instruments in force to which the sick industrial company is a party or which may be applicable to such sick industrial company immediately before the date of such an order. Where any clause in the licence agreement is, in the opinion of the BIFR, detrimental to the interests of the sick company, operation of that clause may be suspended by the BIFR. However, such powers shall be exercised by the BIFR only post registration of the reference filed by the sick industrial company, albeit even prior to declaration of sickness by BIFR.

Under the provisions of both the Companies Act 1956 and the Companies Act 2013, in the event of a winding-up petition being filed before the court and upon a provisional liquidator being appointed by the court, until the making of the winding-up order the provisional liquidator so appointed takes into its custody or control all the assets (including licences), properties, effects and actionable claims to which the company is entitled.

## 2.2 Powers of administrators, receivers or trustees in the licensor's bankruptcy

The licences and intellectual property of a company are part of its assets, and under Section 22A of the Sick Industrial Companies (Special Provisions) Act 1985 the BIFR has power to issue a directive to the sick industrial company not to dispose of its assets without the permission of the BIFR. The operating agency appointed under the provisions of the 1985 act does not have any power to deal with the assets of the sick company.

However, in terms of the provisions of Chapter XIX of the Companies Act 2013 (new legislation), upon an application being filed by any secured creditor or by the company for determination of sickness, the company is restrained from disposing of, or entering into any obligation with respect to, its assets, except as required in the normal course of business. Furthermore, the interim administrator appointed under Section 256(1) of the Companies Act 2013 may be directed by an NCLT tribunal to take over the management of the company and to protect and preserve the assets of the company.

The company administrator appointed in terms of Section 259(1) of the Companies Act 2013 to prepare a rehabilitation scheme for the revival of a sick company may be directed to take over the assets or management of the company. With respect to those assets, the company administrator is only empowered to prepare an inventory of them and, if required, to prepare a valuation report of them. Neither the interim administrator nor the company administrator is empowered to terminate or sell the licences, but the tribunal is empowered under Section 264(1) of the 2013 act to terminate a licence agreement.

In the event of a winding-up filed before the high court, the liquidator appointed by the court has the power to:

- sell the moveable and immoveable property of the company;
- sell the entire undertaking of the company;
- raise money on security of the assets of the company; and
- do all such things that may be necessary for the winding-up of the affairs of the company and the distribution of its assets.

Until such time as that process has been completed, the liquidator has the power to ensure that the licence agreement continues in full force and that all rights with respect to the intellectual property are protected and preserved. Indeed, in the *Oomerbhoy* case,[6] the court held that:

> *in law and for all practical purposes, the Receiver stands in the shoes of the owner and must be entitled to do all such acts necessary for preservation and the protection of the property, including the trademarks for which he is appointed a Receiver.*

Furthermore, administrators, receivers or trustees will not have a right to terminate a licence agreement unless there is breach of the terms of the licence agreement by the licensee and such breach cannot be cured.

## 2.3 Effects on licence agreements in the licensee's bankruptcy

As mentioned above, in the absence of any specific provisions relating to insolvency

---

6 *Court Receiver, High Court of Bombay v RR Oomerbhoy Pvt Ltd* 2003(27) PTC 555 (Bom)

in intellectual property legislation, licence agreements are generally governed by the provisions of contract law (see particularly the Indian Contract Act 1872).

However, in the absence of any clause relating to termination of a licence agreement in the event of bankruptcy, the agreement will continue to remain in force and may get assigned to the acquirer of the licensee company. Indeed, it is important that an acquirer of a licensee company fulfils its obligations and complies with all the terms of the licence agreement.

If the licence agreement restricts or prohibits assignment or transfer of the licence agreement to any third party or the acquirer of the licensee company (and which may lead to termination of the agreement), such a licence agreement is automatically terminated.

### 2.4 Powers of administrators, receivers or trustees in the licensee's bankruptcy

When there is no specific termination clause in the licence agreement, and unless specifically directed by an NCLT tribunal regarding modification, suspension or termination of a clause in the licence agreement, an appointed administrator, receiver or trustee only has the power to oversee that the licence agreement continues in force and all rights with respect to the intellectual property are protected and preserved.

### 2.5 Impact of registration

The registration of a licence agreement does not grant any additional rights to any party in the event of insolvency. However, the registration of a licence agreement helps the parties in getting the terms of the agreement enforced, especially when the existence of the agreement itself is brought into dispute.

## 3. Licence agreements in the phase after declaration of bankruptcy

### 3.1 Treatment of intellectual property rights

There is no specific difference, laid down under current law, with respect to treatment of intellectual property rights in the event of bankruptcy. Also, it should be noted that the relevant provisions of Chapter XV and Chapter XIX of the Companies Act 2013 (which deal with compromises, arrangements and rehabilitation of sick companies, respectively) have still not been promulgated [and it has to be seen as to how the courts would treat different kinds of intellectual property assets in the cases of insolvency (and, more importantly, under the patents law, which has provisions relating to compulsory licensing).

### 3.2 Effects on licence agreements in the licensor's bankruptcy

As mentioned in section 2 above, licensor bankruptcy may have an effect on the licence agreement only when the licence agreement contains clauses with respect to:

- termination of the licence in the event of insolvency or bankruptcy; and/or
- prohibition on transfer/assignment of the licence agreement to any third party in any event which may lead to termination of the agreement.

In the absence of any specific clause in the agreement regarding termination, in the event of a licensor's bankruptcy the agreement remains in full force and the liquidator may sell it to the licensee. When the licence is sold to a third party, the said party steps into the shoes of the original licensor and the same terms and conditions between the new licensor and the existing licensee continue as they existed before the transfer.

### 3.3 Powers of an administrator, receiver or trustee in the licensor's bankruptcy

As described in section 2.4 above, an administrator, receiver or trustee only has the power to ensure that the licence agreement continues in force and that all rights with respect to the intellectual property are protected. Where the licensor is wound up and there is no clause in the agreement that protects the rights of a licensee, the liquidator may sell the agreement to the licensee or a third party but otherwise the agreement will be terminated.

However, *in the Oomerbhoy* case,[7] the court held that:

*in law and for all practical purposes, the Receiver stands in the shoes of the owner and must be entitled to do all such acts necessary for preservation and the protection of the property, including the trademarks for which he is appointed a Receiver.*

Furthermore, administrators, receivers or trustees will not have a right to terminate a licence agreement unless there is breach of the terms of the licence agreement by the licensee and such breach cannot be cured.

### 3.4 Powers and rights of creditors in a licensor's bankruptcy

In case of bankruptcy or insolvency, secured creditors have a first right over the intellectual property assets of the insolvent entity and will be free to deal with the assets in the same manner as the owner. However, the creditors will be bound by the terms of any licence agreement and may terminate the agreement only in accordance with the provisions of the agreement (unless the agreement is automatically getting terminated because of the insolvency or bankruptcy of the licensor). Further, the creditors will be entitled to receive royalty payments from the licensee as provided for in the agreement.

### 3.5 Effects on licence agreements in the licensee's bankruptcy

In the case of the winding-up of a licensee, the intellectual property of the licensee may be sold and the sale proceeds be utilised to cover the debts owed by the company. However, any sale must be subject to the rights of the licensee under the licence agreement, unless the licence agreement contains clauses with respect to its automatic termination in the event of insolvency or bankruptcy.

### 3.6 Powers of an administrator, receiver or trustee in the licensee's bankruptcy

As licensing rights are an asset of a company, those rights stand vested in the administrator, receiver or trustee. As such, under the direction of the court an administrator, receiver or trustee may sell or transfer the licensing rights.

---

7 See fn 6 above.

### 3.7 Powers and rights of creditors in a licensee's bankruptcy

If licensing rights are transferable, then the creditors in a licensee insolvency can enforce those rights. However, where a termination clause in the licensing agreement exists, the licensor may terminate the agreement.

### 3.8 Exclusive and non-exclusive licences

A non-exclusive licence is generally treated as personal and non-assignable, unless the terms of the agreement mention assignment or transfer. Accordingly, if the terms of the licence agreement do not mention 'assignment' or 'transfer', a non-exclusive licence cannot be transferred. Under such circumstances the agreement shall stand terminated in the event of a licensee's bankruptcy. In the case of a licensor's bankruptcy, the licence is dealt by the liquidator in the same manner as any other licence, as discussed in earlier sections of this chapter.

It is strongly suggested (based upon experience from other jurisdictions) that an exclusive licence agreement may, in the absence of any specific prohibition, be assigned or transferred in an event of bankruptcy.

### 3.9 Perpetual and non-perpetual licences

There does not appear to be any distinction between a perpetual or non-perpetual licence in terms of its treatment by an administrator or liquidator in the event of a bankruptcy.

### 3.10 Effects on a sub-licence in a licensor's bankruptcy

Where a sub-licence has been granted with the consent of the licensor, the sub-licence remains in force, subject to the terms of the sub-licence agreement, even when the licensor goes bankrupt. If the licence is sold by the liquidator as part of the winding-up process, the rights and obligations of the sub-licensee in relation to the new licensor remain the same. However, if the licence is terminated, then all the underlying rights, including any sub-licensee's rights, stand terminated.

### 3.11 Effects on a sub-licence in a licensee's bankruptcy

In general, a sub-licence agreement should be treated in the same manner as any other licence agreement, and the terms of the licence and sub-licence agreement will prevail. However, if the licence agreement between the licensor and a licensee is terminated as a result of the insolvency or bankruptcy of the licensee, any sub-licence agreement automatically comes to an end.

### 3.12 Impact of registration

The registration of a (sub)-licence agreement does not grant any additional rights to any party in the event of insolvency.

## 4. Contractual arrangements in deviation from the law

### 4.1 Exceptions

Licence agreements are generally governed by contract law. Licence agreements depending upon the nature of the licence (and protection available under the relevant intellectual property statute) may have certain additional clauses to protect the interests of both the parties and facilitate effective utilisation of the licensed product (under the licence agreement).

A licence stands automatically terminated on the occurrence of a licensee's bankruptcy if a clause setting out such a provision exists in the licensing agreement.

### 4.2 Scope to alter statutory mechanisms

Any contract that is in contradiction of India's statutory provisions is liable to be struck down by the courts and become legally unenforceable.

### 4.3 Termination rights and automatic reversions

The parties to a licence agreement are free to have a clause relating to termination and automatic reversion of rights in the event of bankruptcy or insolvency of a licensee. It is a common practice to have such clauses in the licence agreements in India.

Indeed, at present there are no provisions under the law that either restrict or facilitate the reversion of rights to the licensor in the event of bankruptcy or insolvency of a licensee. The reversion of rights to the licensor will be primarily governed by the licence agreement executed between the parties.

## 5. Cross-border aspects

### 5.1 Foreign law

Intellectual property law in India, including that covering licences granted for use of such intellectual property, is territorial in nature. Indian courts (including insolvency administrators) are not bound by the election of foreign law in licence agreements.

India has adopted neither the Model Law of UNCITRAL (the United Nations Commission on International Trade Law) nor any of the EU regulations relating to insolvency.

### 5.2 Foreign jurisdiction

India's insolvency laws do not have any extraterritorial jurisdiction; nor do they recognise the jurisdiction of foreign courts except in the manner laid down under Sections 13 and 44A of India's Code of Civil Procedure, which is the legislation applicable for the recognition of foreign judgments and proceedings in reciprocating countries as conclusive, barring certain exceptions such as fraud, judgment not based on the merits of the case, no competent jurisdiction, etc. As such, an insolvency administrator or a court in India is not bound by the election of foreign jurisdiction in a licence agreement.

# Ireland

**Martin Kelleher**
Mason Hayes & Curran

## 1. Overview

### 1.1 Relevant legislation governing intellectual property and bankruptcy

There is no single legislative instrument governing the treatment of intellectual property during bankruptcy in Ireland. Instead, Irish law provides for a number of separate instruments, which govern not only different categories of intellectual property but also the insolvency of different types of legal entities.

The primary pieces of national legislation governing intellectual property are as follows:

- the Trade Marks Act 1996;
- the Patents Acts 1992 to 2012;
- the Copyright and Related Rights Acts 2000 to 2007; and
- the Industrial Designs Act 2001.

The primary pieces of national legislation governing legal entities in Ireland during bankruptcy are as follows:

- the various Companies Acts;
- the Personal Insolvency Act 2012;
- the Deeds of Arrangement Act 1887; and
- the Bankruptcy Acts 1988 to 2011.

This legislation is supplemented by secondary legislation, known as statutory instruments, and the judicially developed principles of common law. In addition, as a member state of the European Union, Ireland is subject to European legislation including, in particular, the provisions of Council Regulation (EC) 1346/2000 of May 29 2000 on insolvency proceedings (hereinafter the Insolvency Regulation).

### 1.2 Types of insolvency procedure

The insolvency procedures applicable to corporate entities are known as examinership, receivership and liquidation:

- *Examinership* is a period of court protection for a company which is designed to facilitate the survival of companies that are (or are likely to be) unable to pay their debts. The process involves the appointment of a third party, called an examiner, who is responsible for reviewing the affairs of the company and preparing a scheme of arrangement in respect of the company's debts, for approval by the company's creditors.

- *Receivership* is the process whereby the holder of a charge over specified assets of a company appoints a party called a receiver to sell or manage those assets in satisfaction of the debt owed by the company to the charge holder.
- *Liquidation* is the process of winding up a company by a party called a liquidator. The liquidator is responsible for collecting the company's assets, paying the outstanding debts, and distributing the remaining surplus (if any) to the members. On completion of the liquidation, the company is dissolved.

A separate set of insolvency procedures is applicable to natural persons.

### 1.3 Grounds of bankruptcy

The grounds for a company to avail itself of the corporate insolvency procedures noted in section 1.2 are as follows:

- Examinership is available where it appears to the court that a company that is (or is likely to be) unable to pay its debts has a reasonable prospect of survival as a going concern, either in whole or in part. At the time the petition is presented to the court, there must be no order or resolution subsisting to wind up the company, nor can a receiver have been in place for more than three days. However, satisfying these criteria does not guarantee court protection, as the court retains discretion to refuse to make an order.
- There are two ways in which a secured creditor may appoint a receiver over the assets of the company. First, the terms of the debenture document may contain an express power for the debenture holder to appoint a receiver on the occurrence of a specified event of default by the company. Secondly, if the debenture document does not contain a contractual right to appoint a receiver, the debenture holder may apply to the court to have a receiver appointed pursuant to statute.
- Liquidations may be divided into 'voluntary' and 'official' liquidations:
    - Voluntary liquidations – which may further be categorised into "members' voluntary liquidations" in the case of solvent companies and "creditors' voluntary liquidations" in the case of insolvent companies – are commenced by way of the members of the company passing a special resolution that the company be wound up.
    - Official liquidation, also known as 'compulsory liquidation', arises in circumstances where the company is put into liquidation by an order of the High Court. The most common ground that creditors seeking an order to wind up a company plead is that a company is 'unable to pay its debts'. This phrase has been defined in legislation to mean any of the following three situations: a demand for a sum exceeding €1,269.74 has been served on the company and has not been met within three weeks (with no dispute of the debt arising in that period); a court order in respect of a debt remains unsatisfied after attempted execution; or it is proved to the satisfaction of the court that the company is unable to pay its debts.

## 1.4 Filing for bankruptcy

The following persons may seek to avail themselves of the corporate insolvency procedures:

- A petition to have a company placed into examinership may be brought by the company itself, its directors, one or more shareholders holding between them at least one-tenth of the paid-up voting capital, or any current, contingent or prospective creditor (including an employee).
- A registered debenture holder may apply to have the company placed into receivership.
- The relevant party in the case of a liquidation depends on the type of liquidation sought. Only the members of the company may commence a members' voluntary liquidation or a creditors' voluntary liquidation. An application to the High Court to commence a compulsory liquidation may be brought by any of the following:
  - the company itself, although this is comparatively rare in light of the availability of the voluntary liquidation processes;
  - any person who may be liable to contribute to the assets of the company, provided the company in question does not have the minimum number of members prescribed by law for a company of that type;
  - a creditor, including a contingent or prospective creditor (although a contingent or prospective creditor must first provide the court with security for costs and establish a *prima facie* case for winding-up); and
  - the Director of Corporate Enforcement where it appears to him that, on the basis of a report, information or documentation received by him in accordance with the provisions of the Company Act 1990, a petition should be presented to have the company wound up. Then the director may apply to court to have the company wound up on just and equitable grounds.

Qualifying small and medium-sized enterprises (SMEs) may apply for examinership in either the circuit court or the High Court. Other companies may only apply for examinership in the High Court.

Where it is proposed to appoint a receiver as a result of an express power contained in a debenture document, it is unnecessary for the creditor to apply to court. Notice of the appointment should be filed with the Companies Registration Office within seven days of the appointment and advertised in the *Irish State Gazette* and in at least one daily newspaper circulating in the district where the registered office of the company is situated. Failure to make such notices will not invalidate the appointment.

Where a creditor seeks to appoint a receiver as a consequence of a court order, the application may be made to the circuit court or the High Court. However, as each circuit court is a court of local and limited jurisdiction, it is not permitted to hear applications for the appointment of a receiver where the debt involved exceeds €38,092.14.

Applications for a compulsory liquidation must, in all cases, be made to the High Court.

## 1.5 Administrators and other appointed persons

### *(a)* *Examinerships*

The examinership process is commenced by way of petition to the Central Office of High Court or, where a qualifying SME elects to do so, to the office of the relevant circuit court. On the same day that the petition is presented, the petitioner must apply *ex parte* to the court for direction as to the proceedings. Although the court has the power to treat this initial *ex parte* application as the full hearing, it rarely exercises this discretion and will wait to hear the creditors before deciding whether an examiner should be appointed.

However, in "exceptional circumstances outside of the control of the petitioner", the court has the power to appoint an interim examiner and place the company under the interim protection of the court for a period of up to 10 days. This power is subject to the condition that, where the company is indebted to the National Asset Management Agency (NAMA) or a NAMA group entity, the petition must have been served on NAMA and NAMA must be heard during the *ex parte* hearing.

An examiner is only appointed following a court hearing. The court can adjourn the hearing of the petition until any parties that it considers should be notified have indeed been notified of the presentation of the petition. An examiner's essential functions are to formulate proposals for a scheme of arrangement, convene meetings of the members and creditors for the purpose of voting on the proposed scheme of arrangement, and report his findings to the court. The appointment of an examiner does not automatically serve to displace the directors, who will continue to manage the business during the period of court protection. However, an examiner may apply to court for an order that the powers vested in the directors are transferred to, and only exercisable by, the examiner – although such orders are very rare in practice.

### *(b)* *Receiverships*

A receiver is appointed upon the acceptance by a proposed receiver of his appointment under the terms of a debenture document or as a result of a court order. The position of the receiver is governed by the terms of the debenture document under which he is appointed. Similar to the appointment of an examiner, the appointment of a receiver does not automatically displace the powers of the directors; however, the terms of the debenture may provide that the receiver will act as manager of the company and carry on the business of the company in place of the directors. It is also common for debentures to provide that the receiver acts as agent for the company, with a power of attorney to execute contracts on its behalf.

Irish law does not provide for an interim or provisional receiver. In the case of a receiver appointed as a result of an express power in a debenture document, the appointment does not take effect until it is accepted by the receiver. In the case of a receiver appointed by court order, the receiver is not appointed until the making of the final order after the hearing of the application.

### *(c)* *Liquidation*

In a case of compulsory liquidation, a provisional liquidator may be appointed by the court at any time between the presentation of a petition to have the insolvent company wound up and the appointment of the official liquidator. The most common reason for the appointment of a provisional liquidator is to prevent the directors of the company from disposing of its assets pending the appointment of the official liquidator.

In a compulsory liquidation, the liquidator is appointed by the court following the making of a winding-up order. In a voluntary liquidation the liquidator is appointed following the passing of a special resolution of the members – although the liquidator may be replaced by the creditors' choice of liquidator in a creditors' voluntary winding-up.

In contrast to examiners and receivers, the appointment of a liquidator leads to the automatic cessation of the directors' powers, although in a voluntary winding-up the members or creditors (as appropriate) may authorise some further uses by the directors of their powers.

The purpose of the liquidator is to wind up the company and to realise and distribute its assets in accordance with the law.

## 2. Licence agreements in the phase between filing and declaration of bankruptcy

### 2.1 Effects on licence agreements in the licensor's bankruptcy

The making of an application for the appointment of an examiner, receiver or liquidator does not in itself as a matter of law operate to automatically terminate any contracts to which a company is party. However, the terms of individual contracts may contain contractual provisions that provide for the termination of a licence agreement or the reversion of rights in the event that an insolvency application is filed. A contractual provision that purports to transfer a company's intellectual property assets in the event of its insolvency can, though, be held to be void.

An examinership provides some protection for companies because in an examinership, for a period of 70 days from the date of the petition (which can be extended by a further 30 days), the creditors of the company that is subject to the examinership are prevented from taking action to enforce any judgments or any security against the company.

### 2.2 Powers of administrators, receivers or trustees in the licensor's bankruptcy

An interim examiner has the same powers as an examiner appointed after a full hearing of a petition for licensor insolvency. See section 3.3 for more information on the powers of an examiner.

The powers of a provisional liquidator will depend in each case on the terms of the court order of appointment. Under the Companies Acts, the court has a specific authority to limit and restrict the powers of a provisional liquidator by the order of appointment.

### 2.3 Effects on licence agreements in the licensee's bankruptcy

The making of an application for the appointment of an examiner, receiver or liquidator does not in itself operate to automatically terminate any contracts to which a company is party. However, the terms of individual contracts may provide for the termination of the agreement or the reversion of the rights licensed in such circumstances. In particular, it is common for licence agreements to provide the licensor with a right to terminate the licence agreement in the event of the licensee's insolvency.

### 2.4 Powers of administrators, receivers or trustees in the licensee's bankruptcy

The same arrangements apply as are given in section 2.2 above.

### 2.5 Impact of registration

Irish law does not provide for the registration of commercial licences. Where the licence has been registered in a foreign jurisdiction, consideration will need to be given as to whether the laws of that jurisdiction apply to the licence. See section 5 below for more information.

A patent licence may be registered with the Irish Patents Office in order to highlight the interests of a sub-licensee. This registration does not have any impact on how the licence is treated in the event of insolvency of the licensor and/or licensee.

## 3. Licence agreements in the phase after declaration of bankruptcy

### 3.1 Treatment of intellectual property rights

There is no distinction in how different intellectual property rights are treated in the event of a bankruptcy.

### 3.2 Effects on licence agreements in the licensor's bankruptcy

The appointment of an examiner, receiver or liquidator to a company does not in itself operate to automatically terminate any contracts to which the company is a party. However, the terms of individual contracts may provide for the termination of the agreement or the reversion of the licensed rights in such circumstances.

Where it can be argued that the licence itself contains such unfavourable terms as to constitute an onerous contract, an examiner or a liquidator may make an application to disclaim the contract. A licence which requires the licensor to incur costs (such as patent maintenance fees) is potentially an onerous contract that the examiner or liquidator of the licensor would look to disclaim.

The effect of a disclaimer is to relieve the licensor of its obligations, but the licensee will retain an equitable interest in the intellectual property. The licensee could then make an application to court to have the legal interest in the intellectual property transferred to it, on such terms as the court may think just, on the basis that it is entitled to the property or it is just and equitable that the property should vest in it.

## 3.3 Powers of an administrator, receiver or trustee in the licensor's bankruptcy

### (a) *Examinerships*

The appointment of an examiner operates to prevent creditors taking steps to recover debts owed by the company. However, an examiner may 'certify' expenses incurred during the period of protection – with the effect that such costs take priority over all other debts, including sums secured by a fixed charge. In addition, on application to the court, an examiner may borrow on behalf of the company and pay specified debts incurred prior to the period of protection.

An examiner may apply to the court to dispose of property and licence agreements which are subject to security. The court may grant the application if it is satisfied that the disposal would be likely to facilitate the survival of the whole or part of the company as a going concern.

During its period of protection, but subject to the consent of the court, a company may repudiate any licence agreement under which some element of performance other than payment remains to be rendered by both the company and one or more other parties.

### (b) *Receiverships*

The powers of a receiver will depend on the terms of the court order or debenture document under which the receiver is appointed and whether the receiver is appointed purely as a receiver, or as a receiver-manager with the power to run the business in place of the directors. A receiver appointed through a court order usually has only limited powers to collect and sell the charged assets, while a receiver appointed through a debenture document usually has more expansive powers, such as the power to take possession.

### (c) *Liquidations*

The powers of a company's directors automatically cease on the appointment of a liquidator. A liquidator may exercise all of the powers of the directors, subject to a limited number of circumstances in which the consent of the members or the committee of inspection is required. Liquidators enjoy powers additional to those of directors, such as a power to apply to the court to disclaim onerous contracts.

A distinction can be drawn between liquidators appointed in a members' or creditors' voluntary liquidation and liquidators appointed in a compulsory liquidation. The former may exercise a much wider range of powers than the latter – for example, the power to carry on the business of the company without the necessity to seek consent.

## 3.4 Powers and rights of creditors in a licensor's bankruptcy

### (a) *Examinerships*

In an examinership, the rights of creditors are restricted in that they are prohibited from taking steps against the company during the period of examinership to recover outstanding debts.

The primary right of creditors during an examinership is to vote on the compromise or scheme of arrangement prepared by the examiner, which may include proposals in connection with the licence agreement. In order to bring the scheme to the court, at least one class of creditors whose claims are impaired by the proposed scheme must have accepted the proposed scheme at a creditors' meeting. To carry a vote, a majority in number, representing a majority in value, of claims represented at a creditors' meeting (either in person or by proxy) must vote in favour of the proposed scheme.

*(b)* ***Receiverships***

Provided the terms of the security document are sufficiently broad, a secured creditor may be able to exercise some control over the licence agreement by the appointment of a receiver. Although a receiver does not possess the power to disclaim contracts, the receiver will be able to deal with underlying intellectual property assets where they fall within the scope of the debenture document.

*(c)* ***Liquidations***

In the event that a licence agreement does not provide for automatic termination in the event of a liquidation, a creditor may apply to the liquidator to disclaim the contract, or the court may make an order rescinding the contract and providing for damages for non-performance by the company.

In a creditors' voluntary winding-up, the liquidator may only take certain actions with the consent of the creditors or, if appointed, the committee of inspection.

**3.5 Effects on licence agreements in the licensee's bankruptcy**

The appointment of an examiner, receiver or liquidator to a company does not in itself operate to automatically terminate any contracts to which a company is party. However, the terms of individual contracts may provide for the termination of the agreement in such circumstances. In particular, it is common for licence agreements to provide the licensor with a right to terminate in the event of a licensee's insolvency. If this right is exercised, the insolvent licensee is no longer required to pay the licence fee but remains liable for fees which were outstanding at the time of termination.

Reversion of rights, while possible, are subject to the anti-deprivation principle under Irish common law, which provides that there cannot be a valid contract that a person's property shall remain his until his bankruptcy, and on the happening of that event shall go over to someone else and be taken away from his creditors. A licence agreement arrangement may fall foul of the anti-deprivation principle if it has the commercial objective of depriving the creditors of an insolvent company of the benefit of a particular asset (such as a licence to use intellectual property) and takes effect as a consequence of the insolvency of the company.

**3.6 Powers of an administrator, receiver or trustee in the licensee's bankruptcy**

For a general discussion of the powers of examiners, receivers and liquidators, see section 3.3 above.

### 3.7 Powers and rights of creditors in a licensee's bankruptcy

A licensee's creditors have limited rights with regard to a licence agreement in the event that an insolvency practitioner is appointed, because insolvency practitioners rarely act as agents for the creditors. See also section 3.4 above.

### 3.8 Exclusive and non-exclusive licences

There is no distinction between exclusive and non-exclusive licences as a matter of law. However, from a licensee's perspective, the holder of an exclusive licence – particularly in the case of an exclusive worldwide licence that does not terminate in the event of a bankruptcy – is in a much stronger position in relation to an examiner, receiver or liquidator than the holder of a non-exclusive licence in terms of both any negotiation to purchase the underlying intellectual property and any application to a court to have the intellectual property vested in the licensee.

### 3.9 Perpetual and non-perpetual licences

There is no distinction between perpetual and non-perpetual licences as a matter of law. However, in the case of a non-perpetual licence it may be possible (as noted in section 3.2 above) for the liquidator or examiner to disclaim such a contract as onerous property when the licensee has ongoing payment obligations.

### 3.10 Effects on a sub-licence in a licensor's bankruptcy

There are no specific legislative rules or established case law in Ireland governing the effect on a sub-licence in the event of a licensor's bankruptcy.

However, it is generally understood that general legal principles will apply and that a sub-licence will normally be terminated at the same time as the main licence is terminated, unless there is a specific provision to the contrary in the licence. It is likely that the Irish courts will follow English case law in support of this position.

### 3.11 Effects on a sub-licence in a licensee's bankruptcy

See the comments in section 3.10 above.

### 3.12 Impact of registration

Irish law does not provide for the registration of commercial licences. Where the licence has been registered in a foreign jurisdiction, consideration will need to be given as to whether the laws of that jurisdiction may apply to the licence. See section 5 below for more information.

## 4. Contractual arrangements in deviation from the law

### 4.1 Exceptions

There are no statutory rules that are applicable only to certain types of licence agreement.

However, for some categories of agreement, case law has developed a number of implied terms, which will apply where there is no express agreement to the contrary. For example, a court can imply an undertaking to publish within a reasonable time where there is an agreement to publish without a specified date for publication.

## 4.2 Scope to alter statutory mechanisms

Article 3(1) of Regulation (EC) 593/2008 of June 17 2008 on the law applicable to contractual obligations (known as the 'Rome I Regulation') permits parties, by agreement, to deviate from the default rules for determining the law applicable to licence agreements.

Where the applicable law of an agreement is Irish law, then parties may only contract out of particular statutory mechanisms where, and to the extent that, the underlying statute expressly permits parties to do so.

## 4.3 Termination rights and automatic reversions

A licence agreement may provide for a termination right or an automatic reversion of rights to the licensor if the licensee becomes bankrupt. While a termination right is likely to be upheld by the court as a mere qualification of the licensee's right, the position is less clear in the case of a purported reversion. The anti-deprivation principle is more likely to apply in the case of a reversion of rights triggered by the bankruptcy of the licensee where the purpose of the reversion was to defraud the licensee's creditors. Conversely, the reversion is more likely to be upheld where it can be shown there were *bona fide* commercial reasons behind its inclusion.

The insolvency of the licensor will not normally operate to transfer the benefit of the licensed property to the licensee. In such instances, it is for the examiner, receiver or liquidator of the licensor to dispose of the property for the benefit of the licensor's creditors.

# 5. Cross-border aspects

## 5.1 Foreign law

Examiners, receivers and liquidators must be conscious of the law governing both contractual and non-contractual claims in connection with a licence agreement.

Contractual claims are governed by the Rome I Regulation. The general rule, as set out in Article 3(1), provides that a licence agreement will be governed by law chosen by the parties. This general rule is subject to the provisions of Article 21, which provides that the application of a provision of the law of any country specified in the Rome I Regulation may only be refused if such application is manifestly incompatible with the public policy of the forum. We are not aware of any cases in which Article 21 has been applied in Ireland.

Non-contractual claims are governed by Regulation (EC) 864/2007 of July 11 2007 on the law applicable to non-contractual obligations (known as the 'Rome II Regulation'). Contrary to the approach adopted under the Rome I Regulation, Article 8(1) of the Rome II Regulation overrides any choice-of-law clause agreed between the parties by requiring the law applicable to a non-contractual obligation arising from an infringement of an intellectual property right to be the law of the country for which protection is claimed. Article 8(3) contains an express prohibition on the derogation of this clause by agreement between the parties.

An Irish liquidator will only apply Irish law in relation to licence agreements that are subject to non-Irish law when required to do so under the applicable rules of private international law.

### 5.2 Foreign jurisdiction

As with a choice-of-law provision, an examiner, receiver or liquidator will also generally be bound by the election of a foreign jurisdiction in the licence agreement. However, there are a number of circumstances in which the Irish courts may accept jurisdiction irrespective of the venue selected in the licence agreement. Such circumstances include where:

- the licence agreement contains a non-exclusive jurisdiction clause and the court otherwise has jurisdiction to hear the dispute;
- proceedings are commenced in the Irish courts and the defendant enters an unconditional appearance to the claim brought in the Irish court; or
- neither party is domiciled in a state that is party to Regulation (EC) 44/2001 of December 22 2000 on jurisdiction and the recognition and enforcement of judgments in civil and commercial matters (known as the 'Brussels I Regulation') or the convention on jurisdiction and the enforcement of judgments in civil and commercial matters of September 16 1988 (known as the 'Lugano Convention'), and Ireland has the most real and substantial connection to the action.

It must also be noted that in cases challenging the validity or registration of a patent, trademark, design or other similar right required to be deposited or registered, Article 22(4) of the Brussels I Regulation provides exclusive jurisdiction for the court of the EU member state in which the impugned intellectual property right has been deposited or registered.

# Israel

**Yuval Horn**
**Keren Kanir**
Horn & Co., Law Offices

---

## 1. Overview

### 1.1 Relevant legislation governing intellectual property and bankruptcy

The Israeli insolvency rules are embodied in:

- the Companies Ordinance (New Version), 5743-1983;
- the Companies Regulations (Liquidation), 5747-1987;
- the Bankruptcy Ordinance (New Version), 5740-1980;
- the Companies Law, 5759-1999; and
- the Companies Regulations (Application for Arrangement of Reorganisation), 5762-2000.

Israeli bankruptcy legislation does not specifically and separately refer to matters of intellectual property in bankruptcy. Therefore, when bankruptcy proceedings are invoked, intellectual property and related agreements are treated as any other property or commercial agreement, as applicable, with the required adjustments.

### 1.2 Types of insolvency procedure

Israeli law refers to several winding-up procedures:

- A court-ordered liquidation – This is the most common liquidation route. The court manages the liquidation, appoints a liquidator and oversees its operations. The liquidator's role is to collect creditors' claims, realise the company's assets and pay the company's debts using the proceeds obtained following a realisation of assets in accordance with creditors' preferences.
- Recovery – 'Recovery' is a reorganisation process in which the company may seek a stay of proceedings while it pursues a recovery scheme. The Companies Law together with the related regulations promulgated thereunder (and listed in section 1.1 above) govern creditors' arrangements and plans for reorganisation, which in all cases are court-supervised procedures with the intention of reaching a recovery of the company as an ongoing concern. Over the years, Israel's insolvency body of law has moved its focus from liquidation to reorganisation procedures. Accordingly, recent amendments to the Companies Law, enacted in 2013, provided a set of tools for the court-appointed officer administering a company during rehabilitation. Among others, under Section 350h(b) of the Companies Law, during the stay of proceedings a party to an agreement may not terminate the agreement for reason of the insolvency.

- Voluntary liquidation – This is managed either by the company's shareholders or by its creditors. The conditions for voluntary liquidation are as follows:
  - The board of directors must prepare a solvency declaration whereby the board has enquired and come to the conclusion that the company will be able to meet its obligations during the 12-month period following commencement of voluntary liquidation.
  - The said solvency declaration must be sent to the Registrar of Companies.
  - Only after a copy of the solvency declaration has been provided to the Registrar of Companies, the company must convene a meeting of the shareholders in order to resolve with respect to the liquidation of the company, which is to be managed by the shareholders of the company.

In the event that any one of the aforesaid conditions has not been met, the voluntary liquidation is instead managed by the creditors of the company.

Generally, voluntary liquidation is managed out of court. The company (eg, its shareholders) voluntarily appoints a liquidator, who is responsible for winding up the company's business, subject to the company's compliance with certain conditions (such as solvency).

However, the court may issue an order that the voluntary liquidation becomes court supervised, although in practice this method is not typically preferred. This procedure is appropriate when disputes exist among a company's shareholders, or between its shareholders and its creditors. The court supervises the liquidation process, and may appoint an additional liquidator (on top of the one appointed by the shareholders of the company) to manage the liquidation.

In addition, voluntary liquidation may be transformed into a court-ordered liquidation at the request of:

- any shareholder or creditor of the company, to the extent that the court is convinced that the voluntary liquidation might adversely affect the rights of any shareholder or creditor of the company; or
- the Official Receiver or the Attorney General of the State of Israel, to the extent that the court is convinced that the rights of any shareholder or creditor of the Company require that the liquidation be managed by the court (rather than voluntarily, as set forth above).

### 1.3 Grounds of bankruptcy

Under Israeli law, 'bankruptcy' is not a term used when referring to companies. Rather, under Israel's Companies Ordinance the court may commence liquidation proceedings in each of the following cases:

- The company has adopted a special resolution that it be liquidated by the court;
- The company has not commenced its business within one year following its incorporation, or has ceased its business for a period of one year;
- The company has become insolvent;
- The court believes that it is just and fair that the company be dissolved.

Israel's Companies Ordinance defines a company as insolvent in each of the following events:

- A creditor to which the company has a debt in an amount of more than NIS5 (approximately €1) that has become due and payable, has provided the company with a written demand for the repayment of the debt, and the company has not paid or otherwise come to an arrangement with the creditor within three weeks following such written demand.
- A court order in a creditor's favour remains wholly or partly unsatisfied.
- It has been proven to the satisfaction of the court, taking into account the company's contingent and future liabilities, that the company is not able to pay its debts.

### 1.4 Filing for bankruptcy

Liquidation proceedings may be commenced either by the court, voluntarily by the company, or under court supervision.

A petition for a court-ordered liquidation may be filed by each of the following:

- the company, based on each of the grounds set forth in section 1.3 above;
- a creditor of the company, including a contingent or future creditor, based on each of the grounds set forth in section 1.3 above;
- a shareholder of the company, including anyone who was a shareholder of the company during the 12 months preceding the petition, based on each of the grounds set forth in section 1.3 above;
- the Attorney General of the State of Israel, in the event that any one of the following events has occurred:
  - the company has not commenced its business within one year following its incorporation, or has ceased its business for a period of one year;
  - it is deemed just and fair that the company be dissolved; and
  - the company has not been registered with the Registrar of Companies;
- the Official Receiver of the State of Israel, in the event that:
  - the company has commenced voluntary liquidation; and
  - the rights of the creditors or shareholders require that the liquidation is transformed into a court-ordered liquidation; and
- the Registrar of Companies, in the event that:
  - a financial sanction imposed on the company was not paid in a timely fashion (in that financial sanctions may be imposed by the Registrar when a company violates any of its duties under the Companies Law or any instruction given by the Registrar, such as failure to make the required filings in a timely fashion, failure to pay annual fees, etc); and
  - within three years of the imposition of such sanction, the Registrar has imposed an additional financial sanction on the company, which was also not paid in a timely way.

The district courts in Israel (which rank above magistrates' courts and below the Supreme Court) have jurisdiction over a debtor's liquidation and reorganisation proceedings. The debtor's seat or main place of business determines the district in which the case is heard. The bankruptcy procedure will take place in the court of the debtor's district of residence or its main place of business or assets.

### 1.5 Administrators and other appointed persons

Upon filing for liquidation, the court may appoint a temporary liquidator for the purpose of securing the company's assets until the appointment of a permanent liquidator. Since the company's management is still in charge of operational activity at this point, the authority of the temporary liquidator is more limited and narrower than that of the permanent liquidator and does not include ongoing management of the company's business unless specifically granted by court order. The court may grant the temporary liquidator such authorities as the court may deem fit, in order (for instance) to protect the assets of the company or to preserve the existing state of affairs and prevent damage to the petitioner filing for liquidation.

In a court-ordered liquidation, upon the court order for the liquidation of the company (the equivalent of a declaration of bankruptcy), the court may appoint the Official Receiver[1] to act as a temporary liquidator until a permanent liquidator is appointed as described below. Soon after the grant of a court order for liquidation, separate meetings of shareholders and creditors are convened to elect a permanent liquidator. If different candidates for liquidators are proposed by the shareholders and the creditors, the court will appoint the candidate it deems fit. If no liquidator has been appointed by the court, the Official Receiver acts as the liquidator.

Once appointed, the liquidator acts under the supervision (and in accordance with the instructions) of the Official Receiver, in order to realise the company's assets and distribute the proceeds among the company's creditors. Any instruction provided by the Official Receiver may be appealed before the court within 30 days. Any person that is harmed by a resolution of the liquidator may also address the district court within 30 days. The liquidator may request the court to provide instructions in any matter arising out of the liquidation.

In reorganisation proceedings, once the court approves a petition for a stay of proceedings, a trustee is appointed to perform and carry out the approved reorganisation scheme. The trustee may be either an officer of the company or a third party, as the court deems fit. During the stay-of-proceedings period, the trustee appointed by the court to administer the company is equipped with various authorities, as determined by the court on a case-by-case basis, that enable the trustee to preserve the company's business as a going concern.

In the absence of any specific ruling with respect to the authority of the trustee, the trustee has the same authority and duties that apply to a liquidator in the event of liquidation of a company. The court is further authorised to nominate the current management to continue to operate the company throughout the rehabilitation period and preserve the company's business as a going concern. In the event that the

---

1 The Official Receiver is a state official at Israel's Ministry of Justice, entrusted with managing insolvency procedures, including the bankruptcy of individuals, liquidation proceedings of corporations, recovery proceedings of corporations and creditors' arrangements.

court does not appoint a trustee, the management of the company will have the same authority and duties as a trustee.

## 2. Licence agreements in the phase between filing and declaration of bankruptcy

### 2.1 Effects on licence agreements in the licensor's bankruptcy

Following the filing of a request for liquidation of a company and prior to the granting of an order for liquidation by the court, a temporary liquidator may be appointed by the court in order to secure the company's assets until the appointment of a permanent liquidator. Generally, at that time the courts respect the validity of agreements entered into by the company; however, the court may terminate certain types of transactions retroactively, following the declaration of bankruptcy – for further details, see section 3.2 below.

### 2.2 Powers of administrators, receivers or trustees in the licensor's bankruptcy

Following the filing of a request for liquidation of a company and prior to the granting of a liquidation order by the court, a temporary liquidator may be appointed by the court in order to secure the company's assets until the appointment of a permanent liquidator. Since the company's management is still in charge of operational activity at that stage, the authority of the temporary liquidator is more limited and narrower than that of the permanent liquidator and does not include the ongoing management of the company's business unless it was specifically granted by a court order. The authority of the permanent liquidator to manage the ongoing business of the company includes, among other things, the authority to file claims or defend the company in any legal action, to make payments to debtors, and generally to manage the business of the company as may be required in order to efficiently dissolve the company.

### 2.3 Effects on licence agreements in the licensee's bankruptcy

Following the filing of a request for liquidation of an insolvent licensee and prior to the granting of an order for liquidation by the court, a temporary liquidator may be appointed by the court in order to secure the licensee's assets until the appointment of a permanent liquidator. Generally, at such a time the courts respect the validity of agreements entered into by the company; however, the court may terminate certain types of transactions retroactively, following a declaration of bankruptcy – for further details please see section 3.2 below.

### 2.4 Powers of administrators, receivers or trustees in the licensee's bankruptcy

Following the filing of a request for liquidation of an insolvent licensee and prior to the granting of an order by the court, a temporary liquidator may be appointed by the court in order to secure the licensee's assets until the appointment of a permanent liquidator. Since the licensee company's management is still in charge of operational activities at that stage, the authority of the temporary liquidator is limited and narrower than that of the permanent liquidator and does not include the ongoing management of the company's business unless it was specifically granted by a court order. A temporary liquidator will be appointed in those cases where the court believes there is an urgent need to seize the company's assets, and will only have the specific authorities granted to him/her by the court. Such powers will rarely include the authority to dispose of the assets of the company.

The authority of the permanent liquidator to manage the ongoing business of the company, includes, among other things, the authority to file claims or defend the company in any legal action, to make payments to debtors, and generally to manage the business of the company as may be required in order to efficiently dissolve the company.

## 2.5 Impact of registration

Section 87 of Israel's Patents Law stipulates that a licence with respect to a patent shall be considered void to any party other than the parties to the licence agreement itself, unless it is duly registered in accordance with the provisions of the Patents Law.

An Israeli district court has previously ruled[2] that if a licensee that received an exclusive licence wishes to ensure its ability to prevent infringement of its rights by third parties, or enforce its rights under the exclusive licence in any other manner against third parties, the licensee must register its licence with the Patent Registry. Otherwise, under Israeli law the court might not recognise the licensee's rights in the licensed patent outside the scope of the licence agreement, and the relationship between the parties thereto (ie, against third parties). Accordingly, in the event of the licensor's bankruptcy, and in the absence of registration of a licence granted with respect to a patent, a licensee might find itself with a restricted ability to protect and enforce the rights granted to it under the licence against third parties.

Although Section 87 of the Patents Law requires registration of a licence with respect to a patent, it should be noted that in practice such registration is commonly neglected because companies prefer to save the costs associated with registration and removal of registration, and also because Israeli patents are usually considered less significant (ie, compared with US or European patents, for example).

Under Israel's Copyright Law, 5768-2007, copyrights are not required to be registered in Israel in order to be recognised, and there is no registry of copyrights. Section 37(c) of the Copyright Law states that the granting of a licence with respect to copyrights requires an agreement in writing.

Section 50(a) of Israel's Trade Marks Ordinance,5732-1972, states that the registered owner of a trademark may allow another party to make use of such trademark, and Section 50(b) of the same ordinance requires that such right to use be registered in the trademark register.

---

2 C.C. (Tel Aviv) 1188/95 *Yu Zheng and Others v. El Shai Import and Marketing Ltd.* and others (10.2.1999) (Published in Nevo – online Legal Data-Base)

## 3. Licence agreements in the phase after declaration of bankruptcy

### 3.1 Treatment of intellectual property rights

Under Israeli law, there is no distinction between different intellectual property rights in the event of bankruptcy.

Many Israeli technology companies receive financial support from the Office of the Chief Scientist (the OCS) at the Israeli Ministry of Economy. Under the Israeli Encouragement of Industrial Research and Development Law, 5744-1984, any company that has developed intellectual property using funds received from the OCS (a so-called 'OCS-supported company') is subject to certain restrictions. Among them, an OCS-supported company must notify the relevant OCS official in the event that a request for liquidation or a stay of proceedings is filed against the company. In addition, generally, the production of any product developed by an OCS-supported company with the funds received from the OCS must be conducted in Israel. In order to be able to transfer the production of such product abroad, the OCS-supported company first must receive the approval of the applicable R&D committee, and will be obligated to pay the OCS certain royalties (as prescribed by the Encouragement of Industrial Research and Development Law and the regulations promulgated thereunder).

### 3.2 Effects on licence agreements in the licensor's bankruptcy

In general, the declaration and commencement of bankruptcy does not automatically result in an automatic stay of proceedings, nor eventually in the termination of the bankrupt entity's contractual rights and obligations. Israeli courts have clarified that where a party has a contractual right to exploit intellectual property owned by another party, it should not take advantage of the fact that the other party has been declared bankrupt in order to avoid making payments due under the agreement. Licence agreements are not treated any differently.

Israeli courts respect the validity of agreements entered into by a company prior to the filing of an application for bankruptcy. There are, however, several sets of circumstances in which transactions made by a bankrupt company may be terminated by the court, as follows:

- if the transaction was entered into:
  - with an intention of granting a creditor undue advantage; and
  - within the three-month period prior to filing an application for bankruptcy;
- if the transaction was entered into after the filing of a bankruptcy application (unless made in arms' length terms and in good faith); and
- if the liquidator views the agreement as an 'encumbering asset' as defined by law. Under the Companies Ordinance, an 'encumbering asset' is defined as each of the following:
  - real estate with burdensome conditions or restrictions;
  - shares of a company, which have not been fully paid for;
  - contracts with no profit; or
  - any other asset that cannot be sold, easily or altogether, since it requires the holder thereof to perform a burdensome act or to pay an amount of money.

### 3.3 Powers of an administrator, receiver or trustee in the licensor's bankruptcy

Under Israeli law, the administrator in bankruptcy is authorised, subject to the approval of the court, to 'waive' an encumbering asset. In other words, the administrator may cause the detraction of an asset from the assets that are to be realised and distributed to the shareholders and creditors of the company, but only do so in those cases where the encumbering asset is counterproductive to the liquidation process.

One such encumbering asset that may be waived is an agreement. The administrator is authorised, subject to the approval of the court, to release the company from a contractual obligation by waiving the agreement, on the grounds that the disadvantages for the company involved in the agreement outweigh the benefits.

The waiver by the administrator of an encumbering agreement entails the waiver of both obligations and rights under the agreement. In such cases, when approving the waiver of the agreement the court may condition such waiver upon the payment of compensation to the party harmed by the waiver of the agreement. Once the court instructs the payment of such compensation, the party harmed by the waiver of the agreement is deemed a creditor of the company and has a valid claim against the company in the process of liquidation. Such a claim is settled in accordance with the general preference of liquidation, and is generally not considered a secured debt.

The administrator cannot waive only a portion of an asset – so, for instance, it is impossible to waive only the contractual obligations and keep the contractual rights and benefits.

The waiver of the encumbering asset may harm the rights and obligations of a third party only to the minimum extent required in order to release the company from its liabilities.

### 3.4 Powers and rights of creditors in a licensor's bankruptcy

Creditors do not have powers or rights with regard to any of a licensor's assets in bankruptcy, including any licence agreement. The administrator acts to realise and distribute all the assets, including the licence agreement.

### 3.5 Effects on licence agreements in the licensee's bankruptcy

In general, the declaration and commencement of bankruptcy does not automatically result in the termination of the bankrupt entity's contractual rights and obligations. In such circumstances, to the extent such contractual rights and obligations are not terminated by the court, Israeli courts have clarified that where a party has a contractual right to exploit intellectual property owned by another party, it should not take advantage of the fact that the other party has been declared bankrupt in order to avoid making payments due under the agreement. Licence agreements are not treated any differently.

To the extent that an agreement itself sets forth insolvency as a cause for termination, the situation is likely to be treated differently. It should, however, be noted, that under Section 350h(b) of the Companies Law, during the stay of proceedings a party to an agreement is not permitted to terminate the agreement as a result of the insolvency. This means that even in cases where the agreement itself sets insolvency as grounds for termination, such termination is proscribed during a stay of proceedings within the recovery framework.

### 3.6 Powers of an administrator, receiver or trustee in the licensee's bankruptcy

Under Israeli law, an administrator in bankruptcy is authorised, subject to the approval of the court, to 'waive' an encumbering asset. In other words, an administrator may cause the detraction of an asset from the assets that are to be realised and distributed to the shareholders and creditors of the company, but only in those cases where the encumbering asset is counterproductive to the liquidation process.

One such encumbering asset that may be waived is an agreement. The administrator is authorised, subject to the approval of the court, to release the company from a contractual obligation by waiving the agreement on the grounds that the disadvantages for the company involved in the agreement outweigh the benefits.

The waiver by the administrator of an encumbering agreement entails the waiver of both obligations and rights under the agreement. In such cases, when approving the waiver of the agreement, the court may condition such waiver upon the payment of compensation to the party harmed by the waiver of the agreement. Once the court instructs the payment of such compensation, the party harmed by the waiver of the agreement is deemed a creditor of the company and has a valid claim against the company in the process of liquidation. Such a claim is settled in accordance with the general preference of liquidation and is generally not considered a secured debt.

The administrator cannot waive only a portion of an asset – so, for instance, it is impossible to waive only the contractual obligations and keep the contractual rights and benefits. The waiver of the encumbering asset may harm the rights and obligations of a third party only to the minimum extent required in order to release the company from its liabilities.

The ability to waive an encumbering agreement constitutes an exception to the basic rule that a party to an agreement may not unilaterally be released from its contractual undertakings unless the other party to the agreement is in breach (all in accordance with Israeli legislation regarding contracts). According to the provisions of the Company's Ordinance, the right to waive an asset does not include the right to sell the asset without the approval of the owner of the asset – or, in this case, the right to waive an agreement does not include the right to sell the agreement without the approval of the other party to the agreement.

Notwithstanding the foregoing, certain provisions in the licence agreement itself with respect to the ability to assign the agreement may allow the administrator to sell the licence without seeking the prior approval of the licensor. The administrator of the licensee's assets may, subject to the approval of the court, waive the license agreement (i.e. when the license agreement is deemed to be an encumbering asset), subject to and in accordance with terms set forth hereinabove.

### 3.7 Powers and rights of creditors in a licensee's bankruptcy

The creditors in a licensee's insolvency do not have powers or rights with regard to any of the licensor's assets, including the licence agreement. The administrator of the bankrupt licensee estate acts to realise and distribute all the assets, including the licence agreement. The license agreement itself is deemed an asset of the insolvent licensee, which the administrator of the licensee acts to realise and distribute.

### 3.8 Exclusive and non-exclusive licences

There is no distinction between exclusive and non-exclusive licences in the event of a bankruptcy.

### 3.9 Perpetual and non-perpetual licences

There is no distinction between perpetual and non-perpetual licences in the event of a bankruptcy. However, in a perpetual licence, to the extent the licensed asset does not require any maintenance (such as ongoing payment of fees with respect to registered patents) the licensee may be able to continue to exploit the licence even following the winding-up of the licensor.

In addition, there is no distinction between perpetual and non-perpetual licences, in the event of a bankruptcy, with regard to the ability of the administrator to waive the licence agreement (subject of course to court approval), as further set forth earlier in this section 3.

### 3.10 Effects on a sub-licence in a licensor's bankruptcy

The effects on a sub-licence in a licensor's bankruptcy are similar to the effect on the licence itself, in addition to any contractual claims that may be brought by the sub-licensee against the licensee. In the absence of any provisions to the contrary in the agreement, to the extent the licence agreement is terminated the rights will revert to the licensor, and the effect on a sub-licensee will be similar to the effect on the licensee itself.

### 3.11 Effects on a sub-licence in a licensee's bankruptcy

The court is authorised to rule and provide instructions in cases where, owing to the waiver of an agreement, third parties' rights are affected. For example, in the event of termination of a licence agreement as a result of such a waiver in bankruptcy, a sub-licensee's right under the licence agreement will expire – that is, unless the licence agreement and the sub-licence agreement both stipulate that in the event that the licensee ceases to operate, the sub-licence will survive. In such cases, the sub-licensee may request the court to instruct the assignment of the licensee's rights under the licence agreement to the sub-licensee.

### 3.12 Impact of registration

Section 87 of Israel's Patents Law stipulates that a licence with respect to a patent shall be considered void to any party other than the parties to the licence agreement itself, unless it is duly registered in accordance with the provisions of the Patents Law.

An Israeli district court has previously ruled[3] that if a licensee that received an exclusive licence wishes to ensure its ability to prevent infringement of its rights by

---

3 See footnote 2 above.

third parties, or enforce its rights under the exclusive licence in any other manner against third parties, the licensee must register its licence with the Patent Registry. Otherwise, under Israeli law, the court might not recognise the licensee's rights in the licensed patent outside the scope of the licence agreement, nor the relationship between the parties thereto (ie, against third parties). Accordingly, in the event of licensor's bankruptcy, and in the absence of registration of a licence granted with respect to a patent, a licensee might find itself with a restricted ability to protect and enforce the rights granted to it under the licence against third parties.

Although Section 87 of the Patents Law requires registration of a licence with respect to a patent, it should be noted that in practice such registration is commonly neglected, because companies prefer to save the costs associated with registration and removal of registration, and also because Israeli patents are usually considered less significant (ie, compared with US or European patents, for example).

Under Israel's Copyright Law, copyrights are not required to be registered in Israel in order to be recognised, and there is no registry of copyrights. Section 37(c) of the Copyright Law states that the granting of a licence with respect to copyrights requires an agreement in writing.

Section 50(a) of Israel's Trade Marks Ordinance states that the registered owner of a trademark may allow another party to make use of such trademark, and Section 50(b) of the same ordinance requires that such right to use be registered in the trademark register.

## 4. Contractual arrangements in deviation from the law

### 4.1 Exceptions

Under Section 123 of Israel's Bankruptcy Ordinance (which applies to people, as opposed to corporations), where the assets of a bankrupt person include copyrights, or any rights in connection with copyrights, that require the payment of royalties to the creator, the trustee in bankruptcy may not exploit such rights without paying the creator the royalties due, and may not assign such rights without ensuring that the creator will receive all amounts due to him.

Pursuant to Section 353 of the Companies Ordinance, the foregoing applies *mutatis mutandis* to insolvent corporations that are in the process of liquidation.

### 4.2 Scope to alter statutory mechanisms

Israel's Contracts Law adopts a flexible approach that allows the parties to a commercial contract to freely choose the terms of the agreement, provided that such terms do not contradict mandatory statutes. It should be noted, though, that the mandatory provisions of the Contracts Law mainly prohibit the entering into of any contract whose content or purpose is illegal, immoral or contradicts public policy. Upon any breach of a contract, Israeli law further provides the party that suffered as a consequence of the breach to elect between termination or enforcement of the contract, as well as compensation for damages caused by the breach.

The bankruptcy legislation in Israel is mandatory and therefore may not be contradicted by a licence agreement (or any other agreement); any contradictory contractual condition is considered void. For example, where a licence agreement includes an explicit or implicit condition by which the validity of the agreement is contingent upon the continued existence or solvency of the parties, the bankruptcy of either party to the agreement might lead to the termination of the agreement. Notwithstanding, upon liquidation of either licensor or licensee, the other party might become a debtor of the bankrupt party, and thus its rights regarding amounts owed will be in accordance with the priorities of the debtors set out in applicable law, such that the licensee whose licence is contractually terminated upon insolvency of the licensor has an unsecured claim. Although, therefore, the parties might agree with respect to certain terms of the licence agreement, their agreement cannot deviate from the mandatory bankruptcy rules that would otherwise apply.

### 4.3 Termination rights and automatic reversions

Israeli licence agreements typically include a provision stating that in the event that the licensee becomes bankrupt (and remains so for a certain period of time), the agreement will automatically terminate and the rights granted to the licensee thereunder will automatically revert to the licensor.

## 5. Cross-border aspects

### 5.1 Foreign law

The administrator has no authority to rule with respect to questions arising from the licence agreement. According to rulings by the Israeli Supreme Court, when discussing agreements (including licence agreements) in bankruptcy procedures the competent Israeli court must differentiate between procedural provisions and substantive aspects regarding the rights of the parties. There are two different types of substantive questions that may arise: the general law applicable to the conflict (contract law, property law, etc); and the applicable bankruptcy laws.

The Israeli Supreme Court ruled[4] that in questions of substantive law – such as matters regarding the validity of a contract and the interpretation thereof arising from claims brought as part of insolvency proceedings (such as a claim for a debt) – the rules of private international law will apply, and the parties' election of foreign law in the agreement shall prevail.

Matters that involve the substantive provisions of the bankruptcy laws will be examined by the Israeli court on a case-by-case basis, and may or may not be subject to the foreign law elected by the parties in such case. When dealing with procedural provisions, such as the filing date of a debt claim in insolvency proceedings, the provisions of Israeli law will apply exclusively, being the law of the forum (the *lex concursus*).

### 5.2 Foreign jurisdiction

According to Israeli law, the Israeli courts have jurisdiction over cases involving the

---

4 C.A. 8946/04 *Warner Bros. International Television Distribution v. Zvi Yuchman, CPA, Trustee and Special Administrator of Tevel, Gvanim and Gvanim Krayot and Others*, Tak-El 2010(3) p.1001 [1.8.2010]

insolvency of an Israeli company operating and located in the State of Israel. Where a foreign jurisdiction applies, the Israeli courts respect such election.

Notwithstanding the foregoing, parties' ability to choose a jurisdiction is not unlimited and cannot overrule the mandatory insolvency laws. The court may or may not respect the election of a foreign jurisdiction by the parties to a licence agreement, considering among other things the logic and purpose of the agreement, the parties' intent, the procedural implications (such as multiple plaintiffs or creditors), whether the relevant assets are located in Israel and whether the relevant party is registered in or operates in Israel.

# Italy

**Pietro Masi**
**Davide Petris**
Portolano Cavallo Studio Legale

## 1. Overview

### 1.1 Relevant legislation governing intellectual property and bankruptcy

In Italy, intellectual property is basically governed by Legislative Decree No 30 dated February 10 2005 concerning licences and trademarks, and by Law No 633 dated April 22 1941 and subsequent amendments, which is on copyrights.

The main law governing insolvency in Italy is Royal Decree No 267 of March 16 1942. This law (hereinafter the Bankruptcy Law) has recently undergone a major reform, implemented through several acts – mainly:

- Law Decree No 35 dated March 14 2005 (ratified by Law No 80 dated May 14 2005);
- Legislative Decree No 5 dated January 9 2006;
- Legislative Decree No 169 dated September 12 2007 (effective as from January 1 2008); and
- Law No 134 dated August 7 2012.

EU Regulation (EC) 1346/2000 of May 29 2000 on insolvency proceedings also needs to be mentioned as legislation governing insolvency in Italy.

### 1.2 Types of insolvency procedure

A debtor company facing financial distress can choose from several options under Italian law in terms of how the company's distress will be handled. These options are each outlined next.

#### *(a) Plan of reorganisation*

A company undergoing a situation of temporary financial distress may implement a plan aimed at the so-called 'reorganisation' of the company's activity – in particular with respect to the contractual and debt obligations. This is the least intrusive of the possible pre-insolvency proceedings, since it neither provides complex procedures nor involves the court, the receiver or other public officers entitled to manage or supervise the company. The legal basis for a plan of reorganisation is Article 67(3)(d) of the Bankruptcy Law.

The content of the plan may include access to new leverage, a rescheduling of the amortisation plan of bank debts, a new business plan, a change to key personnel, and individual out-of-court agreements with creditors. The plan must be accompanied by a certification of an accounting or auditing firm attesting that the plan is reasonably adequate to rehabilitate the business, to pay debts and to reinstate a safe financial situation.

The main advantage of the plan is that, in the event of subsequent bankruptcy, payments made by the company in accordance with the plan are not subject to clawback actions. This allows the distressed company to run its business in a normal fashion without being expelled from its market – enterprises generally avoid the closing of deals where they risk being required to give money back at a later stage, and this will not apply to transactions during a reorganisation.

The downside of this procedure is that it is not binding on all creditors, with the consequence that creditors enforcing their claims might jeopardise the exact performance of the plan.

***(b) Debt restructuring agreement***

A distressed company can also seek court authority to implement a debt restructuring agreement approved by creditors holding at least 60% of the company's liabilities. This process is based on Article 182bis of the Bankruptcy Law.

When petitioning the insolvency court for approval to proceed with the agreement, the debtor is required to file a report that is certified by an expert and that sets forth the terms of the agreement and clarifies how the receivables of dissenting creditors will be paid. Indeed, under the Bankruptcy Law any creditors not approving the debt restructuring agreement have to be paid the entire amount of their receivables within 120 days of the approval of the agreement by the insolvency court.

This procedure – aimed at restructuring and relaunching the company's business – is more expeditious than a creditor composition (see (c) below) and enables the distressed company to avoid the more elaborate voting requirements governing compositions. Another advantage over creditor composition is that it does not require payment in full to secured creditors and does not involve external bodies managing/supervising the company (a significant cost saving for the debtor).

As with a plan of reorganisation, should the potentially insolvent company subsequently be declared bankrupt, payments and other transfers or dispositions to any creditor (whether or not party to the agreement) performed as part of the debt restructuring agreement are not subject to clawback actions.

The downside is that debt restructuring agreements are binding only on accepting creditors. Dissenting minority creditors are not bound by the agreement and may issue enforcement proceedings against the debtor (except for a period of 60 days from the date of publishing of the debt restructuring agreement in the Register of Enterprises, during which lawsuits and enforcement proceedings are temporarily frozen).

***(c) Creditor composition***

If the recourse to proceedings for a plan of reorganisation or a debt restructuring agreement is for some reason not possible, the debtor may seek to implement a creditor composition (see Articles 160–186 of the Bankruptcy Law), under which the debtor company may propose:

- a debt restructuring and satisfaction of creditor claims by any means, including asset transfers, assumption of liabilities, or other transactions;
- liquidation of the business; or
- a combination of the preceding two solutions.

The proceedings for the approval of a creditor composition consist of three main phases:

- The debtor files a draft proposal with the local court and the court verifies that all formal requisites set forth by the law are satisfied. If the court accepts the proposal, it appoints a supervisor (in Italian, *commissario giudisiale*) and the proceedings start.
- The creditors are convened to approve or reject the proposed creditor composition. For approval, the favourable vote of the creditors representing a majority of the claims is required; no minimum number of creditors is required. The list of 'admitted' claims is compiled by a judicial officer based on the company's financial records.
- If none of the creditors challenges the validity of the resolution approving the composition, the court gives its final seal of approval. However, if the creditors' resolution approving the composition is challenged, the matter is adjudicated by the competent court. If the challenge is rejected, the composition is approved; if the challenge is accepted, the judge may decide to set aside a provision to satisfy the creditors and approve the composition or, alternatively, to not approve the composition.

Pending the proceedings, the debtor maintains possession of the business and operates under the supervisor as administrator. Actions exceeding the ordinary course of business require prior approval of the court.

### *(d)* *Bankruptcy*

If the debtor does not have access to any of the above pre-insolvency proceedings (because its distress is so serious that all of above proceedings cannot work), or if any one of those fails, the debtor is declared bankrupt.

Generally, the proceedings run as follows:

- filing of the petition before the competent court;
- issuance of a judgment declaring the bankruptcy of the company and the appointment of a public receiver (in Italian, *curatore fallimentare*) who replaces the governance body of the company;
- drawing-up of the creditors' list and rank order;
- liquidation of the debtor's assets and filing of clawback actions; and
- distribution of the proceeds of the bankruptcy estate (if any) to the creditors.

The main effects of bankruptcy are the following:

- The debtor cannot continue to run its business, unless the court expressly authorises this for a limited period of time;
- The debtor is dispossessed (cannot use/sell/perform any acts on its goods);

- The court appoints a public receiver, and directors are removed from their positions;
- There is an immediate suspension of the payment of all debts and liabilities of the debtor;
- Any legal actions brought by creditors are frozen; and
- Some payments made, securities given or transactions entered into by the debtor prior to the declaration of insolvency – within the so-called 'look-back period' – can be set aside by the receiver under certain conditions.

*(e)* ***Extraordinary administration***

Where a legal entity meets certain conditions, so-called 'extraordinary administration' should apply instead of bankruptcy. Those conditions are that the legal entity has at least 200 employees, and the total amount of the debts exceeds two-thirds of the turnover and/or the total assets of the entity.

The procedure and the rules for extraordinary administration are very similar to those for bankruptcy. However, the goal of this procedure is to relaunch the business instead of winding it up through the sale of its assets.

### 1.3 Grounds of bankruptcy

Business legal entities and individual entrepreneurs are subject to the dispositions concerning bankruptcy, provided that three mandatory dimensional requisites are met, namely:

- The aggregate value of the business assets and investments of the debtor in any of the previous three fiscal years exceeds €300,000;
- The average gross annual turnover in any of the previous three fiscal years exceeds €200,000; and
- The aggregate liabilities of the debtor (whether or not yet due) are equal to or higher than €500,000.

In addition to these dimensional requisites, the debtor must be deemed insolvent according to the definition given by the Bankruptcy Law (ie, unable to pay its debts on a regular basis by way of a common means of payment). Usually, any transitory and/or non-material illiquidity or financial difficulty that is likely to be resolved in the short term neither compels the debtor nor gives creditors reason to file for the entity's bankruptcy. There is, though, no clear-cut definition of 'transitory' or 'non-material' with regard to illiquidity.

If even one of the requisites is not met, the debtor is not subject to bankruptcy proceedings and any single creditor is individually entitled to recover its credit.

### 1.4 Filing for bankruptcy

Bankruptcy may be applied for by any one of the following groups:

- unsatisfied creditors that, for the satisfaction of their claims, see no alternative to an orderly winding-up of the business under the control of a court-appointed receiver;
- the debtor itself (as an initiative of the governing body generally, but not

compulsorily authorised by the shareholders' meeting) when it seeks the protection of bankruptcy proceedings against the risk of individual enforcement actions of its creditors; or

- the public prosecutor, when the insolvency arises out of either a criminal proceeding where the public prosecutor is party or a civil proceeding if the prosecutor holds that the public interest is better protected by a filing for insolvency even in the absence of any criminal liability. In the latter case, the public prosecutor is informed by the judge.

The competent court is the tribunal of the place where the company has its main office. Normally, this is the registered office of the company; however, according to the majority of doctrine and case law, in a case of multiple offices the 'main office' is the place where the executive and administrative offices are based. The changing of registered offices does not affect the competent court if the change occurred during the year before the date of the petition for bankruptcy.

### 1.5 Administrators and other appointed persons

When bankruptcy is declared, the relevant tribunal appoints a public receiver. The latter has the power to collect assets, bring legal actions in relation to the debtor's claims and otherwise manage the debtor's assets.

During the procedure the receiver, under certain conditions, may be replaced ex officio by the tribunal. The public receiver may also be replaced, upon either the request of the committee of creditors or the request of the judge delegated to monitor the bankruptcy procedure and to control its correctness.

## 2. Licence agreements in the phase between filing and declaration of bankruptcy

Even if a request for bankruptcy has been filed, the effects of bankruptcy (mainly summarised above) take place only after the latter is declared by the competent court. As a result, between a filing and a declaration of bankruptcy the licence agreements are not affected and the relationship between the licensee and licensor remain regulated by the agreement. Indeed, although clawback action is applicable before a declaration of bankruptcy, payments properly performed (ie, by cash, cheque or other normal means of payment) and in compliance with the licence agreement are not affected by any clawback action.

That said, it must be pointed out that during the proceedings aimed at declaring the bankruptcy, upon request of the interested party, the competent tribunal is entitled to issue interim and conservatory measures in order to protect the assets of the legal entity or individual entrepreneur that is going to be declared bankrupt. These measures are effective up until the judgment declaring the bankruptcy of company, and the measures can be confirmed or repealed through the same judgment.

## 3. Licence agreements in the phase after declaration of bankruptcy

### 3.1 Treatment of intellectual property rights

The Bankruptcy Law does not provide for specific rules regarding the treatment of intellectual property (IP) rights during insolvency. Assuming that the holder of these rights goes bankrupt and there are no licence agreements regulating the use of these rights, the public receiver is entitled to use the rights in the most profitable way according to the best interests of the creditors.

Thus, the receiver can:

- sell the IP rights directly (often at auctions, in accordance with specific formalities provided by the Bankruptcy Law);
- sell the IP rights along with the business unit of which the rights are a part; or
- enter into licence agreements.

The first and the second options (sale of the rights) are preferable since they are more suitable to the likely timetable of the bankruptcy proceedings.

### 3.2 Effects on licence agreements in the licensor's bankruptcy

The Bankruptcy Law governs the effects of the bankruptcy on pending contracts when one of the parties goes bankrupt. In particular, that law provides the general principles applicable to all pending contracts and for specific regulation of some types of contract (lease agreements, insurance agreements etc). The latter prevails over the general principles in a case of conflict.

According to Section 72 of the Bankruptcy Law, as a general principle in a case of bankruptcy by one of the parties a contract remains suspended until the public receiver decides either to become a party to the contract for the time in which the bankruptcy proceeding lasts – and, as a consequence, to be bound by all the duties and obligations provided therein – or to terminate the contract.

That said, licence agreements are not subject to specific regulation under the Bankruptcy Law. As a result, the general principles would apply as a default rule. However, according to some doctrine and case law, licence agreements should be regulated by the following provisions, as set forth in Section 80 of the Bankruptcy Law for lease agreements. In particular, according to that part of doctrine and case law, in the case of bankruptcy of a licensor the licence agreement automatically continues between the public receiver (which is in charge of managing the bankrupt company's assets) and the licensee. As a consequence on the basis of this opinion, the receiver would not have any power over the outstanding agreement. In the alternative, another part of quoted doctrine considers that the licence agreement is to be managed according the above-mentioned general principles, by which the receiver could decide to either become a party of the agreement (through the prior authorisation of the creditors' committee) or terminate it.

### 3.3 Powers of an administrator, receiver or trustee in the licensor's bankruptcy

As explained in section 3.2 above, according to the first opinion of the doctrine, the public receiver automatically becomes a party to a licence agreement and as a consequence is bound by all the obligations established therein without having any specific power to terminate or modify the agreement.

However, on the basis of the other doctrinal thesis, the public receiver would have the powers outlined in sections 3.5 and 3.6 following.

### 3.4 Powers and rights of creditors in a licensor's bankruptcy

According to the opinion that retains applicability of Section 80 of the Bankruptcy Law, creditors do not have specific powers or rights over the licence agreement in the case of the licensor's bankruptcy. The decision as to whether or not to continue the agreement lies exclusively with the receiver.

According to the alternative doctrine (which, in the light of the application of Section 72 of the Bankruptcy Law, requires the receiver to obtain the prior authorisation of the creditors' committee to continue the agreement), the creditors will have the power to authorise the continuation of the agreement. The authorisation of the creditor's committee is binding on the receiver. Note also that, in this case, the receiver has the full power to decide to terminate the contract without prior authorisation of the creditors' committee.

### 3.5 Effects on licence agreements in the licensee's bankruptcy

Different from the case of bankruptcy of the licensor, the majority of doctrine and case law deems that, in a licensee bankruptcy, the public receiver is entitled to decide whether to:

- continue the commercial relationship with the licensor under the same terms and conditions agreed by the parties (subject to prior authorisation of the creditors' committee); or
- terminate the agreement – where, in this case, bankruptcy procedure requires that the licensor receive 'fair indemnification' as a preferred claim.

### 3.6 Powers of an administrator, receiver or trustee in the licensee's bankruptcy

As described in section 3.5 above, the public receiver is entitled to decide whether to continue or terminate the licence agreement.

The receiver is personally liable for any damages or unfair prejudice suffered by the creditors, the debtor declared bankrupt or any third party involved in the bankruptcy proceedings – but only when such damages or unfair prejudice are due to a lack of care by the receiver in performing his obligations.

### 3.7 Powers and rights of creditors in a licensee's bankruptcy

The description in section 3.4 applies, *mutatis mutandis.*

### 3.8 Exclusive and non-exclusive licences

According to some accepted doctrine, in a case of bankruptcy of an exclusive licensee, in addition to what has been explained above, the licensor is granted the right to set a term within which the licensee's public receiver has to restart directly or indirectly commercialising the intellectual property rights licensed through the licence agreement and, as a consequence, to pay the licence fee agreed in the contract.

Where the public receiver fails to commercialise the IP rights by the end of the term provided by the licensor, the latter is entitled to terminate the agreement. Indeed, in this respect it has been pointed out that, even if the agreement can provide for a minimum of royalties as consideration for the exclusive use of the IP rights, the lack of use of the licence rights can trigger damages to the licensor that cannot be compensated by the payment of only the minimum guaranteed licence fee.

### 3.9 Perpetual and non-perpetual licences

First, it must be outlined that a 'perpetual' licence agreement (ie, one where there is an upfront payment and no further payments) is not commonly used in Italy. Indeed, licence agreements are usually based on the payment of royalties depending on the number of goods sold.

The payment method does not have any impact on a licence agreement in the event of the bankruptcy of one of the parties. However, in a case of bankruptcy of a licensee it is likely that the public receiver would opt for continuing the perpetual licence instead of terminating it since the consideration of the contract has been already paid in its entirety.

### 3.10 Effects on a sub-licence in a licensor's bankruptcy

Where a licence agreement provides that the licensor can transfer the licence right to a third party through a sub-licensing agreement, the bankruptcy of the licensor does not affect that agreement. Indeed, the public receiver will automatically continue the contract, replacing the party which went bankrupt.

### 3.11 Effects on a sub-licence in a licensee's bankruptcy

In the event of a licensee's bankruptcy, the effects on the sub-licence depends on the two alternative resolutions of the public receiver in relation to the licence agreement. Indeed, if the licence agreement remains valid and in force, a sub-licence agreement will continue to bind the sub-licensor and the sub-licensee.

Alternatively, should the public receiver terminate the licence contract, the sub-licence agreement is deemed automatically terminated because of its direct connection to the licence agreement.

### 3.12 Impact of registration

Official registration does not have any impact on licence agreements or sub-licence agreements in cases of insolvency.

Thus, the receiver and the creditors' committee have the above-mentioned powers on the outstanding contracts irrespective of whether the licence and sub-licence are registered.

## 4. Contractual arrangements in deviation from the law

### 4.1 Exceptions

Different from all other licence agreements relating to intellectual property, publishing agreements are expressly regulated by the Bankruptcy Law.

In particular, according to Section 83 of the Bankruptcy Law, the effects of the bankruptcy of a publisher on a publishing agreement are provided under Law No 633/1941 dated April 22 1941. Pursuant to Section 135 of that 1941 law, the bankruptcy of the publisher does not trigger the earlier termination of the publishing agreement. However, the contract is deemed as terminated should the receiver not continue or transfer the business within a year starting from the declaration of its bankruptcy.

### 4.2 Scope to alter statutory mechanisms

The Bankruptcy Law is mandatory and cannot be modified or altered by any agreements entered into. That particular law is indeed qualified as one of the public-order regulations, which are those not allowed to be derogated by any party.

The qualification as public-order law is due to the fact that bankruptcy law serves the purpose of protecting all those directly or indirectly involved in (and damaged by) the crisis of the company (such as creditors, stakeholders and contractual counterparties), by balancing the personal interests and rights of each involved entity with the general interest (ie, public order).

### 4.3 Termination rights and automatic reversions

Section 72(6) of the Bankruptcy Law expressly provides that a contractual clause allowing the termination of the contract by one party because of the other party's declaration of bankruptcy is null and void. As a result, considering the equivalent effects, automatic reversion is also deemed invalid according the principles of Italian law.

## 5. Cross-border aspects

### 5.1 Foreign law

Generally speaking, the Bankruptcy Law is mandatory and cannot be bypassed by any agreement between the parties. In compliance with this general principle, where bankruptcy proceedings take place in Italy the effects of the proceedings on any licence agreement are ruled by Italian Law.

In contrast, the choice of law agreed by the parties will apply in governing the contract and, in particular, the obligations established by the parties therein. Also, from an EU law standpoint the law of the country in which the bankruptcy proceedings take place governs the entire proceedings as well as the effects of bankruptcy on the contracts entered into by the debtor.

### 5.2 Foreign jurisdiction

According to Section 24 of the Bankruptcy Law, the Italian tribunal competent to make a declaration of bankruptcy has authority over all the disputes deriving from the bankruptcy proceedings. However, the majority of the doctrine and case law deems that if the licence agreement continues between the receiver and the licensor/licensee and a dispute arises after the declaration of bankruptcy, that dispute will be adjudicated by the court or arbitral tribunal chosen by the parties in the licence agreement.

In contrast, if the receiver terminates the agreement and the other party intends to challenge such termination, the dispute is submitted to the court of bankruptcy.

# Japan

**Shinnosuke Fukuoka**
**Toshihide Haruyama**
Nishimura & Asahi

## 1. Overview

### 1.1 Relevant legislation governing intellectual property and bankruptcy

In Japan, each type of intellectual property right is governed by a separate act:

- patent rights are regulated under the Patent Act, Law No 121 of 1959;
- design rights under the Design Acts, Law No 125 of 1959;
- utility model rights under the Utility Model Act, Law No 123 of 1959;
- trademark rights under the Trademark Act, Law No 127 of 1959;
- circuit layout rights under the Act on the Circuit Layout of a Semiconductor Integrated Circuits, Law No 43 of 1985; and
- copyrights under the Copyright Act, Law No 48 of 1970.

The Act on Amendments to the Patent Act (hereinafter the Patent Amendments Act) was promulgated on June 8 2011 and came into force on April 1 2012. Under the Patent Act and other related acts in Japan, there are two types of licence: exclusive licences and non-exclusive (also known as 'regular' or 'ordinary') licences. One of the purposes of the amendments is to enhance the position of non-exclusive patent licensees, given that under the pre-amended version of the Patent Act a non-exclusive licence was weaker than a registered exclusive licence (as discussed further in section 3.1).

Court procedures for insolvency in Japan are categorised into:

- liquidation procedures, which include bankruptcy (governed by the Bankruptcy Act, Law No 75 of 2004) and special liquidation proceedings (governed by a section of the Companies Act, Law No 86 of 2005); and
- restructuring procedures, which include civil rehabilitation (governed by the Civil Rehabilitation Act, Law No 225 of 1999) and corporate reorganisation proceedings (governed by the Corporate Reorganisation Act, Law No 154 of 2002).

### 1.2 Types of insolvency procedure

As stated in section 1.1 above, court procedures for insolvency in Japan are categorised into four proceedings.

Bankruptcy proceedings are similar to the proceedings prescribed in Chapter 7 of the US Bankruptcy Code. In bankruptcy proceedings, a court-appointed trustee disposes of the assets of the debtor and builds up a bankruptcy estate. The trustee makes distributions to creditors in accordance with the order of priority prescribed by law during the final stage of the proceedings. Creditor approval is not needed for those distributions.

So-called 'special liquidation' is a procedure whereby insolvent stock companies can be liquidated. Unlike in bankruptcy proceedings, the debtor maintains the power to dispose of its assets, and the competent court does not appoint a trustee for the debtor filing for special liquidation. The debtor will make distributions to creditors in accordance with a plan that has been confirmed by the court and approved by the creditors by a two-thirds majority (based on the amount of claims) at a creditors' meeting.

Both civil rehabilitation proceedings and corporate reorganisation proceedings are similar to the proceedings prescribed in Chapter 11 of the US Bankruptcy Code. In civil rehabilitation proceedings, as a general rule, the debtor maintains the power to manage its business and dispose of its assets even after an order for rehabilitation proceedings has been made – the so-called 'DIP' (debtor in possession) system.

In contrast, as a general rule in corporate reorganisation proceedings the debtor's business is managed by a court-appointed trustee. This is a procedure that impairs not only the claims of unsecured creditors, but also the claims of secured creditors. In both procedures, distributions to creditors will only be made after a rehabilitation plan or a reorganisation plan has been approved by a statutory majority at a creditors' meeting and has been confirmed by the court.

In this chapter we focus on bankruptcy proceedings, civil rehabilitation proceedings and corporate organisation proceedings, which are the most important procedures in Japanese insolvency practice (collectively hereinafter, 'insolvency proceedings').

## 1.3 Grounds of insolvency proceedings

### *(a) Bankruptcy proceedings*

Bankruptcy proceedings are available for both individuals and corporations and can be commenced if either a debtor is generally and continuously unable to pay past due debts because of an inability to make payment, or a debtor's debts exceed its assets.

### *(b) Civil rehabilitation proceedings*

Civil rehabilitation proceedings are available for both individuals and corporations and can be commenced if there is a possibility that a debtor will be faced with a situation constituting grounds for the commencement of bankruptcy proceeding, or a debtor is unable to pay its past due debts without significantly hindering the continuation of its business.

Nonetheless, a petition for the commencement of civil rehabilitation proceedings will be dismissed if the court finds that:

- the expenses for the rehabilitation proceedings have not been prepaid;
- bankruptcy proceedings or special liquidation proceedings are pending before the court, and enforcement of either of the proceedings accords with the common interests of the creditors;

- it is apparent that a proposed rehabilitation plan is unlikely to be prepared or approved or that the rehabilitation plan is unlikely to be confirmed; or
- the petition for commencement of rehabilitation proceedings has been filed for an unjustifiable purpose or has not been filed in good faith.

#### *(c) Corporate reorganisation proceedings*

Corporate reorganisation proceedings are only applicable to stock companies and can be commenced under the same circumstances as civil rehabilitation proceedings. A commencement order will generally be issued within approximately one month from the date of filing a petition for the commencement of corporate reorganisation proceedings.

A petition for the commencement of corporate reorganisation proceedings will, however, be dismissed if the court finds that:

- the expenses for the reorganisation proceedings have not been prepaid;
- bankruptcy proceedings, civil rehabilitation proceedings or special liquidation proceedings are pending before the court and enforcement of one of such proceedings accords with the common interests of creditors;
- it is apparent that a proposed reorganisation plan outlining the measures for the continuation of business is unlikely to be prepared or approved or that the reorganisation plan outlining the measures for the continuation of business is unlikely to be confirmed; or
- a petition for commencement of reorganisation proceedings has been filed for an unjustifiable purpose or has not been filed in good faith.

### 1.4 Filing for insolvency proceedings

Insolvency proceedings can be filed at court by both debtors and creditors. In the case of a creditor filing a petition for bankruptcy proceedings or civil rehabilitation proceedings, which is referred to as an 'involuntary petition', the petitioner can file such a petition regardless of the amount of the claims that the petitioner holds.

After a petition for bankruptcy proceedings or civil rehabilitation proceedings has been filed with a court, the court will order commencement of the proceedings if the court finds grounds for bankruptcy. Generally, the court is bound by the selection of the proceedings made by the petitioner; however, if a petition for commencement of rehabilitation proceedings is dismissed, the court, upon discovering the existence of facts constituting grounds for commencement of bankruptcy proceedings with regard to the same debtor can, by its own authority, issue an order for commencement of bankruptcy proceedings in accordance with the Bankruptcy Act.

A petition for commencement of corporate reorganisation proceedings can be filed not only by debtors and creditors, but also by shareholders. In order for a creditor to file a petition for the commencement of such proceedings, the creditor is required to have a claim that amounts to not less than one-tenth of the amount of the debtor's stated capital. In order for a shareholder to do so, the shareholder must hold voting rights that account for not less than one-tenth of the total voting rights held by all shareholders.

If a petition for commencement of corporate reorganisation proceedings is dismissed, the court, upon discovering the existence of facts constituting grounds for commencement of bankruptcy proceedings with regard to the same debtor can, by its own authority, issue an order for commencement of bankruptcy proceedings in accordance with the Bankruptcy Act.

In Japan, insolvency proceedings are not commenced automatically simply by filing for them; they are commenced by court order, which is only made once a court has reviewed a petition and found grounds for the commencement of the procedure filed for. Nonetheless, in cases where insolvency proceedings are filed by a debtor (in voluntary petitions), commencement orders are generally given on the same day or within a few days for bankruptcy proceedings, within approximately one week for civil rehabilitation proceedings, and within approximately one month for corporate reorganisation proceedings. By contrast, in involuntary petitions, although the timing of the commencement of procedures varies depending on the case, it takes more time to obtain a commencement order than in voluntary petitions because in most cases debtors usually argue that they are not insolvent.

## 1.5 Administrators and other appointed persons

In insolvency proceedings, the court that has jurisdiction over those proceedings appoints attorneys with broad experience in such matters to act as trustees, supervisors or other agents in accordance with the Bankruptcy Act, the Civil Rehabilitation Act and the Corporate Reorganisation Act (collectively hereinafter, the 'Insolvency Acts'). In what follows, we explain the role of trustees, provisional trustees and supervisors.

### *(a) Trustees*

Under the Bankruptcy Act and the Corporate Reorganisation Act, once bankruptcy proceedings or corporate reorganisation proceedings have been commenced by a court, the debtor is prohibited from making payments to its creditors (under the Bankruptcy Act and the Corporate Reorganisation Act, payments to creditors can only be made by the trustee through distribution proceedings.[1]) Instead, the court appoints a trustee simultaneously with making the order for commencement of bankruptcy proceedings or corporate reorganisation proceedings, and specifies the period during which claims can be filed by creditors and the date of the creditors' meeting.

A court-appointed trustee in bankruptcy proceedings and corporate reorganisation proceedings has the sole authority to administer and dispose of the assets of the debtor and its estate. (In contrast, in civil rehabilitation proceedings, the courts appoint trustees only in rare cases, such as when the property management by

1 It should be noted that the payment of administrative expenses, which are the highest-ranking claims in insolvency proceedings, may not be impaired. In other words, even after insolvency proceedings are filed, the payment of administrative expenses is given top priority over the payment of other claims. Administrative expenses will be fully paid as long as the debtor's estate is sufficient to do so; otherwise, the administrative expenses will only be partially paid to the extent permitted by the debtor's estate. 'Administrative expenses' are defined as including remuneration for trustees, fees necessary to conduct the proceedings, and expenses incurred after the proceedings are commenced (such as rent or licence fees that may be incurred after the commencement of the proceedings).

the debtor is inadequate.) In bankruptcy proceedings, the trustee makes distributions to the creditors, whereas in corporate reorganisation proceedings, the trustee prepares and implements a reorganisation plan and is required to obtain court approval to carry out certain important actions that do not fall within the ordinary course of business. The duties of the trustee are to convert the assets of the debtor into cash so that distributions to creditors can be made, to examine proofs of claims filed by creditors to the court, and to object to the allowance of any improper claims.

A single trustee is generally appointed in bankruptcy proceedings, while it is common for two trustees to be appointed in corporate reorganisation proceedings. In corporate reorganisation proceedings, an attorney-at-law is usually appointed as the 'legal' trustee, and a businessperson from a company sponsoring the debtor is dispatched as the 'business' trustee.

### *(b)* ***Provisional trustees***

In addition to the foregoing, a provisional trustee may be appointed, mainly in corporate reorganisation proceedings, to control the debtor's property and estate from the time a petition for commencement of corporate reorganisation proceedings is made until an order for commencement of the proceedings is given. The provisional trustee has the sole power to administer and dispose of the debtor's property during such term. In most cases, the provisional trustee becomes the court-appointed corporate reorganisation trustee after an order for commencement of the proceedings is made.

It should be noted that a provisional trustee does not have the right to terminate contracts (known as 'executory contracts') with bilateral obligations that neither the debtor nor the counterparty has completely performed, as described below.

### *(c)* ***Supervisors***

In civil rehabilitation proceedings, the debtor in possession generally remains in control and has the power to manage its business and dispose of its assets after the commencement of the rehabilitation proceedings. However, in most cases a supervisor is appointed by the court under the Civil Rehabilitation Act in order to oversee the conduct of the debtor.

After the court appoints a supervisor, any actions designated by the court in the commencement order will require the supervisor's consent. The court-appointed supervisor monitors the rehabilitation debtor's conduct by examining each application for consent, although activities in the ordinary course of the debtor's business generally do not require the supervisor's consent.

The supervisor also has a duty and the power to express its opinion in regards to the report prepared by the rehabilitation debtor concerning the debtor's financial status and the investigation of liabilities associated with the misconduct of its management. In addition, the supervisor is required to express its views to the court regarding the debtor's proposed rehabilitation plan. After taking into account the supervisor's opinion, the court then decides whether the proposed rehabilitation plan is adequate and legitimate. If the rehabilitation plan is approved in accordance with the Civil Rehabilitation Act, the supervisor will oversee the implementation of that plan.

## 2. Licence agreements in the phase between filing and declaration of bankruptcy

### 2.1 Effects on licence agreements in the licensor's bankruptcy

The act of filing for insolvency proceedings does not in itself affect the validity of licence agreements.

### 2.2 Powers of administrators, receivers and trustees in the licensor's bankruptcy

Between the filing for and commencement of insolvency proceedings, in both bankruptcy proceedings and civil rehabilitation proceedings the court generally does not appoint a provisional trustee; however, the court will generally appoint a provisional trustee in corporate reorganisation proceedings.

As discussed in section 1.5 above, between the filing for and commencement of insolvency proceedings (especially corporate reorganisation proceedings), the court appoints a provisional trustee in a provisional administration order so as to control the debtor's estate from the time a petition for commencement of corporate reorganisation proceedings is made up until an order for commencement of the proceedings is issued.

The provisional trustee has the sole authority to administer and dispose of the debtor's assets within the ordinary course of business, from the time the petition is filed until commencement of the proceedings is ordered, but a provisional trustee does not have the right to terminate executory contracts (including licence agreements).

### 2.3 Effects on licence agreements from the licensee's bankruptcy

The act of filing for insolvency proceedings itself does not affect the validity of licence agreements. There are no differences in procedure across bankruptcy, civil rehabilitation and corporate reorganisation proceedings for licensors and licensees.

### 2.4 Powers of administrators, receivers and trustees in the licensee's bankruptcy

As stated in sections 1.5 and 2.2 above, between the filing for and commencement of insolvency proceedings (especially corporate reorganisation proceedings), the court can appoint a provisional trustee in a provisional administration order to control the debtor's estate from the time a petition for commencement of corporate reorganisation proceedings is made up until an order for commencement of the proceedings is issued. There are no differences in procedure across bankruptcy, civil rehabilitation and corporate reorganisation proceedings for licensors and licensees.

A provisional trustee has the sole authority to administer and dispose of the debtor's assets within the ordinary course of business from the time the petition is filed until commencement of the proceedings is ordered, but the provisional trustee does not have the right to terminate executory contracts (including licence agreements) since exercising such a right does not fall within the definition of 'the ordinary course of business'.

If the court does not appoint a provisional trustee, the debtor controls its estate between the time of the petition and the commencement of the proceedings.

However, the debtor – regardless of whether a licensor or licensee – cannot terminate or modify licence agreements after filing for insolvency proceedings unless that was agreed.

A provisional trustee or debtor cannot claw back any payment of licence fees or other payments that have been made in a legitimate manner before the commencement of insolvency proceedings.

### 2.5 Impact of registration

As mentioned in sections 2.1 and 2.3 above, the act of filing for insolvency proceedings does not in itself have any effect on the validity of licence agreements; nor does registration of an agreement have any effect on any insolvency proceedings. Therefore, whether a licence is registered or not is unrelated to the validity of the licence agreement.

## 3. Licence agreements in the phase after declaration of bankruptcy

### 3.1 Treatment of intellectual property rights

#### *(a) The right to terminate executory contracts*

In insolvency proceedings (excluding special liquidation), a trustee or debtor under the Bankruptcy Act, the Civil Rehabilitation Act or the Corporate Reorganisation Act (collectively, 'the trustee/debtor') has the right to terminate so-called executory contracts, which (as explained earlier) are bilateral contracts under which one or more of the main obligations have not been completely performed by both the debtor and the creditor.

A trustee/debtor usually terminates executory contracts when it believes that maintaining such contracts could become detrimental or is unnecessary. In the event that an executory contract is terminated, the Insolvency Acts provide that the other party has an unsecured claim (not a preference claim) for damages. When, alternatively, the trustee/debtor determines that continuing an executory contract is advantageous or necessary, even after the proceedings commence, the trustee/debtor can allow the contract to remain in force. In such cases, the trustee/debtor can request that the counterparty perform its obligations, and the trustee/debtor will perform the debtor's counter-obligations accordingly. This obligation falls under administrative expenses and is therefore protected, as explained in section 1.5 and footnote 1 above. However, the counterparty cannot terminate the executory contract and is bound by the trustee/debtor's decision.

As the circumstances in which a trustee/debtor can terminate an executory contract are not prescribed in the relevant legislation of Japan, they are generally thought to have a right to terminate executory contracts at their discretion. Additionally, there is a judicial precedent[2] that held that the termination of an executory contract by a trustee/debtor is invalid where the termination will significantly harm the counterparty and lead to an extremely unfair result. Whether

2 *X v Y*, 54 MINSHÛ 553 (Sup Ct, February 29 2000).

or not the termination of an executory contract will significantly harm the counterparty and lead to an extremely unfair result depends on whether:

- the termination imposes a tremendous burden on the counterparty;
- it is easy for the counterparty to recover the damages; and
- the obligations that have not been completely performed by the debtor are essential.

It should be kept in mind that the fact that an obligation of one party has already been performed in full (for example, payment of a licence fee in a licence agreement) prior to the commencement of insolvency proceedings is not enough to conclude that the termination will significantly harm the counterparty.

Exercising the rights to terminate and assume executory contracts sometimes requires court permission. Under the Bankruptcy Act, court permission is generally required for a trustee to assume an executory contract but is not required for a trustee to terminate such a contract. However, if it is likely that the amount of the payments to be made pursuant to the assumption of an executory contract will not exceed ¥1 million (around US$10,000), court permission will not be required as an exception.

In contrast, under the Civil Rehabilitation Act and the Corporate Reorganisation Act the courts may order that court permission or the supervisor's consent should be obtained for a trustee/debtor to terminate an executory contract. However, in practice in civil rehabilitation proceedings the courts tend to exclude both assumption and termination of executory contracts from the acts for which court permission should be obtained (and even in such cases the courts tend to indicate that termination is an act for which the supervisor's consent should be obtained); furthermore, in corporate reorganisation proceedings the courts tend to exclude assumption of executory contracts, but include termination of executory contracts, as one of the acts for which court permission should be obtained.

### *(b) Termination of licence agreements as executory contracts*

The commencement itself of insolvency proceedings, like the act of filing for commencement of insolvency proceedings, does not change or amend intellectual property rights. However, a licence agreement is understood to be a contract under which the owner of intellectual property rights permits a licensee to use and exploit its intellectual property under the terms and within the scope of the agreement in return for the payment of royalties. Therefore, a licence agreement that has been concluded by the time of commencement of insolvency proceedings is usually dealt with as an executory contract.

Before the Patent Amendments Act, in the event that a licensor became subject to insolvency proceedings, the bankruptcy trustee or debtor could terminate a licence agreement where the licence had not been registered; in addition, if a patent was transferred to a third party, non-exclusive licensees that had not registered their licence could not assert their rights against the new patent owner, whereas the holder of an exclusive licence, which could only be vested through registration, could assert its rights against the new patent owner. Despite the fact that a non-exclusive licensee always faced the risk of suddenly being unable to assert its rights, the registration system for non-exclusive licences was not widely used in Japan as licensors disliked registration for the following reasons:[3]

- Registration procedures and the associated expenses were costly;
- Both licensors and licensees usually do not want the existence and content of licence agreements to become publicly known as a result of registration;
- In comprehensive cross-licensing agreements, the target patent rights are not identified by a patent number, which makes them difficult to register; and
- Both the licensor and the licensee were required to apply for registration – although a non-exclusive licensee had no right to force the licensor to cooperate with the registration.

In order to protect the rights of non-exclusive licensees, amendments were introduced to the Patent Act via the Patent Amendments Act. Following implementation of the amendments, in the event of a licensor's insolvency the trustee/debtor is no longer permitted to terminate non-exclusive licence agreements for patents. Furthermore, the amendments enable non-exclusive licensees to assert their rights against third parties without registration. The articles that provide for the creation of the registration system are contained in the Utility Model Act and the Design Act. Therefore, the amendments regarding the registration system also apply to these acts. In contrast, the licence registration system for trademarks and circuit layouts has not been amended and there is no registration system for copyrights and know-how; therefore, licensees of those rights are still not protected from insolvency proceedings.

It should be noted, however, that there is controversy regarding whether all of the terms and conditions of a licence agreement are inherited automatically by a third party without the agreement of the licensor and licensee, or whether they are maintained between the trustee/debtor and the licensee. The outcome depends on the details of the terms and conditions or the circumstances of each case.

### 3.2 Effects on licence agreements in the licensor's bankruptcy

As discussed in section 3.1, licence agreements for patents, utility models and designs cannot be terminated by a trustee/debtor as executory contracts in insolvency proceedings. In contrast, licence agreements for other intellectual property can indeed be terminated by a trustee/debtor as executory contracts in insolvency proceedings.

As the circumstances in which a trustee/debtor can terminate an executory contract are not prescribed in the relevant acts, trustees/debtors are generally thought to have a right to terminate executory contracts at their discretion. However, as noted in section 3.1(a), there is a judicial precedent[4] that held that termination of an executory contract by a trustee/debtor is invalid where the termination will significantly harm the counterparty and lead to an extremely unfair result.

---

3 See Hitomi Iwase and Yoko Kasai, Jan 2012, 'Japan Recent amendments to the Patent Act', IP Value 2012, published by Globe White Page Ltd.

4 *X v Y*, 54 MINSHÛ 553 (Sup Ct, February 29 2000).

### 3.3 Powers of administrators, receivers and trustees in the licensor's bankruptcy

As mentioned in sections 3.1 and 3.2 above, when insolvency proceedings are filed by a licensor and are subsequently commenced, a trustee/debtor has a right to assume or terminate licence agreements.

### 3.4 Powers and rights of creditors in a licensor's bankruptcy

In principle, creditors in insolvency proceedings cannot intervene in the trustee/debtor's disposal of the debtor's assets, and creditors do not have the right to exert an influence on licence agreements. In bankruptcy and civil rehabilitation proceedings, security holders with mortgages, liens and pledges can foreclose collateral and receive a preferred payment from the proceeds, even after the commencement of the proceedings. Therefore, if creditors have security interests in the intellectual property rights that are held by the licensors, such creditors can dispose of those rights. In contrast, foreclosure of collateral by security holders is prohibited in corporate reorganisation proceedings, and creditors can only receive payment by means of a distribution in accordance with a reorganisation plan.

### 3.5 Effects on licence agreements in the licensee's bankruptcy

As noted in sections 3.1 and 3.2 above, licence agreements for patents, utility models and designs cannot be terminated by a trustee/debtor as executory contracts in insolvency proceedings.

In contrast, licence agreements for other intellectual property that is not registered can be terminated by a trustee/debtor as executory contracts in insolvency proceedings.

There are no differences between the bankruptcy, civil rehabilitation and corporate reorganisation proceedings for licensors and licensees. However, there is a judicial precedent[5] that held that the termination of an executory contract by a trustee/debtor is invalid where the termination will significantly harm the counterparty and lead to an extremely unfair result.

### 3.6 Powers of administrators, receivers and trustees in the licensee's bankruptcy

As mentioned in sections 3.1, 3.2 and 3.3 above, when Insolvency proceedings are filed by a licensee and are subsequently commenced, the trustee/debtor has a right to assume or terminate licence agreements. There are no differences between the bankruptcy, civil rehabilitation and corporate reorganisation proceedings for licensors and licensees. However, there is a judicial precedent[6] that held that the termination of an executory contract by a trustee/debtor is invalid where the termination will significantly harm the counterparty and lead to an extremely unfair result.

### 3.7 Powers and rights of creditors in a licensee's bankruptcy

As stated in section 3.4 above, in principle creditors in insolvency proceedings cannot intervene in the trustee/debtor's disposal of the debtor's assets, and creditors do not have the right to exert any influence on licence agreements.

---

5 *Id.*
6 *Id.*

### 3.8 Exclusive and non-exclusive licences

There are two types of licence for intellectual property rights: exclusive licences and non-exclusive licences. Both types come into force upon, at a minimum, the creation of an agreement between a licensor and a licensee.

Exclusive licences of patent rights, utility model rights and design rights must be registered to become enforceable and for the licensees to assert their rights against third parties. A registered exclusive licence can exclude others (including the licensor) from exercising the licensed rights under the terms and conditions of the agreement. On the other hand, a non-exclusive licence cannot exclude the licensor and others from exercising the licensed right, and such licence can in principle be granted to others – under the terms of an agreement, a non-exclusive licensee can be given an exclusive right with the stipulation that the licensor cannot grant the same licence to others.

As mentioned in section 3.1 above, both exclusive and non-exclusive licence agreements are executory contracts as a general rule, and in cases where a trustee/debtor believes that maintaining an executory contract could become detrimental or is unnecessary, the trustee/debtor will usually terminate that contract. However, as discussed in section 3.1 above, trustees and debtors do not have the right to terminate licence agreements for exclusive licences that have been registered or for non-exclusive licences for patents, utility models or designs and registered trademarks and circuit layouts.

### 3.9 Perpetual and non-perpetual licences

In insolvency proceedings, whether a licence agreement is perpetual or not has no bearing on whether or not the licence agreement can be terminated. Even if a licence is given in perpetuity, it is possible for the licence agreement to be terminated pursuant to the principle mentioned in section 3.8 above.

### 3.10 Effects on a sub-licence in a licensor's bankruptcy

A sub-licence agreement is conceptually understood as involving the direct grant of a licence by the original licensor, but the sub-licence is limited in scope by the original licence agreement. Therefore, as long as a sub-licence agreement is a registered exclusive agreement or a non-exclusive agreement for patent rights, utility model rights or design rights, a sub-licensee can assert its rights under the sub-licence agreement even if a trustee/debtor tries to terminate the original licence agreement.

Alternatively, if the original agreement is a non-exclusive agreement for trademarks and circuit layouts that have not been registered, or if it is a non-exclusive agreement for copyright and know-how, a sub-licensee cannot assert its rights because the sub-licensor cannot assert its rights against the original licensor.

### 3.11 Effects on a sub-licence in a licensee's bankruptcy

As a sub-licence agreement is conceptually understood to involve the direct grant of a licence by the original licensor, with respect to a registered exclusive agreement or a non-exclusive agreement for patent rights, utility model rights or design rights, even if the sub-licensor (the original licensee) is subject to insolvency proceedings, a trustee or debtor cannot exercise its right to terminate the sub-licence agreement.

### 3.12 Impact of registration

The effects of registration can be summarised in three regards:

- An exclusive licence is enforceable against third parties and trustees/debtors once it has been registered.
- Non-exclusive licences for patent rights, utility model rights or design rights are not required to be registered in order for licensees to assert their rights against third parties or trustees/debtors.
- Non-exclusive licences for trademarks and circuit layouts must be registered before rights against licensors, trustees/debtors or other third parties can be asserted.

## 4. Contractual arrangements in deviation from the law

### 4.1 Exceptions

As has been mentioned earlier in the chapter, an unregistered licence agreement is not protected from a new owner of intellectual property rights (such as copyrights and know-how) in an agreement terminated by a trustee/debtor. In Japan, know-how is protected as intellectual property but only as a trade secret under the Unfair Competition Prevention Act.

### 4.2 Scope to alter statutory mechanisms

Licensors and licensees cannot alter the statutory mechanisms described in this chapter regarding a trustee/debtor's rights or the registration systems under the Patent Act and other intellectual property laws.

However, there is a judicial precedent[7] that provides an exception to the right of a trustee or debtor to terminate executory contracts in cases where termination would significantly harm the counterparty or would lead to an extremely unfair result. In such cases, it is possible that termination by a trustee/debtor would be declared void.

### 4.3 Termination rights and automatic reversions

In insolvency proceedings in Japan, rules regarding so-called *ipso facto* clauses (contractual provisions that make the bankruptcy or insolvency of one contracting party grounds for termination of the contract by the other party), such as those in the US Bankruptcy Code, do not exist. Even so, the rules regarding such clauses have been accepted in past cases by Japanese courts. Therefore, given these precedents, if a licensor and licensee include a provision in an agreement regarding termination rights and stipulate the terms and conditions that come into force owing to a filing for insolvency proceedings, it is possible that the provision will be deemed invalid by the court (not the competent court for the insolvency proceedings, but the court that has jurisdiction over the contract in general).

Additionally, it should be noted that the judicial precedents are limited only to termination, not modification; so the judicial precedents may not apply to licence

---

7 *Id.*

agreement clauses that do not terminate the agreement. Even so, it is still possible that the court will deem such clauses invalid.

## 5. Cross-border aspects

### 5.1 Foreign law

When insolvency proceedings are commenced, executory contracts, including licence agreements, can be terminated by a trustee/debtor. However, there is currently no consensus on whether a foreign trustee/debtor can exercise the right to terminate executory contracts when foreign insolvency proceedings are commenced. This issue depends on the construction and circumstances of each case.

The general opinion regarding executory contracts is that this issue should be decided by the local laws under which the insolvency proceedings are commenced and that the law governing a licence agreement should have no influence on any conclusion.

### 5.2 Foreign jurisdiction

There are several arguments currently in play on this issue among legal experts, but the majority opinion is that trustees/debtors and the courts are bound by the jurisdiction clauses in licence agreements even if a licence agreement is terminated by exercising the trustee/debtor's termination right.

There are, nonetheless, a few exceptions. In particular, litigation in connection with bankruptcy claims and litigation with respect to avoidance actions are subject to the jurisdiction of the bankruptcy court in Japan because the insolvency proceedings have exclusive jurisdiction over these types of litigation.

# Mexico

**Gustavo A Alcocer**
Olivares

## 1. Overview

### 1.1 Relevant legislation governing intellectual property and bankruptcy

The relevant legislation on intellectual property in Mexico is the Industrial Property Law and its regulations. On August 2 1994 the Industrial Property Law was published in the *Federal Government Gazette*, and it entered into full force and effect on October 1 1994.

In respect of bankruptcy legislation, the Commercial Insolvency Law is the only regulation governing the procedures for orderly liquidation of the assets and rights of a merchant. On May 12 2000 the Commercial Insolvency Law was published in the *Federal Government Gazette*, and it entered into full force and effect the next day.

Under the Commercial Insolvency Law, each insolvency case referred to the courts is assigned to a federal judge. This judge is assisted by specialists appointed by the Federal Institute of Commercial Insolvency Specialists (IFECOM), which was created for the purpose of guiding federal judges through the bankruptcy process, and of maintaining lists of people authorised to act as specialists (such as auditors, conciliators or trustees) in insolvency proceedings.

IFECOM designates such specialists to insolvency proceedings, determining the specialists' fees and overseeing their performance. In this sense IFECOM also provides continuing education to judges and lawyers. It also acts as a mediator between a debtor and its creditors when asked to do so.

### 1.2 Types of insolvency procedure

Pursuant to the Commercial Insolvency Law, the insolvency procedure consists of two successive stages, known as conciliation and bankruptcy.

Notwithstanding the foregoing, and taking into consideration the principles of the Commercial Insolvency Law, an additional previous stage, which can be identified as a preliminary stage of insolvency, needs to be considered in order to determine whether a merchant or company can be declared commercially insolvent. During this stage of the procedure, no special measures take place, unless either of the parties requests a judge to order measures for a company to file for insolvency and liquidation for, among other reasons, the general inability to pay debts and meet obligations when due.

#### *(a) Conciliation*

One of the main purposes of the Commercial Insolvency Law is to create a regulatory framework that allows the conservation of assets and companies and to avoid general non-compliance with payment obligations jeopardising the financial viability of such companies and the continuation of their business. Consequently, the Commercial Insolvency Law has introduced mediation and conciliation to preserve a company's operations while the relevant parties attempt to negotiate and draft a mutually agreeable reorganisation or restructuring plan for the payment of the company's liabilities during a reasonable term.

In order for a restructuring agreement to be valid, it must be approved by:

- the debtor;
- more than 50% of the recognised claims of all unsecured recognised creditors; and
- the recognised claims of all secured or preferential creditors.

Furthermore, in order for any restructuring agreement to be approved, the judge in the case must determine that the agreement treats all creditors within the same class equally, does not contravene public policy and meets all requirements under the Commercial Insolvency Law.

If a restructuring agreement is reached and approved by the judge, the insolvency proceedings end. If during the conciliation stage the reorganisation plan being proposed becomes infeasible, the second stage, formally known as bankruptcy, is initiated.

The conciliation stage can last for up to 185 days and it may be extended for two 90-day periods; in no circumstances may conciliation last more than 365 days.

### *(b) Bankruptcy*

The bankruptcy stage is the liquidation process for a company declared bankrupt. It includes the selling of the assets in order to obtain the greatest payment for the creditors. The phase will last until all of the debts are paid or all of the assets of the company declared in bankruptcy are sold in order to apply the funds from such sales to pay the company's creditors, in accordance with statutory preference.

Pursuant to the Commercial Insolvency Law, a debtor subject to commercial insolvency is declared insolvent if:

- the debtor so requests;
- the period of conciliation has expired and a reorganisation agreement has not been submitted for the judge's approval;
- the reorganisation agreement violates any public order provisions and is therefore not approved by the judge; or
- the conciliator requests a declaration of insolvency.

Basically, the triggering of the bankruptcy stage suspends the ability of the debtor to perform any legal acts on behalf of the company; therefore, all legal acts performed by the debtor after the bankruptcy stage has begun are invalid. In fact, during the bankruptcy stage the administration of the debtor's assets is turned over to a trustee, who may elect to continue or discontinue the debtor's business pending final liquidation, having full authority to manage the business and dispose of the debtor's assets for the benefit of the recognised creditors.

## 1.3 Grounds of bankruptcy

Pursuant to the Commercial Insolvency Law, individuals or legal entities that are considered merchants according to Mexico's Commercial Code may be subject to commercial insolvency proceedings.

Under Articles 9 and 10 of the Commercial Insolvency Law, individuals whose normal occupation is commerce, and business corporations, may be subject to bankruptcy proceedings if they fail to meet their obligations to pay two or more distinct creditors, and at least one the following conditions is present:

- their matured obligations have been due for at least thirty days past and they represent 35% or more of all of the company's obligations, as of the date on which the demand or application for bankruptcy is filed; or
- the company does not have liquid assets, such as cash on hand and on-sight deposits, term deposits and investments whose due date is not greater than 90 calendar days following the admittance date of the demand or application for bankruptcy.

In this regard, the Commercial Insolvency Law also states that a merchant is presumed to have defaulted in meeting its payment obligations if any of the following occurs:

- insufficient assets to seize when enforcing an attachment order resulting from the failure to pay a debt, when enforcing a final judgment entered against the merchant;
- failure to pay two or more creditors;
- hiding or absence without appointing someone who may satisfy current and future obligations to manage or operate the business in similar circumstances;
- closing the stores of the company;
- engaging in misleading, fraudulent or false practices to satisfy or avoid debts;
- failure to meet payment obligations contained in agreements entered into by the merchant; and
- in any other similar instance.

The Commercial Insolvency Law states that branches of foreign companies may be declared insolvent. However, the declaration can only encompass the goods and rights that are located in, and that may be demanded in, the national territory of Mexico, and will only apply to creditors whose transactions have been conducted with such branches.

## 1.4 Filing for bankruptcy

The bankruptcy process may be requested by any of the following persons:

- the company itself;
- any of the company's creditors; or
- the District Attorney Office.

In this regard, Article 21 of the Commercial Insolvency Law states that if a judge, during the course of a commercial lawsuit, warns that a company appears to be within any of the scenarios that could lead to a company being declared commercially insolvent, the judge must notify the competent authorities so that, if applicable, the district attorney may file for a declaration of insolvency.

According to the Commercial Insolvency Law, the district judge with jurisdiction over the place in which the company has its domicile or where its principal place of business is located has jurisdiction over the insolvency proceedings, unless a declaration of insolvency has been previously promoted against one of the subsidiary companies or against a holding company – in which case the judge of competent jurisdiction is deemed to be the one that had tried the original case.

## 1.5 Administrators and other appointed persons

It is important to point out that upon and after the filing of a request for bankruptcy, the operations of the debtor continue unaffected, regardless of that request. Nevertheless, under the Commercial Insolvency Law the parties described next take special roles in the management of the debtor's company during the two stages of conciliation and bankruptcy. That law states further that they are required to be registered professionals.

### *(a) Inspectors*

Once an action for commercial insolvency has been filed and after a district judge has approved a valid request for reorganisation, the judge gives notice to IFECOM, which in turn appoints an inspector (in Spanish, *visitador*), who is a specialist with experience in the accounting, auditing and interpretation of financial statements and who must review the debtor's books, accounting records and financial statements, as well as any other document that contains information relating to the financial or accounting state of the company, in order to determine whether the debtor is eligible for reorganisation.

Additionally, the inspector may request the judge to grant precautionary measures prohibiting the debtor or its managers or board from selling or encumbering the principal assets of the company.

### *(b) Conciliators*

Once the conciliation stage has been triggered, the judge in the case will request IFECOM to designate a specialist called a conciliator (in Spanish, *conciliador*), who will be responsible for preparing a reorganisation plan and will also act as a mediator between the debtor and its creditors. In addition, the conciliator will monitor the administration of the company and will present a list of the company's creditors to the judge, including acknowledgement and classification of their claims. The conciliator will also negotiate a restructuring agreement with the parties involved.

During the conciliation stage, the debtor will continue to manage its company under the supervision – and, in some cases, the explicit authorisation – of the conciliator. The conciliator will oversee the keeping of the books and all of the operations performed by the merchant or his administrator. Furthermore, the conciliator will decide on the termination of pending contracts and will approve, having gained the opinion of a receiver (a person appointed by the creditors with oversight capacity – see also subsection (c) below), if any, the contracting of new credits, the establishment or substitution of guarantees and the sale of assets of the merchant's company.

If the conciliator believes that the continuation of the existing management is not in the best interests of the merchant's creditors, it may request the managers' removal and may be authorised to itself assume responsibility for managing the debtor. In this regard, if the motion seeking the removal of the managers from the management of the company is granted, the conciliator will indeed assume the powers and obligations relating to the management of the company in addition to his other responsibilities.

#### *(c)* *Receivers*

Under the Commercial Insolvency Law, a receiver (in Spanish, *interventor*) represents the interests of the creditors and is responsible for overseeing the actions of the conciliator, as well as the actions of the debtor or his administrator in relation to the operation of the company. In this regard any creditor or group of creditors that represents at least 10% of the value of the amounts owed by the debtor has the right to request that the judge in the case appoint a receiver.

#### *(d)* *Trustees*

Once the bankruptcy stage has been declared, the judge in the case will request IFECOM to appoint a trustee (in Spanish, *síndico*) or confirm the conciliator as such. It is important to point out that if conciliation fails and the bankruptcy stage begins, the legal capacity of the debtor to manage its business is suspended; consequently, the trustee is entrusted with the management and selling of the company's assets.

For the performance of these functions, the trustee has the broadest authority and powers available under law. All of the assets of the debtor must be turned over to the trustee, and the debtor is prohibited from making any payments or delivering any goods without the trustee's authorisation. Furthermore, the Commercial Insolvency Law states that any acts that the debtor or its representatives perform without the written authorisation of the trustee, as of the declaration of bankruptcy, will be null and unenforceable.

## 2. Licence agreements in the phase between filing and declaration of bankruptcy

### 2.1 Effects on licence agreements in the licensor's bankruptcy.

In accordance with Mexican legislation, the rights and obligations between the parties (in this case licensor and licensee) are construed and governed by what is set forth in the agreements entered into by them. According to Mexico's Civil Code, each party is bound in a way and by the terms to which each party intended to be bound.

In this sense, the Commercial Code also recognises the freedom of the parties to negotiate and reach an agreement and to decide independently their rights and obligations under the negotiated agreement. Thus, there is no specific statutory protection for a licensor or licensee in the event of insolvency.

As a general rule applicable in any bankruptcy proceeding, contracts entered into by the licensor, and any other obligations assumed thereby, continue to be valid in their terms unless otherwise agreed by the parties.

### 2.2 Powers of administrators, receivers or trustees in the licensor's bankruptcy

Mexican legislation provides for two broad categories of powers of attorney: special powers of attorney (ie, those restricted to a specific matter or area stipulated in such power) and general powers of attorney (eg, for lawsuits and collections, the management of assets or the exercising of acts of ownership). These categories apply to any representative, including an administrator, conciliator or trustee.

During the first stage of bankruptcy proceedings, the licensor's administrator will continue to perform his activities with the same powers (whether special or general) as were granted by the licensor and regardless that an action for commercial insolvency has been filed.

### 2.3 Effects on licence agreements in the licensee's bankruptcy

As mentioned earlier, regardless that bankruptcy proceedings have been initiated, a licence of any industrial property rights is valid and enforceable between the parties from the moment it is executed. In this sense, the only formality that the licensee needs to fulfil in order to make such agreement enforceable against third parties is the recordal of the licence agreement before the Mexican Institute of Industrial Property (the IMPI).

### 2.4 Powers of administrators, receivers or trustees in the licensee's bankruptcy

As mentioned in section 2.2 above, during bankruptcy proceedings the same rules that apply to the licensor's administrator or conciliator regarding the different levels of authority and powers apply to a licensee's representative, administrator or conciliator. Therefore, the licensee's administrator or conciliator may assume or determine to assign or terminate the licence agreement, in accordance with the terms of that agreement.

It is customary for licensees to be limited as to any assignment to third parties without the prior approval of the licensor.

### 2.5 Impact of registration

Mexican law provides that the owner of a copyright or an industrial property right such as a trademark, patent or industrial design right may assign or grant a licence authorising its use, including patent and trademark applications (which always remain subject to the granting of a registration). Either a licensor or licensee may apply for registration.

In order to be effective and enforceable against third parties, licence agreements (including franchise agreements) and the assignment of intellectual property must be recorded at the IMPI when the underlying asset is industrial property, and at the National Copyright Institute (known as INDAUTOR) when the underlying asset is a copyright. In certain scenarios, trademark renewal is dependent upon proof of use in the territory by its titleholder. Use by a licensee is available to meet this test provided that the licence is registered. In the case of marketing authorisations for pharmaceutical products, the regulatory approval process imposes on each applicant the need to give evidence of title or recorded licence of the related patents.

Registering an agreement with the IMPI provides the following advantages: it makes the trademark or patent licence agreement enforceable against third parties; and it enables the trademark holder to prove trademark use made by the registered licensee.

Notwithstanding the foregoing, an assignment or licence of any industrial property right is effective between the parties from the moment it is executed, regardless of its registration with the IMPI or INDAUTOR.

## 3. Licence agreements in the phase after declaration of bankruptcy

### 3.1 Treatment of intellectual property rights

There is no distinction between intellectual property rights of different kinds in an insolvency context. Automatic termination of intellectual property licence agreements when any one of the parties is in bankruptcy is not provided under Mexican legislation. Furthermore, there is no distinction or explicit mention of intellectual property rights in the Commercial Insolvency Law; thus, all intellectual property rights are considered as assets of the company subject to the bankruptcy proceedings. In this sense, such intellectual property rights (as intangible rights) may be transferred by means of an assignment or a licence agreement.

Following Mexico's principles of civil law, private parties are bound by the terms of the agreed-upon provisions. There are no express provisions on the effect of bankruptcy on intellectual property rights or any contracts concerning them.

### 3.2 Effects on licence agreements in the licensor's bankruptcy

Based in the contracting freedom provided by Mexico's Civil Code, the contracting parties are bound by the terms and conditions they deem necessary. Furthermore, and given that no specific provision applies in cases of industrial property contracts (such as licence agreements), there is no effect on licence agreements if the licensor is subject to bankruptcy proceedings.

### 3.3 Powers of an administrator, receiver or trustee in the licensor's bankruptcy

Once a declaration of bankruptcy has been declared by the judge in the case, such a declaration implies the full removal of the licensor from management of the company. The bankrupt licensor is then replaced by the court-appointed trustee, who has the broadest of powers of authority and control granted by law.

The trustee is entitled to adopt any necessary measures for the safety and conservation of the licensor's company. Therefore, if termination of the licence is a necessary measure to protect the licensor and its business, the trustee may terminate the licence in accordance with the terms of the licence agreement but not by virtue of his capacity as an administrator/trustee.

Once the bankruptcy stage has been declared, the trustee will proceed to sell the property and rights of the licensor, procuring the greatest possible return from their sale in order to pay the licensor's debts.

**3.4 Powers and rights of creditors in a licensor's bankruptcy**

As a general rule that is stated in the Commercial Insolvency Law, upon the declaration of bankruptcy proceedings, creditors will not be able to create or perfect any additional encumbrance or security interest on the debtor's assets in order to secure their unpaid claims. However, the judge in the case may take any step that he deems advisable so as to protect the integrity of the licensor's assets.

Notwithstanding the foregoing, a creditor has the right at all times to request that action be taken to avoid any impairment that may be caused to its collateral as a result of the debtor's liability or negligence. Such protective actions can include the maintenance or repair of specific assets, the hiring of insurance or other similar measures.

**3.5 Effects on licence agreements in the licensee's bankruptcy**

As mentioned earlier, pursuant to the Commercial Insolvency Law there are no specific provisions stating any special effects regarding agreements (such as licences) relating to intellectual property. Parties might therefore only have the right to terminate their agreement as set out therein, including the triggering of bankruptcy proceedings in any of the parties if the agreement encompasses such a provision.

In a case of bankruptcy, failure to comply with the terms of the agreement, if not specifically agreed by the relevant parties, might bring termination of the agreement and the payment of damages and lost profits.

**3.6 Powers of an administrator, receiver or trustee in the licensee's bankruptcy**

Pursuant to the Commercial Insolvency Law, upon declaration of the bankruptcy of a licensee, the management of the company is handed over to a trustee and the declaration suspends the ability of the licensee to perform any legal acts on behalf of the company. In this context, the trustee has the most extensive powers permitted by law in order to run the licensee's business and sell the property and rights that form the licensee's estate, procuring the greatest possible return from their sale.

**3.7 Powers and rights of creditors in a licensee's bankruptcy**

Once bankruptcy proceedings have started, under the Commercial Insolvency Law the creditor is entitled to ask the conciliator whether he will oppose compliance with the agreement. If the conciliator responds that he will oppose it, or if he fails to respond in a 20-day period, the non-affected party (licensor or licensee) is entitled to terminate the agreement.

**3.8 Exclusive and non-exclusive licences**

Pursuant to Mexican legislation regarding bankruptcy proceedings, there are no specific provisions relating to exclusive or non-exclusive licence agreements.

### 3.9 Perpetual and non-perpetual licences

Mexican law does not have specific provisions governing perpetual and non-perpetual licences. In the case of patents, though, note that a 'perpetual' licence would be limited to no more than the lifespan of the underlying patent.

### 3.10 Effects on a sub-licence in a licensor's bankruptcy

If there is no provision otherwise agreed by the parties, a licence would continue to be in effect, and no reversion of rights or termination would apply in the event of the licensor's bankruptcy.

### 3.11 Effects on a sub-licence in a licensee's bankruptcy

See section 3.10 above. In Mexico, it is common to establish a contractual provision in a case of bankruptcy.

### 3.12 Impact of registration

As mentioned in section 2.5 above, the only formality required in relation to registration is that a licence must be registered with the IMPI or INDAUTOR in order to be effective and enforceable against third parties. If an agreement is not registered with the IMPI, the registered owner is the only one entitled to enforce or defend the intellectual property rights.

## 4. Contractual arrangements in deviation from the law

### 4.1 Exceptions

The owner of a copyright, or other industrial property right such as trade or industrial secrets and related agreements such as know-how and technical assistance and support, may also be subject to licence agreements, but would not be subject to a different regime.

Any assignment or licence that involves a trademark, patent, design or copyright must be registered with the IMPI or INDAUTOR in order to be effective and enforceable against third parties.

### 4.2 Scope to alter statutory mechanisms

Freedom of contract is the basic principle of all contract law in Mexico; therefore, the contracting parties are bound in the manner and under the terms in which they appear to have undertaken their obligations. The parties may stipulate the terms and conditions of any agreement they wish to enter, provided only that they do not:

- breach any public statute;
- waive a statutory right that, according to the law, may not be waived; or
- stipulate a term that is contrary to good practices or affects third parties' rights – and in this regard the parties may not, according to Mexican legislation, validly agree on a stipulation to invalidate certain provisions of a statute considered in the public interest and therefore not subject to waiver in law.

Furthermore, Mexican law does not provide specific limitation regarding the termination or reversion rights agreed by parties. Customary contractual stipulations include events of bankruptcy by any of the parties as early-termination events, among others.

### 4.3 Termination rights and automatic reversions

Given that the principle of freedom of contract applies in Mexico, neither the Civil Code or the Commercial Insolvency Law provide for a prohibition or limitation to any right of termination or automatic reversion that is agreed by the parties.

## 5. Cross-border aspects

### 5.1 Foreign law

According to Mexican legislation, there are no restrictions on licence agreements being governed by foreign law: the parties would be governed by the law agreed upon in their agreement. So regardless of the choice of law governing a licence agreement, if the bankruptcy proceeding is brought in Mexico, the insolvency administrator would act based on the Commercial Insolvency Law and would have to enforce the licence agreement based in the foreign applicable law.

### 5.2 Foreign jurisdiction

The Commercial Insolvency Law includes several provisions for cooperation in international proceedings. According to general laws on reciprocity, a Mexican court will recognise the effects of proceedings initiated in a foreign jurisdiction if that foreign jurisdiction recognises proceedings initiated in Mexico.

# Netherlands

**Marcel Willems**
Kennedy Van der Laan

## 1. Overview

### 1.1 Relevant legislation governing intellectual property and bankruptcy

Intellectual property rights in the Netherlands are governed by various acts, the most relevant of which are the Patents Act 1995, the Benelux Convention on Intellectual Property, the Databank Act, the Copyright Act and the Neighbouring Rights Act.

The Insolvency Act governs insolvency proceedings in the Netherlands. It came into force in 1896 and was amended from time to time, but was never revised as a whole. Neither the respective acts on intellectual property, nor the Insolvency Act contain any specific provisions for intellectual property rights or licence agreements in a case of insolvency.

### 1.2 Types of insolvency procedure

The Insolvency Act differentiates between three types of insolvency: bankruptcy, suspension of payments, and debt reorganisation of a natural person. The last in the list is of less relevance for this chapter.

Bankruptcy aims at liquidation of the estate – ie, the sale of any or all assets of the debtor, whether as a going concern or piecemeal, and the distribution of the proceeds to the creditors in accordance with their ranks. The main goal of a suspension of payments is to keep the debtor's business alive by overcoming temporary liquidity issues and avoiding a reorganisation or restructuring (including the possibility of offering a scheme of arrangement to the creditors).

### 1.3 Grounds of bankruptcy

A debtor that is unable to pay its debts as they become due may be declared bankrupt, either at its own request or upon petition of its creditors. If a creditor petitions for bankruptcy, the petitioning creditor must show to the court that at least one other creditor is left unpaid. The public prosecutor is also permitted to request that a debtor be declared bankrupt, but only for public interest reasons.

A debtor who foresees that it will not be able to pay its debts as and when they fall due may request to be granted a suspension of payments. Suspension of payments can be requested only by the debtor himself.

### 1.4 Filing for bankruptcy

If a debtor is a company, the management of that company may file for insolvency. However, there is no statutory obligation to do so – not even in the event that the company becomes insolvent. If the company is a limited liability company, the management of the company may request a declaration of bankruptcy only if the general meeting of the shareholders has resolved to file for bankruptcy. The management is then entitled to request a suspension of payments, unless the articles of association of the company require prior approval by the general meeting of shareholders.

The competent court in both cases (bankruptcy and suspension of payments) is the district court of the statutory seat of the company.

### 1.5 Administrators and other appointed persons

The court will process a request for suspension of payments immediately, without a hearing. This means that the suspension is (in most cases) granted within hours of filing. No administrator (In Dutch, *bewindvoerder*) is appointed in the meantime.

The court decides on a petition for bankruptcy only after a hearing (in principle a hearing *ex parte* – ie, without the creditor who filed the petition). A bankruptcy hearing takes place within weeks of the filing. In the event that the creditor files the petition, it will usually be within three weeks, because the debtor has to be notified of the petition and the hearing. If the debtor itself files for bankruptcy, the hearing will be on the first Tuesday after the filing.

In bankruptcy cases, a trustee is appointed by the court upon the declaration of bankruptcy (and not before).

## 2. Licence agreements in the phase between filing and declaration of bankruptcy

### 2.1 Effects on licence agreements in the licensor's bankruptcy

The filing for insolvency in itself has, in principle, no impact on the licence agreement; it is still enforceable. The grant of rights stays in place and the licensee continues to be obligated to pay the licence fee. Neither a termination nor a reversion of rights occurs.

This is different, however, in the event that the parties to the licence agreement have agreed that, either upon filing for or upon declaration of insolvency, the licence agreement automatically terminates or may be terminated by one of the parties. Such a provision is valid under Dutch law and is common licensing practice in the Netherlands.

### 2.2 Powers of administrators, receivers or trustees in the licensor's bankruptcy

As indicated in section 1.5 above, no administrator or trustee is appointed in the phase between filing and declaration of insolvency.

### 2.3 Effects on licence agreements in the licensee's bankruptcy

The filing for insolvency in itself has, in principle, no impact on the licence agreement; it is still enforceable. The grant of rights stays in place and the licensee continues to be obligated to pay the licence fee. Neither a termination nor a reversion of rights occurs.

This is different, however, in the event that the parties to the licence agreement have agreed that, either upon filing for or upon declaration of insolvency, the licence agreement automatically terminates or may be terminated by one of the parties. Such provision is valid under Dutch law and is common licensing practice in the Netherlands.

### 2.4 Powers of administrators, receivers or trustees in the licensee's bankruptcy

As indicated in section 1.5 above, no administrator or trustee is appointed in the phase between filing and declaration of insolvency.

### 2.5 Impact of registration

While licence agreements for some intellectual property (IP) rights, particularly patents and trademarks, can be – and usually are – registered, this has no effect on how they are treated in the phase between the filing and opening of insolvency proceedings.

## 3. Licence agreements in the phase after declaration of bankruptcy

### 3.1 Treatment of intellectual property rights

There is no distinction between different intellectual property rights in terms of how they are treated in the insolvency of either the licensor or the licensee.

### 3.2 Effects on licence agreements in the licensor's bankruptcy

Unless agreed otherwise, in a suspension of payments all contracts remain in full force and effect. This means that the licensor must continue the licence and the licensee must pay the licence fee.

In bankruptcy, a distinction has to be made between 'executory' and 'non-executory' contracts, whereby executory contracts are those that have not been completely performed by either of the parties (eg, the licence term is still continuing and licence fee payments are still due) and non-executory contracts are contracts that have been fully performed by either party or both parties.

In an executory contract, the licensee may demand that the trustee declares within a reasonable time (in writing) whether or not he will continue to live up to the contractual obligations. If the trustee declares he will not do so, or in the event that he does not declare to do so within a reasonable time period, the trustee loses the right to demand from the creditor that he complies with the agreement. In other words, the agreement does not become void, but no party can any longer demand performance from the other party. Should the trustee declare that he is going to continue (on behalf of the estate) to fulfil the obligations of the debtor under the agreement, he has to provide suitable security to the other party (eg, a bank guarantee or, uncommonly, a personal suretyship). Should the trustee declare (or not make the declaration within a reasonable time) that he is not going to perform according to the licence agreement, the licensee will have an unsecured claim in the bankruptcy for damages.

In a non-executory contract, whereby the licensee has fulfilled its obligations prior to the bankruptcy of the licensor, the situation is unclear. Until 2006 the general opinion was that the trustee would step into the shoes of the debtor and thus would be bound by any and all contractual obligations of the debtor, unless the Insolvency Act provided otherwise. In 2006, however, the Dutch Supreme Court rendered a judgment that seemed to imply a sea change in this respect.[1] Although the judgment was in respect of the lease of real estate and did not refer to licences, the attorney-general of the Supreme Court in his advice to the court expressly mentioned licences by way of analogy. If this analogy were to be followed, it would mean that the trustee in the bankruptcy of the licensor could simply disregard any rights that the licensee might have under the licence agreement. There has been much discussion among legal scholars in the Netherlands about the implications of this judgment. Further, the CJEU (the Court of Justice of the European Union) ruled in the *UsedSoft case*[2] that licensors to a certain extent exhaust their copyrights when offering software for download and including a perpetual licence. This implies that a trustee is also bound by this limitation when it comes to software licences.

### 3.3 Powers of an administrator, receiver or trustee in the licensor's bankruptcy

As mentioned in section 3.2 above, the trustee is basically bound by the position that the debtor was in at the moment the debtor was declared bankrupt. Other than as mentioned in that section, the trustee does not have special powers.

### 3.4 Powers and rights of creditors in a licensor's bankruptcy

Under the Insolvency Act the creditors have hardly any say in what happens. The Insolvency Act provides for the possibility of appointing a creditors' committee in bankruptcies, but this hardly ever happens. Besides, even in the event that the trustee consults the creditors' committee, he is not bound by their advice. Individual creditors, on the other hand, may at all times address the supervisory judge in the bankruptcy with a request to order the trustee to take a specific action or to abstain from an action envisaged by him. However, creditors often do not know what is going on in the bankruptcy on a day-to-day basis, because a trustee is not obliged to inform them individually. The only obligation the trustee has is to report to the court (which report is publicly available) periodically (ie, every 3–6 months) about the status and the progress of the insolvency.

### 3.5 Effects on licence agreements in the licensee's bankruptcy

As explained in section 3.2 above, in a suspension of payments, unless agreed otherwise, all contracts remain in full force and effect. This means that the licensor must continue the licence and the licensee must pay the licence fee. In the event that the administrator finds that it has insufficient funds in the estate to do so, he must

1 HR 3 November 2006, ECLI:NL:HR:2006:AX8838

2 *UsedSoft GmbH v Oracle International Corp*, CJEU case C-128/11, judgment of July 3 2013.

request the court to convert the suspension of payments into bankruptcy. If he does not request for conversion and the estate would not be able to pay the licence fee as of the date of the suspension of payments, the administrator might be held personally liable for those fees.

### 3.6 Powers of an administrator, receiver or trustee in the licensee's bankruptcy

A trustee in a bankruptcy of a licensee has limited powers. If the licensor has performed and is performing his obligations, there is no issue: the licence remains valid unless the parties have agreed otherwise. Should, however, the licensee be in default (and this default not being able to be cured to the benefit of the estate), the trustee has no option but to request conversion of the suspension of payments into bankruptcy or, in the event the licensee was in bankruptcy already, to terminate the licence agreement (or, when being asked by the licensor, to declare that he will not comply with the contractual obligations any more). In these circumstances the licensor has an unsecured claim for damages in the bankruptcy.

### 3.7 Powers and rights of creditors in a licensee's bankruptcy

As set out in section 3.4 above, the creditors have no, or hardly any, direct influence on the fate of a licence agreement. The insolvency administrator is under no obligation to consult with the creditors about the decision to continue or discontinue a licence agreement.

### 3.8 Exclusive and non-exclusive licences

Under Dutch law there is no distinction between exclusive and non-exclusive licences in insolvency scenarios.

### 3.9 Perpetual and non-perpetual licences

If an agreement has not yet been fully performed by both parties, the other party (ie, not the debtor or the trustee) may demand that the trustee declares within a reasonable time whether or not he will continue to live up to the contractual obligations. If the trustee declares he will not do so or in the event that he does not declare to do so within a reasonable time period, the trustee loses the right to demand from the creditor that he complies with the agreement. In other words, the agreement does not become void but no party can demand performance from the other party any more. Should the trustee declare that he is going to continue (on behalf of the estate) to fulfil the obligations of the debtor under the agreement, he has to provide suitable security to the other party (eg, a bank guarantee or, uncommonly, a personal suretyship).

### 3.10 Effects on a sub-licence in a licensor's bankruptcy

A licensor's bankruptcy can have an effect on a sub-licence. This depends on what has been agreed and how far the licensor was involved in the sub-licence agreement.

If a sub-licence was granted with the explicit approval of the licensor, all depends on what was provided in the licence agreement as regards the sub-licence. If the licensor accepted the grant of a sub-licence by the licensee under the condition that the sub-licence would end the moment the (head) licence terminates, the sub-licence will end at the same time that the main licence ends. If nothing to this effect is expressly agreed upon, the question is what the parties to the licence agreement have expressed and what parties reasonably could have expected from each other. In other words, the question is whether the licensee could reasonably have expected to be granted the right to sub-license. If this is not the case, the sub-licensee may have a claim against the sub-licensor, but not against the licensor. Should, however, the sub-licensee in good faith have entered into the sub-licence agreement, it may have a claim against the estate of the licensor, but this will still be an unsecured claim.

### 3.11 Effects on a sub-licence in a licensee's bankruptcy

As described in section 3.10 above, what has been agreed and how far the licensor was involved in a sub-licence agreement will be decisive in relation to the effects on the sub-licence in a licensee's bankruptcy.

If a sub-licence was granted with the explicit approval of the licensor, all depends on what was agreed upon by the licensor as regards the sub-licence. In the event that the licensor accepted the grant of a sub-licence by the licensee but under the condition that the sub-licence would end the moment the (head) licence terminated, the sub-licence will end at the same time as the main licence ends. If nothing to this effect is expressly agreed upon, the question is basically what the parties to the licence agreement have expressed and what the parties reasonably could have expected from each other. In other words, the question is whether the licensee reasonably could have expected to be granted the right to sub-license. If this is not the case, the sub-licensee may have a claim against the sub-licensor, but not against the licensor. Should, however, the sub-licensee in good faith have entered into the sub-licence agreement, it may have a claim against the estate of the licensor, but this will still be an unsecured claim. If the licensee had granted a sub-licence without the consent of the licensor, the sub-licence will terminate at the same time as the termination of the licence of the licensee, and the sub-licensee will principally have a claim against the sub-licensor only.

### 3.12 Impact of registration

While licence agreements for some intellectual property rights may be registered, this has no effect on how they are treated in an insolvency scenario.

## 4. Contractual arrangements in deviation from the law

### 4.1 Exceptions

In essence, Dutch law provides that a security right may be vested in a good (being a receivable or movable/immovable asset) only if it can be transferred freely. As a bankruptcy is considered an attachment on any and all goods of the debtor (the 'estate'), this means that only an asset that is transferable can form part of the bankrupt estate that the trustee has any say about. A copyright is considered a purely personal right. So if someone has written a book, the trustee of the author is not entitled to sell the copyrights to that specific book. This is only different after the moment the author has transferred his rights to a third party (eg, a publisher); after such a transfer, the author is deemed to have given up his personal right.

Apart from that the foregoing, there are no exceptions to the basic rules set out earlier in this chapter.

### 4.2 Scope to alter statutory mechanisms

The statutory mechanisms outlined in the previous sections are pretty much fixed. This means that – apart from the copyright limitation described in section 4.1 above – the parties are reasonably free to make arrangements that suit them, and the trustee is bound by those arrangements. Only if, according to the requirements of reasonableness and fairness, it is unacceptable that the licensee or licensor (as applicable) should be bound by the terms of the agreement, or if the creditors would be prejudiced by such arrangement, can the trustee in bankruptcy revoke the arrangement.

### 4.3 Termination rights and automatic reversions

Under Dutch law it is allowed to agree on either automatic or voluntary termination rights, including reversion rights. Therefore, parties may validly agree that a licence agreement either will be terminated automatically or may be terminated immediately by either party in the event of the other party being declared insolvent or there being an application for insolvency of the other party. Whether such termination gives rise to damages depends on the agreement.

## 5. Cross-border aspects

### 5.1 Foreign law

As a trustee is seen as stepping into the shoes of the debtor, he is generally bound by the election of a foreign law in the licence agreement (as in any agreement) when seeking to enforce rights under the contract. The Insolvency Act is, however, mandatory law. So if the agreement between the debtor and another party is governed by the laws of a jurisdiction other than the Netherlands, the question would be what that law would govern. As to substantive law, the foreign law might prevail; as to insolvency questions, Dutch law would govern.

### 5.2 Foreign jurisdiction

An insolvency administrator is generally bound by the choice of a foreign forum. However, the EU Regulation on insolvency proceedings[3] specifies certain exceptions – eg, for the enforcement of clawback provisions against a party. These can be made pending in the court of the place where the insolvency proceedings have been opened. In general, however, the insolvency administrator can only enforce rights under the licence agreements at the place that is specified in the contract. The insolvency administrator is also bound by arbitration clauses.

---

3 Council Regulation (EC) 1346/2000 of May 29 2000.

# Russia

**Yulia Litovtseva**
**Valentina Orlova**
Pepeliaev Group

## 1. Overview

### 1.1 Relevant legislation governing intellectual property and bankruptcy

#### (a) *Legislation on intellectual property*

The Civil Code is the primary source of regulation for intellectual property. However, other federal laws also contain certain provisions relating to such property – in particular, the federal laws "on the protection of competition", "on commercial secrets", "on joint stock companies" and "on limited liability companies". Additionally, taking account of Article 7(2)(1) of the Civil Code, the grounds that give rise to and the procedure for exercising rights to the results of intellectual activity are also regulated by generally accepted principles, international legal rules and Russia's international treaties – which, according to Article 15(4) of the Russian Constitution, are part of the national legal system.

Russian legislation sets out an exhaustive list of the results of intellectual activity and the means of its identification, which may be legally protected as intellectual property under Article 1225 of the Civil Code. For different items, there are different grounds for legal protection to exist. Copyright items, including computer software, become legally protected as soon as they are created; no formalities like state or other official registration are required. However, if the holder of the copyright to a computer program or database so desires, it may be registered with the federal executive authority for intellectual property.[1]

Legal protection of an invention or trademark is provided from when their state registration is obtained, which is granted further to state expert review.[2] For the results of intellectual activity to be protected as know-how, a special confidentiality regime known as a 'trade secret regime'[3] should be set up and maintained. Legal protection of a trade name starts after a legal entity is registered as the holder of the right to this trade name.[4]

Exclusive rights to different intellectual property items may belong to a broad range of holders. Both individuals and companies may own exclusive rights to copyright items and patent rights. The subject of an exclusive right to a trademark

1 Article 1262 of the Civil Code.
2 Chapter 72(6) and Article 769(2)(3) of the Civil Code.
3 Article 1465 of the Civil Code.
4 Article 1475 of the Civil Code.

may be an individual entrepreneur or a company. The right to a trade name may only be held by a legal entity that is a commercial organisation.

According to Article 1226 of the Civil Code, intellectual property rights – ie, rights to results of intellectual activity and equivalent means of identification – include not only an exclusive right (which is a property right), but also personal non-property and other rights (for example, a right of resale or a right of access) when they are provided for by the Civil Code. Exclusive rights to the results of intellectual activity and the means of its identification continue for a defined time period unless the Civil Code provides otherwise.[5]

General provisions regulating relationships connected with licence and sub-licence agreements are set out in Articles 1235–1238 of the Civil Code. The general provisions on obligations[6] and on contracts[7] also apply to licence and sub-licence agreements.

The Civil Code provides that when a result of intellectual activity or the means of its identification requires state registration, any disposal under an agreement of the exclusive right to such result or means, any pledge of the right or grant of any right to use such result or such means under an agreement, as well as any transfer of the exclusive right to such result or such means without an agreement, also requires state registration. The conditions of and procedure for state registration in this context are established by the Russian Government.[8] Registration is performed through state registration of the relevant agreement.[9] Failure to comply with the requirement regarding state registration may lead to the licence agreement being invalidated.

The right to use intellectual property may also be granted through a franchise agreement.[10] The requirement for state registration applies to these franchise agreements as well.

### *(b) Legislation on bankruptcy*

The primary legislation that regulates insolvency (bankruptcy) in Russia is Federal Law 127-FZ, dated October 26 2002 (hereinafter 'the Bankruptcy Law'). At present, bankruptcy of only one category of debtors, namely credit institutions (which the Bankruptcy Law classifies as financial organisations), is regulated by a separate act: Federal Law 40-FZ on insolvency (bankruptcy) of credit institutions, dated February 25 1999.

## 1.2 Types of insolvency procedure

One of the important features of the Russian legal system is that all procedures in the Bankruptcy Law are used only after the court has initiated insolvency (bankruptcy) proceedings against the debtor; such procedures are performed only in the

---

5 Article 1230 of the Civil Code.
6 Articles 307–419 of the Civil Code.
7 Articles 420–453 of the Civil Code.
8 Article 1232(2) of the Civil Code.
9 Article 1232(3) of the Civil Code.
10 Chapter 54 of the Civil Code.

framework of these proceedings and under the defined control of the court. All bankruptcy cases currently fall under the jurisdiction of Russia's commercial ('arbitration') courts.

The Bankruptcy Law sets out five types of procedure used in a debtor's bankruptcy, and these are described further in the remainder of this section. The five types are set forth in Article 2 of the Bankruptcy Law and are termed:

- supervision;
- financial recovery;
- external administration;
- receivership proceedings; and
- amicable settlement.

Depending on the actual circumstances, all or only some of these procedures may consequently apply to a debtor. As a general rule, the first to occur in practice is always the supervision procedure. Under the Bankruptcy Law, in most situations the meeting of creditors decides which procedure should follow supervision.

### *(a) Supervision*

'Supervision' is a procedure that the commercial court initiates as a general rule after it reviews a bankruptcy petition and finds that it is justified. The supervision procedure is of a preparatory nature and it is used to analyse the debtor's financial condition, to prepare a register of creditors' claims and to hold the first creditors' meeting. The supervision procedure continues for up to six months and the debtor's property is preserved throughout this period.

The outcomes of a supervision procedure are set out in Article 63 of the Bankruptcy Law. The most important of these are as follows:

- Property sanctions under execution orders (including those issued on the basis of a court resolution, taking into account the exceptions specified in this provision) are suspended, and attachments of the debtor's property that were imposed during enforcement proceedings are removed.
- Members' rights are restricted, including by way of a prohibition on rights to payment of a dividend, to have the debtor buy back shares and to have an equity holding split in connection with a member's retirement from the debtor company.

### *(b) Rehabilitation procedures*

The Bankruptcy Law provides for two types of rehabilitation procedure that may be applied to the debtor and that are aimed at restoring its solvency: 'financial recovery' and 'external administration'. The primary difference between these two procedures is that during a financial recovery the debtor's executive bodies continue to perform their functions, albeit in a limited manner and under the control of an administrative manager,[11] while when an external administration procedure is applied the powers of the debtor's chief executive officer and certain other executive

---

11 Article 82(1) of the Bankruptcy Law.

bodies (with some exceptions) are transferred to the external administrator.[12] Each procedure is described further next.

**Financial recovery**: Under Chapter V of the Bankruptcy Law, 'financial recovery' is a procedure that is used to restore the debtor's solvency and to pay its debts according to a financial recovery schedule and a payments schedule approved by the court. This procedure is applied by a commercial court further to a petition drafted as a resolution of the board of creditors or members of the debtor, or of the unitary enterprise that holds the debtor's property. The financial recovery may continue for up to two years.[13] After the debts are paid, the court terminates the bankruptcy proceedings.

**External administration:** Under Chapter VI of the Bankruptcy Law, 'external administration' is a procedure applied to the debtor during bankruptcy proceedings for the purposes of restoring its solvency. The procedure may be applied after supervision or financial recovery. Moreover, under Article 146 of the Bankruptcy Law, if receivership proceedings were initiated against the debtor immediately after supervision, but the receiver identified grounds for restoring the debtor's solvency, the court may, further to a petition by the board of creditors, resolve to change the procedure to one of external administration.

The duration of external administration will not normally exceed 18 months, but a court may extend the period for another six months if it so decides.

If the external administration procedure results in the debtor's solvency being restored and all creditors' claims on the register being settled, the court terminates the insolvency (bankruptcy) proceedings. Should, however, the measures to restore the debtor's solvency fail, the court terminates the external administration procedure further to a petition by the creditors or, when the law so requires, further to a petition by a party to the bankruptcy proceedings, and declares the debtor bankrupt.

### *(c) Receivership proceedings*

Receivership proceedings comprise a procedure where the creditors' claims are proportionally settled, ending in the debtor's liquidation, except for certain special cases (described below). The procedure is applied to the debtor at the same time as the court issues a resolution to declare the debtor insolvent.

Article 124(2) of the Bankruptcy Law sets a six-month term for the receivership proceedings, which a court may extend. Even though the maximum period of extension is limited to six months, completing all measures set out in the law often requires several extensions.

After the bankruptcy estate is formed, the receiver settles creditors' claims. The order of priority of the claims is set out in Article 134 of the Bankruptcy Law. When the receivership proceedings are completed, the claims that could not be paid because the debtor's property was insufficient are treated as discharged.

---

12 Article 94(1) of the Bankruptcy Law.
13 Article 80(6) of the Bankruptcy Law.

When settlements with creditors and other statutory actions are completed, the court issues a ruling that the receivership proceedings are over. This ruling becomes the ground for the debtor's liquidation to be entered in the Companies' Register.

### *(d) Amicable settlement*

In bankruptcy cases, an amicable settlement is a procedure that is used to terminate bankruptcy proceedings and set out in an agreement how the debtor will settle the creditors' claims. An amicable settlement may be made at any stage of the bankruptcy proceedings – ie, during any of the procedures mentioned in subsections (a)–(c) above.

If a court approves the amicable settlement, this leads to the bankruptcy proceedings being terminated.

## 1.3 Grounds for bankruptcy

Russian bankruptcy legislation essentially equates the terms 'bankruptcy' and 'insolvency'. According to Article 2 of the Bankruptcy Law, insolvency (or bankruptcy) is understood as a debtor's inability – recognised by a commercial court – to fully settle creditors' financial claims and/or to make statutory payments.

For companies and individual entrepreneurs, the primary grounds on which a debtor may be declared bankrupt are that the debtor is unable to settle creditors' financial claims and/or to make statutory payments, and that both of the following conditions (under Article 6(2) of the Bankruptcy Law) are simultaneously true:

- These claims and/or payments have not been settled/made within three months from the due date; and
- The aggregate liabilities of the debtor are not less than RUB100,000 (around US$2,800) for companies and not less than RUB10,000 for individuals, including individual entrepreneurs.

An additional requirement for declaring an individual bankrupt is that property is insufficient to settle creditors' claims.

In light of all relevant draft laws that have been issued to date in Russia, the aggregate value of the creditors' outstanding claims required to declare the debtor bankrupt may eventually become much higher.

## 1.4 Filing for bankruptcy

Generally, a debtor, bankruptcy creditor or the competent authorities may submit a bankruptcy petition to the commercial court.[14] That financial claims have been overdue for three months or more should be evidenced by a legally effective resolution of a court of general jurisdiction, a commercial court or an arbitral tribunal that money be recovered from the debtor. That a creditor has made efforts to enforce this resolution is not a required condition for bankruptcy proceedings to be initiated. For a competent authority, it is sufficient for it to be shown to the court that certain measures which the tax legislation sets out for enforcing statutory payments have been taken against the debtor.

---

14 Article 7(1) of the Bankruptcy Law.

According to the Bankruptcy Law, the only persons who have an obligation to submit a bankruptcy petition are a debtor's chief executive officer and an individual entrepreneur. This obligation arises in the following situations:

- Claims of one or more creditors being satisfied results in it becoming impossible for claims of other creditors to be satisfied in full.
- The competent body of the debtor or of the unitary enterprise which holds the debtor's property has resolved that a bankruptcy petition be submitted to the commercial court.
- The debtor's activities would be significantly impeded or made impossible by property being foreclosed.
- The debtor qualifies for insolvency and/or its property is insufficient for all monetary claims to be satisfied and all obligations to be performed in relation to making statutory payments.

A bankruptcy petition may be submitted only to the local commercial court of the debtor (when the debtor is a company) or to the local court (when the debtor is an individual).[15]

The court reviews the bankruptcy petition solely for validity in a court hearing within 30 days from when the petition was submitted. Should the petition be recognised as valid, the court immediately applies the proper procedure to the debtor (and, as mentioned above, this is usually the supervision procedure).

### 1.5 Administrators and other appointed persons

Russian bankruptcy legislation envisages that the procedures used in bankruptcy cases should be managed by court-appointed administrators.[16] In each procedure used during bankruptcy proceedings the administrator has a different title: during the supervision procedure it is 'provisional administrator', during the financial recovery procedure it is 'administrator', while during an external administration it is 'external administrator' and during receivership proceedings it is 'receiver'.

The party that initiates the bankruptcy case should specify in the bankruptcy petition either a particular candidate for the position of the court-appointed administrator or the SRO that could nominate one of its members to be appointed by the court as the provisional administrator or receiver (if receivership proceedings are applied for from the start). When the next procedure (financial recovery procedure, external administration or receivership proceedings) is applied to the debtor, according to Article 45 of the Bankruptcy Law, the creditors' meeting has the right to nominate the administrator or the SRO.

In each specific bankruptcy case, the court-appointed administrator's work is supervised by the creditors and, in certain cases, the court.

---

15 Articles 3 and 33, respectively, of the Bankruptcy Law.

16 It should be noted that in spite of the word that is anglicised as *arbitrazh* being used in the Russian term for 'administrator' in this context, these persons do not belong to any commercial (arbitrazh) courts or arbitral tribunals. Rather, they are individuals who are members of a self-regulating organisation (SRO) of court-appointed administrators and they perform their professional work as private practitioners.

## 2. Licence agreements in the phase between filing and declaration of bankruptcy

The Russian Civil Code does not require that the licensee consents to entering into the agreement to dispose of the exclusive right. At the same time, according to Article 1235(7) of the Civil Code the exclusive right to a result of intellectual activity or a means of its identification being transferred to a new right holder is not treated as a valid reason to amend or terminate the licence agreement that was entered into by the previous right holder.

### 2.1 Effects on licence agreements in a licensor's or licensee's bankruptcy

Russian legislation does not set out any legal consequences for a licence agreement if a bankruptcy case is initiated against the licensee or the licensor. During the period between the bankruptcy petition being submitted and the debtor being declared bankrupt, the licence agreement should be performed by the parties to it without any variations. Accordingly, when bankruptcy proceedings or supervision, financial recovery or external administration procedures are initiated, this does not lead to the agreement or the rights under it being automatically terminated. Moreover, throughout the duration of these procedures the licensor or the licensee (whichever is the debtor) may enter into new licence agreements. No limit is set in the legislation for the duration of such agreements.

### 2.2 Powers of administrators in a licensor's or licensee's bankruptcy

During supervision and financial recovery, the provisional administrator and the administrator respectively do not have any rights to dispose of the debtor's property. Therefore, these categories of administrator may not act to terminate the licence agreement during the respective procedures.

However, if during these procedures the licensor (being the debtor) desires to dispose of its exclusive right to the intellectual property covered by the licence agreement and if the value of the subject matter of the transaction exceeds 5% of the book value of the debtor's assets as of when the respective procedure was applied, this would require the provisional administrator's approval during supervision and the approval of the creditors' meeting during financial recovery.

On the basis of Article 102 of the Bankruptcy Law, within the first three months of an external administration procedure the external administrator may repudiate the licence agreement if the transaction prevents the debtor's solvency from being restored or if the debtor would derive less benefit from the agreement being performed than from similar transactions entered into in similar circumstances being performed. The agreement may, though, be repudiated on behalf of the debtor only provided that the parties have not performed the transaction fully or partially.

A licence agreement that the external administrator declares repudiated is treated as terminated as soon as all parties to such agreement have received the external administrator's notice of repudiation, unless the agreement is subject to registration in connection with rights to use copyrighted items, including computer software and databases. When licence agreements for the use of inventions, utility models, industrial designs, trademarks and service marks are discontinued, this should be registered with the federal executive authority for intellectual property. The agreement to terminate a licence agreement becomes valid when it is registered. The effects of the agreement being repudiated by the licensor will include the licensee having a right to claim that a debtor licensor provides compensation for the damages caused by such repudiation.

The debtor licensor may not repudiate the agreement during external administration if the agreement was entered into during the supervision procedure with the provisional administrator's approval or during a financial recovery procedure that was in line with the Bankruptcy Law's requirements.

### 2.5 Impact of registration

There are no differences in the requirements for the content (ie, terms and conditions) of licence agreements that should be registered with the State authorities and those that should not. The specifics depend on the nature of the result of the intellectual activity or the means of its identification to which the agreement grants the right, as well as on the objectives that the parties to the agreement are pursuing.

The difference is that if the Civil Code sets out that the licence agreement is subject to registration, the agreement should be registered or there is a risk of it being invalidated. Should the parties desire to amend the registered licence agreement, these amendments should also be registered with the Russian authorities because the amendments will not be valid without such registration. If the parties agree to terminate the agreement or if the agreement contains a provision that it may be terminated unilaterally, such termination should also be registered; otherwise, the agreement will be treated as remaining in force. Therefore, under licence agreements that require state registration, exclusive rights are transferred to the new right holder from when the transfer is registered with the federal executive authority for intellectual property matters.[17]

As noted above, the right holder may desire that a computer program or database be registered. However, federal executive authorities for intellectual property do not register licence agreements regarding such registered computer software and databases.

The registration rules for sub-licence agreements are similar to those described above in this section for licence agreements.

## 3. Licence agreements in the phase after declaration of bankruptcy

### 3.1 Classification of rights to intellectual property

Russian legislation does not set out any special rules for classifying rights to intellectual property if the right holder or a user becomes bankrupt. Independently of the type of the particular intellectual property, exclusive rights to this item or to the right to use it become a part of the bankruptcy estate of the licensor or licensee, respectively.

### 3.2 Effects on licence agreements in the licensor's or licensee's bankruptcy

According to Articles 131(1) and 131(2) of the Bankruptcy Law, all of the debtor's

---

17 Articles 1234(4) and 1232(2) of the Civil Code.

property that is available when the bankruptcy proceedings commence or that is identified during the bankruptcy proceedings forms the bankruptcy estate. The following property of a debtor will be excluded from the bankruptcy estate:

- property that has been withdrawn from the market;
- property rights connected with the debtor's personal identity, including rights based on an existing licence to perform certain types of activities; and
- any other property which is defined as such in law.

The receiver disposes of the debtor's property within the limits of its powers, set out in Article 129 of the Bankruptcy Law. According to Article 128 of the Civil Code, protected results of intellectual activity and equivalent means of identification (IP property) are treated as civil rights items, as are property and property rights. In spite of the fact that results of intellectual activity and the means of its identification are not explicitly included in the term 'property', they also may be disposed of as a part of the debtor's bankruptcy estate after the debtor is declared bankrupt.

As a general rule, under Russian legislation the licensor's or licensee's bankruptcy does not lead to the licence agreement being automatically terminated or invalidated. Moreover, the licence agreement should be performed up to when the rights to the results of intellectual activity and the means of its identification are disposed of during the bankruptcy proceedings.

### 3.3 Powers of the receiver in a licensor's or licensee's bankruptcy

In considering here the powers of the receiver, we refer to the licensor and the licensee as the right holder and the user accordingly.

If the licensee is bankrupt, the receiver's powers are similar to those of the licensor's receiver with the exception that during the receivership proceedings for the licensee the item that is being disposed of is not the exclusive right to intellectual property, but the right to use such property.

Just as during an external administration procedure the receiver may repudiate agreements and other transactions in the manner defined in Article 102 of the Bankruptcy Law, so the conditions and procedure for, as well as the consequences of, such repudiations are similar to those described in section 2.2 above.

According to Article 129 of the Bankruptcy Law, the receiver may dispose of the debtor's property in the manner and on the conditions defined by law. Article 139 of the Bankruptcy Law sets out that the debtor's property, including property rights, should be sold in the manner defined by law. Therefore, the rights of the licensor or licensee with respect to the result of intellectual activity or to its use are also subject to sale, and this action is generally performed through competitive bidding.

In exercising its powers, the external administrator or the receiver may dispose of the exclusive rights to the results of intellectual activity or the means of its identification to a new right holder that belongs to the debtor's 'enterprise'. According to Article 132 of the Civil Code, an 'enterprise' is understood to be the set of assets and liabilities which is used for commercial activity. An enterprise is thereby treated as immovable property.

The external administrator exercises its power to sell the debtor's enterprise only provided that the debtor's property is sold in its entirety, because the set of assets and liabilities has been a part of the plan of external administration and this is fixed in a corresponding resolution of the debtor's executive body that, according to the constituent documents, is competent to resolve to enter into large transactions of this nature.

According to Article 110 of the Bankruptcy Law, when the enterprise is sold, all types of property intended for commercial activity are disposed of including the rights to the debtor's means of identification, its products, work and services, as well as the commercial designation, trademarks, service marks and other exclusive rights owned by the debtor, with the exception of those rights and liabilities that must not be transferred to other parties. The trade name is one example of such an exception, which may not be transferred to the buyer of the debtor's property as part of the set of assets and liabilities.

### 3.4 Powers and rights of creditors in a licensor's or licensee's bankruptcy

Russian legislation does not set out any special rights or powers of the creditors regarding licence agreements when the licensor or licensee is bankrupt.

Within the framework of a bankruptcy case, the creditors have the opportunity only indirectly – through participating in the creditors' meeting or committee – to influence the procedure for disposing of exclusive rights to the results of intellectual activity or the means of its identification. According to Article 139(1.1) of the Bankruptcy Law, within one month of when the inventory is taken of the debtor's property and it is assessed, the receiver should table before the creditors' meeting or committee a motion to sell the debtor's property. Through taking part in the vote on a motion submitted by the receiver regarding the procedure for disposing of the debtor's property, a creditor may affect the terms and conditions, as well as the methods for disposing of the debtor's exclusive rights to the results of intellectual activity or the means of its identification. Additionally, should the creditor disapprove of a resolution of the creditors' meeting concerning the procedure for disposing of the debtor's property, that creditor may apply to the commercial court to resolve the difference of opinion.

At the same time, the Bankruptcy Law allows the debtor to transfer the right to an intellectual property (if the debtor is the licensor) or the right to use it (if the debtor is the licensee) to an individual creditor as consideration for that creditor's claim to be terminated.[18] Discharging any creditors' claims by entering into an agreement to give consideration for termination requires the approval of the creditors' meeting or committee.

### 3.5 Exclusive and non-exclusive licences

Russian legislation does not contain any specific rules for exclusive or non-exclusive licences if a licensor or licensee is bankrupt.

---

18 Article 142(9) of the Bankruptcy Law.

### 3.6 Perpetual or non-perpetual licences

Neither Russian legislation nor Russian legal theory employs such concepts as 'perpetual' (prepaid) or 'non-perpetual' licences.

Even so, the range of forms and methods of paying consideration for using a licensed item includes not only royalties (which are the most widely used form) but also a lump sum payment (which is seldom used). A lump sum payment is applied mostly when the licence is acquired by a firm that is unknown in the market and doubts exist as to whether it will be able to successfully launch manufacturing and sales of the product, or when it would be difficult to control the amount of the product manufactured under the licence. The lump sum payments are used when all rights to the licensed item are transferred to the licensee.

Russian law does not contain any differences regarding how licences are treated when either of the parties to the licence agreements is bankrupt, even if different methods have been used to pay for these licences.

### 3.7 Impact of registration

With regard to bankruptcy, certain consequences arise in the case of a franchise agreement that provides for the use of intellectual property.[19]

According to Article 1037(4) of the Civil Code, a franchise agreement should be terminated when a rights holder or user is declared insolvent. However, this does not abolish the requirement for state registration of the agreement being terminated. Supposedly, a competent state authority should perform this independently, without any special application by the parties to the agreement, since the circumstances which have led to the agreement being automatically terminated are regarded as public knowledge. In relation to bankruptcy, this is ensured through the publication of details of all judicial acts, including the decision that the debtor be declared bankrupt, on the website of the Russian Supreme Commercial Court (www.arbitr.ru). The procedure has not yet been regulated for registering a franchise agreement when the rights holder or user is declared insolvent (bankrupt).[20] For this reason, if either party to a franchise agreement becomes bankrupt, the parties should ensure that the state registration of the agreement being terminated has been performed and initiate this process if not.

---

19 Under such agreement a rights holder provides to another user, for a fee and for a fixed or an indefinite period, the right to use in its business activities a set of exclusive rights owned by the rights holder, including rights to any trademarks, service marks or other items covered by exclusive rights as provided in the agreement. By virtue of the direct reference in Article 1027(4) of the Civil Code, the provisions of Section 7 of the code on licence agreements apply to franchise agreements, unless this is inconsistent with any provisions, special rules or the essence of a franchise agreement.

20 The administrative regulations on performance by the Federal Service for Intellectual Property, Patents and Trademarks of its function to register agreements on rights being granted regarding inventions, utility models, industrial designs, trademarks, service marks, protected computer software, databases, topologies of integrated microcircuits and franchise agreements (approved by Order 321 of the Ministry of Education and Science, October 29 2008, and registered by Order 13482 of the Ministry of Justice, March 5 2009) regulate the registration, amendment and termination franchise or sub-franchise agreements. These include a reference to Chapter 54 of the code (clause 9.9.1), which in practice allows registration to be applied for and obtained of franchise agreements being terminated.

## 4. Contractual arrangements in deviations from the law

### 4.1 Exceptions

As noted earlier in the chapter, the law sets out general rules for all licence agreements independently of which type of intellectual property is licensed. However, licence agreements differ depending on the nature of the intellectual property and the parties' objectives. The Civil Code sets out special rules for the following cases:

- Article 1286: "Licence agreement for the right to use a copyright work";
- Article 1287: "Special terms and conditions of a publishing licence agreement";
- Article 1308: "Licence agreement for the right to use a neighbouring rights item";
- Article 1362: "Compulsory licence";
- Article 1367: "Licence agreement on the right to use an invention, utility model or industrial design";
- Article 1368: "Open licence of an invention, utility model or industrial design";
- Article 1423: "A compulsory licence of a selective breeding achievement";
- Article 1428: "Licence agreement for the right to use a selective breeding achievement";
- Article 1429: "Open licence to a selective breeding achievement";
- Article 1459: "Licence agreement regarding the right to use a topology of an integrated microcircuit";
- Article 1469: "Licence agreement regarding the right to use a production secret";
- Article 1489: "Licence agreement of the right to use a trademark"; and
- Article 1539(5) regarding the right to use a commercial designation (in the framework of an enterprise lease agreement or franchise agreement).

Generally, special regulation of licence agreements affects the following areas:

- the form of the agreement;
- the method for entering into the agreement;
- whether or not the agreement is required to be registered with the Russian authorities (see section 2.3 above);
- certain material clauses of the agreement without which the agreement may be treated as not concluded;
- actions which are not treated as violating the licensor's exclusive rights – for example, those regarding rights to a selective breeding achievement;[21]
- whether the right may be granted to any party; and
- additional requirements for the procedure for using the rights.

### 4.2 Scope to alter statutory mechanisms

As mentioned in previous sections, for licence agreements (except for franchise agreements) Russian legislation does not contain any imperative rules that regulate the consequences of the licensor or licensee being bankrupt.

---

21 Article 1422 of the Civil Code.

Article 422(1) of the Civil Code requires that an agreement should be consistent with the rules set out in the Bankruptcy Law and other legal acts which are binding upon the parties on the date of the agreement (known as 'the imperative rules'). Taking this requirement into account, the parties to a licence agreement may not deviate from the imperative rules which are set out, in particular, in civil legislation.

### 4.3 Termination rights and automatic reversions

By virtue of the contractual freedom described in Articles 1 and 421 of the Civil Code, the parties to a licence agreement may add to it a clause that the licensor may terminate the agreement unilaterally should the licensee be declared bankrupt, including out of court. In this case the agreement will be treated as terminated from the date when the event occurred which the parties agreed on – for example, from when the licensee receives the corresponding notice – unless the licence agreement requires Russian State registration. Licence agreements of this kind will be treated as discontinued only after the appropriate state registration is made.

## 5. Cross-border aspects

### 5.1 Foreign law

In bankruptcy procedures, matters relating to the governing law remain less precisely regulated.

According to Article 1(1) of the Bankruptcy Law, this law defines the grounds on which a debtor may be declared insolvent (bankrupt), regulates the procedure to be followed and sets forth the terms and conditions for measures to be taken to prevent the debtor's insolvency and for bankruptcy procedures to be applied, as well as other relationships which arise when a debtor is unable to fully discharge creditors' claims. For debtors that are registered in Russia, the Bankruptcy Law will therefore have a priority regarding these matters.

The few rules which regulate how foreign law is applied include Article 1(5) of the Bankruptcy Law, according to which the provisions of that law apply to relationships it regulates with foreign creditors, unless any international treaty of Russia provides otherwise. Accordingly, if no such international treaty exists, the Bankruptcy Law will apply to such relationships. This primarily involves the provisions of the Bankruptcy Law that regulate how creditors should submit their claims so that they are entered in the register of creditors' claims for the debtor, and how the debtor's transactions with its contractors should be challenged.

At present, the practice of Russian Federation courts and commercial ('arbitration') courts confirms that the Bankruptcy Law has priority with regard to the procedure for how creditors should submit their claims against the debtor in the context of bankruptcy proceedings.

The lack of precise legal regulation with regard to the applicable law for bankruptcy cases means there is a need to rely on the general rules and approaches used in case law. According to Article 1210(1) of the Civil Code, the parties to an agreement contract may select the applicable law both when they enter into the contract and at a later stage. Article 1210(2) of that code states that either the parties should expressly set out their agreement concerning the applicable law, or their intentions should follow unequivocally from the terms and conditions of the agreement or the combined circumstances applying.

It can be stated with confidence that when considering bankruptcy proceedings Russian courts resolve matters regarding contracts being entered into, as well as the duration for which they remain valid, according to the legislation that the parties have agreed on. This rule is also based on Article 13(5) of the Russian Code of Commercial Procedure, which is the basis for a commercial court to apply a foreign law taking into account Russia's international treaties, federal law and an agreement of the parties that has been made in line with the foregoing.

The situation is less clear for assessing whether transactions and the measures taken to perform them are valid. This includes applying special grounds for transactions to be treated as invalid, as set out in Chapter III.1 of the Bankruptcy Law, when the parties have agreed that their agreement will be regulated by a foreign legislation. At present the case law on this matter is still being developed. However, we observe that Russian state courts tend to give priority to national bankruptcy legislation when they consider the special grounds for transactions to be treated as invalid, whether the parties' actions in performing such transactions may be challenged and whether the state commercial court which is considering the debtor's bankruptcy case is competent to resolve this particular dispute.

## 5.2 Foreign jurisdiction

It is common to encounter disputes which arise from contracts being referred to foreign jurisdictions where one or more of the parties are Russian individuals or companies. In these circumstances, the nature of the dispute and whether the debtor is the claimant or defendant dictate whether or not the Russian state court would accept as binding the clause of a licence agreement where a dispute in the event that one of the parties is bankrupt is referred to the jurisdiction of a foreign state or arbitration court.

The Bankruptcy Law refers certain categories of disputes to the exclusive jurisdiction of the commercial court which is considering the bankruptcy case (the local court of the debtor). Such disputes are considered within the framework of the bankruptcy proceedings and not that of the contentious proceedings relating to the dispute. They include court cases regarding whether the debtor's licence agreements are valid and the actions taken to perform such licence agreements if they are challenged by the receiver on certain special grounds.[22] For example, payments made by a debtor licensee for a certain period (up to three years) preceding the date when the bankruptcy case was initiated or after this date may only be challenged within the framework of the bankruptcy case if these payments are classified as suspicious transactions[23] or unfair preference transactions.

On the basis of Chapter 3.1 of the Bankruptcy Law, any claims of one party to a licence agreement against the other party, which has entered into bankruptcy

22 Chapter III.1 of the Bankruptcy Law.
23 Article 61.2 of the Bankruptcy Law.

proceedings, should also be referred only to the debtor's local commercial court; such claims are considered within the framework of the bankruptcy proceedings.

Any disputes which the Bankruptcy Law does not refer to the exclusive competence of the commercial court that is considering the bankruptcy proceedings should be referred to the court or arbitration court that the parties have specified in the arbitration clause of their agreement.

# South Africa

**Hans Klopper**
Independent Advisory

## 1. Overview

### 1.1 Relevant legislation governing intellectual property and bankruptcy

The legislation governing intellectual property rights in South Africa is found in the following Acts of Parliament:

- the Patents Act, No 57 of 1978;
- the Designs Act, No 195 of 1993;
- the Trade Marks Act, No 194 of 1993; and
- the Copyright Act, No 98 of 1978.

The above-mentioned legislation does not contain any specific provisions relating to insolvency. The rights in and to intellectual property under insolvency must therefore be interpreted by taking into consideration the general principles of the laws of insolvency on property and on contracts.[1]

The law regulating insolvency is substantially provided for in the Insolvency Act.[2] The common law of insolvency as contained in Romano-Dutch sources also applies in so far as it is not inconsistent with any legislation.

The effect of insolvency is, however, not unified in a single piece of legislation. The Insolvency Act essentially governs the relationship between creditors and debtors in the insolvent estate of a natural person, trust or partnership. In so far as legislation governing corporate entities such as companies and close corporations does not provide for a specific set of circumstances, the Insolvency Act still applies, as further explained below.

Companies are incorporated in line with the company laws of South Africa, and close corporations in line with the Close Corporations Act.[3] A 2008 Companies Act[4] (hereinafter 'the 2008 Companies Act') came into force on May 1 2011. Although the previous Companies Act[5] (hereinafter 'the 1973 Companies Act') has been repealed,[6] the 2008 Companies Act provides, in terms of a transitional arrangements, that

1 The main source of what is contained herein is E Bertelsman *et al, Mars: The Law of Insolvency in South Africa* (ninth edn, 2008).
2 Act No 24 of 1936.
3 Act No 69 of 1984.
4 Act No 71 of 2008.
5 Act No 61 of 1973.
6 Section 224(1) of the 2008 Companies Act.

Chapter 14 of the 1973 Companies Act continues to apply with respect to the liquidation (also known as the 'winding-up') of companies.[7]

In terms of the 2008 Companies Act, the Close Corporations Act was amended and close corporations that existed as at May 1 2011 were permitted to remain in existence but no new close corporations can be formed thereafter. Therefore, upon the liquidation of a company, the provisions of the aforementioned Chapter 14 of the 1973 Companies Act apply. Even so, in that Chapter 14 of the 1973 Companies Act does not deal with any specific set of circumstances, the provisions of the Insolvency Act apply *mutatis mutandis*.

Furthermore, given that the Close Corporations Act also does not provide for any specific set of circumstances, the provisions of Chapter 14 of the 1973 Companies Act may apply *mutatis mutandis*; and where Chapter 14 of the 1973 Companies Act does not apply, the provisions of the Insolvency Act will apply.

The *concursus creditorum* is one of the key concepts of the South African laws of insolvency in that it entails that the rights of creditors as a group are preferred to the rights of individual creditors. The concept of the *concursus creditorum* ensures that, upon an incidence of bankruptcy either by way of an order of court sequestrating a natural person or an order of court liquidating a company or a close corporation (hereinafter referred to in overall terms as 'insolvency'), the position of the insolvent natural person, company or close corporation (hereinafter referred to as the 'insolvent estate') be crystallised; and it also ensures that once the hand of the law is laid upon the affairs of an insolvent estate, the rights of the general body of creditors have to be taken into consideration.[8]

## 1.2 Types of insolvency procedure

There are three main types of insolvency procedure available in South Africa:

- sequestration of the estates of natural persons, partnerships and trusts;
- liquidation of companies and close corporations; and
- 'business rescue' in respect of companies and close corporations.

### *(a) Sequestration*

In the case of natural persons, partnerships and trusts, a sequestration order is granted pursuant to an application to the High Court of South Africa, a superior court that operates in 14 divisions, with jurisdiction to grant an order placing the estate of a natural person (among others) into sequestration. Such an application would ordinarily be launched by a creditor.

A natural person may even file an application for an order by the court for a so-called 'voluntary surrender' of his estate in line with the provisions of the Insolvency Act. A natural person who applies for voluntary surrender must demonstrate that the estate has sufficient assets that are unencumbered, or not fully encumbered, to ensure that the benefit to creditors will not be negligible. The major consideration here is that the filing of a voluntary surrender must be to the advantage of creditors,[9]

---

7 Schedule 5, paragraph 9 of the 2008 Companies Act.
8 *Walker v Syfret* NO 1911 AD 141.

and this is also a requirement when a creditor launches a hostile sequestration application. The statutory requirement to demonstrate an advantage to creditors to the court, in an application by a creditor for the sequestration of the debtor, would appear to be unique to South Africa.

*(b)* ***Liquidation***

Companies may be liquidated through a resolution or by way of an application to court.

*(c)* ***Business rescue***

The 2008 Companies Act provides for business rescue provisions similar to Chapter 11 provisions in the United States. Under the provisions of Chapter 6 of the 2008 Companies Act, a company may adopt a resolution to be placed under business rescue[10] and, upon filing such a resolution with the Companies and Intellectual Property Commission (the CIPC), the company's business rescue proceedings commence. Business rescue may also commence in terms of an order of the court pursuant to an application to the court.

Upon commencement of business rescue proceedings there is an immediate moratorium[11] against legal action against the company and against any enforcement action against any of its assets.

### 1.3 Grounds of bankruptcy

The grounds for the liquidation of a company are contained in Chapter 14 of the 1973 Companies Act, specifically Section 344. Thus a company may resolve to be placed in liquidation either by way of a members' voluntary[12] winding-up resolution for a solvent company, or by way of a creditors' voluntary[13] winding-up resolution for an insolvent company.

A company may be liquidated by any division of the High Court of South Africa if the grounds for liquidation as set out in Section 344 of the 1973 Companies Act are met and:

- the company has by special resolution resolved that it be wound up by the court;
- the company commenced business before the CIPC certified that it was entitled to commence business;
- the company has not commenced its business within a year of its incorporation, or has suspended its business for a whole year;
- in the case of a public company, the number of members has been reduced below seven;
- three-quarters of the issued share capital of the company has been lost or has become useless[14] for the business of the company;

---

9 Section 12(1)(c) of the Insolvency Act; see also *Meskin & Co v Friedman* 1948 (2) SA 555 (W).
10 See Section 129 of the 2008 Companies Act.
11 See section 130 of the 2008 Companies Act.
12 The term is used herein as it is contained in the1973 Companies Act.
13 *Id.*

- it is unable to pay its debts as described in Section 345 of the 1973 Companies Act;
- in the case of a company considered 'foreign' to South Africa, that company has been dissolved in the country in which it was incorporated, or has ceased to carry on business or is carrying on business only for the purpose of winding up its affairs; or
- it appears to the court that it is just and equitable that the company should be wound up.

In addition, when a company is under business rescue in line with the 2008 Companies Act, the appointed business rescue practitioner may, under certain circumstances, apply to the court for liquidation of the company.

## 1.4 Filing for bankruptcy

An application for liquidation[15] of a company may be made:

- by the company itself (an *ex parte* application);
- by one or more of its creditors (including contingent or prospective creditors);
- by one or more of its members (shareholders);
- jointly by any or all of the parties mentioned in the three bullet points immediately above;
- in the case of any company being wound up voluntarily, by the Master of the High Court or any creditor or member of that company; or
- the business rescue practitioner of a company appointed under the provisions of the 2008 Companies Act.

The only court that is competent to grant an order of liquidation or sequestration is the High Court of South Africa, which operates in 14 divisions in South Africa.

## 1.5 Administrators and other appointed persons

There is no immediate appointment of a trustee of the insolvent estate of a natural person, trust or partnership or a liquidator of a company or close corporation (as appropriate) upon a filing for sequestration or liquidation. A trustee or liquidator is appointed subsequently as determined by the court.

A Master of the High Court[16] is the person appointed by the Minister of Justice to each division of the High Court of South Africa to have jurisdiction over matters referred to that division.[17] Upon the granting of an order by the court as a result of

---

14 Blackman, Everingham and Jooste, *Commentary on the Companies Act* (vol 3), Juta legal and Academic Publishers, 2002 states that the origin of this provision is to be found in Section 13 of the Limited Liability Act of 1855, which imposed a duty on the directors to apply the winding-up of the company once "three fourths of the subscribed capital stock of the company has been lost, or has become unavailable in the course of trade".

15 Section 346 of the 1973 Companies Act.

16 Note the Master is in a separate department in the Department of Justice and not linked to the High Court. The title 'Master of the High Court' is in a way a misnomer in that it was initially formed to oversee the affairs of deceased estates and to look after "widows and orphans". It was later given the responsibility to oversee insolvencies as well.

17 See Sections 1 and 2 of the Administration of Estates Act No 66 of 1965.

which the estate of a natural person, partnership or trust is sequestrated, the ownership of the estate's assets vests in the Master until he appoints a provisional or final trustee to such insolvent estate. Upon the granting of an order by the court as a result of which a company of close corporation is placed into liquidation by way of a provisional or final order, the affairs of the company or close corporation are under the control of the Master until he appoints a provisional or final liquidator.

The Master is the only person enjoined with the appointment of such practitioners (trustees or liquidators) and he is not bound in law to appoint a provisional practitioner immediately upon the granting of an order of court. He may, however, only appoint a provisional practitioner upon a provisional or final liquidation or sequestration order of court being received by him.

A final practitioner is elected at the first statutory meeting of creditors convened by the Master under the terms of the Insolvency Act[18] – at which meeting, among other things, the appointment of a final practitioner is voted on by the proved creditors present at the meeting. The Master is then duty bound to appoint such a person as long as the prospective practitioner is not disqualified from appointment in some way.[19]

If required to do so, the Master ordinarily appoints provisional practitioners based on the wishes of the creditors. Upon receipt of an order of court, the Master opens a file and creditors with claims of more than ZAR1,000 (around US$100) vote for the appointment of a practitioner. The votes of creditors are reckoned in number and value. In certain instances joint practitioners may be appointed, where one practitioner was elected on the number and another on the value of creditors' votes.

## 2. Licence agreements in the phase between filing and declaration of bankruptcy

### 2.1 Effects on licence agreements in the licensor's bankruptcy

During the phase between the filing (also referred to as the 'issuing') of an application to the court for an order of court placing the debtor in insolvency, the control over the affairs, property (including intellectual property rights) and business and trading activities remains under the control of the debtor.

### 2.2 Powers of administrators, receivers or trustees in the licensor's bankruptcy

During the phase between the filing of an application for insolvency and the granting of an order of the court, there is no role for a practitioner. The debtor's affairs remain under the debtor's control, as described in section 2.1 above.

### 2.3 Effects on licence agreements in the licensee's bankruptcy

By virtue of the fact that no practitioner gets appointed upon filing, the licensee remains in control of its own affairs until the actual granting of an order of court placing the licensee in insolvency. The licensee can continue to conduct business, including the payment of licence fees; and a practitioner, once appointed, will not

18 Section 40 of the Insolvency Act and Section 412 of the 1973 Companies Act.
19 Section 55 of the Insolvency Act; Sections 372 and 373 of Chapter 14 of the 1973 Companies Act.

be legally able to challenge such payments because they will be deemed to be made in the normal course of business.

### 2.4 Powers of administrators, receivers or trustees in the licensee's bankruptcy

No practitioner is involved or gets appointed upon the filing of insolvency proceedings, and the debtor will remain in possession of its assets and in control of its own affairs.

### 2.5 Impact of registration

In the phase between filing for insolvency proceedings and a court order being issued that declares insolvency, it makes no difference whether a licence agreement is registered, because it is not possible for a practitioner to get involved until duly appointed under the law.

## 3. Licence agreements in the phase after declaration of bankruptcy

### 3.1 Treatment of intellectual property rights

Where intellectual property rights arise by virtue of an agreement between two parties – whether a licence agreement or any other agreement – in the event of insolvency of any of the parties, such rights are dealt with in terms of the normal principles that apply in the laws of insolvency.

Where intellectual property rights constitute an asset or property in an insolvent estate, such rights are dealt with in exactly the same way that any asset would ordinarily be dealt with under insolvency. These rights may be disposed of by an insolvency practitioner, and a third party can acquire such intellectual property rights from the insolvency in the same manner that any purchaser can acquire any asset from an insolvent estate.

Therefore, the only distinction between the different intellectual property rights and how they are treated in insolvency relates to whether the intellectual property rights accrue pursuant to a contractual arrangement or, alternatively, constitute property in the insolvent estate.

Copyright as an asset is transmissible as movable property by assignment, testamentary disposition or operation of law[20] and the assignment of copyright pursuant to an agreement to transfer copyright out of an insolvent estate is done according to the applicable normal principles. As such, the assignment of copyright or the grant of exclusive licences pursuant thereto require formalities in that such assignment needs to be in writing and duly signed by both parties.[21] Furthermore, a non-exclusive licence to do an act which is subject to copyright may be assigned in writing or in terms of an oral agreement, and may be inferred from the conduct of the parties. However, under these circumstances such rights may be revoked at any time.[22]

The partial assignment of copyright may be limited so as to apply only to some

---

20 Section 22 of the Copyright Act of 1978.
21 Section 22(3) of the Copyright Act of 1978.
22 Section 22(4) of the Copyright Act of 1978.

of the acts which the owner of the copyright has the exclusive right of control over, or to a part only of the term of the copyright, or to a specified country or other geographical area.

As far as future works are concerned, an assignment or licence may be granted or made in respect of the copyright in future work, or the copyright in an existing work in which copyright does not subsist but which will come into being in the future, and the future copyright of any such work is also transmissible as movable property.[23] As is recorded in the *Roopanand Brothers* case:

> *The effect of a valid assignment is to vest the assignee ownership of the copyright in the work or works covered by the assignment and entitles the assignee to sue for infringement of such copyright.*[24]

Practitioners must be mindful of the provisions of the Trade Marks Act of 1993 when disposing of trademarks, and the requirement that purchasers who become entitled by assignment or transmission to a registered trademark need to make application to the registrar of trademarks to register their title.[25] A failure to comply with the provisions of the Trade Marks Act will render the transaction between the practitioner and the purchaser invalid.

In terms of the Designs Act of 1993, an assignment of rights in a design is required to be in writing in order to be valid.[26]

### 3.2 Effects on licence agreements in the licensor's bankruptcy

An express statutory provision may provide that a contract be terminated upon insolvency. An example of this is found in the Insolvency Act, which provides in Section 38 that service contracts with employees may be terminated after consultation with the practitioner. However, in terms of the laws of insolvency in general, a contract is not – and may not automatically be – cancelled or terminated upon the insolvency of one of the parties. As the legislation relating to intellectual property does not contain express statutory provisions in this regard, a licence agreement will not be treated any differently from any other agreement in terms of South Africa's laws of insolvency.

As a licence agreement remains valid even upon insolvency, the practitioner has to choose whether to abide by the agreement or to terminate an unexecuted contract entered into by the insolvent party before insolvency. The practitioner is not bound to perform the contract unless he, in conjunction with the general body of creditors who proved claims and who may direct the practitioner to act in certain manner, considers that performance will be in their best interests. If the practitioner elects to affirm the contract he must perform all that the insolvent party to the contract would have had to have performed. It should be noted that the practitioner cannot be held personally liable where he makes an election pursuant to directions given to him by creditors. The other party to the contract, ie the licensee, does not have a similar right of election.

---

23 Section 22(5) of the Copyright Act of 1978.
24 *Frank & Hirsch (Pty) Ltd v A Roopanand Brothers (Pty) Ltd* 1993 (4) SA 279 (A).
25 Section 40 of the Trade Marks Act of 1993.
26 Section 30 of the Designs Act.

The manner in which the practitioner, after having been appointed, conducts himself is important because the conduct of a practitioner may cause the other party to a contract to infer that the practitioner has made an election to abide by the contract.

There is no room for a practitioner to retract his decision once an election to complete a contract has been made. Once a decision has been made, the practitioner is absolutely bound by that decision.[27] A risk for a practitioner lies therein that, once the above-mentioned election to abide by a contract has been made, the practitioner becomes obliged to fulfil all outstanding obligations of the insolvent estate. These obligations could include unfulfilled past obligations that may be outstanding under the contract.[28] Therefore, unless the practitioner is absolutely sure that he will be able to fully perform his duties in place of the licensor, he would ill advised to make an election or to conduct himself in any manner which may suggest, or from which it may be inferred, that he has elected to abide by the contract. Indeed, Van Winsen AJA stated as follows:[29]

> *The liquidator must make its election within what, regard being had to the circumstances of the case, is a reasonable time. Should he elect to abide by the agreement, the liquidator steps into the shoes of the company in liquidation and is obliged to the other party to the agreement to whatever counter-prestation is required of the company in terms of the agreement.*

The costs relating to the practitioner's decision to abide by the contract will be a cost in the administration of the insolvent estate; and in the event that the proceeds of the realised assets are insufficient to cover such costs, creditors who proved claims against the insolvent estate may become liable to contribute additional monies, *pro rata* to the value of their claims, to such a shortfall.[30] When abiding by a licence agreement, the practitioner therefore needs to be mindful of all the costs involved and be sure that there are no unfulfilled past obligations.

A practitioner's decision not to abide by a contract does not necessarily mean that he may unilaterally cancel a contract; the practitioner is only entitled to refuse to render specific performance in terms of the contract. Under those circumstances, the other party to the contract may accept or reject the repudiation. An acceptance of the repudiation may lead to an unsecured claim for damages against the insolvent estate.

The practitioner also has no right to unilaterally alter or amend the provisions of a contract that was in existence prior to insolvency.

An accrued right of cancellation[31] that arose prior to arrival of insolvency may be enforced, but only a completed right of cancellation will survive the *concursus creditorum*.[32] The effect of this is that if a breach of a provision of the contract has occurred prior to the arrival of insolvency which entitles the other party to cancel, such cancellation may be completed after the date of insolvency.

---

27 *Churchyard v Redpath, Brown and Co Ltd*, 1911 WLD; *Uys v Sam Friedman Ltd*, 1934 OPD; *Gordon NO v Standard Merchant Bank Ltd*, 1983 (3) SA, 68 (A).

28 *Muller NNO v Bryant & Flanagan (Pty) Ltd* 1978 (2) SA 807 (A).

29 *Ibid.*

30 See *Nedcor Investment Bank v Pretoria Belgrave Hotel (Pty) Ltd* 2003 (5) SA 189 (SCA).

31 *See Porteous v Strydom NO* 1984 (2) SA 489 (D).

32 *Roering NNO v Nedbank Ltd* 2013 (3) SA 160 (GSJ).

### 3.3 Powers of an administrator, receiver or trustee in the licensor's bankruptcy

The practitioner of the licensor's insolvent estate is bound by the terms of the licensor's agreement(s) with licensees. Invariably, the affairs of the insolvent estate need to be finalised and wound up and the practitioner would have to either sell the business of the licensor to a third party or enter into alternative arrangements with the licensees.

The practitioner does not have immediate powers to act upon his initial appointment. He needs to obtain powers to sell assets and to generally act in the interest of creditors through directions obtained from creditors at a statutory general meeting of proved creditors.

The practitioner in the insolvent estate of a licensor might be able to assign the rights in and to a licence to a buyer. If there are contractual limitations that prevent the licensor from assigning rights, such issues may have to be addressed and will be the subject of negotiations – failing which, assignment might be problematic.

In practice, and to save time, application is often made to the court for an order in terms of which the practitioner's powers are extended to enable him to sell assets and businesses.

### 3.4 Powers and rights of creditors in a licensor's bankruptcy

The creditors' powers are, as mentioned in section 3.3 above, confined to directions that those creditors may give at a statutory general meeting of creditors.

The creditors' rights to information during the proceedings are limited to the receipt of a report at the second (general) meeting of creditors. However, in extraordinary circumstances supplementary reports are submitted and correspondence may be addressed to the practitioner at any given time to which the practitioner would be duty bound to respond; and the practitioner is bound to adhere to directions provided to him by creditors at statutory meetings of creditors convened for this purpose. Other than the duty to submit a report, there is no specific duty upon the practitioner to provide information to creditors.

### 3.5 Effects on licence agreements in the licensee's bankruptcy

Upon his final appointment at a first meeting of creditors, the practitioner must submit a report and draft resolutions at a second (general) meeting of creditors, which will then be considered by creditors after having received timely notice. Creditors may then give directions as they deem fit on any matter reported to them or any matter relating to the administration or realisation of the estate's assets. Subject to such directions being legal and capable of fulfilment, the practitioner will be duty bound to adhere to them. The directions would ordinarily be known as 'adopted resolutions'.

It is also evident from what is explained earlier in the chapter that the effect on a licence agreement is no different from the position that would prevail upon the insolvency of a licensor. In terms of the principles set out above, contracts between an insolvent licensee and third parties such as its licensor are not automatically terminated by the insolvency of the licensee.

The major effect of the foregoing is that the practitioner, who steps into the shoes of the licensee, cannot be compelled to render a specific performance and has to act in the interests of the general body of creditors. It therefore follows that the practitioner must, within reasonable time, decide (also termed, 'elect') whether he will perform each particular licence agreement or terminate it.

The rights to intellectual property in the nature of the right of the licensee is absolute; but the practitioner, by abiding by an agreement entered into by the licensee, is at risk where he binds creditors for reciprocal obligations arising as a result of the executory nature of a licence agreement. The practitioner, having acted upon directions provided to him by creditors, cannot be held personally liable.

The intellectual property rights held by an insolvent licensee pursuant to a licence agreement are deemed property of the insolvent estate. This is because it has been held in South African courts[33] that intellectual property rights that an insolvent entity acquired during its insolvency fall within the definition of 'property'[34] and form part of the insolvent entity's estate. Then, as would apply to any asset, the practitioner must take control of it, procure a valuation of the rights pursuant to the licence agreement and, once the practitioner obtains the powers as described above, dispose of the rights.

The cost of abiding by the agreement needs to be assessed by the practitioner, and there is no basis upon which the practitioner will be able to abide by the licence agreement where he is uncertain about the financial effect that abiding by the agreement will have on the insolvent estate and consequently the general body of creditors. Where it proves to be too risky or onerous, the practitioner may elect not to abide by the agreement.

### 3.6 Powers of an administrator, receiver or trustee in the licensee's bankruptcy

The practitioner of a licensee's bankruptcy has the same powers as described in section 3.3 above in respect of the practitioner in a licensor's bankruptcy.

### 3.7 Powers and rights of creditors in a licensee's bankruptcy

Creditors have no right to terminate or continue with any agreement; such rights remain with the practitioner. Nonetheless, creditors have the right to provide directions to the practitioner at a general meeting of creditors, as described in section 3.4 above.

The rights of creditors to participate in the process arise when the creditors obtain the necessary *locus standi* by proving claims at a statutory meeting of creditors. The practitioner is duty bound to act in accordance with the directions by creditors, unless such directions are illegal by reason of their being in conflict with either the letter or the spirit of South Africa's insolvency laws. Where creditors therefore deem it appropriate to terminate or continue with a licence agreement, they need to participate as described above.

### 3.8 Exclusive and non-exclusive licences

The general insolvency principles relating to agreements apply to any licence

---

33 See *Haupt t/a Soft Copy v Brewers Marketing Intelligence (Pty) Ltd* 2005 (1) SA 398 (C).
34 See Section 2 of the Insolvency Act.

agreement and there is therefore no distinction between exclusive and non-exclusive licences during the bankruptcy of any of the parties to the licences.

### 3.9 Perpetual and non-perpetual licences

The general insolvency principles relating to agreements apply to perpetual and non-perpetual licences. As the practitioner must make an election as to whether or not to continue with the licence agreement, it is irrelevant whether the licence is perpetual or non-perpetual in nature. The effect of this is that the practitioner may also make an election to reject performance of the agreement upon the insolvency of a licensor, even under circumstances where the licensee has made full payment of licence fees.

The practitioner will act in conjunction with the wishes of creditors as expressed in their directions, provided as described above.

### 3.10 Effects on a sub-licence in a licensor's bankruptcy

A decision to abide by a main contract does not mean that the practitioner has also elected to abide by all subcontracts.[35]

Also, where the insolvent estate was party to a principal contract which was procured by or involved an agent and the practitioner elects to abide by such contract, such election does not necessarily mean that the practitioner has also abided by the contract of agency.[36]

In the event of a licensor's bankruptcy, the practitioner will have to choose whether to abide by or terminate the sub-licence agreement. The effect on the sub-licence may be negligible where the rights in terms of the main agreement are assigned.

### 3.11 Effects on a sub-licence in a licensee's bankruptcy

Where the licensee's practitioner made an election to abide by the agreement and to assign those rights, the effect on the sub-licence may be negligible.

Under circumstances where the licensor's practitioner elects not to continue with the licence agreement with a licensee who entered into a sub-licence agreement, the licensee will have an unsecured claim against the licensor's insolvent estate equal to a damages claim instituted against the licensee by the sub-licensee as a result of the cancellation of the licence agreement and which, in turn, forced the licensee to be unable to perform in terms of its sub-licence agreement.

Practically, the practitioner would ordinarily assign the licence to the licensee where it appears that the insolvent licensor's proved creditors deem it unnecessary or not financially viable to abide by the licence agreement or where a purchaser cannot be found for the licence.

### 3.12 Impact of registration

In terms of the principles identified above, it would make no difference whether a licence has been registered or not.

---

35 *Du Plessis NNO v Rolfes Ltd* 1997 (2) SA 354 (A).
36 *Gore NNO v Roma Agencies CC* 1998 (2) SA 518 (C).

## 4. Contractual arrangements in deviation from the law

### 4.1 Exceptions

There are no licence agreements relating to intellectual property that are subject to a different regime than the one described above.

### 4.2 Scope to alter statutory mechanisms

South Africa's legislation contains no specific provisions relating to statutory mechanisms relating to insolvency, and the principles that apply are the normal insolvency laws relating to contracts and assets. The parties cannot agree to contract out of the insolvency principles.

### 4.3 Termination rights and automatic reversions

As mentioned in section 4.2 above, it is not possible to contract out of provisions resting on the general principles of insolvency law by agreeing to an automatic reversion of rights or automatic cancellation upon insolvency. A provision in any agreement to the effect that the agreement is *ipso facto* terminated upon the insolvency of one of the parties is unenforceable in South African law.

A provision in terms of which rights are reversed pursuant to the insolvency of one of the parties is likewise unenforceable in South African law.

## 5. Cross-border aspects

### 5.1 Foreign law

It is inconceivable that the South African courts would permit two contracting entities based in South Africa to contract out of the provisions of South Africa's laws of insolvency.

A practitioner in South Africa would likewise be duty bound, for with any licence agreement he is administering, to deal with it under South Africa's laws.

### 5.2 Foreign jurisdiction

If a licence agreement contains an attempt to circumvent the South African laws of insolvency by making the rules of a foreign jurisdiction applicable where both parties and the licence agreement are within South African jurisdiction, it would appear that such an agreement would be unenforceable. It has, however, been held in South African case law that local courts do not have jurisdiction to decide claims of infringement of foreign copyrights.[37]

---

37 *Gallo Africa Ltd v Sting Music (Pty) Ltd* 2010 (6) SA 329 (SCA).

# Spain

**Agustín Bou**
JAUSAS

---

## 1. Overview

### 1.1 Relevant legislation governing intellectual property and bankruptcy

Business insolvency legalisation in Spain is governed in the country's Insolvency Act, No 22/2003 of July 9 2003, which has been amended on a number of occasions since its promulgation.

For its part, intellectual property is covered by a wider range of laws, with one governing each specific area:

- the Trademarks Act, No 17/2001 of December 7 2001;
- the Invention Patents and Utility Models Act, No 11/1986 of March 20 1986;
- the Industrial Design Legal Protection Act, No 20/2003 of July 7 2003; and
- Royal Legislative Decree, No 1/1996 of April 12 1996, which approves the revised text of the Intellectual Property Act.

Both sets of regulations – those governing insolvencies and those concerning intellectual property – are independent of one another and do not specifically govern rights available during insolvency proceedings, which creates a difficult fit between these two fields of law.

### 1.2 Types of insolvency procedure

Insolvency proceedings in Spain can be divided into two kinds, depending upon whether it is the debtor itself that voluntarily seeks a declaration that it is insolvent (voluntary insolvency) or one of its creditors that seeks the debtor's declaration of insolvency (compulsory insolvency).

The key differences between the two are that, in the case of voluntary insolvency, the company's managing body retains, in principle, its powers of management and the making use of business assets,[1] albeit subject to the involvement of an insolvency administrator. The procedure requires the insolvency administrator's authorisation or confirmation for the governing body to manage or make use of the company's assets.[2] So, the insolvent business's governing body remains active (during the first phase of the insolvency, known as the 'common' phase), albeit requiring the collaboration and involvement of the insolvency administrator.

---

1 See Article 7 of the Insolvency Act.
2 Article 40.1 of the Insolvency Act.

Generally speaking, the insolvency administrator authorises those acts and operations inherent in the debtor company's normal business, to facilitate its ordinary activities.[3] After completion of the common phase, if the insolvency leads to liquidation, the insolvency administrator will dismiss the governing body and take over administration of the company's liquidation. If, on the other hand, an arrangement with creditors is approved, the insolvency administrator will resign and the company's managing body will remain in place.

In the case of compulsory insolvency,[4] the asset administration and management powers of the management body are suspended at the time of the declaration of insolvency, and that body is replaced by an insolvency administrator,[5] which takes control of the company to continue with its business activities by means of an arrangement with creditors (something fairly uncommon in compulsory insolvencies) or by means of liquidation.

## 1.3 Grounds of bankruptcy

The objective presupposition set by the Insolvency Act for establishing whether a company is insolvent is that it cannot regularly meet its short-term liabilities.[6] Indications of this situation are the failure to pay salaries, suppliers, liabilities against public entities, or short-term credit obligations. As soon as the company knows that it cannot meet any or all of those liabilities, it must submit within a period of two months an insolvency declaration before the relevant commercial court.[7] A debtor's insolvency can either be 'current' (when the business is already aware that it cannot meet its due liabilities) or 'imminent' (when the debtor foresees that it will soon be unable to meet its liabilities).

As soon as a debtor becomes aware or should have become aware of its insolvent position (current or imminent), its management body has a duty to apply for a declaration of insolvency within the above-mentioned two month period. This deadline is mandatory and, if not met, the company's directors can be required by a court to pay any asset deficit should they be ruled culpable.[8]

## 1.4 Filing for bankruptcy

As noted in the preceding section, the body entitled and obligated to seek a company's declaration of insolvency is its management body (or of its liquidation, if the business finds itself in a liquidation situation). Also entitled to seek this declaration of insolvency are any shareholders personally answerable for the company's debts.

Should the debtor company not seek a formal declaration of insolvency when it has a duty to do so, any of its creditors may do so, giving rise (as noted in section 1.2 above) to compulsory insolvency proceedings, which normally involve the suspension of the management body's powers.

---

3 Article 44.2 of the Insolvency Act.
4 Article 40.2 of the Insolvency Act.
5 Article 44.3 the Insolvency Act.
6 Article 2.2 of the Insolvency Act.
7 Article 5 of the Insolvency Act. See also section 1.4 of this chapter.
8 Article 163 and following of the Insolvency Act.

Spain's commercial courts are those with the jurisdiction to hear insolvency applications, specifically those of the territory in which that debtor has its centre of main interests,[9] with the presumption being that this is its business location.

### 1.5 Administrators and appointed persons

After the filing of an application for a declaration of insolvency (voluntary or compulsory), the company will continue to function as usual, governed by its management body, which will carry out its duties as normal until the relevant commercial court issues a ruling declaring it to be insolvent and appointing an insolvency administrator. That ruling will establish the voluntary or compulsory nature of the proceedings, as well as the system of involvement in or the suspension of the management body's powers by the insolvency administrator, which in any case proceeds to inspect the operations of the insolvent company.

## 2. Licence agreements in the phase between filing and declaration of bankruptcy

### 2.1 Effects on licence agreements in the licensor's bankruptcy

It should be stressed that Spain's insolvency system takes as its point of reference, time-wise, for effects before thirds parties, the date of the judicial declaration of insolvency, rather than that of the application therefor by those entitled to do so. Furthermore, it does not provide for any special situation during the period of time between the application and the actual declaration of insolvency. The company will continue to operate normally during the said period, awaiting the formal declaration of insolvency and the appointment of the insolvency administrator, at which point the insolvent business's method of operating will vary, depending upon whether its running is subject to oversight or the suspension of management powers.

Nevertheless, these 'normal operations' should not be confused with complete freedom of operation: they must in all cases be carried on in such a way as not to harm the interests of the body of creditors, prejudicing their chances of collecting their debts. The Insolvency Act establishes that any action outside the normal course of business that is likely to be deemed prejudicial to the assets of the insolvent party's estate, if carried out in the two years preceding the actual declaration of insolvency, may be subject to annulment by the insolvency administrator.[10]

It should be pointed out that, up until the judicial declaration of insolvency, agreements may only be terminated by virtue of the grounds for termination contemplated therein or by specifically applicable regulations (in this case, the intellectual property legislation mentioned in section 1.1 above) governing the contractual relationship. In other words, should any of the cases of breach of contractual duties occur during the period between the application for insolvency and the juridical declaration, the occurrence would entitle the party in compliance or an *in bonis* creditor to seek termination of the agreement or judicial enforcement

9 Article 10.1 of the Insolvency Act.
10 Article 71 of the Insolvency Act.

of compliance pursuant to Article 1.124 of Spain's Civil Code, together with compensation for any financial harm and damages caused by that breach.

In the case of a licensing agreement, when it is the licensor that applies for the declaration of insolvency, the agreement with its licensees remains in place, valid and enforceable for both parties, unless there is a breach by the licensor of its core obligations, such as the payment of registry dues for keeping the intangible asset up to date and allowing the licensees to enjoy peaceful use of the licensed rights, in accordance with the agreement. In this regard, and much as when the insolvency has been declared, Article 61.3 of the Insolvency Act establishes that any provision in an agreement entitling either of the parties to terminate or rescind the agreement due to the mere declaration of insolvency of either of them shall be deemed invalid and unenforceable. This issue is examined in further detail in section 3 below.

### 2.2 Powers of administrators, receivers or trustees in the licensor's bankruptcy

During the period between the application for insolvency and its formal declaration by the relevant commercial court, the company's management body retains full powers to act and make use of its assets, with a duty to ensure due compliance with its social and contractual obligations, just as with any 'going concern' company, including those assumed as a licensor of a brand or patent before its licensees.

The Insolvency Act does not contemplate any automatic declaration of insolvency, nor the immediate appointment of an insolvency administrator upon making the application therefor. Instead, the court must first verify that the requirements set by Articles 5 and 6 of the Insolvency Act regarding the substance and form of the application are met in order for the declaration of insolvency to actually be issued. The ruling declaring the insolvency will appoint the insolvency administrator, which starts to exercise its powers when it accepts office.

It should nevertheless be noted that, at the request of a party entitled to apply for a declaration of compulsory insolvency and provided that the court deems it justified and necessary for the proper conduct of the proceedings, precautionary measures can be ordered by the court to ensure the integrity of the insolvent party's assets, all the while giving the insolvency application leave to proceed. In other words, this can occur before the actual declaration of insolvency.

### 2.3 Effects on licence agreements in the licensee's bankruptcy

The same occurs in the case of the declaration of insolvency of a licensee company, which has the obligation to pay over to its licensor the royalties or fees for the use of the relevant licence, trademark or patent. The licensing agreement will remain valid and fully enforceable for both parties despite the licensee's application for a declaration of insolvency, and any mention in the agreement establishing a power to terminate or rescind it as a result of the licensee company's application to be declared insolvent must be regarded as unenforceable.[11] Only the grounds for termination due to breach of contract noted in section 2.1 above would be valid for the injured party in compliance to seek termination of the agreement with the associated

---

11 Article 61.3 of the Insolvency Act.

compensation for financial harm and damages. In other words, only a breach of contract by the licensee, such as failure to make payment of licence royalties or fees, would entitle the licensor to terminate the agreement, not the mere application for an insolvency declaration on the part of the licensee. This matter is analysed in more detail later in the chapter.

### 2.4 Powers of administrators, receivers or trustees in the licensee's bankruptcy

The situation of the management body of the licensee company that has applied for a declaration of insolvency is the same as that outlined in the case of a licensor company. The body's powers to act remain fully in force until the judicial declaration of insolvency is issued – from which point, depending upon whether it is a voluntary or a compulsory insolvency, the powers of management and use of the company's assets shall be overseen or suspended by the appointed insolvency administrator.

### 2.5 Impact of registration

Licences are not affected by the issue of registration in the period of time until the insolvency is actually declared.

## 3. Licence agreements in the phase after declaration of bankruptcy

### 3.1 Treatment of intellectual property rights

As part of the insolvent party's intangible assets, intellectual property rights are regarded in the insolvency proceedings as just another of the insolvent party's assets, like fixed assets, stocks, etc. No distinction is made nor favour granted between different assets or entitlements, other than the value they have within the estate as a whole. In the case of a licensee company with exclusive rights over a trademark or patent, the asset will be more valuable than that of a company with no exclusive rights – the value of whose licence will accordingly be much lower.

As already noted, intellectual property rights will normally form part of the insolvent company's assets, since they are entitlements owned by the insolvent party by means of acquisition through a licence agreement to exploit them. Nevertheless, express mention should be made of the provision contained in Article 83 of the Invention Patents and Utility Models Act, which establishes the obligation to exploit the patented invention within the established time limits (that is, within a period of not more than four years from the application therefor or three years from the publishing of its granting in Spain's *Official Intellectual Property Journal*). In the absence thereof, a system of obligatory licences is provided for, which must be granted by the Spanish Patents and Trademarks Office.[12]

It is clear that the financial solvency of the owner of patent rights is or may be linked to how properly the invention is exploited. Accordingly, it is possible that a situation of financial insolvency gives rise in the holder of the exclusive rights to a failure to exploit the invention patent, or to properly exploit it. The question is whether this system of obligatory granting of licences should be applied to the

---

12 Articles 86 and following of the Invention Patents and Utility Models Act.

trademark as an asset in the insolvency proceedings. Bearing in mind that the patent will form part of the insolvent company's estate, and by virtue of the criterion of universality established in Article 76 of the Insolvency Act, as well as that of intangibility in Article 43 of the same act, the system of obligatory licences is deactivated in the case of insolvency proceedings.

The foregoing means that, should a competitor or other potentially interested party wish to acquire the intangible assets of an insolvent company (such as licensing rights or trademarks), it must take part in the common phase (see section 1.2 above),[13] acquiring the patent in an advance sale process at the best possible price permitted by both the market and the insolvency proceedings themselves, or, in the liquidation phase, to acquire the patent in an auction process that comprises part of the insolvency administrator's liquidation plan.[14]

In this case, legal doctrine has concluded that the special provisions of the Insolvency Act should be applied in preference to the Invention Patents and Utility Models Act and, when a licensee is declared insolvent, the system established in Articles 86 and following of the Invention Patents and Utility Models Act which related to the granting of mandatory licences is not applicable, in that it represents an undermining of the insolvent party's estate.

### 3.2 Effects on licence agreements in the licensor's bankruptcy

With regard to agreements, the Insolvency Act establishes the general principle that a declaration of insolvency does not imply any interruption to the performance of those agreements or to the continuance of the debtor's normal professional or business activities. So, after a licensor is declared insolvent, in principle any licensing agreements it has entered into with its licensees remains valid and in force as normal.

After the declaration of insolvency, any contracts or agreements to which the insolvent company (in this case, the licensor) is a party may only be terminated due to breach of contract by either of the contracting parties,[15] or when its termination is required by or in the interests of the insolvency proceedings,[16] but never simply because of the declaration of insolvency.

With regard to the first case of termination, namely breach of contract, despite a declaration of insolvency Article 62 of the Insolvency Act entitles the party in compliance to seek termination of the agreement due to breach by the other party. In the case of single-performance agreements (which are complied with once only), all that is permitted is to seek termination due to breach subsequent to the declaration of insolvency; with ongoing performance agreements, the power to terminate may also be executed when the breach is prior to the declaration of insolvency. In the case of a licence agreement that is regarded as an ongoing and long-lasting agreement with reciprocal obligations for both parties, if the party in breach is the licensor owing to its inability to meet the obligations inherent in the licensing agreement prior or subsequent to the declaration of insolvency, any of the

13 Article 43 of the Insolvency Act.
14 Article 148 of the Insolvency Act.
15 Article 62 of the Insolvency Act.
16 Article 61.2 of the Insolvency Act.

injured licensees are entitled to seek termination of the agreement. If, on the other hand, it is any of the licensees that breaches its obligations before the insolvent licensor, the latter (in the case of oversight) or the insolvency administrator (in the case of suspension of powers) may require that the party in breach comply with the agreement or seek termination thereof and the payment of associated compensation. In any case, to seek termination of the agreement the party so seeking must act in good faith and with due cause.

The second case of termination of contract, namely when it is required by or in the interests of the insolvency proceedings, arises from Article 61.2 of the Insolvency Act. The company itself (in the case of overseen voluntary insolvency) or the insolvency administrator (in that of compulsory insolvency with suspension of powers) is entitled, even if there is no breach by either of the parties, to make an application to the commercial court hearing the insolvency proceedings for it to terminate the agreement (in this case a licensing agreement), in the interests of the insolvent estate. This decision to seek termination of the agreement is usually made on the grounds that there is no need to continue with the agreement, given the company's situation, when it cannot formally meet its liabilities due to its ceasing of its activities (particularly if liquidation lies in its near future). It makes no sense for a company about to enter liquidation to continue with certain agreements, as this may entail expenses made out of the estate, which would worsen the cash flow situation and make it more difficult to pay other preferential claims.

Should there be differences of opinion between the parties regarding the termination of the agreement, the matter will be resolved by means of a so-called 'insolvency incident' hearing before the commercial court hearing the insolvency proceedings.

In the contrary sense to Article 61.1 of the Insolvency Act, Article 62.3 of that act contemplates, also in the insolvency estate's interests, that even if there is a breach subsequent to the insolvency (and also prior thereto, in the case of an ongoing performance agreement), the court may resolve to keep the agreement in place and enforceable, obliging in this case the licensee creditor not in breach to continue the contractual relationship with the insolvent licensor. Here, the insolvent licensor would be obliged to accomplish any pending obligation with the party not in breach (the licensee), and any expense related to that must be charged to the estate. Imagine, for example, a case in which the licensee's entire commercial activities revolve around the exploitation of intangible assets licensed by the insolvent licensor company. In such a case, it will be in the insolvency estate's interest that the business activity continues. The presiding judge may enforce the applicability of the licence contract, provided that the licensor has the possibility of continuing in compliance of the contract.

As indicated above, Article 61.3 of the Insolvency Act establishes that any mention made in an agreement of a power to terminate the agreement on the insolvency of either of the parties shall be ineffective. Nevertheless, insolvency proceedings may (and surely will) harm the credibility of the brand owned or licensed by the insolvent company and may provide sufficient grounds for the other party to seek termination. That is why legal doctrine holds that Article 61.3 of the

Insolvency Act must be applied sparingly, such that exploitation of the licensor's assets must not be allowed to be carried on improperly or in a manner causing serious or even irreparable harm to the good name and reputation of its intangibles.

One alternative for skirting the application of Article 61.3 of the Insolvency Act is to demand a level of technical capacity for the performance of a licensing agreement (usually in the case of patent or utility model licensing agreements). This technical capacity may be affected by and linked to a lack of financial solvency on the part of the licensee. In such circumstances, an agreement could include a clause linking this technical capacity to the enforceability of the agreement, which would be perfectly valid provided that it did not automatically come into force on the declaration of insolvency. It is anyway the case that Spanish lawmakers do not permit validity of an agreement to be subject to the mere fact of a declaration of insolvency – although it is not beyond the realm of economic realities that this may arise as a consequence of such a declaration.

### 3.3 Powers of an administrator, receiver or trustee in the licensor's bankruptcy

As described in section 1.2 above, once an insolvency is declared, and depending upon whether it is declared as being voluntary or compulsory in nature, the insolvent company's governing body's powers of actions shall be supervised or suspended, respectively, by an insolvency administrator. In the case of the voluntary insolvency of a branded licensor, the powers of management and use of the assets (which include any trademarks it owns) shall simply be complemented by the insolvency administrator; in other words, the licensor company shall retain its powers. In the case of compulsory insolvency or when the management powers are suspended, any decisions (amongst them those on terminating agreements) shall be taken by the insolvency administrator. Either way, the involvement of the insolvency administrator shall be required to carry out anything as important as the sale of assets or of a production unit during insolvency proceedings.

The Insolvency Act supports, whenever possible, the sale of an insolvent company's assets forming a whole production unit, and this might be on a global basis. Nevertheless, this is not always possible and assets have to be disposed of piecemeal. Trademarks, designs and patents are intangible assets and are closely linked to the company's activities, and they tend to be sold together with the rest of the assets making up the production unit, since the piecemeal sale of a trademark without an intangible asset underlying it makes no sense. Nevertheless, in the case of trademarks, designs and patents of acknowledged prestige in the market, which thereby constitute an asset of great value for the insolvent owner company, there is the possibility of the said asset being disposed of separately from the company to which it belongs.

In both the first phase of proceedings (the common phase) and that of liquidation, preference is given to transactions that seek to maintain the business's activity by means of the sales of the entire asset base, with the insolvency administrator being in all cases responsible for formally carrying out the sale of assets or production units.

## 3.4 Powers and rights of creditors in a licensor's bankruptcy

The creditors of a licensor company, like those of any other company declared insolvent, have no other rights (except for the obvious right to recover part of their credits in so far as the insolvency rules permit) than that of their credits being recognised in the list of creditors and that of challenging any report made by the insolvency administrator with regard to the valuation of assets and/or the ranking or quantification of the list of creditors attached to the said report.

Pursuant to Article 46.2 the Trademarks Act, creditors with rights *in rem* over trademarks benefit from recognition of a credit with a special preference that will enjoy preferred status over the other creditors. Creditors with rights *in rem* over the insolvent licensor company's trademarks are entitled, in situations outside of insolvency proceedings, to enforce their security and take over ownership of the trademark – but they are not entitled to commence enforcement once the licensor has been declared insolvent. Only when an arrangement is reached that does not affect the exercising of this right or when more than a year has passed since the declaration of insolvency without liquidation proceedings having commenced may the secured creditor enforce its security and acquire title over the trademark as part of separate enforcement proceedings.

Nevertheless, a licensee that is a creditor of an insolvent licensor cannot hold, merely as a licensee, any right *in rem* over the trademark, patent or design in question, and is not granted any credit with special preference in the insolvency proceedings. Licensee creditors may only seek termination of their agreement in the case of breach of contract by the licensor, as explained in section 3.2 above. Except in these circumstances, no other type of creditor not a party to the agreement may seek its termination or compliance.

## 3.5 Effects on licence agreements in the licensee's bankruptcy

In the case of the insolvency of a licensee company, in principle and as noted previously, the licence agreement remains in force after the insolvency declaration; but, as it is an ongoing performance agreement, its termination may be sought on the grounds of the licensee's breach of its contractual obligations, both prior and subsequent to the declaration of insolvency.

Nevertheless, as with the case of an insolvent licensor, it may be that the licensee in breach, or its insolvency administrator, applies to the court to keep the licence agreement in force and not leave the licensee without any activity.[17] In this case the court, if it deems it fit to do, will order compliance with the agreement, and any payments or services due by the insolvent company to the licensor harmed by the breach are made out of the estate.

As previously noted with regard to the insolvency of the licensor, it may also be possible to seek the termination of the licence agreement in cases where there has not even been any breach of contract. All of this must be in the insolvency proceedings' interests and pursuant to Article 61.2 the Insolvency Act.

As stated above, it must be noted that any mention made in the agreement of a

17 Article 61.3 of the Insolvency Act.

power to terminate it in the case of the insolvency of either of the parties is deemed invalid. Nevertheless, the personal nature of licence agreements and the fact that such licences are granted by the licensor to the licensee on a markedly *intuitu personae* basis – in other words, based on the personal capacity of the person of the licensee – needs to be borne in mind. So, if the licensor of a trademark of recognised standing or a patent does not collect its royalties, its patent or trademark may suffer serious harm on the market – indeed, much greater harm than any it may suffer through insolvency proceedings as a result of termination of the agreement. An analysis must be undertaken of the relationship of trust between the licensor and the licensee, and whether this was decisive when it came to entering into the agreement. If this was not a decisive condition, the provisions of Article 61.3 of the Insolvency Act would clearly be applicable; in contrast, if the personal capacity of the licence was decisive for the agreement and its insolvency is causing serious harm to the trademark or patent in question, the validity or otherwise of the clause permitting termination of the agreement could be arguable.

### 3.6 Powers of an administrator, receiver or trustee in the licensee's bankruptcy

With regard to he insolvency administrator, its powers in the case of a licensee's insolvency are the same as described in our analysis of the case of an insolvent licensor (see section 3.3 above). The licensee's insolvency administrator has a duty either to attempt to keep the licence agreement in force or to terminate it, depending on whether the insolvency proceedings are on a going-concern or liquidation basis. In the former case, the licence will be the key to the business being able to continue with its activities, whilst if it goes into liquidation it makes no sense to continue with the agreement, which should be terminated as soon as possible so as not to give rise to unpaid royalties.

### 3.7 Powers and rights of creditors in a licensee's bankruptcy

The situation for the creditors of an insolvent licensee company is the same as that of a licensor – see section 3.4 above.

### 3.8 Exclusive and non-exclusive licences

According to the provisions of Article 54 of the Insolvency Act, the licensor (in a case of voluntary insolvency) or the insolvency administrator (in a case of compulsory insolvency) is entitled to be a party to the judicial proceedings against third parties in respect of acts that may be prejudicial to it. For its part, an exclusive licensee must provide notice to the licensor of its wish to pursue any alleged infringing use thereof, in case the latter should wish to participate in the proceedings.

In the case of exclusive licences, pursuant to the provisions of Article 124 of the Invention Patents and Utility Models Act, consistent with Article 42.2 of the Trademarks Act, an exclusive licensee is entitled to act in protection of the rights object of the licence and therefore to seek possible compensation for financial harm and damages it suffers: in other words, it has the right to seek compensation for itself rather than on behalf of the licensor.

The same is not the case for licences granted on a non-exclusive basis. Here, the licensee does not possess any independent entitlement of its own: in other words, a non-exclusive licensee of intangible rights does not enjoy any entitlement in or of itself to protect the licensed rights. Nevertheless, if the licensor has not acted against infringing acts within three months, a non-exclusive licensee may, in a subsidiary capacity, lodge the relevant action.

### 3.9 Perpetual and non-perpetual licences

Normally, 'perpetual' licences are used to license copyrights arising from software. There is, however, no provision in intellectual property legislation regarding perpetual licences in insolvency proceedings, in which they must therefore be treated as part of the insolvent estate. In trading practice, it is in fact more commonplace to use non-perpetual licences – ie, those with successive payments.

The practical consequences are not the same for both cases. Let us imagine a case in which the licensee of a perpetual licence becomes insolvent and the licensor reconsiders the validity of the agreement as a result of the insolvent company lacking the technical capacity (*ius instrumenti*) to properly exploit the licensed intangible asset. In this case, the licensor must reimburse the estate with the amount corresponding to the remaining term of the agreement, previously paid over by the licensee.

### 3.10 Effects on a sub-licence in a licensor's and licensee's bankruptcy

Within the framework of the insolvency of either a licensor or a licensee, the effects on the granting of sub-licences are the same as those analysed for ordinary licences (see above). Therefore, by virtue of the provisions of Article 61.3 of the Insolvency Act and as the general rule, agreements remain in force regardless of insolvency and may be terminated only on the grounds of breach of the obligations arising from the agreement or of the interests of the insolvency proceedings,[18] applying the same presuppositions noted for ordinary licensing agreements.

In any case, should the court hearing the insolvency proceedings deem it fit, it may enforce compliance with or the validity of the licence or sub-licence agreement, as indicated in section 3.2 above, with associated payments always being charged against the insolvent estate.[19]

### 3.11 Impact of registration

#### (a) *Practical implications*

After a declaration of insolvency is issued, that declaration must be noted in those public registers in which the insolvent company's assets and/or entitlements are recorded, to prevent any possible seizures of insolvent party's estate.

The insolvency declaration in itself gives protection to the assets of the company before any new seizure after that declaration. The court order declaring the insolvency of the company will be published in the Companies Register and in all other public registers where the insolvent company would have any particular asset,

18 Article 61.2 of the Insolvency Act.
19 Article 62.3 of the Insolvency Act.

in order to inform all potentially interested parties that, from the moment of the insolvency declaration, any seizure of the insolvent company assets will be possible.

If a particular asset is not duly registered, although it will be protected because of the insolvency declaration, any entity carrying out proceedings against the insolvent company before the insolvency declaration could try to seize the company assets, mainly because it does not yet have information about the insolvency declaration and the prohibition of attempting a seizure.

When a private or public entity has the intention of seizing any asset of a company that has a debt owing to it, before beginning the seizure process it should investigate the situation of the debtor company and its assets. If the debtor company is under an insolvency declaration and has its assets duly registered in the appropriate public registers, the entity trying to seize assets will have direct knowledge of that fact and will not initiate the seizure proceeding because will know that no seizure will prosper because of the insolvency declaration. If any entity tries to accomplish a seizure of assets in those circumstances – which is not legally possible according to the Insolvency Act – it must first submit a request in writing to the insolvency court, as well as to the court or other public entity considering the validity of a seizure, to unblock any proceedings taking place because of the insolvency declaration.

If the asset (in this case, a licence or patent) has been duly registered, any executor entity has information about the insolvency declaration from the outset and should not try to seize any licence or patent. So, duly registered licences or patents, unlike unregistered ones, will be directly and from the outset protected against possible seizure by third parties, and it will not be necessary to attack any such seizure because the seizure party cannot initiate such proceedings.

### *(b) Aspects of legal doctrine*

A licence agreement is an atypical agreement and this has given rise to numerous theories as to whether it is obligational or property-related in nature. Part of legal doctrine holds that the essential characteristics of the licence suggest that it is an agreement with obligational and not properly-related effect. This discussion is not pointless, in that there is a need to establish whether this type of agreement benefits from some kind of credit preference.

Insolvency lawmakers have chosen to distribute credit preferences pursuant to the provisions of Article 89.2 of the Insolvency Act, so as not to alter the general principle of insolvency proceedings of giving the same standing to all creditors. Prevailing legal doctrine has concluded that, by application of Articles 56 and 57 of the Insolvency Act, licence agreements are not recognised as having any credit preference over intangibles, and so a licensee is not for this reason regarded as having any preferential credit in insolvency proceedings.

## 4. Contractual arrangements in deviation from the law

### 4.1 Exceptions

Legislation specifically governing intellectual property does not contemplate a specific system for agreements on intellectual property rights during insolvency, and so the provisions of the Insolvency Act are applicable thereto.

### 4.2 Scope to alter statutory mechanisms for termination rights and automatic reversions

As noted previously in section 3.2, any clause in the licence agreement contemplating the possibility of terminating the agreement automatically as a result of a declaration of insolvency is deemed invalid and unenforceable, pursuant to Article 61.3 of the Insolvency Act.

Ignoring insolvency legislation, contracting parties sometimes tend to include this type of clause in licence agreements for reasons (noted previously in section 3.5 above) regarding technical capacity and the *intuitu personae* nature of the agreement. Nevertheless, should either of the parties wish to terminate the agreement after a declaration of insolvency, the insolvency administrator is entitled to question the validity of this contractual clause and, if necessary, seek its annulment. Despite this, in the interests of the insolvency proceedings it is not uncommon for no position to be taken in this regard and for the clause to remain in place.

It should not be forgotten that Article 61.2 of the Insolvency Act provides that it is possible to terminate an agreement in the interests of the insolvency proceedings. Therefore, allowing the clause to be enforced is to do no more than anticipate events and allow a negotiated clause to act in the same sense as the law.

## 5. Cross-border aspects

### 5.1 Foreign law

Should the parties to a licence agreement submit themselves to the laws of a third country in order to resolve any contractual dispute, it must be this law that is used by the parties to terminate the agreement before the commercial court hearing the insolvency proceedings. Purely procedural issues should always be resolved by the insolvency judge in accordance with Spanish law; nevertheless, when dealing with matters of substance with regard to the licence agreement itself, such as compliance with or breach of obligations, it will be the chosen foreign law that is applied by the commercial court judge, provided that the parties demonstrate they agreed to submit the contract to the foreign law. If not, the judge will apply Spanish law.

### 5.2 Foreign jurisdiction

Submission to the courts of another state in a case of insolvency in Spain is invalidated by the *vis atractiva* (precedence due to an 'attractive power') of the insolvency proceedings in Spain.

The commercial court in Spain has the power to hear all matters regarding the net worth of the insolvent party. Therefore, if it is a company in Spain that is insolvent, it will be the insolvency court in Spain that must hear any matter in this regard, even though the law of the state to which the parties submit themselves may be applied.

# Sweden

**Jennie Klingberg**
**Odd Swarting**
Setterwalls

---

## 1. Overview

### 1.1 Relevant legislation governing intellectual property and bankruptcy

Swedish legislation and case law is limited and to some extent inadequate when it comes to intellectual property (IP) rights and insolvency, and it only contains some isolated regulations. Owing to the lack of general legal rules and case law, the answer of how a licence agreement should be treated when one party becomes insolvent must often be sought in other rules regarding related questions, general principles and legal doctrine.

Swedish insolvency law is mainly regulated in the Bankruptcy Act (1987:672) and the Company Reorganisation Act (1996:764). Answers to insolvency questions are also found in other legal areas – eg, company law, employment law and property law. Indeed, there is a difference between liquidation of an insolvent company and liquidation according to the Swedish Companies Act (2005:551). Other applicable laws are the Rights of Priority Act (1970:979), which governs the priority of claims between creditors, and the Wage Guarantee Act (1992:497), which ensures that employees of a bankrupt company receive their salaries.

### 1.2 Types of insolvency procedure

According to Swedish law there are two primary forms of insolvency proceedings for a company: bankruptcy; and compulsory composition.

In the event of a bankruptcy, the property of an insolvent debtor falls into the hands of an official receiver and is distributed among the creditors. The Bankruptcy Act governs petitions and declarations of bankruptcy, effects of bankruptcy, recovery, claims, duties of the debtor, administration of the bankruptcy estate and supervision of the bankruptcy.

Companies that are unable to pay their overdue debts, or companies that can be assumed to be unable to do so in the near future, can also apply for business reorganisation. There must, however, be reasonable grounds to believe that the reorganisation can achieve its purpose, and the debtor must either be the applicant or agree to the reorganisation.

'Composition' is a special type of court-enforced agreement between an insolvent debtor and a certain majority of creditors, which normally is the most important element of business reorganisation. Under a composition agreement, the debtor is granted a respite or reduction of debts which, provided it has been confirmed by a court, is binding to all creditors.

### 1.3 Grounds for bankruptcy

According to Swedish statutory law, a debtor is considered to be insolvent and may be declared bankrupt when it is unable to pay its debts as they fall due and this inability is not temporary. A petition for bankruptcy may be filed with the court in either of two ways: by the debtor itself or by a creditor.

If the petition is filed by the debtor, the company is normally declared bankrupt on the same day that the petition is filed. Alternatively, when the petition for bankruptcy is filed by a creditor, the debtor's insolvency has to be proved by the creditor – eg, by showing that:

- during the past six months, the Swedish Enforcement Authority has made an attempt to enforce a writ of execution which reveals that the debtor does not have enough assets to cover the claim – in Sweden a writ of execution may be attained, if not disputed, through summary proceedings at the Enforcement Authority or through normal court proceedings;
- the debtor has, under its liability to keep accounts, failed to pay an undisputed and due debt within one week of the creditor's demand for payment and the petition for bankruptcy has been filed within the following three weeks – this will also be the case if the debtor has been liable to keep accounts under the Annual Accounting Act within one year prior to the bankruptcy; or
- the debtor has suspended payments and has informed a substantial number of creditors of such suspension.

### 1.4 Filing for bankruptcy

A petition for bankruptcy may be filed either by the company itself or by a creditor. If the petition is filed by a creditor, the debtor's insolvency has to be proven by the petitioner.

The competent court of first instance in both bankruptcy and reorganisation proceedings is the district court. The decisions may be appealed to the Court of Appeal and ultimately to the Supreme Court. According to Swedish law, the court's jurisdiction is limited to appointing an official receiver and determining the creditors' right to receive payment. The determination of the creditors' right to receive payment will be made by the court after the application for bankruptcy has been filed and the court has decided whether to approve the official receiver's dividend proposal.

Separate proceedings must be initiated in respect of disputes and claims for priority regarding property and the collection of outstanding debts in accordance with the general principles of judicial procedure. As regards the debtor's assets, these are administered independently by the official receiver – ie, they are not part of the district court's jurisdiction.

### 1.5 Administrators and other appointed persons

According to the Bankruptcy Act, an official receiver is appointed by the district court as soon as a decision on bankruptcy has been made. The duties of the official receiver include administering the debtor's property (ie, the bankruptcy estate) and making an inventory of the debtor's assets and liabilities. The inventory is reviewed at an oath administration meeting, where the debtor makes a sworn statement that the information listing assets and liabilities is correct.

During the bankruptcy it is decided whether parts of the business can be continued under new ownership, or if they must be wound up. Decisions taken by the official receiver must be those most advantageous to the creditors. The debtor's property (if any) is sold whereas the proceeds, in so far as they exceed the cost of the bankruptcy, are divided amongst the creditors.

Moreover, the official receiver is also obligated to prepare a trustee's report covering, amongst other things:

- a description of the quality of accounting;
- the reason for insolvency and the time it occurred;
- whether there are grounds for recovery;
- whether any assets have been unlawfully transferred;
- the time required for preparation of a balance sheet for liquidation purposes; and
- whether there are grounds for claiming damages.

## 2. Licence agreements in the phase between filing and declaration of bankruptcy

### 2.1 Effects on licence agreements in the licensor's bankruptcy

There is no specific Swedish statutory legislation regulating how a licence agreement should be treated when either a licensor or a licensee files for bankruptcy. It will most likely be treated as described in section 3.2 below.

### 2.2 Powers of official receivers in the licensor's bankruptcy

According to the Bankruptcy Act, an official receiver is appointed by the district court as soon as a decision on bankruptcy has been made. Thus, in the phase between filing and a declaration of bankruptcy, there is no official receiver.

### 2.3 Effects on licence agreements in the licensee's bankruptcy

The effects are the same as are described in section 2.1 above.

### 2.4 Powers of official receivers in the licensee's bankruptcy

The effects are the same as are described in section 2.2 above.

### 2.5 Impact of registration

A licence agreement of a registered trademark, a plant variety right, a patent right or a design right may be registered with the Swedish Patent and Registration Office; for copyright licences there is no such registration procedure. A registered licensee is presumed to be the licensee in a case of infringement or in an invalidity action, but the validity of a licence agreement does not depend on whether it is registered. Further, registration of a licence agreement does not create a real right towards third-party claims under Swedish law.

The parties to a licence agreement may pledge patents and trademarks as security for obligations in the agreement. Security of patents and trademarks, or applications thereof, may be registered at the Patent and Registration Office by either the pledgor or the pledgee. The pledge is valid in relation to third parties (creditors or anyone who later acquires the right) upon the date of filing for registration. Since registration is not possible if one party has applied for bankruptcy or become insolvent, it is important to register the pledge as soon as possible and, preferably, upon the signing of the licence agreement.

## 3. Licence agreements in the phase after declaration of bankruptcy

### 3.1 Treatment of intellectual property rights

#### *(a) Copyrights*

According to the Act on Copyright in Literary and Artistic Works (1960:729; hereinafter the Copyright Act), a person who creates a literary or artistic work is entitled to copyright to the work. No formality, such as registration or fixation, is required. The originator also has a non-profitable (moral) right to 'pertain' his work, which means that he:

- has the right to be named in conjunction with the work being used, to the extent and in the way required by good practice; and
- may require that the work is not altered or made available to the general public in a form or connection that is damaging to the originator's literary or artistic reputation or distinctive character.

According to the Copyright Act, the person to whom a copyright has been assigned may not alter the work or assign the copyright to others, unless otherwise agreed with the copyright owner. Nevertheless, if the copyright forms part of a business activity, it may be assigned together with the business activity or as part thereof; the assignor will anyhow remain liable for the performance of the agreement. The Copyright Act furthermore states that the copyright may not be subject to seizure to the extent it remains with the author or with any other individual who has acquired the copyright as a result of division of property between spouses, inheritance or will. The same applies to manuscripts and to such works of art which have not been exhibited, offered for sale or otherwise authorised to be made available to the public.

In other words, if the originator has assigned or licensed the copyright (in terms of a monetary right) to a third party, the economic right may be subject to seizure by a third party if the monetary right is transferable according to the acquisition agreement. If such a provision has not been included in the acquisition agreement, the copyright cannot be subject to seizure.

#### *(b) Trade names or established (non-registered) trademarks*

The principles of protection of the trade names – the name under which a business is conducted – resemble those concerning trademarks. A company acquires exclusive right to a trade name through registration or establishment in the market. Under the

Trade Names Act (1974:156), a trade name is not transferable other than in connection with the transfer of the whole business. Therefore, registered trade names cannot be subject to seizure but are nevertheless included in the bankruptcy estate.

According to the Trademarks Act (1960:644), trademarks can be protected through exclusive rights as a result of use or registration. Trademark protection can thus arise by the fact that the trademark has been established on the market. This is the situation when a logo has become known as a symbol for the goods being made available under that logo.

Under Chapter 10, Section 9 of the Trademarks Act, seizure of established (non-registered) trademarks is prohibited. Nevertheless, the right must be included in the bankruptcy estate.

#### *(c) Plant variety rights*

If the holder of a plant variety right has granted a licence, the licensee may only assign the right if it is stated in the agreement. If the licence forms part of a business, however, it may be assigned together with the business or as part thereof, unless there is an agreement to the contrary. If the licence has been assigned in this manner, the assignor remains liable for the performance of the licence agreement.

#### *(d) Other IP rights*

Patents and registered trademarks are assets that can be assigned or leased in whole or in part and may therefore be included in the holder's bankruptcy and can be distrained.

According to the Design Protection Act (1970:485), a licensee may only assign the licence further if there is an agreement to that effect. If the licence forms part of a business, however, it may be assigned together with the business, unless there is an agreement to the contrary. In such cases, the assignor remains liable for the performance of the licence agreement.

### 3.2 Effects on licence agreements in the licensor's bankruptcy

The Swedish law governing insolvency proceedings only sparsely deals with IP rights or IP licences. Nonetheless, the general regulations in the Bankruptcy Act and the Enforcement Code (1981:774), when applied in combination with the applicable IP law, will have certain effects on IP rights and IP licences and may separate them from other types of assets within bankruptcy proceedings. As there are limited directly applicable statutory rules on licence agreements in bankruptcies, answers must be sought in interpretation of the relevant rules, general principles and legal doctrine.

According to insolvency law, an asset is part of the bankruptcy estate if it may be distrained or seized. An asset can be distrained if it is not protected against third-party claims. Different principles are applicable in order to create a real right towards third-party claims:

- a transfer of possession (the most common principle);
- registration of the property in an official register;
- putting a third party on notice; or
- the contract itself.

Since IP rights are intangible assets, transfers of possession, in the traditional sense, are not possible. Instead, IP rights are generally protected from claims made by third parties or creditors upon the signing of an agreement. The general view in legal doctrine is that granted IP licences prevail and are deemed to have effect *in rem*, and they can therefore be enforced by a licensee against the bankruptcy estate (ie, the bankruptcy administrator may not choose to terminate the agreement). This view is built on the interpretation of rules in related areas (such as licences in relation to a pledgee), other general principles and the legal doctrine.

An official receiver is thus generally considered to have the right to assume the agreement's obligations and to use the IP rights. This is on condition that the bankrupt estate can fulfil the terms and conditions of the agreement, since the licensee's right to use the licence endures through the duration of the agreement. According to legal doctrine, such a right does not extend to so-called 'secondary' obligations, such as support, education or know-how. The reason for this is that secondary obligations are considered in a strict sense to be 'service obligations' rather than the licensed asset itself; likewise, secondary obligations often depend on the licensor's personal features and are thus impossible for the estate to fulfil. Hence, the surviving licence may be limited to right of use under the agreement.

It should be noted that if the secondary obligations are of material importance, the licensee may have the right to terminate the agreement if the obligations cannot be fulfilled by the bankruptcy estate. Nonetheless, even though the licensee may claim damages as a result, such damages will have the character of a non-prioritised claim in the bankruptcy.

### 3.3 Powers of an official receiver in the licensor's bankruptcy

The duties of the official receiver include administering the debtor's property – ie, the bankruptcy estate – and to make an inventory of the debtor's assets and liabilities. The inventory is reviewed at an oath administration meeting, where the debtor makes a sworn statement that the information listing assets and liabilities is correct.

Neither the Bankruptcy Act nor the Enforcement Code explicitly addresses an official receiver's ability to adopt, assign, modify or terminate an IP licence in the event of a bankruptcy. Instead, such provisions are located in different IP laws, and the Sale of Goods Act (1990:931) is applicable by analogy. The general principle is that the official receiver has the right to continue performance by entering into the relevant IP licence agreement. This right requires that the agreement has not been terminated before the bankruptcy.

To avoid a breach of contract being committed, the receiver should rather quickly notify the licensee whether the estate intends to enter into the agreement; and if it enters, it should make sure that the estate is able to fulfil the most important commitments.

### 3.4 Powers and rights of creditors in a licensor's bankruptcy

Sweden's Bankruptcy Act does not give creditors any specific rights to impact how the official receiver should manage the bankruptcy estate. The former decision right for creditors in administrative matters has been abolished and now the official receiver alone determines the outcome of the estate. Commercial decisions regarding which agreements the official receiver should keep or terminate are taken solely by the official receiver. The creditors' rights are limited to the power to file for bankruptcy, present evidence in the bankruptcy, and appeal against a dividend proposal from the official receiver and such types of rights.

The official receiver is nevertheless obligated to consult with particularly concerned creditors in certain issues, but this is only an obligation to hear the creditors and not an obligation to actually carry out proposals from the creditors. Furthermore, some creditors have a voting right in composition arrangements. Creditors without deposit or mortgage lien have no right to determine what the official receiver should do with the estate's assets.

Normally, creditors do not need to notify the relevant district court that they have claims, since it is part of the function of the official receiver to establish to which parties the debtor is liable to pay money. However, if the assets of the bankruptcy estate are so large that it can be safely assumed that creditors without a so-called 'priority right' (a right to receive payment ahead of others) will receive payment, the district court has the power to decide that a proof-of-debt procedure should be implemented. This then means that creditors must give notice of their claims to the district court, which they otherwise would not need to do.

### 3.5 Effects on licence agreements in the licensee's bankruptcy

As described in section 1.1 above, the conflict between intellectual property law and insolvency law is complicated, but the conflict is perhaps more complicated when it is the licensee which becomes bankrupt.

Almost all Swedish laws regulating IP rights contain provisions that prohibit the licensee from assigning the licence without the consent of the licensor, since the licensor's interest to control who is using the IP right is considered to be stronger than the bankruptcy estate's interest to exploit the value of the licence. This issue has been discussed by legal experts and the dominant view is that a bankrupt licensee has the right to enter into the licence agreement but not assign the IP right/licence without the licensor's consent. Some claim that the licensor has the right to terminate the agreement owing to the single fact that the licensee files for bankruptcy even if it is not stated in the agreement. Others claim that analogies can be made from the Sale of Goods Act (1990:931), which would mean that the estate should be able to assign the licence if the licensor is thereby provided with a more favourable position and does not explicitly oppose the assignment. The assignment would then be justified by the reduced risk of value destruction. In any case, the estate is obligated to notify the licensor of the assignment.

The conclusion is that, if the agreement in itself does not regulate what will happen if the licensee becomes bankrupt, an answer must be sought from the general principles applicable and will thus depend on the individual circumstances in each case.

### 3.6 Powers of an official receiver in the licensee's bankruptcy

The official receiver has the power to decide whether the estate should enter into a licence agreement and whether the licence agreement should be assigned to third parties or creditors. For more detailed information of an official receiver's rights, see section 3.3 above.

### 3.7 Powers and rights of creditors in a licensee's bankruptcy

See section 3.4 above.

### 3.8 Exclusive and non-exclusive licences

There have been discussions among legal experts as to whether there is a distinction between exclusive and non-exclusive licences in bankruptcies. One opinion is that the bankruptcy estate should be able to enter into an exclusive licence agreement in case production has started or substantial investments have been made. Another opinion is that, since an exclusive licence puts the licensor in a more vulnerable position, where the relationship of trust between the parties is more prominent, the licensor, in the licensee's bankruptcy, should have a strong interest in (and thus a right to) a fast termination of the licence agreement. Under a non-exclusive licence the need for protection of the licensor may be less important, since often the licence has been granted to several companies and the licensor easily may sign a new agreement with another licensee. Because a non-exclusive licence rarely includes know-how, reliance under such an agreement is less prominent compared with reliance under an exclusive licence agreement, where know-how might be a prerequisite. Nonetheless, the licensor may be damaged in the long term if the licensee's estate continues to produce and sell products of inferior quality under the licence, because confidence in the licensor's products may decline.

The conclusion in the literature is that an exclusive and a non-exclusive licence agreement should be treated the same, since it is advantageous that various royalty creditors are treated equally. Moreover, owing to the various intermediate forms between exclusive and non-exclusive licences, it is hard to make a sharp distinction among the different licence forms. The licensor who has granted a non-exclusive licence is often just as careful as the licensor who has granted an exclusive licence.

### 3.9 Perpetual and non-perpetual licences

Under Swedish legislation there is no distinction between perpetual and non-perpetual licences in the event of a bankruptcy. The same principles as are expressed in section 3.8 above apply.

Nevertheless, there has been a discussion among legal experts as to whether a perpetual licence can be terminated by either party providing the other party with a reasonable period of notice of termination. Through analogies from general contract rules and case law, an agreement that is valid until further notice may be terminated if one party provides the other with reasonable notice of termination – unlike an agreement with a fixed term, which cannot be terminated before the contract period ends.

Another opinion is that, when it comes to perpetual patent licences, the licence should be considered valid until the protection of the IP right has ceased, rather than upon reasonable notice of termination. The parties' intentions and objectives at the signing of the agreement must, of course, also be considered.

### 3.10 Effects on a sub-licence in a licensor's bankruptcy

Even though under Swedish legislation there is no established direct statutory law or case law for the scenario, an IP licence will presumably be handled in the same way whether it is the licensee or a sub-licensee which goes bankrupt. The same principles as are set out earlier in this section 3 ought to apply – but, since a sub-licence is conditional on the main licence, the sub-licensee cannot get a superior right than the main licensee.

Thus, if a bankruptcy estate chooses to assign a licence, the licence should be assigned conditional on the sub-licence, and if the licensee terminates the licence agreement, the sub-licence will be terminated as well.

### 3.11 Effects on a sub-licence in a licensee's bankruptcy

See section 3.10 above.

### 3.12 Impact of registration

As mentioned in section 2.5 above, a licence agreement for a registered trademark, a plant variety right, a patent right or a design right may be registered with Sweden's Patent and Registration Office, but for copyright licences there is no such registration procedure. A registered licensee is presumed to be the licensee in a case of infringement or in an invalidity action, but the validity of a licence agreement does not depend on whether it is registered. Security in the form of patents or trademarks, or applications thereof, may be registered at the Patent and Registration Office by either the pledgor or the pledgee, and registration creates a right in rem.

Furthermore, registration of a licence agreement does not create a real right towards third-party claims under Swedish law. Instead, the principle of priority prevails, which means that the party who first acquires the licence will have priority over a subsequent assigner of the licence or the licensed object. The principle of priority is applicable also in relation to creditors and sub-licensees.

Escrow agreements are normally used to secure access to source code, since it is most advantageous for the licensee to deposit the source code with a third party. Such an agreement regulates the conditions under which the source code may be handed over to the licensee, and the agreement normally contains provisions governing how the deposited source code must be stored and updated.

Moreover, patents, trademarks, plant variety rights and registered design rights can all be covered by floating charges. In addition, copyrights – with the exception of those copyrights that cannot be distrained or seized – can also be covered by floating charges. The right to trade names and unregistered designs may not be covered by floating charges.

## 4. Contractual arrangements in deviation from the law

### 4.1 Exceptions

#### *(a) Compulsory licences*

A compulsory licence to (for example) use an invention in Sweden may be granted where:

- three years have elapsed from the grant of the patent and four years have elapsed since the date the patent application was filed;
- the invention is not used to a reasonable extent in Sweden; and
- there is no acceptable reason why the invention is not being used.

According to the Patents Act (1967:837), a compulsory licence may be assigned to someone else only together with the business in which it is exploited or is intended to be used. Additionally, if there is a significant change in circumstances (such as bankruptcy), the court has the power to revoke or modify the terms of the compulsory licence.

***(b) Publishing agreements and copies of copyrighted work***

Through publishing agreements, authors assign to their publisher the right to reproduce and publish their literary or artistic work by means of printing or a similar process. According to the Copyright Act, though, manuscripts or other copies of the work in which the work is being reproduced always remain the property of the author and thus may not be distrained. The reason for this is because manuscripts are associated with a strong personal interest of the author. Similarly, works of art which have not been exhibited, offered for sale or otherwise authorised to be made available to the public are also excluded from seizure. However, once an artwork has been published or made available for sale, the exemption is no longer applicable and the copy may be distrained. An announcement that publication might be performed has the same effect.

The general rule is otherwise the opposite: copies of copyrighted work may be distrained or seized. According to this doctrine, then, the estate of a publisher's bankruptcy may generally continue to fulfil a licence agreement if the copyright has been 'possessed' – ie, the printing of books has started. By analogy with Section 63 of Sweden's Sale of Goods Act, the estate should then be required to provide security for future royalty payments.

***(c) Catalogues, tables or other similar products***

Anyone who has produced a catalogue, table or other similar product in which a large amount of information has been compiled or which is the result of a significant investment has an exclusive right to make copies of the product and to make it available to the public. The holder is not, however, protected against seizure and does not have any moral rights.

## 4.2 Scope to alter statutory mechanisms

The parties to a licence agreement may deviate from most of the statutory mechanisms, but the rules of protection against third-party claims are mandatory in nature and the parties may not agree to something else.

## 4.3 Termination rights and automatic reversions

Swedish legislation distinguishes between contractual termination and extraordinary termination due to breach. Contractual termination is regulated in the agreement itself and may be made at specified occasions – eg, after a number of years or at a certain event. The content of the clauses may be negotiated by the parties relatively freely.

A bankruptcy clause provides the licensor with a right to terminate the contract at the licensee's bankruptcy. It is also possible to include a pre-bankruptcy clause stipulating the right of the licensor to terminate the licence agreement upon early signs of insolvency. Pre-bankruptcy clauses have been confirmed as valid in Swedish case law, although the individual circumstances of each case are considered.

Another type of clause is the so-called '*ipso facto*' clause – ie, one according to which the licence agreement automatically expires if there are signs of insolvency or bankruptcy. In that situation a notice of termination is not required. Such a clause often states that all contractual obligations shall be null and void in the defined circumstances. In general, an *ipso facto* clause is only valid with regard to future obligations, while it is uncertain whether termination may affect rights and obligations that have already arisen under the contract. Furthermore, the clause is only valid if termination is carried out before bankruptcy has been declared. The reason for this is that termination of the agreement after the bankruptcy would entail placing obligations on a third party, namely the bankruptcy estate, which is a separate legal entity. A procedure where an obligation is placed on a third party is in conflict with basic principles under Swedish contract law. Since the validity of an *ipso facto* clause in Sweden is unclear, it is important to discuss the possible effects and scope of such a clause.

## 5. Cross-border aspects

### 5.1 Foreign law

Under Swedish law, a Swedish district court is bound by the parties' choice of law – including foreign law – in a licence agreement that is part of a Swedish bankruptcy. However, insolvency issues arising in Swedish bankruptcies are generally governed by Swedish law, such as Swedish procedural and enforcement issues (eg, the court's composition, the means of appeal, the way to file for bankruptcy, the priority rules when all assets are in Sweden, and who is eligible to file for bankruptcy). The issues will be tried by the court *ex officio* – ie, even if the parties themselves do not plead them.

### 5.2 Foreign jurisdiction

Swedish courts recognise foreign insolvency and rescue procedures. A foreign insolvency estate can bring cases before the Swedish courts.

The courts accept the legal status of insolvency proceedings in foreign jurisdictions, even if those jurisdictions are not signatories to the same international treaties as Sweden. Sweden recognises Regulation (EC) 1346/2000 on insolvency proceedings (commonly known as the Insolvency Regulation), which means Swedish courts automatically accept EU insolvency proceedings. Generally, they accept non-EU insolvency proceedings as well.

# Switzerland

**David Jenny**
**Christian Wyss**
VISCHER AG

---

## 1. Overview

### 1.1 Relevant legislation governing intellectual property and bankruptcy

With respect to intellectual property, there are different laws and related ordinances, depending on the nature of the intellectual property rights involved: the Patents Act, Design Act, Copyright Act, Trademark Protection Act, Plant Variety Protection Act, and the Act on Protection of Topographies of Semiconductor Products.

The relevant bankruptcy legislation consists of the Federal Debt Enforcement and Bankruptcy Act and a number of related laws and ordinances, in particular the Banking Insolvency Ordinance and the Insurance Bankruptcy Ordinance. This chapter focuses on the general rules under the Debt Enforcement and Bankruptcy Act and does not deal with the particularities of bank and insurance insolvencies.

### 1.2 Types of insolvency procedure

The types of insolvency procedures available for companies are bankruptcy, deferral of bankruptcy, and composition proceedings; each is outlined further below. The provisions of the Debt Enforcement and Bankruptcy Act relating to restructuring were revised with effect from January 1 2014. The main goal of the revision was to structure the composition proceedings in a more restructuring-friendly manner and to implement the lessons learned from the insolvency of the former Swiss national airline, Swissair.

#### *(a) Bankruptcy*

Upon declaration of bankruptcy, all assets of the debtor become one sole bankruptcy estate. The debtor loses control and the bankruptcy administrator, usually the cantonal bankruptcy office, assumes authority over the estate. Depending on the estimated value of the estate, the bankruptcy court either orders ordinary bankruptcy proceedings, summary bankruptcy proceedings, or abandons the bankruptcy proceedings for lack of assets. Most bankruptcies are dealt with in the summary proceedings, which are taken care of by the cantonal bankruptcy office and which allow for neither a private bankruptcy administration nor a creditors' assembly.

#### *(b) Deferral of bankruptcy*

Deferral of bankruptcy protects the debtor from further debt enforcement measures. The bankruptcy court grants deferral of bankruptcy if there is a good chance of a successful reorganisation. Upon granting deferral of bankruptcy, the court implements the necessary actions to protect the assets of the debtor and to prevent illegitimate preference of certain creditors. These actions typically include appointing a trustee and allocating the powers between the trustee and the board of directors at the court's discretion. The court determines the duration of the deferral of bankruptcy on a case-by-case basis depending on the restructuring plan submitted and may grant several extensions.

### *(c) Composition proceedings*

Composition proceedings start with a provisional moratorium that, including all extensions, cannot exceed four months. If at the end of the provisional moratorium there are good chances for a successful reorganisation or creditors' composition agreement, the bankruptcy court grants a definitive moratorium. The duration of the definitive moratorium is four to six months and can be extended to up to 24 months. The definitive moratorium leads to a creditors' composition agreement or to bankruptcy, or the moratorium can be cancelled once restructuring measures have been successfully implemented.

Unlike under the previous bankruptcy legislation, the recently amended provisions of the Debt Enforcement and Bankruptcy Act provide the possibility of using composition proceedings just to carry out a restructuring protected from further debt enforcement measures. It is no longer necessary that composition proceedings result in a creditors' composition agreement or bankruptcy.[1] If composition proceedings result in a creditors' agreement, the most common type is the creditors' agreement with assignment of assets aiming at the liquidation of the debtor. Very rarely used in practice is the ordinary creditors' agreement providing for a deferral of payment, a partial waiver of claims, or a combination of both, where the debtor continues its business after completion of the composition proceedings.

## 1.3 Grounds of bankruptcy

A court declares bankruptcy if a company is unable to pay its debts as they fall due or if the company is over-indebted. A company is over-indebted if, either in a liquidation scenario or in a going-concern scenario, the balance sheet shows sufficient assets to cover all of the company's liabilities. Claims that have been properly subordinated are not taken into account when determining the company's liabilities.

## 1.4 Filing for bankruptcy

Each creditor may file for bankruptcy of a debtor if the debtor is unable to pay its debts as they fall due. In addition, a particular creditor may file for bankruptcy of a debtor after this creditor has fully gone through the debt enforcement proceedings against the debtor without being paid.

The board of directors of a company must file for bankruptcy if the company is

---

1 See report of the Swiss Government on the amendment of the Debt Enforcement and Bankruptcy Act from September 8 2010, *FJ* 2010, p6455 and following.

over-indebted. If it is established that there are good chances for an immediate and sustainable restructuring, the board may, however, delay the bankruptcy filing for up to 60 days.[2] The exact duration of the permissible delay depends on the specific circumstances of the individual case.

The auditors of a company must file for bankruptcy if it is clear that the company is over-indebted and the board of directors fails to file for bankruptcy. This obligation applies even if the statutory auditor is a large international audit firm like one of the 'big four'.

Most courts require that a filing for bankruptcy based on over-indebtedness is accompanied by audited financial statements showing that the debtor is over-indebted. This requirement applies also to companies that do not have a statutory auditor, which sometimes leads to practical problems when an insolvent company tries to find an auditor to prepare audited financial statements for the bankruptcy filing.

Based on a shareholders' resolution recorded in a public deed, the board of directors may also file for bankruptcy if the company is unable to pay its debts as they fall due (the so-called 'declaration of insolvency'). The declaration of insolvency does not require audited financial statements. However, some courts require that an advance on court fees be paid before declaring bankruptcy.

Petitions of bankruptcy are received by courts. The cantonal bankruptcy office is not competent for receiving petitions of bankruptcy, but only for administering the bankruptcy proceedings after a declaration of bankruptcy by the court. The venue of the court that is competent for receiving petitions of bankruptcy is determined by the court system of the canton where the insolvent debtor has its registered legal seat. While most cantons have several judicial districts or counties, others provide for just one court that receives petitions of bankruptcy relating to insolvent debtors in the entire canton.

Subject matter jurisdiction – ie, which court is competent within the relevant judicial district or canton – is determined based on cantonal laws on subject matter jurisdiction. Some of these laws explicitly state which court is competent to decide on petitions of bankruptcy; others just indicate which court is competent for so-called 'summary proceedings'. In the latter case, those courts are competent to decide on petitions of bankruptcy because the Federal Civil Procedure Code states that decisions on petitions of bankruptcy are made in summary proceedings.[3] Unless the cantonal laws on subject matter jurisdiction provide that specific courts are competent to decide on petitions of bankruptcy, the jurisdiction is with the court responsible for summary proceedings.

### 1.5 Administrators and other appointed persons

Upon filing for bankruptcy, no administrator, receiver, trustee or other person is appointed. The board of directors remains in charge of the company's business until

2 Peter Böckli, *Schweizer Aktienrecht*, 4th edn, Zurich, 2009, §13 N 777; Roland Fischer, Flavio Delli Colli, *Sanierungsbemühungen bei Überschuldung*, GesKR – Gesellschafts- und Kapitalmarktrecht, 2014 p261.

3 Article 251(a) of the Federal Civil Procedure Code.

the bankruptcy court has issued the declaration of bankruptcy. Depending on the workload of the bankruptcy court, the time between filing for and declaration of bankruptcy can vary between one business day and more than a month. In this period, the board of directors has increased diligence obligations to ensure that no payments are made that could constitute an unlawful preference of certain creditors, and that no assets are sold that could become subject to avoidance actions. In practice, the board of directors must cease to pay the company's creditors, with a few exceptions for privileged creditors such as employees and social security (if it seems clear that their claims will be fully covered) and for what are deemed 'emergency' payments that are absolutely required to maintain the value of the debtor's assets (eg, utility bills, insurance premiums, or lease payments for a car that otherwise would be repossessed by the leasing company).[4] Other ongoing debts (eg, rent) may not be paid.

Upon the court order declaring bankruptcy and opening bankruptcy procedures, all assets of the debtor – in theory all assets worldwide – become one sole bankruptcy estate. The debtor loses control and the bankruptcy office assumes authority over the estate. In summary bankruptcy proceedings, the bankruptcy office becomes the bankruptcy administration of the company. In ordinary bankruptcy proceedings, either the bankruptcy office or a private bankruptcy administrator is appointed as the bankruptcy administration. Private bankruptcy administrators are typically a lawyer or law firm, or an accountant or accounting firm.

The bankruptcy administration assumes all the powers of the board of directors and the management. It also prepares an inventory of the debtor's assets, invites the creditors to file their claims against the debtor, prepares a schedule of admitted claims, maintains and liquidates the debtor's assets, sets up a distribution plan and distributes the proceeds.

## 2. Licence agreements in the phase between filing and declaration of bankruptcy

### 2.1 Effects on licence agreements in the licensor's bankruptcy

The filing for bankruptcy of a licensor does not have any statutory effect on the licence agreement or on any other assets or agreements of the licensor. Only the declaration of bankruptcy has effects on the assets and agreements of the licensor.

A bankruptcy filing remains confidential until the bankruptcy is declared. If a licensee knows by some means that its licensor has filed for bankruptcy, the licensee can use this information to establish that the licensor is insolvent and withhold any upfront or advance payments until the licensee's rights under the licence agreement are secured (see also sections 3.4 and 3.7 below).[5]

### 2.2 Powers of administrators, receivers or trustees in the licensor's bankruptcy

In the phase between filing and declaration of bankruptcy, the board of directors of the debtor remains in charge of the business. Only when the bankruptcy court issues

4 Peter Böckli, *op cit*, §13 N 778 and following.
5 Article 83 of the Code of Obligations.

a declaration of bankruptcy, does the bankruptcy office assume authority over the bankruptcy estate. Swiss law does not provide for the option to appoint any receivers or trustees in this phase of bankruptcy proceedings.

### 2.3 Effects on licence agreements in the licensee's bankruptcy

The filing for bankruptcy of a licensee does not have any statutory effect on the licence agreement or on any other assets or agreements of the licensee. Only the declaration of bankruptcy has effects on the assets and agreements of the licensee.

### 2.4 Powers of administrators, receivers or trustees in the licensee's bankruptcy

In the phase between filing and declaration of bankruptcy, the board of directors of the debtor remains in charge of the business. Only when the bankruptcy court issues a declaration of bankruptcy does the bankruptcy office assume authority over the bankruptcy estate. Swiss law does not provide for the option to appoint any receivers or trustees in this phase of bankruptcy proceedings.

### 2.5 Impact of registration

Swiss law allows the registering of licences on patents, designs, trademarks, plant varieties and topographies of semiconductor products. There is no register in Switzerland for copyrights, so copyright licences cannot be registered.

The registration of a licence avoids the possibility of a third party acquiring in good faith an unencumbered intellectual property right from the licensor. Before declaration of bankruptcy, however, the registration of the licence does not make any difference with regard to bankruptcy-related effects on the licence.

## 3. Licence agreements in the phase after declaration of bankruptcy

### 3.1 Treatment of intellectual property rights

All intellectual property rights of a bankrupt debtor become part of the bankruptcy estate. In the event of a bankruptcy, all unregistered intellectual property rights are treated in the same way – ie, the bankruptcy administration can sell unregistered intellectual property rights unencumbered and free of any obligations to a former licensee. Swiss law provides registration for patents, designs, trademarks, plant varieties, and topographies of semiconductor products. No registration is possible for copyrights.

### 3.2 Effects on licence agreements in the licensor's bankruptcy

In a licensor's bankruptcy, the licence agreement remains valid unless the licensor and the licensee agreed on automatic termination in the licence agreement. Any rights of the licensee under the licence agreement other than the right to receive payments are converted into money claims.[6] This means that despite the continued validity of the licence agreement, the licensee cannot make use of the rights granted under the licence agreement.

---

6 Article 211 of the Debt Enforcement and Bankruptcy Act.

The change of the licence grant into a money claim is technically a conversion and not a damages claim, but it puts the licensee in the same situation as if the licensee had a damages claim due to the licensor's failure to grant a licence. The money claim corresponds to the amount needed to put the licensee financially in the same position as if the licensor had performed its obligations under the licence agreement.[7]

Such money claims form part of the claims in bankruptcy and are compensated with (at most) a dividend payment according to the relevant creditor class. Unsecured claims of trade creditors form part of the third (and last) class, which is subordinated to secured claims and claims related to employment and social security.

### 3.3 Powers of an administrator, receiver or trustee in the licensor's bankruptcy

Immediately after a declaration of bankruptcy, the bankruptcy office assumes authority over the bankruptcy estate. In summary bankruptcy proceedings, the bankruptcy office will assume the bankruptcy administration throughout the entire bankruptcy proceedings. In ordinary bankruptcy proceedings, the creditors' assembly may decide to appoint a private bankruptcy administrator instead of the bankruptcy office.

In general, the bankruptcy administration has the right to assume the licence agreement on behalf of the debtor, which means that the licensee's rights under the licence agreement are not converted into money claims but remain claims for specific performance that are preferential to the claims in bankruptcy. 'Preferential' here means that these claims will be satisfied in preference over unsecured claims that existed when the bankruptcy was declared or that accrued thereafter without the explicit consent of the bankruptcy administration. 'Preferential' does not mean that the bankruptcy administration is personally liable for these claims.

The bankruptcy administration does not have the right to assume a licence agreement if the licence agreement provides for a termination right in the case of the other party's bankruptcy and the other party exercises this termination right.

The bankruptcy administration has the right to extraordinary termination of the licence agreement, which leads to a reversion of rights to the licensor. This extraordinary termination right does not need to be agreed in the licence agreement, but is based on the bankruptcy administration's duty to wind down the licensor's business and liquidate its assets.[8] An extraordinary termination triggers a damages claim of the licensee. This damages claim constitutes a claim in bankruptcy without any preferential rights and is compensated with (at most) a dividend payment according to the relevant creditor class. Unsecured claims of trade creditors form part of the third (and last) class, which is subordinated to secured claims and claims related to employment and social security.

Unless prohibited by the provisions on assignment and transfer in the licence agreement, the bankruptcy administration may assign or transfer the debtor's rights

---

7 Article 211a of the Debt Enforcement and Bankruptcy Act; see also Adrian Staehelin *et al*, *Kommentar zum Bundesgesetz über Schuldbetreibung und Konkurs*, 2nd edn, Basel, 2010, vol 2, §211 N 12.

8 Article 240 of the Debt Enforcement and Bankruptcy Act.

under the licence agreement (or parts thereof) to an acquirer of the underlying intellectual property rights. The bankruptcy administration may also transfer the entire licence agreement to a successor company by way of an asset transfer in accordance with Switzerland's Merger Act.[9]

The trustee in a deferral of bankruptcy cannot terminate a licence agreement.

The trustee in a composition proceeding moratorium has the right to terminate a licence agreement against reasonable consideration for early termination to be paid to the licensee.[10] The licensee's claim for reasonable consideration forms part of the claims in bankruptcy without any preferential rights. It is compensated with (at most) a dividend payment according to the relevant creditor class. Unsecured claims of trade creditors form part of the third (and last) class, which is subordinated to secured claims and claims related to employment and social security.

### 3.4 Powers and rights of creditors in a licensor's bankruptcy

General creditors do not have any powers or rights to influence the duration, validity or enforceability of a licence agreement. The only creditor having such powers is the licensee as party to the licence agreement.

If the licence agreement provides for a termination right in the case of the other party's bankruptcy, the licensee has the right to terminate the licence agreement. In addition, the licensee may suspend the performance of its obligations and request an appropriate security if and to the extent that the bankruptcy jeopardises the creditor's rights under the licence agreement (eg, the prosecution and maintenance of patents). For example, the licensee can withhold royalty payments due after a declaration of bankruptcy – but the licensee can withhold royalty payments due before a declaration of bankruptcy only when the licensor has already failed to perform its corresponding obligations before the declaration of bankruptcy.

If the bankruptcy administration does not assume the licence agreement on behalf of the debtor, the licensee has the right to withhold any payments or performance of other obligations until the licensor has provided a security for the performance of the licensor's obligations. If the licensor does not provide security within a reasonable time, the licensee may terminate the licence agreement.[11] This option is only of interest to the licensee if the licensee fee was considered too expensive or if the licensed or similar rights can be obtained from third parties.

### 3.5 Effects on licence agreements in the licensee's bankruptcy

In the licensee's bankruptcy, the licence agreement remains valid unless the licensor and the licensee agreed on automatic termination in the licence agreement. Any rights of the licensor under the licence agreement other than the right to receive payments are converted into money claims. Licence fee claims – usually the most important claims of the licensor – are already money claims and not affected by the conversion. Other rights of the licensor – for example, the right to request that a

---

9 Article 69 and following of the Merger Act.
10 Article 297a of the Debt Enforcement and Bankruptcy Act.
11 Article 83 of the Code of Obligations.

licensed product be further developed, marketed, and sold in particular territories – will be converted into money claims.

All money claims (including licence fee claims due before and after the declaration of bankruptcy) form part of the claims in bankruptcy without any preferential rights and are compensated with (at most) a dividend payment according to the relevant creditor class. Unsecured claims of trade creditors form part of the third (and last) class, which is subordinated to secured claims and claims related to employment and social security.

### 3.6 Powers of an administrator, receiver or trustee in the licensee's bankruptcy

The bankruptcy administration has the right to assume the licence agreement on behalf of the debtor, which means that the licensor's rights under the licence agreement are not converted into money claims but remain unchanged and become preferential to the claims in bankruptcy. In most cases the bulk of the licensor's rights under a licence agreement are anyway money claims, but specific claims such as information and reporting obligations may survive. If the bankruptcy administration just uses the licensee's rights under the licence agreement without formally assuming the licence agreement on behalf of the debtor, just those rights of the licensor become preferential claims that accrued after the declaration of bankruptcy. All rights of the licensor that accrued prior to the declaration of bankruptcy are deemed claims in bankruptcy and are compensated with (at most) a dividend payment according to the relevant creditor class.

If the licence agreement provides for a termination right in the case of the other party's bankruptcy, the bankruptcy administration cannot maintain the licence agreement after the other party has exercised this termination right.

The bankruptcy administration further has the right to extraordinary termination of the licence agreement, which leads to a reversion of rights to the licensor. This extraordinary termination right does not need to be agreed in the licence agreement, but is based on the bankruptcy administration's duty to wind down the licensee's business and liquidate its assets.[12] An extraordinary termination triggers a damages claim of the licensor. This damages claim constitutes a claim in bankruptcy without any preferential rights and is compensated with (at most) a dividend payment according to the relevant creditor class. Unsecured claims of trade creditors form part of the third (and last) class, which is subordinated to secured claims and claims related to employment and social security.

Unless prohibited by the provisions on assignment and transfer in the licence agreement, the bankruptcy administration can assign or transfer the debtor's rights under the licence agreement (or parts thereof) to an acquirer of the debtor's assets. The bankruptcy administration may also transfer the entire licence agreement to a successor company by way of an asset transfer in accordance with Switzerland's Merger Act.[13]

---

12 Article 240 of the Debt Enforcement and Bankruptcy Act.
13 Article 69 and following of the Merger Act.

### 3.7 Powers and rights of creditors in a licensee's bankruptcy

General creditors do not have any powers or rights to influence the duration, validity, or enforceability of the licence agreement. The only creditor having such powers is the licensor as party to the licence agreement.

If the licence agreement provides for a termination right in the case of the other party's bankruptcy, the licensor has the right to terminate the licence agreement if a licensee is declared bankrupt. In addition, the licensor may suspend the performance of its obligations (eg, the prosecution and maintenance of patents) and request an appropriate security if and to the extent that the licensee's bankruptcy jeopardises the licensor's rights under the licence agreement (eg, lacking royalty payments, or a failure to develop, market and sell the licensed product).

If the bankruptcy administration does not assume the licence agreement on behalf of the debtor, the licensor has the right to withhold the performance of any of its obligations under the licence agreement until the licensee has provided a security for the performance of its obligations. If the licensee does not provide such security within a reasonable time, the licensee may terminate the licence agreement.[14] This option is of particular interest to the licensor if the licence granted was exclusive and third parties are interested in obtaining such a licence.

### 3.8 Exclusive and non-exclusive licences

Under Swiss law, there is no distinction between exclusive and non-exclusive licences when it comes to the consequences of bankruptcy.

### 3.9 Perpetual and non-perpetual licences

Under Swiss law, there is no distinction between perpetual licences ('perpetual' meaning that the licence fee is paid upfront so that, during the lifespan of the licence, no further payments to the licensor have to be made by the licensee) and non-perpetual licences when it comes to the consequences of bankruptcy.[15]

### 3.10 Effects on a sub-licence in a licensor's bankruptcy

The effects on a sub-licence in the event of the licensor's bankruptcy are the same as the effects on the licence (see section 3.2).

### 3.11 Effects on a sub-licence in a licensee's bankruptcy

In the licensee's bankruptcy, the sub-licence agreement remains valid unless the licensee and the sub-licensee agreed on automatic termination in the sub-licence agreement. Automatic termination or termination rights in the licence agreement between the licensor and the licensee do not affect the sub-licence agreement as such, but might affect the sublicense grant and lead to a breach of contract by the licensee under the sub-licence agreement.

For other circumstances relating to a licensee's bankruptcy, the effects on a sub-licence are the same as the effects on a licence in a licensor's bankruptcy (see section

---

14 Article 83 of the Code of Obligations.

15 Roland Fischer, *Lizenzverträge im Konkurs*, Berne, 2008, p259.

3.2). Note that the bankruptcy administration might assume a sub-licence agreement with favourable commercial terms on behalf of the licensee, while the claims of the licensor towards the bankrupt licensee constitute claims in bankruptcy without any preferential rights.

### 3.12 Impact of registration

Exclusive or non-exclusive licences and sub-licences to patents and patent applications, designs, trademarks, plant varieties and the topographies of semiconductor products may all be registered.

The majority of today's Swiss legal scholars argue that the granting of a registered (sub-)licence survives the bankruptcy of the (sub-)licensor – ie, the licensee keeps the right to use the licensed intellectual property and neither the bankruptcy administration nor an acquirer of the underlying intellectual property rights can revoke the licence other than in accordance with the termination provisions, if any, in the licence agreement.[16] The issue is controversial, however, and there is no precedent clearly stating that the licence grant under a registered licence is not converted into a mere money claim in the licensor's bankruptcy.

It is clear that there are situations where it might be very appealing for a bankruptcy administration to follow the minority opinion and decide that the registration does not prevent the bankruptcy administration from selling the underlying intellectual property rights unencumbered and free of any licences. Also, the minority opinion has some merits when it comes to equal treatment of the creditors. In short, a licensee of a registered licence must take into account that the bankruptcy administration might not follow the majority opinion and decide that such licensee's rights, too, will be converted into money claims.

## 4. Contractual arrangements in deviation from the law

### 4.1 Exceptions

For publishing agreements, Article 392(3) of the Code of Obligations states that, in his publisher's bankruptcy, an author may entrust his work to another publisher unless the bankrupt publisher provides a security for the performance of future obligations under the publishing agreement. This mechanism corresponds to the mechanism in Article 83 of the Code of Obligations (see sections 3.4 and 3.7 above).

The licensee under a software licence agreement maintains its right to use the licensed software in the licensor's bankruptcy. Neither the bankruptcy administration nor a later acquirer of the software can prevent the licensee from continuing to use the software. While the majority opinion is that this applies to all software licences,[17] some scholars argue that it applies only to perpetual, fully paid-up, software licences.

---

16 Roland Fischer, *op cit*, pp250-255; Mark Reutter, in Magda Streuli-Youssef, *Urhebervertragsrecht*, Zurich, 2006, p420.

17 Article 12(2) of the Copyrights Act and article 17(1) of the Copyrights Ordinance; Roland Fischer, *op cit*, p258; Georg Rauber, in Magda Streuli-Youssef, *Urhebervertragsrecht*, Zurich, 2006, p255.

### 4.2 Scope to alter statutory mechanisms

Swiss law offers limited possibilities to alter the statutory mechanisms or deviate from the general rules governing the effects of bankruptcy on licence agreements. The licensor can, for security reasons, unconditionally assign and transfer the underlying intellectual property rights to the licensee. Such assignment and transfer prevents the bankruptcy administration from selling the underlying intellectual property rights in violation of the licence agreement. An assignment and transfer conditional upon the licensor's bankruptcy is not enforceable.[18]

In practice, it is rare that parties agree on assigning the underlying intellectual property rights as a security. However, the licensor can, for security reasons, pledge the underlying intellectual property right to the licensee. The pledge provides the licensee with a financial preference right, but it does not secure the licensee's right to actually use the licensed intellectual property rights.

In a sub-licence agreement, the sub-licensee may be granted step-in rights in the event of the licensee's bankruptcy. To validly agree on such step-in rights, the licensor either must sign the sub-licence agreement providing for such step-in rights, or the licence agreement must afford the sublicensee(s) a direct step-in claim towards the licensor.

Finally, the parties may agree that the licensed intellectual property is put into a non-trading bankruptcy remote special purpose vehicle, which reduces (but does not exclude) the risk that the licensor falls into bankruptcy.[19]

### 4.3 Termination rights and automatic reversions

A licensor and licensee may validly agree in the licence agreement on automatic termination of the licence agreement upon the bankruptcy of either party. A licensor and licensee may also validly agree on a termination right in the case of the bankruptcy of the other party or of either party. These contractual agreements lead to the reversion of the rights to the licensor.

The parties may also agree on a termination right or automatic termination that is triggered before any declaration of bankruptcy – eg, upon receipt of a bankruptcy notice by the debtor or upon the filing of a petition for bankruptcy.

An automatic reversion without termination of the licence agreement, or other arrangements that unilaterally affect the balance of performance and consideration in a case of bankruptcy, are not enforceable and are deemed an unlawful preference of one party in the bankruptcy of the other party. In general, termination or reversion rights structured to be excessively disadvantageous for the debtor will be subject to avoidance actions. Automatic reversion of rights in favour of a bankrupt licensor seems possible under Swiss law, but we hardly see any commercial rationale to agree on such a mechanism.

---

18 Roland Fischer, *op cit*, p303.

19 Roland Fischer, op cit, p348 and following.

## 5. Cross-border aspects

### 5.1 Foreign law

An insolvency administrator in Switzerland is bound by the election of foreign law in the licence agreement with regard to issues of contract law – eg, what the rights of each party are under the licensee agreement and what the consequences of a breach of the agreement (subject to *ordre public*) are.

The insolvency administrator is not, though, bound by the election of foreign law in the licence agreement with regard to the effects of the bankruptcy on the debtor and the debtor's assets.

### 5.2 Foreign jurisdiction

An insolvency administrator in Switzerland is bound by the election of foreign jurisdiction in the licence agreement. The election of foreign jurisdiction does not, however, affect the jurisdiction where the other party would have to file its claims against the bankrupt party and where the other party would have to challenge any decisions of the bankruptcy administration. The election of foreign jurisdiction only affects the jurisdiction where one party would have to file a suit against the other party for breach of contract or similar causes of action.

# Turkey

**Orçun Çetinkaya**
**F Müjgan Güngör**
**Merve Karaduman**
**Asena A Keser**
GÜN & PARTNERS

## 1. Overview

### 1.1 Relevant legislation governing intellectual property and bankruptcy

Under Turkish Law, intellectual property is mainly regulated by:

- the Law on Intellectual and Artistic Works, numbered 5846;
- Decree Law on the Protection of Trademarks, numbered 556;
- Decree Law on the Protection of Patent Rights, numbered 551;
- Decree Law on the Protection of Industrial Designs, numbered 554; and
- Decree Law on the Protection of Geographical Indications, numbered 555.

There are also several secondary regulations in relation to implementation of these laws.

As for bankruptcy law, the Enforcement and Bankruptcy Law, numbered 2004, and the Regulation on Enforcement and Bankruptcy Law, published in the Official Gazette dated April 11 2005 and numbered 25783, are the two pieces of legislation that govern bankruptcy-related issues.

### 1.2 Types of insolvency procedure

Pursuant to the Enforcement and Bankruptcy Law, there are two different types of bankruptcy procedure. Creditors of a debtor can either initiate a bankruptcy procedure before an enforcement office (indirect bankruptcy) or they can request the debtor's bankruptcy from a commercial court (direct bankruptcy).

#### *(a) Indirect bankruptcy*

Upon application of a creditor to an enforcement office to initiate the bankruptcy procedure, the enforcement office serves a payment order to the debtor.

Where the debtor does not object to this order within seven days of its notification, the payment order becomes definite. If the receivables of the creditor are secured by negotiable instrument (cheque, bond etc), the creditor may alternatively follow the procedure set forth specifically for these kinds of receivable, where the time period to file an opposition against the payment order is five days instead of seven days.

If no opposition is filed by the debtor against the payment order, the creditor is entitled to request from the commercial court a declaration of the debtor's bankruptcy by filing a lawsuit within one year from the notification date of the payment order. If there is no objection raised by the debtor, the commercial court does not make any examination with regard to the merits of the case – ie, it does not make an examination with respect to the existence of the debt, but only examines whether the debtor raised an objection against the payment order and whether the enforcement procedure has become definite.

As the commercial court is obliged to announce the creditor's bankruptcy request in local and national newspapers, other creditors of the debtor can intervene in this action and question whether the receivable that is subject to the request actually exists and whether the debtor is in a condition to be announced bankrupt. If the court decides that the debtor is not indebted or cannot be declared bankrupt for some reason (eg, the debtor is not a merchant), the court will reject the bankruptcy case. Alternatively, the court orders the debtor to deposit the debt amount, as well as execution expenses and any interest due, to the safe keeping of the court within seven days. If the debtor does not deposit such amount in due time, the court declares the bankruptcy of the debtor, which starts the liquidation process.

If, however, the debtor files an opposition against the payment order within five/seven days following receipt of the payment order, the creditor will be required to request a commercial court to remove the opposition of the debtor and decide on the issue of bankruptcy. In contradistinction to the procedure explained above, the court here examines the merits of the creditor's request – in other words, it researches whether the debt actually exists. If the court decides that the creditor does not have any legal grounds to request such amount from the debtor, the commercial court will reject the case. However, if the court concludes that the debtor has no right to object to the payment order, it will remove the opposition and decide to proceed with the bankruptcy procedure as detailed above.

### *(b) Direct bankruptcy*

According to the Enforcement and Bankruptcy Law, the creditors of a debtor are entitled to directly request the bankruptcy of the debtor if the conditions of bankruptcy are met as detailed under section 1.3 below.

## 1.3 Grounds of bankruptcy

In the direct bankruptcy procedure, if the court determines the existence of the debt and one of the following grounds, it declares the bankruptcy of the debtor:

- the permanent address of the debtor is not known;
- it is highly likely that the debtor can or will run away in order not to pay the debts;
- the debtor takes actions infringing the rights of creditors or it is possible that the debtor would attempt to take such actions;
- the debtor hides its assets during the enforcement process;
- the debtor suspends payments;
- the proposed concordat[1] is removed, not approved or terminated by the court; and
- a debt determined by a judgment cannot be collected through the enforcement process.

The court will also order the debtor to deposit the debt amount to the safe keeping of the court (as in the indirect bankruptcy procedure), and doing so saves the debtor from being declared bankrupt.

However, if the debtor is a joint stock company or limited liability company and its assets are less than its liabilities, then the creditors of such a company can directly request the bankruptcy regardless of the grounds listed above. Furthermore, in this case the debtor cannot save itself from being declared bankrupt by depositing the debt amount to the safe keeping of the court.

## 1.4 Filing for bankruptcy

The creditors of a debtor company may request its bankruptcy based on the grounds explained in section 1.3 above.

Apart from the creditors, the debtor itself, as represented by its board of directors, can request the bankruptcy of the company from a commercial court, based on the ground that its assets are less than its liabilities. In this case, an expert panel is appointed by the court to examine the assets and liabilities of the company.

Alternatively, the debtor is obliged to request its bankruptcy from the competent commercial court if at least half of the debtor's assets are disposed of at the end of an indirect bankruptcy procedure initiated by its creditors, and the remaining assets are not sufficient to pay the debts due or to be due within one year.

In addition to the foregoing, a liquidation officer of a company which is in the liquidation process[2] is also entitled to make a bankruptcy application on behalf of the company.

### *(a) Postponement of bankruptcy*

Although the bankruptcy procedure principally proceeds as outlined above, representatives of a commercial company as well as its creditors may request the postponement of bankruptcy under Article 377 of the Commercial Code and Articles 179 and 179(b) of the Enforcement and Bankruptcy Law. They do so by submitting an 'improvement project' to the commercial court. Where the court considers that the improvement project is appropriate and applicable, it decides to postpone the bankruptcy of the company.

Following the postponement of a bankruptcy decision, all the execution proceedings initiated against the company before the postponement are ceased except for those that are based on pledged assets; further, the creditors are not entitled to initiate new execution proceedings during this period. With a decision to postpone, the court immediately appoints a trustee to act as the representative of the company and takes other relevant measures to protect the assets of the company.

The duration of the postponement is one year at most. However, this period can

---

1 A 'concordat' can simply be defined as a composition agreement with creditors where the debtor or creditor can request from an enforcement court in order to prevent the debtor's bankruptcy. If such application is in accordance with the formal requirements prescribed by the law, the court will grant the debtor a period of time in which to reach an agreement with its creditors.

2 If a company decides to end its business, it may go into the liquidation process in accordance with the provisions of Turkish Commercial Code (numbered 6102). A liquidation officer is appointed to conduct this process.

be extended up to four years by the court upon request. At the end of the postponement period, if the court concludes that an improvement is not possible for the company, it announces the bankruptcy of the company.

### 1.5 Administrators and other appointed persons

In principle, apart from the postponement-of-bankruptcy procedure no administrator, receiver or trustee is appointed by enforcement offices or commercial courts upon filing for bankruptcy. However, commercial courts may decide to appoint a trustee for administration of the company's assets as a precautionary measure, upon at least one creditor's request.

In contrast, when the commercial court declares the bankruptcy of a company and the first creditors' meeting[3] is held, the bankruptcy administration starts representing the company and takes over the right of disposal over all its assets and rights. The bankruptcy administration consists of three persons appointed by the creditors during the first creditors' meeting, and these three persons have the responsibility of carrying through the bankruptcy proceedings until the liquidation is completed.

## 2. Licence agreements in the phase between filing and declaration of bankruptcy

In the phase between filing and declaration of bankruptcy, regardless of whether such filing has been made for the licensor or the licensee, the licence agreement will not be directly affected by the filing unless there is a provision within the licence agreement imposing a penalty (eg, termination of the agreement) as a result of such an application. So if the contracting parties had agreed on termination of the licence agreement when a filing for bankruptcy of one of the parties occurs, the agreement would be automatically terminated. Otherwise, it will remain valid and enforceable during this phase.

During the phase between filing and declaration of bankruptcy, registration of the licence does not play a role. Registration only gains importance in the event of bankruptcy, as explained further in section 3 below.

Although there is no administrator, receiver or trustee appointed in the phase between filing and declaration of bankruptcy, the court can decide to take a wide range of precautionary measures in order to protect the rights of the creditors. The Enforcement and Bankruptcy Law regulates such measures in a vague way by giving a large discretionary right to the court. Although the measures – other than the bookkeeping, which is regulated under Article 159(2) of the Enforcement and Bankruptcy Law – are not expressly stipulated, there are various protective measures applied in practice:

- identifying the assets of the debtor;
- forbidding third parties from making any payments to the debtor (but instead to the court's safe keeping);
- sealing the workshops and storehouses or putting the management of such premises under the governance of the enforcement offices;

3 Please see the explanations as to the first and second creditors' meeting under 3.4. below.

- putting an annotation onto the land registry to prevent the transfer of assets;[4] and even
- ordering a general restraint on the disposal right of the debtor.

As the court has a large amount of discretion on these measures, it decides on the measures to be applied by evaluating the facts of each case.[5] Even though the court primarily aims to protect the rights of the creditors, it should also take into consideration the rights of the debtor. The protective measures are taken in order to prevent the debtor from disposing of its assets. There is no precedent where the court uses its discretionary powers over licence agreements (eg, to terminate), as this would not serve the purposes just outlined.

## 3. Licence agreements in the phase after declaration of bankruptcy

### 3.1 Treatment of intellectual property rights

When it comes to the phase after a declaration of bankruptcy, there is no distinction between the different intellectual property (IP) rights in terms of how they are treated in the event of bankruptcy. The Law on Intellectual and Artistic Works refers merely to the acts of disposal and to contractual relationships through a catch-all point of view without distinguishing any particular IP rights. Besides, the decree laws regulating the different types of IP rights (see section 1.1 above) adopt the same stance among themselves by not regulating the effect of bankruptcy on the IP rights.

The silence of these specific regulations gives rise to the application of the general clauses of the Enforcement and Bankruptcy Law, which means that, in a case of the bankruptcy of an owner of an IP right, these rights pass to the bankrupt's estate; until the liquidation is completed, they remain with the bankruptcy administration.

### 3.2 Effects on licence agreements in the licensor's bankruptcy

Neither the Law on Intellectual and Artistic Works nor the decree laws listed in section 1.1 above touch upon the fate of licence agreements in case of a licensor's bankruptcy.

The provisions of Turkish Code of Obligations[6] on 'usufructuary' lease[7] and the provisions of the Turkish Civil Code on 'usufructuary' right, in relation to non-exclusive licences and exclusive licences respectively, are referred to in the general provisions on licences (namely Article 56) of the Law on Intellectual and Artistic Works. When those provisions are examined, it is seen that the two legal codes mentioned do not provide a specific provision regarding the effect of the principal right owner's bankruptcy on the relevant contractual relation. However, it is accepted among legal scholars that in principle the personality of the licensor is not

---

4 B Kuru, *İcra ve İflas Hukuku El Kitabı* (in English, *Enforcement and Bankruptcy Law Handbook*), 2nd edn, 2013.

5 H Pekcanitez, O Atalay and M Özkan, *İcra ve İflas Hukuku* (in English, *The Enforcement and Bankruptcy Law*), Yetkin Yayinlari, 2011.

6 Numbered 6098.

7 A 'usufructary' lease is an agreement where the lessor undertakes to provide the lessee with use of a thing or a right which gives a yield in return for a price.

the key element for the continuance of the licence agreement, and therefore the licence agreement is not automatically terminated in the event of the licensor's bankruptcy. Here it should be noted that, in terms of agreements granting a know-how licence (ie, licence agreements under which the licensor's personality is of importance), the licence agreement is deemed to be terminated if bankruptcy is declared before the relevant information or data is transferred to the licensee.

In light of the above, it can be concluded that if a licensor has already granted a licence – ie, the licensor has already performed its obligation at the time the licensor is declared bankrupt – the licence agreement would remain in effect between the licensee and bankruptcy administration because all of the bankrupt's rights and obligations pass to the bankrupt's estate. Since the bankruptcy of the licensor does not prevent the licensee from enjoying its rights acquired within the scope of the licence agreement, the licensee can only terminate the agreement on a just cause or in the event of a situation that is specifically stipulated in the licence agreement.

If the licence has not been granted to the licensee at the time the bankruptcy of the licensor is declared, the bankruptcy administration may choose to perform the licensor's obligations. In such a case, the licensee has the right to request a guarantee from the bankruptcy administration and may refrain from performing its own obligations until the acquisition of such a guarantee. However, if the bankruptcy administration does not choose to enter into the licence agreement, the licensee may claim compensation and request registration of this claim on the bankrupt's estate. If this claim is not accepted by the bankruptcy administration, the licensee is entitled to bring its claim before the courts.

If the bankruptcy administration enters into the licence agreement, it does not have any role other than being party to the agreement. The creditors of the licensor do not have any powers or rights with respect to this licence relationship.

### 3.3 Effects on licence agreements in the licensee's bankruptcy

Pursuant to Article 59 of the Law on Intellectual and Artistic Works, which stipulates the conditions with respect to the return of financial rights to the owner (licensor), the licence right of the licensee does not automatically return to the licensor in the event of the licensee's bankruptcy. However, if the personality of the licensee has significance in conclusion of the licence agreement, the licence right returns to the licensor upon the licensee's bankruptcy.

Despite the above provision of the Law on Intellectual and Artistic Works, it is debated among legal scholars whether the usufructuary lease provisions of the Code of Obligations, which provide that the agreement would automatically be terminated by declaration of the lessee's bankruptcy, should apply because of the reference to Article 56 of the Law on Intellectual and Artistic Works. However, in practice the determination of whether the licence agreement is terminated upon the bankruptcy of the licensee is left to the courts, where the judges will evaluate whether the personality of the licensee is significant for conclusion of the agreement. Notwithstanding this, in most of the cases the parties determine the consequences of the bankruptcy of one of the parties under the licence agreement and the agreement therefore is treated in accordance with the parties' will.

Where it is accepted that the agreement is not terminated automatically, the licensor can resort to its right to terminate the agreement with a six-month prior notice period[8] in compliance with Article 368 of the Code of Obligations, provided that the licensor cannot be expected to continue the relationship when it turns out to be an unbearable burden instead of an obligation.[9] However, it may not be possible to argue this since the licensor is able to vest the same rights to others if non-exclusive licences are in question. It should also be noted that the licensor may use this right in return for a proper indemnity.

Moreover, Article 58 of the Law on Intellectual and Artistic Works, which regulates the right of withdrawal, provides a simplified protective solution for the licensor and especially if exclusive licences are in question. Accordingly, if the exercise of licence rights by the licensee becomes impossible for any reason, the licensor may resort to the right of withdrawal even without prior notice.

### 3.4 Powers of an administrator, receiver or trustee and the licensee's creditors in the licensee's bankruptcy

Upon the licensee's bankruptcy, all its financial rights (including the licence right, the use of which is left to him under the licence agreement) are transferred to the bankrupt's estate. After the establishment of the bankrupt's estate, two meetings of creditors are held before the liquidation.

Both disputed and undisputed creditors gather at the first meeting, where the creditors cannot take crucial decisions except for urgent ones.[10] At this meeting, the creditors also choose a bankruptcy administration among themselves. The bankruptcy administration will then have the power to represent the bankrupt and also to conduct the liquidation process.

Until the second creditors' meeting, the bankruptcy administration is entitled to choose to perform the licensor's obligations undertaken within the licence agreement, whereas it can also choose not to perform these obligations, as explained in detail above.[11] In the latter case, the bankruptcy administration can register (partially or in its entirety) the licensee's claim arising from the licence agreement on the bankrupt's estate as a receivable, upon request of the licensee. If the licensee's receivable claim is accepted, the creditors of the bankrupt have the right to object to this registration by filing a court action under Article 142 of the Enforcement and Bankruptcy Law. If the bankruptcy administration decides to enter into the licence agreement, such decision may be discussed during the second creditors' meeting.

The second creditors' meeting is held by the undisputed creditors of the bankrupt. The creditors are entitled to make decisions on:

- pursuing the court actions which were previously put on hold because of the announcement of bankruptcy;
- the type of the liquidation procedure to be followed;

8 Ü Tekinalp, *Fikri Mülkiyet Hukuku* (in English, *Intellectual Property Law*), Vedat, 2012, p469.
9 M Tüysüz, Fikri Haklar *Üzerindeki Sözleşmeler* (in English, *Agreements on Intellectual Property Rights*), Yetkin, 2007, p122.
10 Article 224 of the Enforcement and Bankruptcy Law.
11 Uyar, Talih, Uyar, Alper, Uyar, Cüneyt, İcra ve İflas Kanunu Şerhi El Kitabı, Cilt II, p2556.

- the sale of assets of the bankrupt's estate; and
- all other issues which they deem necessary for the benefit of the bankrupt's estate.

Considering the broad powers of the second creditors' meeting, it can be considered that the creditors are also entitled to reconsider and even withdraw the decision of bankruptcy administration taken with respect to the fate of the licence agreements.

### 3.5 Exclusive and non-exclusive licences

There is no distinction between exclusive and non-exclusive licences in the event of a bankruptcy.

### 3.6 Perpetual and non-perpetual licences

In terms of perpetual and non perpetual rights, theoretically it cannot be said that there is a distinction between the perpetual and non-perpetual licences in the event of bankruptcy. Even so, in practice these are not common types of licence that constitute the subject of a licence agreement.

### 3.7 Effects on a sub-licence in a licensor's bankruptcy

Unless it is agreed by the parties that a sub-licence agreement will be terminated in the event of the licensor's bankruptcy, the sub-licence agreement remains in force even in such circumstances.

### 3.8 Effects on a sub-licence in a licensee's bankruptcy

In the event of a licensee's bankruptcy and where the licence agreement is deemed to be terminated, the sub-licence agreement concluded between the sub-licensor and sub-licensee's also affected by the termination of the licence agreement and is considered terminated.

### 3.9 Impact of registration

The registration of a licence does not play a role in terms of the enforcement of the licence agreement. Moreover, under Turkish law it is not mandatory to register a licence. Indeed, the Law on Intellectual and Artistic Works does not set forth any provisions regarding registration.

Nonetheless, the registration of trademarks is of significance. Accordingly, where there is a registered trademark licence, the licensee will be entitled to claim its rights arising from the trademark licence against third parties, even if the owner of the licence has changed because of the bankruptcy of the licensor.

## 4. Contractual arrangements in deviation from the law

### 4.1 Exceptions

Licence agreements in general are private law contracts which are dependent on the mutual will of the parties. Therefore, the general principles stated in the Code of

Obligations are applied to these agreements by analogy. Furthermore, according to the majority of legal scholars the content of the licence agreements can be determined fully in accordance with the parties' needs, since such agreements are not perceived as a transaction of real rights.[12]

Publishing agreements are specifically addressed in the Code of Obligations. Pursuant to Article 500 of that code, in the case of the bankruptcy of a publisher, the owner of a work can assign another person to publish the work, unless any security has been provided with regard to performance of an obligation that is not yet due and payable. In accordance with Article 500, in the event of the death of the transferee before the work is completed, or his incapacity to complete the work for some other reason, all commitments are cancelled.

### 4.2 Scope to alter statutory mechanisms

As stated above, the terms and conditions of the licence agreements can be determined in accordance with the parties' needs as a consequence of the 'freedom of contract' principle in the Code of Obligations. In line with this, the parties can validly agree that no reversion of rights to the licensor will take place in the event of the licensor's bankruptcy. This freedom does not, however, apply if the agreement is deemed to be against imperative provisions, morals, public order or personal rights, or if the subject of the agreement is infeasible.[13]

In addition, the Decree on the Protection of Trademarks states in the last sentence of Article 21 that the parties cannot agree provisions in an agreement that are in contradiction to that decree and to other related laws, regulations and by-laws. Bearing in mind the contractual nature of the licence agreements and the framework of the freedom-of–contract principle, it is possible to conclude that parties may agree on a dissolving condition that is subject to the bankruptcy of the parties.

### 4.3 Termination rights and automatic reversions

Article 59 of the Law on Intellectual and Artistic Works stipulates the conditions under which the right arising from the licence agreement can return to the owner of the work. Accordingly, the licence rights cannot return to the owner of the work in the event of the decease or bankruptcy of the licensee unless the licensee's personality is of significance in terms of the work. In those latter circumstances, the licence right passes to the inheritors of the owner or to the bankruptcy office.

Article 59 also clearly states that even if the licensor prohibits the transfer of the licence right from the licensee to third persons, the rule set out in the foregoing paragraph will still be applicable. However, Article 59 does not provide any explanation regarding the event of death or bankruptcy of the licensor, since it does not have any effect on the use of licence rights.

---

12 M Tüysüz, *Fikri Haklar ÜzeÜzerindeki Sözleşmeler* (in English, *Agreements on Intellectual Property Rights*), Yetkin, 2007.

13 See Articles 26 and 27 of the Code of Obligations.

## 5. Cross-border aspects

### 5.1 Foreign law and foreign jurisdiction

Under Article 154(2) of the Enforcement and Bankruptcy Law, parties are allowed to conclude agreements in relation to the jurisdiction of enforcement offices where the enforcement and insolvency processes will be conducted. However, in terms of the commercial courts where insolvency cases will be heard, such jurisdiction agreements cannot be concluded, as provided by Article 154(3) of the Enforcement and Bankruptcy Law.

In the event that the parties have agreed a foreign law or jurisdiction within their licence agreement, Article 47 of the International Private and Civil Procedural Law,[14] which regulates the authorisation of the court of foreign countries in terms of contractual relationships, should be taken into account. In addition, Article 47 states that a jurisdiction agreement authorising a foreign court is only valid and enforceable if the subject of the agreement does not fall into the scope of what has been set down in law as requiring the exclusive jurisdiction of Turkey's domestic courts.

Since Article 40 of the International Private and Civil Procedural Law clearly states that international jurisdiction of the Turkish courts is determined by the jurisdiction rules of the domestic law, the Enforcement and Bankruptcy Law should be referred to in order to verify the jurisdiction regarding an insolvency case.

'Enforcement' in its simplest form is the performance of an obligation through the state.[15] Enforcement actions and procedures are subject to the sovereignty of the state involved. Such exercises are carried out in accordance with the state's own legislation and organs. The laws of the state in which the enforcement process is conducted are applicable on the matter. As stated in a decision of the Assembly of Civil Chambers of Court of Appeals in 1998,[16] enforcement is a consequence of the state's own sovereignty and independence. The jurisdiction of the commercial court is regarded as related to public order and therefore foreign jurisdiction selections provided by Article 47 of the International Private and Civil Procedural Law have no legal effect for insolvency cases.

In light of the foregoing, the insolvency administrator would not be bound by both the election of foreign jurisdiction and the election of foreign law in a licence agreement.

---

14 Numbered 5718.

15 E Nomer, "İflas Davalarında Milletlerarası Yetki Anlaşmaları" (in English, "International Authorisation Agreements in Bankruptcy Cases"), *Istanbul Bar Review*, 2011.

16 Assembly of the Turkish Supreme Court's Civil Chambers, reference T.6.5.1988 1998/12-287E 1998/325K.

# United States

**John W Holcomb**
**Lynda Zadra-Symes**
Knobbe Martens

## 1. Overview

### 1.1 Legislation governing US bankruptcy

The US Constitution provides that "The Congress shall have power ... [t]o establish ... uniform laws on the subject of bankruptcies throughout the United States."[1] In 1978, Congress embarked on a major overhaul of America's bankruptcy laws and replaced the out-of-date Bankruptcy Act of 1898 with a new comprehensive Bankruptcy Code.[2] Congress has amended the Bankruptcy Code several times since 1978, but the basic structure of US bankruptcy law has not changed over the past three decades.

In addition to enacting the Bankruptcy Code, Congress also established specialised federal bankruptcy courts to oversee and adjudicate issues that arise in the bankruptcy process. The federal judicial system in the United States is divided into 12 regional circuit courts of appeal,[3] and it is further subdivided into 94 subordinate district courts within those 12 circuits. Each of the 94 judicial districts also includes a bankruptcy court, which is subordinate to the district court.[4] The jurisdiction of bankruptcy courts is strictly limited to bankruptcy cases and proceedings arising under the Bankruptcy Code.[5]

Appeals of the decisions of bankruptcy courts are heard by district courts or by bankruptcy appellate panels (in those circuits that have established such a panel).[6] The regional circuit courts of appeal hear appeals from final decisions of district courts and bankruptcy appellate panels.[7]

In addition to each bankruptcy judge, another government official, the US trustee, is involved in the administration of bankruptcy cases. The US Attorney General is charged with appointing 21 geographically based US trustees, each of whom is responsible for monitoring bankruptcy cases within one or more of the 94 judicial districts.[8] Each US trustee may make an appearance and be heard on any

1 Article I, §8(4).
2 See 11 USC §§101–1532.
3 That is, the geographically based federal appellate courts are the First through Eleventh Circuit Courts of Appeal, plus the District of Columbia Circuit Court of Appeal. One other federal appellate court, the Federal Circuit Court of Appeal, is not geographically based but instead has jurisdiction over particular specialised subject matter, such as patent cases. See 28 USC §1295.
4 28 USC §152.
5 28 USC §157.
6 28 USC §158.
7 *Id.*
8 28 USC §581.

issue in any bankruptcy case in the judicial districts for which he is responsible.[9] One of the US trustee's most important duties is to maintain a panel of qualified individuals who serve as trustees in bankruptcy cases.[10]

## 1.2 Types of bankruptcy procedure

Legal entities such as corporations, partnerships and limited liability companies[11] may choose to file a bankruptcy petition under Bankruptcy Code Chapter 7,[12] which provides a process for the liquidation of the entity, or under Chapter 11,[13] which provides for the reorganisation of the entity's finances; these two options are outlined further below. US bankruptcy law also provides for Chapter 9 cases for municipalities,[14] Chapter 12 cases for family farmers and fishermen with regular annual income,[15] and Chapter 13 cases for individuals with regular income.[16]

### (a) *Chapter 7: liquidation*

The purpose of a Chapter 7 bankruptcy case is to liquidate the property of the bankruptcy estate. The primary duties of the trustee in a Chapter 7 case are to wind down the debtor's financial affairs, to liquidate the non-exempt property of the bankruptcy estate, and to distribute the proceeds to creditors and others, as appropriate under the Bankruptcy Code.[17]

### (b) *Chapter 11: reorganisation*

The general purpose of a Chapter 11 bankruptcy case is to reorganise the finances of the debtor. A successful Chapter 11 bankruptcy case results in the confirmation of a plan of reorganisation.[18] A plan of reorganisation is a detailed document that sets forth, among other things:

- how creditors (secured and unsecured) are to be paid, including the amount and the timing of those payments;
- how the debtor will operate its business and use the property of the estate;
- how the debtor's management structure will change; and
- how the debtor's ownership structure will change.[19]

Obtaining confirmation of a plan of reorganisation is often a long and complicated process, involving the preparation and dissemination of a disclosure statement that explains the proposed plan of reorganisation[20] and the solicitation of the votes of creditors and equity holders in favour of the plan.

---

9 11 USC §307.
10 28 USC §586.
11 The Bankruptcy Code prohibits certain types of business enterprise, such as banks and insurance companies, from obtaining bankruptcy protection. See 11 USC §109.
12 11 USC §§701–728.
13 11 USC §§1101–1174.
14 11 USC §§901–946.
15 11 USC §§1201–1231.
16 11 USC §§1301–1330.
17 11 USC §704.
18 11 USC §§1121–1129.
19 11 USC §1123.
20 11 USC §1125.

## 1.3 Grounds for bankruptcy and the filing process

### *(a) Involuntary bankruptcy*

If an entity's creditors believe that the entity is insolvent – meaning generally that the entity's liabilities are greater than its assets[21] – then they may file an involuntary bankruptcy petition with respect to that entity.[22] In that instance, if the entity does not consent to the commencement of the bankruptcy case, the bankruptcy court will determine whether the entity is indeed insolvent and, if it is, the court will grant the creditors' petition and enter an 'order for relief', which commences the bankruptcy process.[23] If the bankruptcy court denies the creditors' involuntary bankruptcy petition and declines to enter an order for relief, the petitioning creditors can be held liable for the entity's costs or attorney's fees. Furthermore, if the bankruptcy court finds that the creditors filed the involuntary bankruptcy petition in bad faith, the bankruptcy court can enter a judgment against the petitioning creditors for the entity's damages proximately caused by the filing or for punitive damages.[24]

### *(b) Voluntary bankruptcy*

It is a relatively easy matter for an entity to seek and obtain bankruptcy protection. If an entity is insolvent, or even if it is not insolvent but experiencing financial problems, it may file a voluntary bankruptcy petition under Chapter 7 or Chapter 11 of the Bankruptcy Code.[25] The entity's filing of a voluntary bankruptcy petition constitutes the entry of an order for relief;[26] unless a party in interest challenges the entity's qualification for bankruptcy protection, the bankruptcy court does not adjudicate the propriety of the filing.

The vast majority of bankruptcy cases in the United States are voluntary cases.

## 1.4 Administrators and other appointed persons

Shortly after a debtor commences a bankruptcy case, the bankruptcy court will set a date for an initial meeting of creditors (sometimes called a '341(a) meeting', referring to the section of the Bankruptcy Code that provides for this meeting).[27] The US trustee conducts and presides over this 341(a) meeting, at which the individual debtor, or the representatives of a corporate debtor, must appear under oath and answer questions posed by creditors concerning the debtor's financial affairs and other issues pertaining to the bankruptcy case.[28]

One of the most important benefits to a debtor in bankruptcy is that all efforts by creditors to attempt to collect on a claim against the debtor or against property of the bankruptcy estate are automatically stayed.[29] The debtor need not therefore take

21 11 USC §101(32).
22 11 USC §303.
23 *Id.*
24 11 USC §303(i).
25 11 USC §301(a).
26 11 USC §301(b).
27 11 USC §§341–343.
28 *Id.*
29 11 USC §362.

any additional action to prevent, for example, the commencement or continuation of a lawsuit against it or foreclosure proceedings against the property of its estate.

### (a) *Chapter 7: liquidation*

Whether or not a trustee is appointed to administer the bankruptcy estate depends upon the type of bankruptcy case. Shortly after a debtor commences a Chapter 7 case, the US trustee will appoint an interim trustee to administer the bankruptcy estate.[30] At the 341(a) meeting, creditors may call for an election of some other individual as trustee,[31] but usually the interim trustee is confirmed and becomes the representative of the bankruptcy estate for all purposes, with the capacity to sue and be sued.[32]

### (b) *Chapter 11*

The US trustee does not appoint a trustee in a Chapter 11 case; instead, the debtor is considered a 'debtor in possession',[33] with authorisation to operate the debtor's business[34] and with all of the rights, powers and duties of a trustee.[35] Any party in interest in a Chapter 11 case may ask the bankruptcy court to appoint a trustee to replace the debtor in possession for cause, such as fraud or mismanagement by the debtor in possession,[36] but such appointments are rare.

## 2. Licence agreements in the phase between filing and declaring bankruptcy

In the United States, a bankruptcy case is considered 'declared' upon the entry of an order for relief. As discussed in section 1.3(b) above, the debtor's filing of a voluntary bankruptcy petition constitutes the entry of an order for relief;[37] thus, there is no phase between the debtor's filing of a voluntary bankruptcy petition and the declaration of bankruptcy. Accordingly, the issues addressed in this section 2 arise only in connection with involuntary bankruptcy cases, in the period between the creditors' filing of an involuntary bankruptcy petition and the bankruptcy court's entry of an order for relief.

### 2.1 Effects on licence agreements in the licensor's bankruptcy

During the phase between the creditors' filing of an involuntary bankruptcy petition and the bankruptcy court's entry of an order for relief, "any business of the debtor may continue to operate, and the debtor may continue to use, acquire, or dispose of property as if an involuntary case concerning the debtor had not been commenced".[38] Indeed, the only legal effect on the debtor's financial affairs that arises during this

---

30 11 USC §701.
31 11 USC §702.
32 11 USC §323.
33 11 USC §1101.
34 11 USC §1108.
35 11 USC §1107.
36 11 USC §1104.
37 11 USC §301(b).
38 11 USC §303(f).

phase is the imposition of an automatic stay of all efforts by creditors to attempt to collect on a claim against the debtor or against property of the bankruptcy estate.[39] Accordingly, the only effect on a debtor–licensor's licence agreement arising from the creditors' filing of an involuntary bankruptcy petition is that licensees may not commence or continue any lawsuit against the debtor to seek damages or other remedies for the debtor–licensor's alleged breach of that licence agreement.

## 2.2 Powers of administrators, receivers, or trustees in the licensor's bankruptcy

During the phase between the creditors' filing of an involuntary bankruptcy petition and the bankruptcy court's entry of an order for relief, a party in interest may ask the bankruptcy court to order the US trustee to appoint an interim trustee to take possession of the property of the bankruptcy estate and to operate the business of the debtor.[40] The bankruptcy court will grant such a request only if the appointment of an interim trustee is "necessary to preserve the property of the estate or to prevent loss to the estate".[41] If no party in interest seeks the appointment of an interim trustee, the debtor will continue to operate its business during this phase.

## 2.3 Effects on licence agreements in the licensee's bankruptcy case

Similarly as discussed in section 2.1 above, during the phase between the creditors' filing of an involuntary bankruptcy petition and the bankruptcy court's entry of an order for relief, a debtor–licensee continues to operate its business and to use, acquire or dispose of property of the estate.[42] However, the automatic stay prevents creditors from attempting to collect on any claim against the debtor or against property of the bankruptcy estate.[43] Consequently, the only effect on a debtor–licensee's licence agreement arising from the creditors' filing of an involuntary bankruptcy petition is that the licensor may not commence or continue any lawsuit against the debtor in order to seek damages or other remedies for the debtor–licensee's alleged breach of that licence agreement.

## 2.4 Powers of administrators, receivers, or trustees in the licensee's bankruptcy

See section 2.2 above, as the same provisions apply for a licensee's bankruptcy.

## 2.5 Impact of registration

In general, any party may register an intellectual property (IP) licence agreement by recording it in the US Patent and Trademark Office (USPTO), in the file of the patent or trademark that is the subject of the licence. During the phase between the creditors' filing of an involuntary bankruptcy petition and the bankruptcy court's entry of an order for relief, the debtor may record such IP licence agreements because the debtor may continue to conduct its business as usual. However, the non-debtor

---

39 See 11 USC §362(a): "a petition filed under section ... 303 of this title ... operates as a stay, applicable to all entities ...".

40 11 USC §303(g).

41 *Id.*

42 11 USC §303(f).

43 See 11 USC §362(a): "a petition filed under section ... 303 of this title ... operates as a stay, applicable to all entities ...".

party's action in recording an IP licence agreement during this phase would likely be held void as a violation of the automatic stay.[44]

The registration or recordation of an IP licence agreement provides third parties with constructive notice of the existence of the licence. In general, the primary benefit of providing such constructive notice is to prevent third parties from claiming the status of a '*bona fide* purchaser without notice', who could potentially take an interest in the intellectual property at issue that would be superior to the debtor's interest.

## 3. Licence agreements in the phase after declaring bankruptcy

US bankruptcy law provides debtors who are licensors or licensees of IP rights with powerful tools to maximise the value of the intellectual property at issue. However, US bankruptcy law is also teeming with pitfalls for the unwary. Choosing the best course of action, for debtors and for non-debtor parties, requires an understanding of several specialised bankruptcy concepts, including 'executory contracts' and their potential 'assumption', assignment and rejection – see further below.

### 3.1 Treatment of intellectual property rights

The treatment of IP licences under US bankruptcy law is an extension of the general treatment of a debtor's contracts in bankruptcy. Section 365 of the Bankruptcy Code generally provides that a trustee or debtor in possession may 'assume' (ie, take responsibility for) or reject the debtor's pre-petition executory contracts. That is, broadly speaking, if a trustee or debtor in possession perceives that the net consideration that the bankruptcy estate will receive post-petition from a pre-petition contract is worthwhile and valuable, the trustee or debtor in possession will likely want to assume that contract so that it stays in force and so that the trustee or debtor in possession may enjoy its benefits. Alternatively, if that pre-petition contract saddles the bankruptcy estate with burdensome and expensive obligations, the trustee or debtor in possession will likely desire to reject it.

The option of a trustee or debtor in possession to assume or reject arises only with respect to executory contracts, which are explained further next.

#### *(a) Executory contracts*

The Bankruptcy Code does not define the term 'executory contract', but most bankruptcy courts use the following definition:

> *a contract under which the obligation of both the [debtor] and the other party to the contract are so far unperformed that the failure of either to complete performance would constitute a material breach excusing the performance of the other.*[45]

Under this definition, most IP licences are quintessentially executory contracts – that is, in a typical IP licence the licensor's unperformed material obligation is to

---

44 See 11 USC §362(a); but also see *In re Acelor* 169 BR 764, 765 (Bankr SD Fla 1994) (notwithstanding the express language in §362(a), finding that the automatic stay is triggered in an involuntary case when the order for relief is entered, not when the involuntary petition is filed).

45 V Countryman, *Executory Contracts in Bankruptcy: Part I*, 57 *Minn L Rev* 439, 460 (1973); see also *NLRB v Bildisco & Bildisco* 465 US 513, 522 n6, 104 S Ct 1188, 1194 n6 (1984).

refrain from suing the licensee for infringement of the IP at issue,[46] and the licensee's unperformed material obligation is to make royalty payments.[47]

Even if the IP licence at issue does not call for the licensee to make periodic royalty payments (if, for example, it is a so-called 'paid-up' licence), usually other unperformed material obligations exist that cause the contract to be 'executory'. Such unperformed material obligations in many standard IP licence agreements include duties of confidentiality, duties to give notice of lawsuits or of potential infringement by others, and duties to defend and indemnify.[48]

### *(b) Assumption, assignment and rejection*

If a pre-petition contract is executory, then the trustee or debtor in possession may generally choose to assume or reject it. In a Chapter 7 case, the trustee must make this election relatively early – within 60 days of the entry of the order for relief – or the executory contract at issue will be deemed rejected.[49] However, the trustee may seek an extension of that 60-day deadline, for cause.[50] In a Chapter 11 case, the trustee or debtor in possession may delay making the assume-or-reject election until a relatively late point – before the confirmation of a plan of reorganisation.[51] However, any party in interest may ask the bankruptcy court to shorten the time for the trustee or debtor in possession to make that election.[52]

Trustees and debtors in possession have broad discretion to assume or reject executory contracts; bankruptcy courts generally apply the business judgment rule to challenges to these decisions.[53] Under this discretionary standard, a court should only overturn the assumption or rejection of a contract if it finds the decision to be "so manifestly unreasonable that it could not be based on sound business judgment, but only on bad faith, or whim, or caprice."[54]

If a trustee or debtor in possession chooses to assume an executory contract, then the rights and obligations of the contract remain in force and any damages caused by a subsequent breach by the trustee or debtor in possession receive administrative expense priority.[55] Often, a debtor in possession will wish to generate cash for future operations by selling property of the bankruptcy estate, which the Bankruptcy Code permits under certain conditions.[56] One of the assets that a debtor in possession may

---

46 See, eg, *Spindelfabrik Suessen-Schurr Stahlecker & Grill, GmbH v Schubert & Salzer Maschinenfabrik Aktiengesellschaft* 829 F2d 1075, 1081 (Fed Cir 1987) (holding that a patent licence is nothing more than a promise by the licensor not to sue the licensee for patent infringement).

47 See, eg, *Lubrizol Enters, Inc v Richmond Metal Finishers, Inc* 756 F2d 1043, 1046 (4th Cir 1985).

48 See, eg: *id* at 1045; and *Everex Sys, Inc v Cadtrak Corp (In re CFLC, Inc)*, 89 F3d 673, 677 (9th Cir 1996) (holding that a patent licence was an executory contract where the licensee had an ongoing obligation to mark products made under the patent).

49 11 USC §365(d).

50 *Id.*

51 *Id.*

52 *Id.*

53 See, eg, *Orion Pictures Corp v Showtime Networks (In re Orion Pictures Corp)* 4 F.3d 1095 (2d Cir 1993).

54 *In re Pomona Valley Medical Group, Inc* 476 F3d 665, 670 (9th Cir 2007) (quoting *Lubrizol*, 756 F2d at 1047); see also *In re Prestige Motorcar Gallery, Inc* 456 BR 541, 545 (Bankr ND Fla 2011) (denying motion to assume an unexpired lease because the trustee failed to show sufficient benefit to the estate).

55 See *NLRB* 465 US at 532, 104 S Ct at 1199; *In re BankVest Capital Corp*, 360 F3d 291, 296 (1st Cir 2004); and *Adventure Res Inc v Holland*, 137 F3d 786, 793 (4th Cir 1998).

56 11 USC §363.

desire to sell is its rights under an executory contract; indeed, licensee rights under an IP licence may be particularly valuable. In order to assign such rights under an executory contract, a debtor in possession must first assume them.[57]

If a debtor (pre-petition) or debtor in possession (post-petition) is in default of an executory contract, then the debtor in possession may not assume that contract unless it first:

- cures the default (or provides adequate assurance that it will promptly cure);
- compensates the other party for the actual pecuniary loss resulting from the default; and
- provides adequate assurance of its ability to perform under the contract in the future.[58]

In addition, as discussed in more detail below, the debtor in possession may be prohibited from assuming a contract that is personal in nature (such that applicable non-bankruptcy law would excuse the other party from accepting performance from an entity other than the debtor), unless the other party consents to the debtor in possession's assumption of that contract.[59]

If a trustee or debtor in possession chooses to reject an executory contract, then such rejection constitutes a breach, which gives rise to a general unsecured claim, as of the petition date, by the other party to the contract.[60] In other words, generally the only adverse consequence that arises from the rejection of an executory contract is an increase in amount of the general unsecured claims against the bankruptcy estate. In most instances, in both Chapter 7 and Chapter 11 cases, insufficient funds exist to pay unsecured creditors in full – indeed, if excess funds exist, the debtor probably would not need to be in bankruptcy in the first place – and so an increase in the amount of general unsecured claims caused by the rejection of an executory contract usually is of little concern to a trustee or debtor in possession, particularly when the rejection of that contract sheds the bankruptcy estate of a burdensome ongoing obligation. Thus, the ability of a trustee or debtor in possession to choose to assume or reject executory contracts is a powerful tool.

A debtor in possession must assume or reject an entire executory contract; piecemeal assumptions are not permitted.[61]

### *(c) Treatment of different intellectual property rights*

Different types of IP licences are treated differently under US bankruptcy law. Since 1988, 11 USC §365(n) of the Bankruptcy Code has provided IP licensees with significant protection against the threat and uncertainty arising from their licensors' potential bankruptcy, as discussed further below. However, the definition of 'intellectual property' under the Bankruptcy Code is limited to:

- trade secrets;

57 11 USC §365(f)(2)(A).
58 11 USC §365(b)(1).
59 11 USC §365(c)(1).
60 11 USC §365(g).
61 See *Stewart Title Guar Co v Old Republic Nat'l Title Ins Co* 83 F3d 735, 741 (5th Cir 1996).

- Inventions, processes, designs, and plants protected under Title 35 of the US Code;
- patent applications;
- plant varieties; and
- copyright rights and mask works protected under Title 17 of the US Code.[62]

Notably absent from this list are trademark rights and IP rights arising under foreign (ie, non-US) law. Accordingly, trademark licensees and licensees of non-US IP rights are still at risk that their licensors may extinguish their licensee rights by filing a bankruptcy petition and rejecting the relevant licence agreements. A split currently exists among the 12 US legal circuits regarding the protection of trademark licensees under bankruptcy law.[63]

**Exclusive and non-exclusive IP licences:** On its face, US bankruptcy law does not distinguish between exclusive and non-exclusive IP licences. However, whether an executory contract may be assumed by a trustee or debtor in possession depends in part upon whether the contract could be assigned under applicable non-bankruptcy law. In turn, whether an IP licence is assignable under non-bankruptcy law depends upon whether the licence is exclusive or non-exclusive.

Whether or not an exclusive IP licence is assignable or assumable by a licensee also depends upon the type of intellectual property at issue. With respect to copyright law, some courts cite the Copyright Act for the proposition that the holder of an exclusive copyright licence is entitled to all of the rights and protections of the copyright owner to the extent of the licence.[64] Accordingly, those courts conclude that an exclusive copyright licence is not personal in nature, and they permit a debtor–licensee to assign such licences.[65] However, at least one other court (although not in a bankruptcy context) has held that an exclusive copyright licensee may not assign its licensee rights without the consent of the licensor.[66]

In the patent context, courts have held that, even though exclusive patent licensees convey more rights to a licensee than non-exclusive licences, exclusive patent licences are still personal in nature, such that patent licensors maintain the right to control the identity of their licensees.[67] Accordingly, those courts conclude that a debtor–licensee of an exclusive patent licence may not assign away its licensee rights without the consent of the licensor.

Research has revealed no reported cases in which a debtor–licensee of exclusive trademark rights has attempted to assign those rights without the trademark licensor's consent. However, in view of the more intimate nature of trademark rights,

---

62 11 USC §101(35A).
63 See *Sunbeam Products, Inc v Chicago Am Mfg, LLC* 686 F3d 372, 377 (7th Cir) cert. denied, 133 S Ct 790 (2012) (disagreeing with *Lubrizol* and concluding that a debtor–licensor's rejection of a trademark licence did not terminate the licensee's right to use the trademark); see also J. McCarthy, *McCarthy on Trademarks and Unfair Competition*, §18:30 at 18–68 (3rd edn, 2014).
64 See *In re Patient Educ Media, Inc* 210 BR 237, 240 (Bankr SDNY 1997) (citing 17 USC §201(d)(2)).
65 See *In re Golden Books Family Entm't, Inc* 269 BR 311, 319 (Bankr D Del 2001).
66 See *Gardner v Nike, Inc* 279 F3d 774 (9th Cir 2002).
67 See, eg, *In re Hernandez* 285 BR 435, 439–440 (Bankr D Ariz 2002).

which involve the transfer of goodwill associated with the mark, it would be logical and consistent for courts to treat non-exclusive and exclusive trademark licensees equivalently and to deny a debtor–licensee the unfettered ability to assign away those rights.

Table 1 summarises the status of US law with respect to assignability for different types of IP rights – patent, copyright, and trademark – for exclusive and non-exclusive licences.

**Table 1: Assignability of different types of IP rights**

| Patents | | Copyrights | | Trademarks | |
|---|---|---|---|---|---|
| Exclusive | Non-exclusive | Exclusive | Non-exclusive | Exclusive | Non-exclusive |
| Probably no | No; licence is personal in nature | Maybe; courts are split | No; licence is personal in nature | No reported cases, but probably no | No; licence is personal in nature |

### 3.2 Effects on licence agreements in the licensor's bankruptcy

Aside from the decision of a trustee or debtor in possession to assume or reject an executory contract, as discussed in detail in section 3.3 below, the debtor–licensor's bankruptcy case does not affect the validity, enforceability or termination of an IP licence agreement.

### 3.3 Powers of a trustee or debtor in possession in the licensor's bankruptcy

One of the most valuable powers of a trustee or debtor in possession is the ability to choose whether to reject or to assume an IP licence agreement.

#### *(a) Rejection*

In 1983, when the Bankruptcy Code was still relatively new, the court in the *Lubrizol* case[68] held that a debtor–licensor could reject a prior patent licence and enter into a more lucrative deal with another licensee. Under the analysis described above, the *Lubrizol* case was correctly decided at that time: the licence was an executory contract and the debtor in possession reasonably exercised its business judgement in rejecting that agreement in timely fashion. However, the *Lubrizol* decision created an uproar in the intellectual property community because it caused licensees and prospective licensees to realise that their IP licensee rights could be easily snatched away from them if their licensor simply filed a bankruptcy petition and chose to reject the licence. Accordingly, in response to a lobbying effort by those IP interests, in 1988

68 *Lubrizol Enters, Inc v Richmond Metal Finishers, Inc*, 756 F2d 1043 (4th Cir 1985).

the US Congress amended the Bankruptcy Code to add a provision that permits IP licensees to retain their licensee rights even if the debtor–licensor seeks to reject the licence agreement.[69]

Specifically, §365(n) of the Bankruptcy Code now provides that if a "trustee [or debtor in possession] rejects an executory contract under which the debtor is a licensor of a right to intellectual property," then the non-debtor licensee may elect to retain its licensee rights; but the licensee must not only continue to make its royalty payments, as applicable under the licence agreement, but also waive any right of set-off or administrative claim against the bankruptcy estate.[70] Even so, the licensee's rights are limited to those that it possessed under the licence on the petition date,[71] so the licensee cannot enforce any ongoing affirmative obligations that the debtor–licensor may have under the licence, such as the duty to maintain the intellectual property or to make improvements.[72]

### *(b) Assumption*

If a trustee or debtor in possession that is a licensor of IP rights desires to assume that licence (and, presumably, to continue to receive royalty payments from its licensee), that debtor in possession must meet the following requirements:

- the IP licence at issue must be an executory contract;
- if the debtor in possession is in default, then it must cure the default, compensate the other party on account of the default, and provide adequate assurance of future performance;[73] and
- the IP licence at issue must not be personal in nature, such that applicable non-bankruptcy law would excuse the licensee from accepting performance from an entity other than the debtor.[74]

As discussed above, most IP licences are quintessentially executory contracts, satisfying the first condition. Additionally, the third condition, regarding whether the IP licence is personal in nature, is usually not an issue for debtor–licensors because applicable non-bankruptcy law – here, IP law – does not generally prevent IP licensors from assigning away their licensor rights.[75] Thus, the second condition – overcoming any default – is usually the only significant hurdle that a debtor–licensor must clear when it desires to assume, or to assume and assign, an IP licence.

## 3.4 Powers and rights of creditors in the licensor's bankruptcy

As discussed in section 3.3(a) above, the *Lubrizol* decision in 1983 caused creditors who were licensees and prospective licensees to realise that they could easily lose

---

69 11 USC §365(n).
70 11 USC §§365(n)(2)(B) and (C).
71 11 USC §365(n)(1)(B).
72 *Id.* See also *In re Exide Tech* 607 F3d 957, 966 (3rd Cir 2010) (Ambro J, concurring) ("Thus, in the event that a bankrupt licensor rejects an intellectual property license, §365(n) allows a licensee to retain its licensed rights – along with its duties – absent any obligations owed by the debtor–licensor."); and *Encino Bus Mgmt, Inc v Prise Frise, Inc (In re Prise Frise, Inc)*, 32 F3d 426, 429 (9th Cir 1994).
73 11 USC §365(b)(1).
74 11 USC §365(c)(1).
75 See *Armstrong Pump, Inc v Hartman* 745 F Supp 2d 227 (WDNY 2010).

their IP licensee rights if their licensor filed a bankruptcy petition and rejected the licence. Accordingly, in 1988 the US Congress amended the Bankruptcy Code to add §365(n), which permits IP licensees to retain their licensee rights even if the debtor–licensor seeks to reject the licence agreement.

In order for a licensee to invoke 11 USC §365(n) and thereby retain its IP licensee rights, the licensee must not only continue to make its royalty payments, as applicable under the licence agreement, but also waive any right of set-off or administrative claim against the bankruptcy estate.[76] Even so, the licensee's rights are limited to those that it possessed under the IP licence on the petition date,[77] so the licensee cannot enforce any ongoing affirmative obligations that the debtor–licensor may have under the licence, such as the duty to maintain the intellectual property or to make improvements.[78]

Any party in interest, including a creditor, may object to a decision by a trustee or debtor in possession to assume or to reject an IP licence. However, a party making such an objection must prove that the trustee's or debtor in possession's decision violates the business judgement rule.[79] This is a difficult standard to meet, requiring the objecting party to show the assume-or-reject decision to be "so manifestly unreasonable that it could not be based on sound business judgment, but only on bad faith, or whim, or caprice".[80]

### 3.5 Effects on licence agreements in the licensee's bankruptcy

Aside from the decision of the trustee or debtor in possession to assume or reject an executory contract, as discussed in detail in section 3.3 above, the debtor–licensee's bankruptcy does not affect the validity, enforceability or termination of a licence agreement.

### 3.6 Powers of a trustee or debtor in possession in the licensee's bankruptcy

One of the most important powers of a trustee or debtor in possession is the ability to choose whether to assume or to reject an IP licence agreement.

#### *(a) Rejection*

A debtor–licensee may reject an IP licence agreement, just as it may do so with any other executory contract. As discussed in section 3.1(b) above, if a debtor–licensee rejects an IP licence agreement, then such rejection constitutes a breach, which gives rise to a general unsecured claim, as of the petition date, by the licensor.[81] An increase in the amount of general unsecured claims caused by the rejection of an IP licence usually is of little concern to a debtor–licensee, particularly when the rejection of that licence eliminates from the bankruptcy estate a burdensome ongoing obligation.

76 11 USC §§365(n)(2)(B) & (C).
77 11 USC §365(n)(1)(B).
78 *Id.*
79 See *Pomona Valley* at footnote 54 above, at 669–70.
80 *Id* at 670 (quoting *Lubrizol*, 756 F2d, at 1047).
81 11 USC §365(g).

### (b) *Assignment*

Assuming that the IP licence at issue is an executory contract (as most are) and that the debtor–licensee is not in default (or that the trustee or debtor in possession can cure the default, compensate the other party on account of the default, and provide adequate assurance of future performance[82]), the analysis for assignability turns on whether the IP licence is personal in nature, such that applicable non-bankruptcy law would excuse the licensor from accepting performance from an entity other than the debtor–licensee.[83]

US law is well established that non-exclusive patent,[84] copyright,[85] and trademark[86] licences are personal in nature and therefore they are non-delegable and non-assignable. Accordingly, non-bankruptcy law excuses a non-debtor–licensor that does not consent to an assignment from accepting performance from an entity other than the debtor–licensee; and, consequently, the Bankruptcy Code prohibits a trustee or debtor in possession from assigning away its licensee rights under a non-exclusive patent, copyright, or trademark licence.[87] The law is somewhat less clear regarding the ability of a debtor–licensee of an exclusive IP licence to assign away its licensee rights. As discussed in detail in Section 3.1(c) above, different types of exclusive IP licences may be assignable.

### (c) *Assumption without assignment*

As discussed in Section 3.1(b) above, in order for a trustee or debtor in possession to assign an executory contract such as an IP licence, that trustee or debtor in possession must first assume it.[88] Accordingly, if a particular executory contract is not assumable, it is unequivocally not assignable. Conversely, one of the greatest current debates in US bankruptcy law is whether an executory contract may be assumable, even if it is not assignable.

Circuit courts generally follow one of two primary tests to determine whether a licence is assumable even if it is not assignable: the 'actual test' or the 'hypothetical test'. The relevant statutory provision, 11 USC §365(c), provides pertinent information in part, as follows:

> ...
>
> *(c) The trustee [or debtor in possession] may not assume or assign any executory contract ... of the debtor, whether or not such contract ... prohibits or restricts assignment of rights or delegation of duties, if –*
>
> *(1)(A) applicable law excuses a party, other than the debtor, to such contract ... from accepting performance from or rendering performance to an entity other than the debtor or the debtor in possession, whether or not such contract ... prohibits or restricts assignment of rights or delegation of duties; and*
>
> *(B) such party does not consent to such assumption or assignment ... .*

---

82 11 USC §365(b)(1).
83 11 USC §365(c)(1)(A).
84 See, eg, *CFLC*, 89 F.3d at 679 (summarising cases).
85 See, eg, *In re Valley Media, Inc* 279 BR 105, 135 (Bankr D Del 2002).
86 See, eg, *In re XMH Corp* 647 F3d 690, 695 (7th Cir 2011).
87 11 USC §365(c)(1)(A).
88 11 USC §365(f)(2)(A).

The *Perlman* case,[89] heard in the ninth circuit, effectively describes each test. In *Perlman*, the court began its analysis by noting that "federal patent law makes nonexclusive patent licences personal and nondelegable".[90] Accordingly, the ninth circuit concluded that the condition set forth in §365(c)(1)(A) was satisfied. Furthermore, the licensor objected to the debtor–licensee's assumption of the patent licences, so §365(c)(1)(B) was also satisfied.[91] The ninth circuit then focused its analysis on the words "assume or assign" in §365(c) and noted that some courts interpret that language according to the so-called 'actual test'. Under the 'actual test' view of §365(c), a court should prohibit a trustee or debtor in possession from assuming and assigning a non-exclusive patent licence only if the trustee or debtor in possession actually intended to assign away its licensee rights. If the trustee or debtor in possession merely intended to assume those rights and to continue to enjoy the benefits of the licence itself, then, under the 'actual test' view:

- the non-debtor party would not have to accept performance from an entity other than the debtor;
- the whole reason for prohibiting assumption and assignment was absent; and
- accordingly, the trustee or debtor in possession should be permitted to assume the licence.[92]

The ninth circuit observed that the first circuit,[93] and many lower courts, had adopted the actual test for §365(c) analyses.[94] The ninth circuit, however, chose to follow the so-called 'hypothetical test'. Under this test, a court literally reads §365(c) to prevent assumption or assignment of the executory contract at issue if the conditions set forth in subparagraphs (A) and (B) of §365(c)(1) are present – ie, the bankruptcy court asks the hypothetical question as to whether applicable non-bankruptcy law would excuse the other party to the contract from accepting performance from an entity other than the debtor (regardless of whether the trustee or debtor in possession actually intends to assign away the contract rights to such an entity). If so, then, under the 'hypothetical test' view, the trustee or debtor in possession may not even assume that executory contract without the licensor's consent.[95]

While the US ninth circuit decided to adopt the hypothetical test, a split remains among the circuits, with several remaining undecided.[96] Notably unique, though, is the Second Circuit Court of Appeals, which includes the Southern District of New York, a popular bankruptcy forum for companies located in New York. The second

---

89 *Perlman v Catapult Ent'm't, Inc (In re Catapult Ent'm't, Inc)* 165 F3d 747 (9th Cir 1999).
90 *Id* at 750.
91 *Id* at 750–51.
92 *Id* at 751.
93 See *Institut Pasteur v Cambridge Biotech Corp*, 104 F3d 489, 493 (1st Cir 1997).
94 See *Catapult* at footnote 89 above, at 749 n2.
95 *Id* at 749.
96 Circuits adopting the 'actual test': first circuit (see *Institut Pasteur v Cambridge Biotech Corp* 104 F3d 489 (1st Cir 1996)); fifth circuit (see *Bonneville Power Admin v Mirant Corp (In re Mirant Corp)* 440 F3d 238 (5th Cir 2006)). Circuits adopting the 'hypothetical test': third circuit (see *In re West Elecs, Inc* 852 F2d 79 (3rd Cir 1988)); fourth circuit (see *RCI Tech Corp v Sunterra Corp (In re Sunterra Corp)* 361 F3d 257 (4th Cir 2004)); ninth circuit (see *Perlman* 165 F3d 747); and the 11th circuit (see *City of Jamestown v James Cable Partners (In re James Cable Partners)* 27 F3d 534 (11th Cir 1994)). Unsettled circuits: sixth circuit, seventh circuit, eighth circuit, 10th circuit, and the DC circuit.

circuit itself has not ruled on this issue regarding the right of a debtor–licensee to assume an executory contract, but one bankruptcy court within the second circuit has taken a novel approach to the issue, although not in an IP context. Instead of the actual test or the hypothetical test being used, the *Footstar* court[97] granted the motion of the debtors in possession to assume a potentially non-assignable executory contract by focusing on the word 'trustee' in §365(c), which provides that "the trustee may not assume or assign any executory contract ...".[98] Specifically, the Footstar court reasoned that §365(c) and its prohibitions on the ability of trustees to assume and assign executory contracts do not apply to debtors in possession, such as the *Footstar* entities.[99] Accordingly, under the *Footstar* analysis, a Chapter 11 debtor in possession does not need to satisfy the conditions set forth in §365(c) before assuming an executory contract.

At least one other bankruptcy court in the Southern District of New York has followed the *Footstar* approach and has permitted a debtor in possession to assume an executory contract without conducting an analysis under §365(c).[100]

Thus, it appears that whether a debtor–licensee will be permitted to assume a non-exclusive IP licence over the objection of the licensor is currently venue-dependent. The US Supreme Court has acknowledged the split among the circuit courts of appeal on this issue, but it has not yet granted certiorari to resolve the dispute.[101]

### 3.7 Powers and rights of creditors in the licensee's bankruptcy

As discussed in detail in section 3.6 above, a creditor who is the licensor of IP rights may object to the debtor–licensee's election to assume, or to assume and assign, an IP licence. Whether the bankruptcy court will permit the debtor–licensee to assume, or to assume and assign, the IP rights at issue, over the licensor's objection, will depend upon whether the licence is exclusive or non-exclusive – and currently it may even depend upon the circuit in which the bankruptcy case is pending.

Any party in interest, including a creditor, may object to a decision by a trustee or debtor in possession to assume or to reject an IP licence. However, a party making such an objection must prove that the decision of the trustee or debtor in possession violates the business judgement rule.[102] This is a difficult standard to meet, requiring the objecting party to show the assume-or-reject decision to be "so manifestly unreasonable that it could not be based on sound business judgment, but only on bad faith, or whim, or caprice".[103]

### 3.8 Exclusive and non-exclusive licences

As stated in section 3.7 above, whether a debtor may assume and assign an IP licence depends in part upon whether the licence is exclusive or non-exclusive. Under US law,

---

97 See *In re Footstar, Inc*, 323 BR 566 (Bankr SDNY 2005).
98 11 USC §365(c).
99 See *Footstar*, at 571–75.
100 See *In re Adelphia Commc'ns Corp* 359 BR 65, 72 (Bankr SDNY 2007).
101 See *NCP Mktg Group, Inc v BG Star Prods, Inc* 556 US 1145, 129 S Ct 1577 (2009) (statement of Kennedy J respecting denial of cert).
102 See *Pomona Valley* at footnote 54 above, at 669–70.
103 *Id* at 670 (quoting *Lubrizol*, at 1047).

non-exclusive IP licences are generally considered personal in nature, and they cannot be assumed and assigned by a debtor–licensee. Depending upon the type of intellectual property that is the subject of the licence, and as discussed in Section 3.1(c) above, a debtor–licensee may in some instances assume and assign an exclusive licence.

### 3.9 Perpetual and non-perpetual licences

US bankruptcy law treats perpetual and non-perpetual licences in the same manner. The key issue is whether the IP licence at issue is an executory contract,[104] not whether it is perpetual.

### 3.10 Effects on a sub-licence in a licensor's bankruptcy

US bankruptcy law does not directly address sub-licences, and courts have not resolved the extent to which 11 USC §365(n) applies to sub-licensees.[105] In view of courts' treatment of potentially analogous portions of the Bankruptcy Code, such as 11 USC §365(h) pertaining to real property leases, if a debtor–licensor rejects the original licence and the original licensee declines to elect to maintain its licensee rights under §365(n), then a sub-licensee may be left to the protections of non-bankruptcy law. Under non-bankruptcy law, the termination of the original licence ordinarily results in the termination of the sub-licence.

### 3.11 Effects on a sub-licence in a licensee's bankruptcy

US bankruptcy law does not directly address sub-licences, and courts have not resolved the extent to which 11 USC §365(n) applies to sub-licensees.[106] In view of courts' treatment of potentially analogous portions of the Bankruptcy Code, such as 11 USC §365(h) pertaining to real property leases, if a debtor–licensee rejects the original licence, then a sub-licensee may be left to the protections of non-bankruptcy law. Under non-bankruptcy law, the termination of the original licence ordinarily results in the termination of the sub-licence. However, if the debtor–licensee assumes the original licence but then attempts to reject the sub-licence, the fact that the sub-licence is a separate IP licence may entitle the sub-licensee to invoke the protection of 11 USC §365(n).

### 3.12 Impact of registration

As discussed in section 2.5 above, any party may register an IP licence agreement by recording it at the US Patent and Trademark Office. The registration or recordation of an IP licence agreement provides third parties with constructive notice of the existence of the licence. In general, the primary benefit of providing such constructive notice is to prevent third parties from claiming the status of a '*bona fide* purchaser without notice', who could potentially take an interest in the intellectual property at issue that would be superior to the debtor's interest.

---

104 See section 3.1(a) above.

105 See Michelle M Harner and David A Beck, "Sublicensing from a Distressed Company", *ABI Journal* 25(7), September 2006; and Gregory W Wekheiser, "Intellectual Bankruptcy?", *Delaware Lawyer* 26(3), Winter 2008–09.

106 *Id.*

Recordation of licences with the US Patent and Trademark Office is not mandatory. Trademark licences may be recorded in the discretion of the Commissioner of Patents and Trademarks, even though such recordation does not transfer title to the mark or convey the entire title or interest in the business with which the mark is used.[107] Trademark licences may be recorded in the public interest to give other parties notification of a record of equitable interest or of other matters relevant to the ownership of a mark. The US Patent and Trademark Office does not examine the substance of the document, nor its effect on the title of the mark.[108]

## 4. Contractual arrangements in deviation from the law

### 4.1 Exceptions

No specific exceptions exist for individual types of intellectual property under US bankruptcy law.

### 4.2 Scope to alter statutory mechanisms

A bankruptcy court may enforce a contractual provision through which a non-debtor party provides pre-petition consent to the post-petition assumption and assignment of the contract.[109] Accordingly, generally speaking, if a contractual provision works to deprive the debtor of some right or benefit as a consequence of the existence of the bankruptcy case, that provision is likely to be unenforceable. However, if the contractual provision conveys some right or benefit to the debtor as a consequence of the existence of the bankruptcy case, then a bankruptcy court is likely to enforce it. See also section 4.3 below.

### 4.3 Termination rights and automatic reversions

Many contracts contain provisions that cause the termination of the agreement, or cause a party to lose certain rights, if that party becomes insolvent or files a bankruptcy petition. The Bankruptcy Code is extremely hostile to parties' pre-petition attempts to contract around bankruptcy law through the use of such provisions.

With respect to property of the bankruptcy estate, 11 USC §541(c)(1) provides that any interest of the debtor in property becomes part of the bankruptcy estate notwithstanding any provision that either restricts the transfer to the bankruptcy estate or conditions forfeiture or modification of the interest in the insolvency of the debtor, the appointment of a trustee or the commencement of a bankruptcy case.[110]

Likewise, with respect to executory contracts, 11 USC §365(e)(1) provides that no provision, right or obligation under an executory contract can be terminated or modified by a provision in the contract conditioned on:

- the insolvency of the debtor;

---

107 37 CFR §3.11.

108 See J Thomas McCarthy, *McCarthy on Trademarks and Unfair Competition*, §18:12 at 18–33 and 34.

109 See *Metropolitan Airports Comm'n v Northwest Airlines, Inc (In re Midway Airlines, Inc)* 6 F3d 492 (7th Cir 1993).

110 11 USC §541(c)(1).

- the commencement of a bankruptcy case; or
- the appointment of a bankruptcy trustee.[111]

## 5. Cross-border aspects

In 2005, the US Congress amended the Bankruptcy Code by adding Chapter 15, which is entitled "Ancillary and Other Cross-Border Cases".[112] The Bankruptcy Code itself states, "The purpose of this chapter [15] is to incorporate the Model Law on Cross-Border Insolvency so as to provide effective mechanisms for dealing with cases of cross-border insolvency ... ."[113] In sum, Chapter 15 permits the representative of a debtor in a foreign bankruptcy or insolvency proceeding to seek US recognition of that foreign case and thereby to obtain bankruptcy protection.

To commence a Chapter 15 case, a foreign representative must file in a US bankruptcy court an application for recognition of the foreign bankruptcy proceeding.[114] If the application meets relatively modest requirements, then the bankruptcy court will enter an order recognising the foreign proceeding,[115] which will immediately provide the foreign representative with certain relief, including the automatic stay of all efforts by creditors to attempt to collect on a claim against the foreign debtor and the ability to operate the foreign debtor's business.[116]

The foreign representative may also apply to the bankruptcy court for other relief, including the ability to assume or reject executory contracts.[117] The bankruptcy court has discretion to grant or to deny additional relief, as it sees fit, "to protect the assets of the debtor or the interests of the creditors".[118] In addition, the Bankruptcy Code provides that "nothing in this chapter [15] prevents the court from refusing to take an action governed by this chapter [15] if the action would be manifestly contrary to the public policy of the United States".[119]

### 5.1 Foreign law

US bankruptcy law is well equipped to recognise foreign bankruptcy proceedings and to protect the interests of foreign debtors. Nevertheless, when foreign debtors' interests conflict with US law and with the concerns of domestic creditors and other interested parties, US courts will carefully balance the parties' interests, and they may decline to apply foreign bankruptcy law.

Applying this balancing test, a circuit court recently held that when a foreign debtor attempted to reject patent licences held by US licensees, the licensees could retain their licensee rights under 11 USC §365(n), contradicting the applicable foreign law.[120]

---

111 11 USC §365(e)(1).
112 See 11 USC §§1501–1532.
113 11 USC §1501(a).
114 11 USC §§1504, 1509, & 1515.
115 11 USC §1517.
116 11 USC §1520.
117 11 USC §1521.
118 11 USC §1521(a).
119 11 USC §1506.
120 See *Jaffe v Samsung Elecs Co, Ltd* 737 F3d 14, 32 (4th Cir 2013), petition for cert filed, No 13-1324, 2014 WL 172586 (US April 30 2014). The fourth circuit affirmed the district court's conclusion based upon its balancing of the various parties' interests, but it did not adopt the district court's alternative public policy ground for applying 11 USC §365(n).

### 5.2 Foreign jurisdiction

In general, a contractual provision cannot waive a debtor's right to receive protection under the Bankruptcy Code.[121] Thus, a debtor's right to seek bankruptcy protection in the United States will not be restricted by a contract purporting to elect a foreign jurisdiction. However, a bankruptcy court's jurisdiction is limited to certain issues sufficiently related to the debtor's bankruptcy case, and that jurisdiction may not extend to general contract disputes involving a licence agreement.[122]

Outside any bankruptcy issues, contractual elections of foreign jurisdiction are generally enforceable under US law.[123]

121 See *In re Huang* 275 F3d 1173, 1177 (9th Cir 2002).

122 See *In re Ray* 624 F3d 1124, 1130 (9th Cir 2010) (discussing the scope of a bankruptcy court's jurisdiction and holding that a contract claim fell outside the proper scope of that jurisdiction).

123 See *M/S Bremen v Zapata Off-Shore Co* 407 US 1, 15 (1972); see also *Martinez v Bloomberg LP*, 740 F3d 211, 217 (2nd Cir 2014).

# About the authors

**Gustavo A Alcocer**
Partner, Olivares & CIA
gustavo.alcocer@olivares.com.mx

Gustavo A Alcocer joined Olivares as a partner in 1999. He manages the corporate and commercial law group and is co-chair of the life sciences and pharmaceuticals group. Before joining Olivares, he acted as in-house counsel for Banamex for 11 years in various positions, including vice president of international legal affairs in New York and executive vice president and assistant general counsel for Grupo Financiero Banamex in Mexico City.

Mr Alcocer possesses a wealth of transactional experience in mergers and acquisitions, finance and business law, and advises clients on complex mergers and acquisitions, finance, asset sales and acquisition, licensing, franchising, real estate transactional work and regulatory work. Clients routinely turn to him for sophisticated strategic advice regarding structuring, maintaining and expanding operations in Mexico and IP valuation and monetisation. In addition, Mr Alcocer has worked with international companies in Foreign Corrupt Practices Act and anti-bribery compliance, as well as privacy and personal data protection.

**Axel Anderl**
Partner, DORDA BRUGGER JORDIS
axel.anderl@dbj.at

Axel Anderl heads DORDA BRUGGER JORDIS's IT/IP and media department. His practice covers the drafting and negotiation of international IT-related contracts, outsourcing, license, franchising and distribution contracts, social media advice, as well as IT/IP and media litigation.

Dr Anderl is the author of numerous expert publications on IT and IP law and contributed to the standard commentary on the Austrian Unfair Competition and Copyright Act. He also lectures on a regular basis and is a member of the Austrian Bar Association and ITechLaw.

Dr Anderl graduated from the University of Vienna (*Mag iur* 2000, *Dr iur* 2004) and completed his LLM in IT law with distinction in 2001. With his admission to the Austrian Bar in September 2005, he joined DORDA BRUGGER JORDIS as a partner.

Dr Anderl is recognised by international directories such as *Legal 500* and Chambers, and in national rankings as a leading IT lawyer.

**Peter Armstrong**
Partner, Harbottle & Lewis LLP
peter.armstrong@harbottle.com

Peter Armstrong is a partner at leading London-based law firm Harbottle & Lewis LLP, which is best known for its work advising clients involved in the creation, development and exploitation of IP and other rights, including leading names in the entertainment, media and technology industries.

Mr Armstrong acts for a number of major Hollywood studios on IP rights and production legal matters, as well as for independent film and television producers and other rights owners in the United Kingdom and abroad. He is a past co-chair of the IP and Entertainment Law Committee of the International Bar Association.

**Gusztáv Bacher**
Partner, Szecskay Attorneys at Law
gusztav.bacher@szecskay.com

Gusztáv Bacher is a Hungarian attorney admitted to the Budapest Bar Association. He joined Szecskay Attorneys at Law in 1999, and specialises in civil, competition, advertising and IP law and litigation. In 2012 Dr Bacher was elected as president of the International League of Competition Law, having served as secretary general (2007-2010) and as first vice president (2010-2012). He became chairman of the Ethics Commission of the Hungarian Advertising Association in 2011. Furthermore, he is a member of the IP Expert Committee and Copyright Expert Committee attached to the Hungarian Patent Office, the National Board Against Counterfeiting and Piracy and the board of the Hungarian Association for the Protection of Industrial Property and Copyright. He is vice chairman of the Hungarian Group of the International Association for the Protection of Intellectual Property.

**Mark Bedford**
Partner, Boughton Peterson Yang Anderson
in association with Zhong Lun Law Firm
mbedford@bpya.com.hk
markbedford@zhonglun.com

Mark Bedford is a partner specialising in commercial dispute resolution at Boughton Peterson Yang Anderson. He was admitted as a solicitor in England and Wales in 1990 and practised in London for several years before relocating to Hong Kong, where he was admitted as a solicitor in 1998. His practice focuses on domestic and international litigation and arbitration. He advises Hong Kong, Mainland Chinese and international clients on disputes concerning debt recovery, sale of goods and international trade, construction and engineering, professional negligence, employment and shareholders, as well as on insolvency issues.

**Agustín Bou**
Partner, JAUSAS
abou@jausaslegal.com

Agustín Bou is a partner of Spanish law firm JAUSAS and director of its restructuring and insolvency department. He is a renowned expert in providing legal advice to troubled companies on temporary receivership and bankruptcy proceedings. He has been involved in some of the biggest insolvency proceedings in Spain as insolvency administrator or representing debtors and creditors.

Further, Mr Bou has extensive experience in M&A and other special corporate operations. He has been a pioneer in promoting the purchase of productive units during bankruptcy proceedings as the best way to invest in a sector. He was co-chairman of the Insolvency, Restructuring and Creditors' Rights Section of the International Bar Association from 2004 to 2006.

He is a regular columnist in general and specialist newspapers and magazines, with a focus on restructuring and insolvency, as well as corporate matters.

**Christopher R Brown**
Barrister, Lonsdale Chambers, Melbourne
cbrown@vicbar.com.au

Christopher Brown practises in commercial law, particularly in the areas of insolvency, banking and finance, corporations and securities, and equity. He has an extensive business background and holds an MBA from Melbourne Business School and a JD from Melbourne Law School. He appears in many commercial matters in all jurisdictions, but mostly appears in trials and interlocutory hearings in the Supreme Court of Victoria, the Supreme Court New of South Wales, the Federal Court of Australia and the Federal Circuit Court of Australia.

Mr Brown is co-author of *Australian Corporation Law Principles and Practice* (LexisNexis) and *Bankruptcy Law and Practice* (LexisNexis). He is also a nationally accredited mediator, mediating in most areas of commercial law, and a full member of the Australian Restructuring Insolvency and Turnaround Association.

**Arly Carlquist**
Partner, Bech-Bruun, Copenhagen
ac@bechbrunn.com

Arly Carlquist, a partner in the IP and technology department of Bech-Bruun, represents a wide range of clients within the IP, IT and other technology-related industries.

Mr Carlquist is highly experienced in intellectual property, including all copyright law issues, and has extensive experience in the enforcement of IP rights in relation to cases concerning the illegal copying of software, music, computer games and films.

Moreover, Mr Carlquist has extensive experience with respect to IT law, such as system development and delivery, outsourcing, hosting and cloud computing. He also advises clients on the drafting of software and patent licence agreements, as well as in connection with other technology-based fields.

Mr Carlquist is co-author of the book *Retshåndhævelse af immaterialrettigheder*, covering all aspects of IP rights enforcement in Denmark.

**Orçun Çetinkaya**
Partner, GÜN + PARTNERS
orcun.cetinkaya@gun.av.tr

Orçun Çetinkaya is a disputes partner advising on a broad range of issues, including shareholder and partnership disputes, joint venture, agency, professional negligence and employment disputes, contractual claims and defamation. His work often involves multi-jurisdictional actions in Russia, the United States, Europe and worldwide. He advises local and multinational companies in complex fraud, bribery, corruption and tax cases, as well as on anti-corruption schemes and procedures. He advises on the local implications and interpretations of the US Foreign Corrupt Practices Act and the UK Anti-bribery Act.

He has a significant presence in the construction and real estate sectors and advises and represents project sponsors, contractors, financiers and government bodies on major construction, engineering and project-financings in Turkey and Russia.

**Carsten Ceutz**
Partner, Bech-Bruun, Copenhagen
cac@bechbruun.com

Carsten Ceutz, a partner in the restructuring department of Bech-Bruun, represents financial creditors with exposure through financial and operational leasing, loans to and charges over cooperative housing associations in distress, possession and administration of receivable charges and floating company charges, as well as the initiation and administration of company restructuring procedures.

As supervisor, administrator or trustee of many restructured businesses and estates in bankruptcy, Mr Ceutz employs his substantial professional expertise to safeguard the interests of estates in bankruptcy and creditors. He has vast experience in administering the bankrupt estates of travel agencies and in the management of information technology, rights and employees in connection with company restructurings and insolvency.

Mr Ceutz and his partners work with specialists in order to reach the best possible solutions for companies and creditors. They have developed a comprehensive national and international network of contacts, providing quick access to accountants, engineers, consultants and appraisers so that they can assemble a multi-disciplinary team of legal and business professionals at short notice.

**Tim Creek**
Senior associate, Davies Collison Cave Law
tcreek@davies.com.au

Tim Creek's practice involves contentious and non-contentious IP law matters, with a focus on the commercialisation of IP rights.

His non-contentious practice includes the preparation and negotiation of commercial agreements for all IP and related rights across a variety of industries, including telecommunications, broadcasting and entertainment, financial, arts, medical device and pharmaceuticals, and he has also acted for government and non-profit organisations. Mr Creek regularly advises on consumer protection and trade practice issues. He has also worked as in-house counsel where he advised on, among other thing, licensing, distribution and finance arrangements, privacy, corporate law and governance issues.

Mr Creek is a member of the Licensing Executives Society of Australia and New Zealand, the Intellectual Property Society of Australia and New Zealand and the Australian Corporate Lawyers Association.

**Rodney De Boos**
Consultant, Davies Collison Cave Law
rdeboos@davies.com.au

Rodney De Boos' major area of practice is the commercial exploitation of IP rights. His practice includes the negotiation and preparation of commercial agreements, covering the full spectrum of IP rights and transactions. He also practises in the trade practices (antitrust) area. He provides advice and has acted for both companies and individuals in prosecutions by and applications to the Australian Competition and Consumer Commission.

Mr De Boos has lectured in IP licensing at a postgraduate level for many years and is the author of many published articles, both in Australia and internationally, as well as the chapter on the exploitation of patents in *Laws of Australia* (Law Book Company).

In 1998 Mr De Boos was president of the Licensing Executives Society International, and was subsequently awarded the society's Gold Medal.

**Amélie Dorst**
Associate, BMH Avocats
adorst@bmhavocats.com

Amélie Dorst is a member of the corporate/restructuring group of BMH Avocats in Paris.

She specialises in international transactions (cross-border mergers and acquisitions, distressed mergers and acquisitions and corporate finance) and in corporate restructurings and reorganisations.

Her experience includes advising banks, funds, insolvency practitioners and companies in relation to a wide range of transactions, including financial restructurings, cross-border acquisition finance and general bank lending.

**Anja Droege Gagnier**
Partner, BMH Avocats, Paris
adroege@bmhavocats.com

Anja Droege Gagnier, admitted to the Paris Bar in 1994, is head of the corporate/restructuring group of boutique law firm BMH Avocats in Paris.

Ms Droege Gagnier has gained broad experience for more than 20 years in international transactions (cross-border mergers and acquisitions, joint ventures, distressed mergers and acquisitions and corporate finance) and in corporate restructurings and reorganisations (out-of-court and formal insolvency proceedings) in various industries (real estate, printing, steel, aeronautic, automotive, nuclear, petrol/oil refinery business, cogeneration energy, transport and infrastructure projects, medical instruments, life science, biotech, and luxury goods). She advises mainly foreign corporations, financial institutions, stakeholders and insolvency practitioners.

Ms Droege Gagnier is vice chair of the Insolvency Section of the International Bar Association and is a member of INSOL Europe. She was part of the experts group set up by the Universities of Heidelberg and Vienna retained by the European Commission for the evaluation study of the EU Insolvency Regulation and the reform proposals addressed to the European Commission in November 2012.

**Gabor Faludi**
Of counsel, Szecskay Attorneys at Law
gabor.faludi@szecskay.com

Gabor Faludi is of counsel at Szecskay Attorneys at Law, a law firm with an international clientele and scope of activities, and specialises in civil and commercial law, particularly IP and e-commerce law. As one of the firm's most accomplished attorneys, he is a highly recognised expert in the field of copyright law, having gained extensive experience with the Hungarian Copyright Protection Agency. He also provides advice and assistance in connection with the protection of copyright relating to, among other things, literary, musical, commercial, software and database protection and licensing.

Dr Faludi is an associate professor of law at Eötvös Loránd University. He is also a board member of the Hungarian Association for the Protection of Industrial Property and a member of the Copyright Experts Committee, the Council for the Protection of Intellectual Property attached to the National Patent Office and the Electronic Telecommunications Arbitration Board.

**Shinnosuke Fukuoka**
Partner, Nishimura & Asahi
s_fukuoka@jurists.co.jp

Shinnosuke Fukuoka is a partner in the restructuring/insolvency group of Nishimura & Asahi. He has been involved in numerous restructuring and insolvency cases, representating both debtor parties and creditor parties. Most recently, he represented Japan Airlines as a legal cousel of the debtor and Takefuji and Elpida as a creditor's counsel. He has also contributed to many publications relating to restructuring and insolvency, including *An Overview of Chinese Insolvency Law*, *Legal Practice of Turnaround ADR and DIP Type Corporate Reorganization* and *An Overview of the United States Bankruptcy Law*.

**Rahul Goel**
Partner, Dhir & Dhir Associates, Advocates & Solicitors
rahul.goel@dhirassociates.com

Rahul Goel is a partner and his practice focuses on IP law, competition/antitrust law, international trade and World Trade Organisation law (including anti-dumping law), IT law media and broadcasting law, telecommunications law, privacy and data protection law and food and drug law. Mr Goel has completed an LLM in information technology, media and e-commerce laws at the University of Essex, United Kingdom. He was recently nominated by *Indian Lawyer 250* (published by Law Business Research) as a leading Indian lawyer under 45.

**F Müjgan Güngör**
Associate, GÜN + PARTNERS
mujgan.gungor@gun.av.tr

Müjgan Güngör is an associate in the dispute resolution department of GÜN + PARTNERS since 2012. She mainly concentrates on commercial dispute resolution, debt collection matters and other commercial law issues. She also takes part in construction and real estate-related projects and labour law-related disputes of both national and international companies investing and doing business in Turkey.

**Sandeep Kumar Gupta**
Associate partner, Dhir & Dhir Associates, Advocates & Solicitors
sandeep.gupta@dhirassociates.com

Sandeep Kumar Gupta is an associate partner in Dhir & Dhir Associates, Advocates & Solicitors. He is a qualified chartered accountant with 20 years' extensive experience in banking, project finance and debt restructuring of entities in distress, both through the corporate debt restructuring mechanism and on a bilateral basis. He is part of the firm's corporate consultancy team, advising clients on matters related to settlements with lenders and other insolvency-related issues.

**Toshihide Haruyama**
Attorney, Nishimura & Asahi
t_haruyama@jurists.co.jp

Toshihide Haruyama is an attorney at law at Nishimura & Asahi. He has worked in various areas of practice, including product liability disputes, US litigation involving cross-border discovery issues, cross-border M&A transactions, corporate restructuring and bankruptcy matters. He is a graduate of Keio University (LLB, 2009) and was admitted to practise law in Japan in 2010.

**Craig J Hill**
Partner, Borden Ladner Gervais LLP
chill@blg.com

Craig J Hill is a partner and Toronto region leader in the insolvency and restructuring group of Borden Ladner Gervais LLP. Mr Hill specialises in advising trustees, receivers, monitors and other court-appointed officers with respect to various insolvency proceedings and, in particular, advising trustees in bankruptcy and compensation funds regarding insolvencies of regulated securities firms. Most recently, Mr Hill acted for the trustee in bankruptcy of MF Global Canada and has acted for customer compensation funds in various other securities firm insolvencies, including First Leaside Securities. He acted for the monitor in the Companies' Creditors Arrangement Act proceedings relating to the C$36 billion ABCP restructuring, the largest restructuring in Canadian history. Mr Hill is a member of the Insolvency Institute of Canada, co-chair of the Insolvency Institute of Canada (IIC) Task Force on Pension Reform relating to insolvency matters and a member of the IIC's Joint Task Force on Insolvency Review regarding proposed amendments to the Bankruptcy and Insolvency Act.

**John W Holcomb**
Litigation partner, Knobbe, Martens, Olson & Bear, LLP
john.holcomb@knobbe.com

John Holcomb is a partner in the Irvine, California office of Knobbe Martens. For the past 20 years he has litigated all types of IP dispute in state and federal court, including cases involving patents, copyrights, trademarks, trade secrets and unfair competition. Mr Holcomb also counsels clients on bankruptcy and insolvency matters, particularly as they affect IP rights. Mr Holcomb earned an engineering degree from the Massachusetts Institute of Technology and law and business graduate degrees from Harvard University. Before beginning private practice, Mr Holcomb clerked for Bankruptcy Judge Ronald Barliant in Chicago. Mr Holcomb serves on a number of bar organisations and committees, including the boards of the local chapters of the Federal Bar Association and the Association of Business Trial Lawyers. Mr Holcomb also volunteers his time as a member of the Attorney Mediation Panel and the Magistrate Judge Merit Selection Panel of the Central District of California.

**Felix Hörlsberger**
Partner, DORDA BRUGGER JORDIS
felix.hoerlsberger@dbj.at

Felix Hörlsberger is head of DORDA BRUGGER JORDIS's restructuring and insurance/insurance litigation department.

Dr Hörlsberger is the author of numerous expert publications, mostly related to insurance law, data privacy, banking and corporate law. He also lectures at seminars on compliance, directors' duties, directors' and officers' insurance and cash pooling.

He graduated from the University of Vienna (*Dr iur* 2003 with distinction) and from the Vienna University of Economics and Business Administration (*Mag rer soc oec* 2003). He was admitted to the Austrian Bar in 2006 and became a partner in 2009. He is a member of the Austrian Lawyers' Club and the International Bar Association (insurance, litigation). Dr Hörlsberger is a founding member and vice president of the Young Austrian Commercial Litigation Association.

Dr Hörlsberger is recognised for his insurance and litigation expertise in *Legal 500* (Dispute Resolution: recommended), *Chambers Europe* (Dispute Resolution: Band 4) and PLC *Which Lawyer* (recommended).

**Yuval Horn**
Founder, Horn & Co – Law Offices
yhorn@hornlaw.co.il

Yuval Horn is the founder of Horn & Co, Law Offices, a leading technology practice based in Tel Aviv, Israel. The firm comprises 14 lawyers and two articled clerks, and represents Israeli and international technology-focused companies, founders, investors and board members. The firm regularily advises its clients on private and public financings (in the United States, the United Kingdom and Israel), mergers and acquisitions, and international corporate reorganisations, and on all legal aspects of operations of high-tech and life sciences companies, including licensing and sale of technology, joint ventures, commercial transactions and labour law issues. Mr Horn is the former chair of the Life Sciences Subcommittee of the International Bar Association Technology Committee. He is a member of the Institutional Review Board (Helsinki) Committee at the Sheba Medical Centre in Tel Hashomer, Israel, and has been ranked as a leading Israeli practioner in various international publications. Mr Horn was identified by *The International Who's Who of Life Science Lawyers* 2013 as one of five leading individuals worldwide in life sciences transactions.

**Pekka Jaatinen**
Senior partner, Castrén & Snellman Attorneys Ltd
pekka.jaatinen@castren.fi

Throughout his long career Pekka Jaatinen has specialised in mergers and acquisitions, insolvency and corporate law. He has advised large financial institutions and other clients, acting as a leading legal counsel in relation to both domestic and international transactions, restructurings and insolvency proceedings. He is well recognised for acting as a trustee and administrator of the majority of the largest Finnish bankruptcy estates and restructuring proceedings. Mr Jaatinen is also a board member of several domestic and international companies. He is the co-chair of the Insolvency Section of the International Bar Association and a Finnish member of the International Insolvency Institute. *Chambers Europe*, *Chambers Global*, *Best Lawyers* and PLC *Which Lawyer* have ranked Mr Jaatinen among Finland's leading legal experts.

**David Jenny**
Partner, VISCHER AG
djenny@vischer.com

David Jenny is a partner of VISCHER AG, a major Swiss law firm with offices in Basel and Zurich. He has been advising and representing corporations since 1991 in transactions and corporate and commercial matters. In the insolvency field, he acts as a liquidator and advises governing bodies of corporations and creditors. Mr Jenny is one of the authors of the leading commentary on the Swiss Bankruptcy Code, and also acts as an arbitrator. He is a member of various boards of directors and foundation councils. Mr Jenny was president of the Basel Bar Association and co-chair of the Insolvency, Restructuring and Creditors' Rights Section, now the Insolvency Section, of the International Bar Association. He holds *lic iur* (1984) and *Dr iur* (1988) degrees from the University of Basel and an LLM (1989) from the University of Michigan Law School.

**Keren Kanir**
Partner, Horn & Co – Law Offices
kkanir@hornlaw.co.il

Keren Kanir has been a partner with Horn & Co (formerly Baratz, Horn & Co) since January 2007. Ms Kanir is an expert in corporate finance and commercial transactions relating to intellectual property.

Ms Kanir has significant expertise in the representation of public and private companies and venture capital funds. Ms Kanir has advised parties to complex cross-border transactions, mergers, private rounds of investment led by major venture capital funds and angel investors, licensing and joint development agreements involving academic institutions and companies, the incorporation of companies and ongoing representation of their corporate and commercial interests.

Ms Kanir has been a member of the Israel Bar Association since 2001 and a member of the New York State Bar Association since 2004. She is a graduate of Tel Aviv University (LLB, 1999; BA in Middle East studies, 2000) and received her LLM from Northwestern University (with honours) in 2003.

**Merve Karaduman**
Associate, GÜN + PARTNERS
merve.karaduman@gun.av.tr

Merve Karaduman is an associate in the corporate and commercial law department; dispute resolution, construction and real estate, business crimes and anti-corruption practice groups of GÜN + PARTNERS since 2009. She concentrates on commercial dispute resolution, preparation and negotiation of contracts, IP law matters and other commercial law issues. She has extensive experience on construction and real estate-related projects and disputes, expropriation, lease, debt collection matters, insolvency procedures and business crimes, and she has handled various disputes where these practice areas overlap. She has represented and assisted a number of multinational companies investing and doing business in Turkey, especially in their real estate investment projects.

**Martin Kelleher**
Partner, Mason Hayes & Curran
mkelleher@MHC.ie

Martin Kelleher is a partner in the firm's corporate group and head of life sciences. He has extensive experience in corporate and commercial law, with particular focus on acting on technology transactions in the information and communications technology and life sciences sectors.

Mr Kelleher's broad corporate practice includes advising on domestic and cross-border mergers and acquisitions, venture capital and private equity transactions, reorganisations and fundraisings. He also has significant experience in the commercialisation of intellectual property, and represents technology companies, state bodies and third-level universities in this specialist area.

Mr Kelleher has an MBA from Cranfield University, School of Management and was a recipient of the JP O'Reilly Scholarship from the Law Society of Ireland.

**Dávid Kerpel**
Associate, Szecskay Attorneys at Law
david.kerpel@szecskay.com

David Kerpel is a Hungarian attorney admitted to the Budapest Bar Association. He joined Szecskay Attorneys at Law in 2008. Dr Kerpel specialises in advertising, consumer protection, IP law, insolvency law and civil law. He received his JD, *cum laude*, from Eötvös Loránd Faculty of State and Legal Sciences in 2008. In addition to his university studies he participated in a four-semester course of the *Université Panthéon-Assas Paris II*, which focused mainly on French law and the EU legal system. During his studies, Dr Kerpel worked as a trainee at Köves Clifford Chance and at Dr Sági Law Firm, working primarily in the areas of real property transactions and the law of business organisations. He participated in the preparation of the Corporate Governance Guidance and Principles for Unlisted Companies in Europe issued by ecoDa. He is fluent in English and conversant in French.

**Asena A Keser**
Associate, GÜN + PARTNERS
asena.keser@gun.av.tr

Asena A Keser has been an associate in the corporate and commercial law department of GÜN + PARTNERS since 2011. Her practice mainly focuses on advising and representing both national and international clients in their commercial law, construction and real estate-related disputes. She also advises on labour law issues in relation to employment contracts, personnel management, re-employment actions and various employer-employee disputes. Her practice also includes white collar crime, administrative, tax and regulatory and insolvency procedures.

**Hans Klopper**
Managing director, Independent Advisory
hansk@corprecover.co.za

Hans Klopper is an attorney admitted in South Africa specialising in restructuring and insolvency law. He is actively involved in the establishment of a culture of business rescue in South Africa and has presented workshops, lectures and initiatives in this regard. He is a director of the South African Restructuring and Insolvency Practitioners Association and serves on the Board of Directors of INSOL International, a worldwide federation of national associations for accountants and lawyers specialising in turnaround and insolvency.

A major milestone in his career in recent years was his appointment as joint liquidator to Consolidated News Agencies, one of the largest and most controversial liquidations in recent times in 2002.

Mr Klopper chaired the Northern Provinces Law Society's Committee for Insolvencies and Liquidations for five years. He served on the Insolvency Standing Committee of the Law Society of South Africa.

**Jennie Klingberg**
Advokat, Setterwalls Advokatbyrå
Jennie.klingberg@setterwalls.se

Jennie Klingberg's main areas of practice are life sciences, corporate law and IP law. Ms Klingberg has experience of handling complex litigations within these areas and regularly assists both Swedish and international companies in a number of different industries with contract negotiations, acquisitions and legal investigations. Ms Klingberg has vast experience in the areas of healthcare, pharmaceuticals and medical devices, and regularly advises clients in contract negotiations and the procurement process.

**Kevin Lee**
Partner and head of private client
Boughton Peterson Yang Anderson
in association with Zhong Lun Law Firm
klee@bpya.com.hk/kevinlee@zhonglun.com

Kevin Lee is a qualified solicitor in Hong Kong, England and Wales and British Columbia, Canada. He obtained his LLB from Dalhousie University, Halifax, Nova Scotia in 1984 following which he was admitted to the British Columbia Bar in 1986. Mr Lee practised in Vancouver before relocating to Hong Kong, where he has been with Boughton Peterson Yang Anderson since October 1989. Mr Lee was admitted as a solicitor of England and Wales in September 1992, and was subsequently admitted as a solicitor of the Supreme Court of Hong Kong in October 1993.

Mr Lee's core areas of practice include tax, trusts, private client practice, corporate and commercial law, private equity, cross-border transactions, business law and intellectual property.

**Yves Lenders**
Partner, Lydian
yves.lenders@lydian.be

Yves Lenders is a partner in the commercial and litigation practice, where he heads the ports and logistics team.

He joined Lydian on January 1 2002 and specialises in commercial law, litigation, port projects and logistics. He handles complex construction litigation matters and has experience in post-acquisition litigation work. Mr Lenders's work also includes shareholders disputes. He regularly acts as trusted adviser to his clients on commercial matters, including advising, drafting and implementing legal documentation for his clients' businesses. Further, he advises clients faced with insolvent or near insolvent counterparts. He is a trained mediator.

**Yulia Litovtseva**
Head of dispute resolution and mediation practice group, Pepeliaev Group
y.litovtseva@pgplaw.ru

Yulia Litovtseva specialises in applying entrepreneurial legislation to all areas of business. She represents businesses at all levels of the commercial courts and courts of general jurisdiction in a range of economic disputes. These include disputes over property, lender-borrower relationships, commodity supplies, power supplies and contractor agreements. She is also competent in resolving disputes arising from public law relationships, including challenging regulatory and non-regulatory acts and decisions of officers and companies. Mr Litovtseva has an extensive track record resolving disputes over corporate registration, reorganisation and liquidation, title to shares and equity interests, and invalidating transactions entered into by legal entities. She also successfully protects businesses in commercial arbitration.

Ms Litovtseva has experience of drafting and performing legal analyses of sale and purchase agreements, leases, investment agreements, general contractor and sub-contractor agreements (public procurement), and agency agreements. She has drafted and analysed, with a view to identifying litigation risks, numerous sale and purchase agreements, leases, investment agreements, general contractor and subcontractor agreements (public procurement) and agency agreements. She has also provided legal support on M&A transactions.

Ms Litovtseva is a professional mediator and has experience of mediating at both the pre-trial stage and in the context of litigation. She has more than nine years' experience as a judge of Kaluga Region State Commercial Court and as an attorney at law.

**Rhys Llewellyn**
Partner, Harbottle & Lewis LLP
rhys.llewellyn@harbottle.com

Rhys Llewellyn is a partner at leading London-based law firm Harbottle & Lewis LLP, which is best known for its work advising clients involved in the creation, development and exploitation of IP and other rights, including a number of leading names in the entertainment, media and technology industries. Mr Llewellyn advises on a full range of corporate and commercial issues and has particular experience of private company share and business sales and acquisitions, start-up, investment, joint venture and shareholder arrangements> He also provides advice on limited liability partnerships and restructuring and insolvency issues. He is recommended in *Legal 500* (2013 edition) for his "excellent commercial acumen".

**Pietro Masi**
Associate, Portolano Cavallo Studio Legale
pmasi@portolano.it

Pietro Masi mainly provides consultancy services, including arbitration, with particular reference to contractual matters and corporate law. He has particular experience in assisting companies involved in insolvency proceedings, and in the drafting and negotiation of restructuring agreements and arrangements with creditors. He also handles litigation involving bankruptcy matters assisting creditors in their claims before insolvency courts and in clawback actions brought by public receivers and commissioners.

He undertakes out-of-court activity, with a particularly strong background in ventures and shareholder agreements.

He is co-author of *Q&A Arbitration Italy* and *Q&A Dispute Resolution* (Practical Law Company).

**Anu Monga**
Principal associate, Dhir & Dhir Associates, Advocates & Solicitors
anu.monga@dhirassociates.com

Anu Monga is a principal associate and her practice focuses on IP and licensing law, antitrust and competition law, international trade and World Trade Organisation law (including anti-dumping law), foreign investment law, information technology, media and communication law and environment and climate change law. Ms Monga advises and assists companies in protecting, prosecuting and acquiring IP rights and licensing agreements.

**Annick Mottet Haugaard**
Partner, Lydian
annick.mottet@lydian.be

Annick Mottet Haugaard is a partner in the commercial and litigation practice, where she heads the IP team.

Her practice encompasses the full range of areas linked to the launching and marketing of products and services, including privacy issues related to personal data protection, distribution, franchising, advertising, product regulations, consumer protection and intellectual property (trademarks, copyright, designs and patents).

She acts for numerous prestigious international companies and has solid experience in litigation and negotiations, including with authorities.

Since January 2010 she has been a member of the Belgian Council for Intellectual Property.

Between July 2010 and June 2012 she was president of the European Communities Trademark Association.

**Matthias Nordmann**
Partner, SKW Schwarz
m.nordmann@skwschwarz.de

As a certified expert for corporate and commercial law, Matthias Nordmann focuses on strategic transactions and mergers and acquisitions. He is frequently recommended or named as a leading lawyer by many prominent lawyer rankings for information technology/e-business law in Germany. Dr Nordmann is a member of the Executive Committee and a past chair of the IP and Entertainment Law Committee of the International Bar Association.

**Valentina Orlova**
Head of IP and trademarks practice,
Pepeliaev Group
v.orlova@pgplaw.ru

Valentina Orlova is among Russia's leading experts in intellectual property and the protection of exclusive rights, including trademark rights, with more than 30 years' experience in the field. Ms Orlova focuses on advising clients on IP matters, including the registration of both domestic and international trademarks, the use of IP assets, including franchising and licensing agreements, e-commerce and advertising law. She has an extensive track record of acting for Russian and foreign clients in the pre-trial settlement of IP issues, preparing documents to be used for administrative appeals and producing expert opinions for court hearings on cases involving the protection of intellectual property, including infringement of trademarks and industrial designs. She was part of the team which drafted and commented on the Russian legislation on means of individualisation (company names, trademarks, geographical indications and trade names). At present, Ms Orlova is a member of the working group for the development of individualisation strategies under the non-commercial partnership 'Facilitating the development of corporate law'. Ms Orlova is also a member of the Innovation Working Group on Intellectual Property of the US-Russia Bilateral Presidential Commission created by Presidents Medvedev and Obama. She was also a member of the Russian delegation that negotiated Russia's accession to the World Trade Organisation.

**Elina Pesonen**
Associate, Castrén & Snellman Attorneys Ltd
elina.pesonen@castren.fi

Elina Pesonen advises clients on all aspects of insolvency law. Her main areas of practice also include general corporate and contract law. Ms Pesonen has participated in various large bankruptcy and restructuring proceedings, both assisting the administrator and representing the creditors. Ms Pesonen also has experience in drafting and negotiating contracts as well as in other questions related to contract law. She is a member of INSOL Europe. In addition to her law degree from the University of Helsinki, Ms Pesonen has studied business law at the ESADE Business School in Spain.

**Davide Petris**
Associate, Portolano Cavallo Studio Legale
dpetris@portolano.it

Davide Petris assists Italian and foreign clients with disputes in ordinary courts and arbitration tribunals. He has developed particular expertise in litigation involving bankruptcy matters, commercial contracts disputes in the industrial and intellectual property fields, unfair competition and unfair commercial practice.

He is co-author of *Q&A Arbitration Italy* (Practical Law Company) and the *Doing Business Report: Enforcing Contracts* (the World Bank and the International Finance Corporation).

Mr Petris graduated in law from the Luigi Bocconi School of Economics in Milan in 2009. He was the Bocconi University delegate at Willem C Vis International Commercial Arbitration Moot, an international arbitration competition.

**Ulrich Reber**
Partner, SKW Schwarz
u.reber@skwschwarz.de

Ulrich Reber assists and represents domestic and foreign enterprises in the field of civil and commercial law, in particular in litigation and dispute resolution matters. A special focus lies on cross-border lawsuits and representation in the competent courts. Clients from the publishing, music and games industry rely on Dr Reber's competence in the fields of media, entertainment and copyright law. He also assists clients in bankruptcy and restructuring matters.

**Nilesh Sharma**
Partner, Dhir & Dhir Associates, Advocates & Solicitors
nilesh.sharma@dhirassociates.com

Nilesh Sharma is a partner in Dhir & Dhir Associates, Advocates & Solicitors. He is a law graduate and a chartered accountant, and looks after the firm's restructuring and insolvency practice. His association with the firm and his experience in this practice area has lasted more than two decades. His experience includes providing advice on restructuring and insolvency issues, negotiated settlements, cross-border insolvency issues and representation before the bankruptcy courts. He is a member of INSOL India and the AAIFR-BIFR Association of India.

**Brian Sullivan**
Lawyer, W&H Law Firm
brian@whlaw.cn

Brian Sullivan is a member of the insolvency and restructuring team at W&H in Beijing and a graduate of Renmin University of China.

**Odd Swarting**
Partner, Setterwalls Advokatbyrå
Odd.swarting@setterwalls.se

Odd Swarting has a wide variety of experience in corporate insolvency and restructuring, beginning in 1985, including appointments as bankruptcy trustee for companies quoted on the Stockholm Stock Exchange, stockbroker companies under the supervision of the Swedish Financial Supervisory Authority, production companies and real property companies, and restructuring work for industrial, IT, real property, development and other companies.

Mr Swarting also has particular experience of international insolvency issues and has been the Swedish representative at international seminars held by the American Bar Association, the International Bar Association and the International Insolvency Institute. He has been chairman of the Swedish Restructuring and Bankruptcy Trustees Association since 2003 and has been an expert on Swedish government committees reviewing the insolvency law (2009-2011) and rights *in rem* issues for movable goods (since 2013).

Mr Swarting's main areas of work also include advising commercial clients, particularly within the pharmaceutical and pulp and paper business on regulatory, commercial and corporate law. Since 2010 he has been the chairman of UNICEF Sweden.

**Marcel Willems**
Partner, Kennedy Van der Laan
marcel.willems@kvdl.nl

Marcel Willems started his professional career in 1988. In 1992 he co-founded Kennedy Van der Laan, now one of the leading firms in the Netherlands. Mr Willems has broad experience in insolvency, banking and finance and dispute resolution, mostly in a cross-border setting. He publishes and lectures regularly. Mr Willems has been active in the Insolvency, Restructuring and

Creditors' Rights Section of the International Bar Association for a number of years, and and is currently senior vice chair conference quality.

**Christian Wyss**
Managing associate, VISCHER AG
cwyss@vischer.com

Christian Wyss is managing associate with VISCHER AG, a major Swiss law firm with offices in Basel and Zurich. He specialises in drafting and negotiating contracts for the biotech and pharmaceutical industries. Mr Wyss regularly leverages his experience to advise clients in other technology-driven industries such as software and new media. His activities include licensing, technology transfer, research collaborations, manufacturing, distribution, joint ventures and IP issues in M&A transactions. Mr Wyss also gained in-depth insolvency experience when assisting the trustee of a 100-person company from insolvency filing until completion of the liquidation proceedings. He holds a *lic iur* degree (2000) from the University of Basel and an LLM (2005) from Wake Forest University School of Law.

**Lynda Zadra-Symes**
Partner, Knobbe, Martens, Olson & Bear, LLP
lynda.zadrasymes@knobbe.com

Lynda Zadra-Symes is a litigation partner in Knobbe Martens' Orange County, California office, where she has practised for more than 20 years. She represents clients through all stages of US litigation, from pre-action through trial and appeal, in federal courts throughout the country and before the Trademark Trial and Appeal Board of the US Patent and Trademark Office. Ms Zadra-Symes's practice involves all types of intellectual property, including patents, trade secrets, trademarks and trade dress, copyrights, false advertising, unfair competition and rights of publicity. She also advises on customs and anti-counterfeiting issues, international trademark and copyright matters, advertising and competition issues. Her clients come from a wide variety of industries, from beverages, toys and fashion to medical devices, computer chips, software, e-commerce and video games. Ms Zadra-Symes was called to the Bar of England and Wales in November 1989 and admitted to the California Bar in 1991.

**Yin Zhengyou**
Senior partner, W&H Law Firm
yinzy@whlaw.cn

Yin Zhengyou is a senior partner of W&H Law Firm and is widely considered a leading practitioner with respect to restructuring and insolvency matters in Mainland China. He has handled nearly 100 restructuring and insolvency cases, and has played an important role in the drafting of relevant judicial interpretations of the Enterprise Bankruptcy Law. Dr Yin is chairman of the Restructuring and Insolvency Committee of the All-China Lawyers Association, the official organisation for all 230,000 lawyers in China. He also holds positions in several other bankruptcy and legal organisations: executive chairman, China Bankruptcy Law Forum; vice president and secretary general, Beijing Bankruptcy Law Society; secretary general, China Chapter of East Asian Association of Insolvency and Restructuring; and vice chair, Insolvency Committee, Inter-Pacific Bar Association.

Additionally, Dr Yin has authored five books in the field of insolvency and has acted as chief editor of seven volumes of papers from the China Bankruptcy Law Forum.